D1282437

The Shadow in the Cave

Anthony Smith

The Shadow in the Cave

The Broadcaster, His Audience, and the State

University of Illinois Press
Urbana Chicago London

Published by agreement with George Allen & Unwin Ltd.
Manufactured in the United States of America
© 1973 by Anthony Smith

Library of Congress Cataloging in Publication Data:

Smith, Anthony, 1938-
    The shadow in the cave.

    Bibliography: p.
    1. Television broadcasting.   2. Radio broadcasting.
I. Title.
HE8689.4.S64   384.54   73-18146
ISBN 0-252-00442-6

In Memory of My Mother
ESTHER
1898–1965

'This is a strange image, he said, and they are strange prisoners.
Like ourselves, I replied; and they see only their own shadows, or the shadows of one another, which the fire throws on the opposite wall of the cave.
True, he said: how could they see anything but the shadows if they were never allowed to move their heads?
And of their objects which are being carried in like manner they would see only the shadows?
Yes, he said.
And if they were able to talk with one another, would they not suppose that they were naming what was actually before them?'

PLATO *The Republic* Book VII

Acknowledgements

The people who are principally responsible for this book are the producers and broadcasters of radio and television throughout the world, among whom I have worked for a dozen years. Scores of colleagues, past and present, have helped consciously or unconsciously, to construct the line of thinking which I have tried to develop within these covers; it is impossible to name more than a small corps even of those who gave specific help in the course of composition.

My thanks are especially to be recorded to Mr Huw Weldon and Mr John Grist of the BBC Television Service who put up with me, with little complaint, for ten happy and fruitful years and then enabled me to make my departure equally happy and fruitful; to Raymond Carr, the Warden, and the Fellows of St Antony's College, Oxford, who then admitted me to their company for two productive and restorative years; to Lord Murray of Newhaven, formerly Director of the Leverhulme Trust Fund, whose generosity made, as they say, the whole thing possible. Two distinguished broadcasters, each unknown to the other, share roughly equal responsibility for urging me to take the plunge—Robert McKenzie and Malcolm Muggeridge. I spent many useful weeks as the guest of Dean Elie Abel at the Graduate School of Journalism at Columbia University in New York, an institution which pulsates with the dynamic enthusiasm of Professor Fred Friendly and the hospitality of his wife, Ruth. I have enjoyed advice, critical comment, hospitality and direct help during the course of composition from Yehoshua Allmogg, Moshe Arad (and Rivka), Eliane Arari, Donald Baverstock, Jay Blumler, Mike Burns, Rex Cathcart, Tem Conway, David Croom, James Day, John Dekker, Ann Doe, Jonathan Dubois, Desmond Fisher, Ernest Fuhr, Tom Hardiman, Leofranc Holford-Strevens, Barbro Hallström, Nicholas Johnson, Peter Lance, Jim McGuiness, Robert McKenzie, Jill Mortimer, Haggai Pinsker, John Redwood, Werner Rulf, Ann Saldich, Michael Starks and Brian Winston.

My thanks are due to Professor Herbert Nicholas of New College, who read and commented on the manuscript, to Dr Janet Morgan of Nuffield College, who did likewise and offered much detailed help, and to Professor Stuart Hood whose wise criticism has been invaluable. The only aspect of the work which has enjoyed unqualified praise from all quarters has been the typing of the manuscript, which was the task of Mrs Pat Kirkpatrick. Two friends, Gudie and Joachuin Romero-Maura, have watched the project grow from its inception; without their companionship and light-hearted encouragement the project would have been neither started nor completed.

Preface

On 13 November 1969 the Vice President of the United States, Spiro T. Agnew, rose to his feet at a Republican party meeting at Des Moines, Iowa, and delivered a speech which fell into the world of broadcasting like a large rock into a small pond. 'The purpose of my remarks tonight,' he said, 'is to focus your attention on this little group of men who not only enjoy right of instant rebuttal to every Presidential address, but, more importantly, wield a free hand in selecting, presenting and interpreting the great issues in our nation. . . . They decide what 40 to 50 million Americans will learn of the day's events in the nation and the world. We cannot measure this power and influence by the traditional democratic standards, for these men can create national issues overnight. They can make or break by their coverage and commentary, a Moratorium on the war. They can elevate men from obscurity to national prominence within a week. They can reward some politicians with national exposure and ignore others. . . . The American people would rightly not tolerate this concentration of power in government. Is it not fair and relevant to question its concentration in the hands of a tiny, enclosed fraternity of privileged men elected by no one and enjoying a monopoly sanctioned and licensed by government?'[1]

Only a few hours before the Vice President had reached Des Moines, the three major American television networks had jointly made a decision to cancel their scheduled evening news programmes, forfeiting much advertising revenue, and transmit instead, live, the whole of the Agnew denunciation. The speech rapidly became a basic text in the international debate about broadcasting. Within days his key phrases were being repeated in newsrooms and broadcasting board rooms from Berlin to Santiago, in Dublin, London and Tokyo, in every place in which the instrument of broadcasting has added its special complications to an age-old argument between politicians and journalists. It was not by any means the beginning of the tension between broadcasters and politicians but it helped both sides to make their dispositions around the globe and prepare for a long war of curses and threats. Agnew was trying to blame American television for the 'credibility gap' between government and people; the networks in their turn invoked the First Amendment and clasped it bravely to their bosoms. Dr Frank Stanton, President of the Columbia Broadcasting System, sprang to his network's defence: 'Because a federally licensed medium is involved, no more serious episode has occurred in government–press relationships since the dark days in the fumbling infancy of this Republic when the ill-fated Alien and Sedition Acts forbade criticism of the government and its policies on pain of exile or imprisonment.'[2]

Within a month of his outburst the Vice President received nearly 80,000 letters supporting his stand, and less than four thousand attacking it. The networks themselves received 150,000 letters, dividing two-to-one in favour of Agnew. The correspondence analysts at the networks noticed the large number of letter-writers who had chosen to express themselves with special virulence. Columbia University's Graduate School of Journalism in New York analysed a pile of 2,500 of these 'hate-letters' and found that a quarter accused the networks of communism, 11 per cent were antisemitic and 10 per cent antiblack; 15 per cent contained a threat to 'make trouble' for the networks, a few made threats of actual violence. One station in the south-west[3] was visited by four men who announced that they had come to beat up anti-Agnew newsmen. Other stations found it prudent to lock their doors after office hours. Broadcasting was under siege.[4]

In the years that followed broadcasting has developed a siege mentality in many places. Tensions between the broadcasters, the politicians and the vast audience which they jointly share have increased. The purpose of this book is to point out the origins of those tensions in the history of broadcasting and of the institutions inside which broadcasting has been placed.

Broadcasting can no longer be ignored by political science. Its problems are encoded versions of the political issues which confront societies. The second part of the book therefore is an attempt to unravel these 'codes' in a number of countries and to show how the broadcasting systems of the world conceal layer upon layer of suppressed conflict; many of the unresolved neuroses from which nations suffer can be found reflected in the ways they choose to organise radio and television.

Thirty years ago R. S. Lambert summed up his experiences in the first decade of broadcasting in Britain with a picture of the broadcasting institution as the centre of a web of social contacts. Every group contending for the attention of the new mass audience had to find a path to its door. 'Today, the BBC holds—in the field of art, intellect and politics—the power once exercised by the Court. It has become the main indirect organ of Government, all the more potent because its influence *is* indirect. . . . No doubt the tendency is inevitable—and we are doomed, in this twentieth century, to see individualism in art, music, drama, literature and journalism disappear and in its place a kind of corporative system, within which the formerly independent thinker, writer, performer will have to seek absorption.'[5] Lambert wrote before the era of television. The feeling that broadcasting introduced a strong element of corporation into the whole of culture is of course much greater today. I do not believe that this is attributable to the naked technology itself, but to the legal and organisational formulae that have been adopted to clothe and control it. We have reached a point at which the various institutions and legal devices created around the world are ceasing to satisfy many of the parties involved in their creation. At the same time a new source of independent pressure has sprung up among the creative workers of broadcasting who have become much more conscious of themselves as a special interest within the debate than ever before. Furthermore the politicians, the network officials, Government, and the new range of broadcasting pressure groups are all of them choosing to speak in the name of 'freedom', in one sense or another. The debate is thus complicated because all the participants are employing the same shibboleths.

One simple and perhaps obvious problem bedevils all broadcasting. The broadcaster reaches a vast and incoherent audience, the entire audience which the geography of the wavelength permits. When he has reached it he has created a source of power for himself which no society can possibly allow him to wield without supervision or control. If the instrument is used for means of clear personal expression, the position of the broadcaster is socially unacceptable. If it is used merely to create the maximum audience the product becomes culturally and ultimately politically unacceptable. Under the weight of this problem the structure of the ethics which is believed to be skeletal to twentieth-century culture—that of individual artistic and informational freedom—simply disintegrates. Broadcasting therefore either takes place on a territory of enforced neutrality which becomes intellectually meaningless or it becomes a tyranny. When it finds a level of taste at which it can successfully aggregate its audience it becomes culturally valueless; when it occupies a higher ground in a spirit of dedicated intellectual exclusiveness it fails in its purpose of serving the entire society. Those are the horns of the broadcasting dilemma.

Television sets are purchased by individuals to entertain themselves in their non-working time, usually in surroundings of domestic privacy. They become members of a 'mass' as a result of the kind of messages they receive, not as a result of the kind of people they are. When a man acquires a television set, even more acutely than when he buys a mass-circulation daily paper, or votes as a member of a mass franchise, he enters into a set of cultural, political and social transactions of kinds more far-reaching than those of which he is aware. During the last two decades an instrument which entered our home as a means of entertainment has become the means by which an enormous range of other forces enter our lives; we did not invite them there, but they came. Because of that network of forces the question of controlling the messages is becoming a more contentious and often a more bitterly fought issue than almost any other. The Agnew affair was an archetypal example of the daily testing of power which goes on between communicators and political figures within the electronic–informational systems of the world.

One intention of this book is to examine the way in which television has gradually acquired these 'ulterior' powers and meanings. I shall draw examples from various parts of the world, although, necessarily, most of my knowledge is derived from the countries in whose television systems I have worked, namely America and Britain. My descriptions of broadcasting institutions in various parts of the world are not comprehensive;[6] I select those of their characteristics and problems which illustrate my main underlying arguments, and these it might be of help to readers to summarise at the start.

Firstly, I think that the actual technical development of broadcasting took directions which were dictated by a new configuration of market forces and social beliefs about the nature of mass society; broadcasting thus arrived in the 1920s in a form which seemed to offer solutions to the fears existing at that moment about the volatile nature of mass society. Broadcasting had to find a way to inform and entertain without overstimulating its audience.

My second observation is that broadcasting arrived encrusted in the assumption that it was an instrument by which a few voices addressed a multitude, without response. It was necessary to contain and control the minds and energies of these few, and the new technology thus came to be housed in institutions on which was imposed an 'ideology' of a kind which would help keep them out of trouble—that ideology is variously described as 'objectivity' or 'impartiality', and it is instructive to observe the ever-changing meanings which these words are given as each broadcasting organisation struggles for survival in the sceptical political environment.

Thirdly, broadcasting, in the process of rapid growth over half a century, has acquired a role of such magnitude that it (and its controllers) can steer the course of entire cultures; just as an economy can be manipulated today by a few who control the major offices in a few large corporations, so can a culture be oriented in certain directions by a tiny group of broadcasting impresarios whose main motive is the preservation of their own institutions intact rather than the actual 'good' of the culture concerned.

Fourthly, broadcasters are dominated by their collective assumptions about their own audience. The supposed nature and interests of the audience dominate all the thinking inside broadcasting; beliefs about 'what the audience can take' and 'what people want' float about within broadcasting and dominate all its decisions, the development of its cultural genres, its entire output. But the institution itself defines those characteristics of the audience which are most important to it and therefore broadcasters tend to see their audiences through a haze of professional and institutional assumptions.

Fifthly, I believe that any useful development of broadcasting must be based upon a return to an examination of the idea of freedom: we have to find ways to steer the various systems of broadcasting in ways which actually relate to the newly identified needs and demands of society.

A. S.

Contents

Acknowledgements		*page*	11
Preface			13
1	The Riddle of the Masses		21
2	Building Citadels in the Air: The Broadcasting Institution		47
3	News—The Ugly Mirror		73
4	Sharing the Labours of Statesmanship		111
5	Broadcasting Autonomy Under Threat		140
6	France and the ORTF: Personal Power plus Television Monopoly Equals Gaullism		155
7	America: The People's Air		187
8	American Viewers in Revolt: Talking Back to the Networks		215
9	Japan: The Television of Hard-Training		246
10	The Dutch System: The Pillars of Hilversum, the Issue of 'Access'		264
11	The Last Resource of Freedom		279
Notes			287
A Broadcasting Bibliography			313
Index			339

Chapter One

The Riddle of the Masses

'The great men of culture are those who have had a passion
for diffusing, for making prevail, for carrying from one end
of society to the other, the best knowledge, the best ideas of
their time; who have laboured to divest knowledge of all
that was harsh, uncouth, difficult, abstract, professional,
exclusive; to humanise it, to make it efficient outside the
clique of the cultivated and learned . . .'
Matthew Arnold, *Culture and Anarchy* 1869 (Cambridge
University Press, 1969, p. 70)

'Just because I and a taxi-driver and an estate agent have
watched the same programme the night before, I have never
found that we have shared an area of common experience:
we are just as far removed from each other as if we were
discussing an article in *Mind*.'
Henry Fairlie, *Encounter* (March 1962)

I

In the summer of 1896 a young Irish-Italian Guglielmo Marconi
first succeeded, in a demonstration on Salisbury Plain, in
making a wireless wave travel beyond the horizon. At first it
went a hundred yards, then a mile, then six miles.[1] 'The calm
of my life ended there', he later wrote.[2] During the same
summer in France, the sociologist Gabriel Tarde was at work
systematising all the existing accepted data in the new and
fascinating field of crowd-psychology for a book entitled
Les Lois de l'Imitation;[3] his book rapidly influenced the contemporary discussion about the ways in which crowds responded
to communication. 'The general laws governing imitative
repetition . . . are to sociology what the laws of habit and
heredity are to biology, the laws of gravitation to astronomy

21

and the laws of vibration to physics,' Tarde wrote. 'Society is imitation and imitation is a kind of hypnotism.'[4] The invention of radio was to add a new medium to those which were already informing and entertaining the new mass audience. The nature of that audience puzzled and frightened the social psychologists and political scientists of the time. Two decades later the World War accelerated and dramatised Marconi's technology and exploited the potential for wartime propaganda in the social theories of Tarde.

Certain social, cultural, educational and political dilemmas had been apparent in mass society for a generation. Those dilemmas, still to this day unresolved, have dominated all the decisions which have shaped the development of Marconi's wireless discoveries. The story of broadcasting therefore can be read as the story of the interaction of a series of inventions with a series of beliefs about the nature of twentieth-century mass societies. The organisation of broadcasting, the institutions which govern it, the divisions of labour within it, the methods of financing it, the development of the very types of programme used in radio and television, all the conscious and unconscious assumptions of which the business of broadcasting is compounded, can be made to reveal, like geological strata, the successive encrustations of the argument about the culture and government of a society of masses. The earliest crucial decisions made about broadcasting bear the mark of the prevailing ideas about how a modern society worked.

The last generation of Victorians inherited a world of social thought in which mankind had been relegated to the status of one among many evolving species.[5] Charles Darwin's ideas had quickly taken root (the soil had already been very well prepared by others for his Theory of Evolution) in the 1860s and had left his contemporaries with the burgeoning sense of *environment*, of human society, as well as that of other species, existing in a continuum of time and space. The methods of the new biologists were being assimilated to the tasks of social and political observation. But psychology remained several steps behind. Darwin had explained the process of physical evolution in a manner which left in its wake a very mechanical explanation of animal behaviour. When the lessons of the history of the animal kingdom were applied to the human domain, the same simple psychological mechanisms were thought to apply. Human conduct was deemed to be as mechanical and impulse-based as the conduct apparent in beasts. 'To observe from outside (as one observes an ants' nest through a magnifying glass) the "struggle for life" or the working of the "gregarious instincts" in human society seemed to the contemporaries of Darwin to be a much more "scientific" method than to analyse the minutiae of one's own feelings.'[6] That was how Graham Wallas later summed up the efforts of the post-Darwinian school of psychologists (he might have been speaking of the Positivists too). Walter Bagehot's *Physics and Politics* was Wallas' main target. 'The propensity of man to imitate what is before him is one of the strongest parts of his nature', Bagehot had written, in a book which treated social organisation principally as a manifestation of the instinct of imitation.[7] A human society, it was thought, must be rather the same as a nest of ants – to understand it, one ignored the individual and looked at the mass, and its primal imitative behaviour.

Since imitation was a primal instinct, then public instruction became inevitably a primary social duty. The whole discussion of mass psychology was heavily tinged with 'educationism'. The newly enfranchised workers after the reforms of 1867, the growing armies of the literate, the new readerships for magazines and cheap fiction, had all arrived at the gates of Society but had not yet been admitted. Their presence, however, was profoundly felt throughout the worlds of culture and politics. Wilkie Collins had expressed the feeling that a redefined audience, *The Unknown Public*, would in future determine the course of English fiction. 'The members of it are evidently, in the mass, from no fault of theirs, still ignorant of almost everything which is generally known and understood among readers whom circumstances have placed, socially and intellectually, in the rank above them.'[8] The middle-class writers who were attempting to reach out towards this new audience felt the masses as an environment as much as a readership; the importance of communicating with it resulted from its growing power, its potential to alter all the settled elements of society. But lack of direct contact between the new communicators and their audience changed the nature of cultural relationships.[9] In politics similar gaps were opening up between politicians and the new mass electorate.

The working class had produced its own writers who had enjoyed, like Cobbett, overwhelming success in their relationship with a vast working-class readership. Middle-class writers, intent upon 'improving' their audience, and socially frightened of it, made heavy weather of the task of discovering the correct level of style. 'It was the conviction of these middle-class enthusiasts that the world, or, as a good and vital start, the English working classes were to be made over in their image. And they set to propagating all their ideas. They propagated religion, morals, art, temperance, charity, respectability, prudence, emigration, progress, political economy. . . . And the middle-classes, with the best will in the world, made certain their own defeat. They were condescending and condemnatory when they had no intention of being so. They tried to impose their standards and criteria on people whose needs were different. Calm assumptions were inherent in their confidence, embedded in their psychological theories.'[10] As an educator himself, Matthew Arnold was fundamentally involved in the same task. But he saw the class at closer quarters. As a school-inspector the problem of indoctrination was a practical as well as a moral matter. He uses the words of the reformers but turns them. 'The men of culture are the true apostles of equality.'[11] He juxtaposes the need for quality with the task of mass distribution and foreshadows with an eerie exactness the arguments of the broadcasting age, the perplexities of the mass communicator who fears to lose his audience by giving them 'the best' which will go over their heads, and equally to keep his audience by adulterating and perhaps intellectually invalidating his material. 'Culture works differently', is Arnold's confident advice. 'It does not try to reach down to the level of inferior classes; it does not try to win them for this or that sect of its own, with ready-made judgments and watchwords. It seeks to do away with classes; to make the best that has been thought and known in the world current everywhere.'[12] The literary intelligentsia had assumed a more or less educational role in England as the new technologies of print bound them to a wider but less well understood audience. Arnold constantly returns to the idea of making the best 'prevail'; culture, when applied to the masses, was not a superior form of entertainment, nor a means of simple spiritual communication between an artist and an audience – its aim was to communicate in order to infiltrate, to dominate. It was to entertain because it had to educate by stealth. Arnold's language is that of the school-master but also that of the politician contemplating the potential of an enfranchised mass which failed to share the same moral terms of reference as its masters.[13] 'Culture' therefore, through its role as a means of mass education, as a way of spreading certain moral ideals in a manner that committed the recipient to them, became profoundly political. 'Plenty of people will try to give the masses, as they call them, an intellectual food prepared and adapted in the way they think proper for the actual condition of the masses. The ordinary popular literature is an example of this way of working on the masses. Plenty of people will try to indoctrinate the masses with the set of ideas and judgments constituting the creed of their own profession or party. Our religious and political organisations give an example of this way of working on the masses. I condemn neither way; but culture works differently.'[14]

Industrialisation was transforming an old tradition of popular literature into a mass literature; the point of cultural control was shifting from audience to communicator or, rather, the new processes were now forcing and regimenting more rigidly the distinction between the two. The growth of adver-tising and the growth of new forms of political communication suited to the new voters showed how rapidly the new mass psychology had spread and how inadequate it was; the distinc-tion between the communicator and the mass audience grows with the distorted and oversimplified version of the latter held by the former. As Raymond Williams puts it, 'There are in fact no masses; only ways of seeing people as masses.'[15]

Nonetheless in the Victorian city the sociologists of the late nineteenth century saw vivid illustration of their analysis of mass behaviour. Advertisement-writing had become a respect-able profession. Drapers instructed their employees in sophisti-cated techniques of salesmanship, involving 'voice-magnetism'.

25

Travellers returning from the East explained with scientific enthusiasm how hypnotic methods could be used to enforce obedience within crowds of simple people. The notion of Suggestion was a subject of considerable interest to sociologists who saw its political potential.[16] Society itself no longer seemed to correspond to the simple mechanical model of Hobbes and Bentham; it was a mysterious, fickle, organic and ever-evolving creature, and at its heart was the megalopolitan mass. Bagehot had, as an opponent of the franchise reforms of 1867, tended to exaggerate the imitative instinct of the masses; Carlyle thought that the situation merely reinforced the need for strong leadership of society from the traditional ruling class.[17] Matthew Arnold saw a chance for the creation of mass responsibility through self-discipline resulting from inspired education. Fabians like Graham Wallas, when they saw how trouble-free had been the passage of the masses to political power, took up positions recognisable today as 'Welfare State' attitudes towards the issues presented by mass society. Modern politics created the need for a new psychology, one that applied to the special needs of politicians as well as of voters in the mass-franchise systems of Europe and America.

Wallas wanted to place the study of human nature once again in the centre of the study of politics; he argued that a much cooler view of crowd behaviour could be taken than that being urged by 'Latin' psychologists like Tarde and le Bon. 'My own observation of English politics suggests that in a modern national state, this panic effect of the combination of nervous excitement with physical contact is not of great importance. . . . A crowd in a narrow street is more likely to get 'out of hand', and one may see a few thousand men in a large hall reach a state approaching genuine pathological exaltation on an exciting occasion, and when they are in the hands of a practised speaker. But as they go out of the hall they drop into the cool ocean of London, and their mood is dissipated in a moment.'[18]

The argument between the alarmists and the anti-alarmists was fundamentally an argument about the nature of communication with the newly enfranchised. The year of Marconi's experiment on Salisbury Plain was also the year in which

Northcliffe purchased the *Daily Mail* and turned the mass audience into a source of vast wealth and political power. The mass communicator had to discover a tone of voice which was adjusted both to the new democracy and to the economic exigencies of a newly defined market. The new entertainment technologies, beginning with the mass press and the cinema, have had to provide the writer, the artist, the film-maker with a ready-made level of style and interest which when mastered guarantees the physical participation of the audience. The most important characteristic of the mass audience is that it is undifferentiated, unknown in terms of its human nature to the communicator; it is seen distantly as through a telescope compounded of a series of accumulated commercial assumptions.

One of the earliest models of a mass communication process was Mudie's Circulating Library. Mudie dominated the literary scene of London throughout the half century in which the three-volume novel thrived; from the 1840s tens of thousands of readers would absorb the literature of the time in the reading rooms set up by Mudie. So great was the influence of the circulating library as a *method of distribution* that Mudie was able to dictate the size, print-order and choice of Victorian fiction. He also tried to dictate its moral values. Together with W. H. Smith in 1894, at a stroke of the pen, Mudie destroyed the three-volume novel.[19] In the circulating library we have an example of what was simply a technique of distribution becoming the main determining factor of the content of an entire cultural genre. It remained in the hands of a man who could determine the content, because he had already discovered or determined (through the social level at which he directed the mechanism of his reading rooms), the kind of public that could reach the product. At the same moment, Mudie's library became a mechanism which guaranteed the author a certain size and type of audience (which the author would ignore only at the peril of his livelihood), and which guaranteed the audience a certain product which was 'what it wanted'. There was no real choice for either party. The middle-man had become king.

Mudie was well able to defend his position as that of servant not dictator to his readers: 'The title under which my library was established . . . implies this: – the public know it and subscribe accordingly and increasingly. They are evidently willing to have a barrier of some kind between themselves and the lower floods of literature.'[20] All Mudie did was to protect his readers against violations of the Victorian moral code. In order to maintain his standards he recruited and trained a staff of professional readers whose skill and highly developed taste were a tribute to Mudie's ability to induce in them his own high set of standards; Mudie's employed readers had a similar relationship to him and the system which he ruled as the producers within Reith's BBC to it. The crucial although unnoticed essence of broadcasting was that the editorial power was fused with the ownership of the means of disseminating the product.

Until the First World War the increasingly felt presence of the mass audience and the mass market for goods represented new challenges in the field of culture, the task of elevating rather than degrading the taste of the masses was an obligation of a social or a religious nature. Psychologists speculated without great clinical experience on the extent of the potential for persuasion of the masses. Hypnotism and telepathy developed as stunts.[21] Jokes were made about the possible future development of the telephone as an instrument of mass persuasion; there is a cartoon in the New York *Daily Graphic* in 1877 entitled 'Terrors of the Telephone' which depicts a screaming tyrant bellowing into a black box from which lead wires connecting him with audiences around the world in Peking, San Francisco, Boston, Dublin and London. But although the speaker looks like an early version of Hitler, the audiences are sitting in rows, some solemn, some smiling – these are not urban rabbles hysterically roused by exploitation of the new technology for malign purposes.[22]

It was the World War which suddenly presented the mass audience to the propagandist as mere victim. The propagandists recruited to fight on both sides arrived at their work surrounded by an aura of secret power. Mass manipulation was widely believed to be one of the major tools of war-making. The propagandists on both sides achieved enormous prestige which they took with them to the new public relations industries which sprang up when they became militarily redundant.[23] But the wartime propaganda created in its immediate aftermath a deep and widely felt distrust of propaganda especially in the Western democracies. In the United States European propaganda was blamed for dragging the Americans into the war. So great was the distrust that wholly new techniques had to be developed in the Second World War. In the Depression years the accusation of cynical manipulation of the masses became itself part of the ammunition of the class war.[24]

In the twenties there developed a widespread feeling that within mass society the individual has less and less influence on the flow of events. The psychological distance between the governed and the political élite grew greater. The specialist became powerful, the man who is 'qualified' to make the very judgements which are supposed to be the newly won prerogative of the voting masses. Politicians constantly emphasise the importance of a well-informed public; they insist that the man-in-the-street possesses all the facts necessary to make a particular political decision, but simultaneously the sense of mass impotence grows and with it the feeling that political events possess the inexorability of natural events.[25] Politics seem to move helplessly outside the range of morals; the scope for personal moral involvement diminishes. Some observers of the interwar years remark on the decline of indignation in politics. The viciousness of First World War propaganda changed the entire range of feelings with which the new mass communicator faced his audience. 'Under the impact of propaganda', wrote Walter Lippmann, 'not necessarily in the sinister meaning of the word alone, the old constants of our thinking have become variables. It is no longer possible, for example, to believe in the original dogma of democracy, that the knowledge needed for the management of human affairs comes up spontaneously from the human heart. When we act on that theory we expose ourselves to self-deception, and to the forms of persuasion that we cannot verify. It has been demonstrated that we cannot rely upon intuition, conscience or the accidents of casual opinion if we are to deal with the world beyond our reach.'[26] Lippmann constantly emphasised the nature of the mass audience as *an environment*, and indeed acknowledges his indebtedness to Graham Wallas for this important concept.[27] The ability to conduct mass persuasion through the new mechanical media, with the help of big finance, turned public opinion into the raw material of political life as much as the determinant of it. The industry of news-gathering, assisted by armies of public relations men and press agents (a survey conducted before the war revealed that there were already 1200 of these operating in New York alone[28]) was responsible for the evolving complexity of 'public opinion'. 'Within the life of the generation now in control of affairs persuasion has become a self-conscious act and a regular organ of popular government. None of us begins to understand the consequences, but it is no daring prophesy to say that the knowledge of how to create consent will alter every political calculation and modify every political premise.'[29]

In fact the war had ensured that every single one of the new technologies had been exploited for national purposes. In Britain there had been 5000 cinemas operating before hostilities commenced, and 17 mass circulation daily papers. 20 million people visited the cinema every week, but it was still a 'low-status' medium and only half-way through the war years did it spring into use as a propaganda medium with the formation of the Topical War Film Committee.[30] The cumbersome equipment meant that the camera was not particularly efficient as a tool of reporting, but its obvious impact on an audience enabled it to be used as an important tool for reinforcing the official propaganda line. The cinema during the war made much more effective use of the cartoon to encourage nationalistic stereotypes and build up the sense of solidarity.

Northcliffe in *The Times* and the *Daily Mail*, and Rother-mere, his brother, in *The Daily Mirror*, *The Leeds Mercury* and *The Glasgow Record* had created a four-year fiction of German terrorism and bestiality. They described the German army's reprisal actions in Belgium as an orgy of torture and debauchery, inventing atrocities where their reporters were unable to find them. The Northcliffe newspapers depicted the work of German soldiers in images which are the familiar material of horror stories: babies being lifted on bayonets, nuns raped on tables. Public sentiment was whipped into a frenzy of anti-German hatred. 'If your waiter says he is Swiss, ask to see his passport.' Horatio Bottomley in *John Bull* called for a war of extermination against the Kaiser as 'the soul of Satan'. In the early years of peace the whole business of propaganda earned well justified public resentment.[31]

Propaganda is one means by which mass society fuses culture and politics. The experience of the propagandists of the First World War coupled with the ensuing reaction against the black art they had perfected were among the profoundest influences on the men who came to lay the foundations of broadcasting in the early nineteen-twenties. Among the belligerent nations there was no doubt that any new machinery for linking a communicator with the mass audience would need to involve public authorities of some kind in controlling the content of the message. At the same time the founders of broadcasting feared equally the direct control of the medium by the government of the day. The discussion in Britain and Europe was in the main about what kind of public control there should be, not whether there should be any. It seemed inevitable that the technology of broadcasting should be developed as a means for *mass communication* rather than minority; the potential for two-way communication was ignored. The telephone was not the archetype for the new medium, based though it was on reproducing the human voice, but rather the record industry and the cinema.[32] 'The outstanding feature of radio-telephony', says one of the opening passages of the Report of the Sykes Committee, 'is that it enables a single voice to reach innumerable ears. It can carry speech and melody into every home. It can bring isolated towns and villages into close touch with the great centres of population, and thereby alleviate one of the severest drawbacks to rural life. . . . Broadcasting is a mode of distribution of music and information which at present excels in cheapness anything hitherto conceived. . . .'[33]

Broadcasting was founded with certain interim solutions in mind to the nineteenth-century quandary about the right levels of taste and tone with which to address the new mass audience. The problems to which Matthew Arnold and Mudie had in their different ways addressed themselves still beset an age which had a series of new information technologies on its hands, and decisions to make which would clearly be destined to be of far-reaching social importance. The immediate past offered only a very poor example of how mass media could best be organised and controlled. One thing seemed certain, or at least was so deeply ingrained that it did not have to be argued – that the mass audience was homogeneous and huge and was susceptible to unpleasant influences from which it should be protected. Nonetheless the mood of the twenties remained in Britain and Europe fairly optimistic about the potential for enforced enlightenment of the mass audience. The Report of the 1925 Broadcasting Committee under the Chairmanship of Lord Crawford which urged the transformation of the British Broadcasting Company into a Commission (and in fact helped to found the BBC very much as we know it today), wrestled with the problem of the height of brow which has bedevilled the entire history of discourse about broadcasting: 'The listener is entitled to latitude. He must not be pressed to assimilate too much of what he calls "highbrow" broadcast, and the Commission would not be wise in transmitting more educational matter than licensees are prepared to accept. We are assured by musicians eminent in their art and versed in this very problem, that the gradual infusion of improved standards will be welcomed by listeners – unconsciously at first, but with growing appreciation amongst those who will instinctively learn to desire better performances.'[34]

Broadcasting spoke a gentle language, that of uncles and aunts.[35] 'In any event', wrote Reith, the founder of the BBC, 'it was better to over-estimate than to under-estimate. If another policy had been adopted – that of the lowest common denominator – what then? Probably nobody would have protested.'[36] Radio came to alleviate loneliness rather than satisfy a mass craving for non-stop entertainment. In every country to which it came it had to respond to the needs of soc .. bewildered by the new force of the mass audience. 'The multitude has suddenly become visible, installing itself in the preferential positions in society. Before it existed, it passed unnoticed, occupying the background of the social stage; now it has advanced to the footlights and is the principal character. There are no longer protagonists; there is only the chorus.'[37]

The tone of voice which broadcasting adopted and spread was a mixture of the elementary schoolteacher, the social planner and the psychologist. The institutions which were created in the early twenties to house and control the broadcasters were all concerned to avoid the pitfalls of commercialism which, in the growth of a society of mass consumer goods, had already degraded the language of mass communication. (Even in the United States, Coolidge and Hoover tried to minimise the quantity of advertising.) Broadcasting was born with a sense of social responsibility, and the duty was imposed on the communicator to be aware of the nature of the audience. Only very rarely was the audience itself expected to get up out of its seat and speak. Marconi had made waves travel through the air and enabled the telephone to be split into two halves, one half for the communicator and one for the audience. Nearly all the energy which went into the creation of broadcasting went into the task of processing the messages, of choosing voices which would address the listening multitude. This meant that broadcasting automatically inherited another major conundrum, the problem of freedom, the question of how mass society could cope with its own libertarian ideals.

II

In 1870 James Fitzjames Stephen set off on the long voyage to India where, for two years, he was to act as a member of the Legislative Council; he was already a distinguished member of the London legal world and author of *A General View of the Criminal Law of England*; in his trunk he took with him a copy of John Stuart Mill's already famous *Essay on Liberty*,[38] published in 1859 and well established as a classic document of the English view of democracy. Stephen pondered its highminded and influential idealism as he wrestled with the problems of helping to rule an empire of 150,000,000 people armed only with the ideals of English government and the tools of English law. He determined to write a denunciation of Mill, systematic and total, and completed it as his ship sailed through the Red Sea on the voyage home. He published the first version of his attack in a series of articles in *The Pall Mall Gazette* and then turned them into a book. Alas, his target died a few months after the book *Liberty, Equality, Fraternity* was published and

Stephen never discovered what Mill thought of its arguments. But their dialogue – that of liberty versus coercion – provided arguments and the shibboleths for a debate about how far freedom of discussion and action can be allowed to go in societies which depend, because of their complexity, on the centralisation of Order. It is, of course, a very old debate; British and American literature and politics had provided a series of superb examples of its expression for centuries before Mill and Stephen presented Victorian London with their extreme and eloquent versions of the opposing cases. Nonetheless their two essays expressed the dilemma in the language of men confronting urbanised society and a multi-racial empire, modern nations living in daily fear of modern revolutionaries, of demagogues suddenly whipping up semi-literate mobs into acts of frenzy, of suburbs full of idealists demanding the opportunity to spread reform. They were dealing with the problem of discussion and disorder in what was in essence a world we understand today. Stephen saw that coercion in the end was the only effective tool of order – all else was hypocrisy or revolutionism: 'All the great political changes which have been the principal subject of European history for the last three centuries have been cases of coercion in the most extreme form.'[39] It was force which determined the nature of the relationships between human beings; the place of toleration was to mitigate struggles, not to mislead people into thinking that they could be avoided.

Mill was expressing his thoughts, he believed, in a society which had come to accept that rulers were now 'tenants and delegates',[40] revocable at their subjects' pleasure. His object was to assert one very simple principle: 'that the sole need for which mankind are warranted, individually or collectively, in interfering with the liberty of action of any of their number, is self-protection. That the only purpose for which power can be rightfully exercised over any member of a civilised community, against his will, is to prevent harm to others.'[41] Stephen's voice can almost be heard scoffing down the years at such vapid and dangerously optimistic a view of human nature. 'What is all morality, and what are all existing religions in so far as they aim at affecting human conduct, except an appeal either to hope

34

or fear, and to fear far more commonly and far more emphatically than to hope?'[42]

Mill had created a model of society consisting of freely circulating ideas as a free market consists of freely circulating goods. 'But the peculiar evil of silencing the expression of an opinion is, that it is robbing the human race; posterity as well as the existing generation; those who dissent from the opinion, still more than those who hold it. If the opinion is right, they are deprived of the opportunity of exchanging error for truth; if wrong, they lose, what is almost as great a benefit, the clearer perception and livelier impression of truth, produced by its collision with error.'[43] Stephen had a totally different picture in his mind of the workings of society: coercion, not liberty, was the mechanism by which ideas moved into and out of ascendancy. 'A struggle for ascendancy does not mean mere argument. It means reiterated and varied assertion persisted in, in the face of the wheel, the stake and the gallows, as well as in the face of contradiction.'[44]

In the decades that followed the Mill–Stephen controversy a vast section of the population previously excluded from power entered it. Political discussion was no longer confined to the drawing room; the abstract discussion about a vague 'right of expression' was translated into a complex set of issues concerned with the organisation of freedom *within the world of the press*. In a society in which individual rights were widely spread the problem of the right to know, the right to obtain information itself, rather than the right to hold and express opinions of one's own, became more important. The press thus became the carrier throughout society of great quantities of factual material, and freedom was on the one hand something which had to be delegated to a professional and organised group, a specialised industry in fact, and on the other an issue between government and governed concerning the release of information.[45] After the opening up of all posts in the civil service to competitive examination, a new type of central government bureaucracy came into being whose function was to monitor the regulations of a complex modern state.[46] The model of a 'free' society drawn up by Mill was accepted as a matter of faith by the citizens of the modernised British state, but in practice two sets of middlemen intervened in the flow of facts and ideas – the press and the bureaucracy.

Wilbur Schramm dates the growth of what he calls The New Theory of mass communication from that point (in England under Walpole) when the spread of printed material swamped the ability of government to preserve itself from sedition by prior censorship of everything in circulation.[47] Printing had been born into an authoritarian society in which all discussion was subordinated automatically to the needs of the state. Plato had stated the case for a powerful code of culture which would control all poetry and all writing prior to publication. Sheer bulk of material, however, forced a situation at the end of the seventeenth century in which governments had to resort to punishment after the fact of publication rather than relying on the licensing of presses.[48] 'If every dreamer of innovations may propagate his projects, there can be no settlement; if every murmurer at government may diffuse discontent, there can be no peace; and if every skeptick in theology may teach his follies, there can be no religion. The remedy against these evils is to punish the authors; for it is yet allowed that every society may punish though not prevent, the publication of opinions which that society shall think pernicious,'[49] wrote Samuel Johnson in an effort to resolve the vexing problem of uniting order with freedom. The solution to the impossibility of prevention was to elevate publishing at peril into an organised system.

The period of the Enlightenment brought of course a renewed sense of individuality and diversity which almost destroyed the older forms of authoritarianism. Paine, Erskine and Jefferson revived the Miltonic notion of the self-demonstrating power of truth. In the cut and thrust of rational discussion, true doctrine will always survive. 'The discernment they have manifested between truth and falsehood, shows that they may safely be trusted to hear everything true and false, and to form a correct judgment between them,'[50] said Jefferson, anticipating the 'free market' notion of Mill. The New Theory could survive intact the growth of improved distributive technology of printed material, but was inevitably called again into question with the advent of a society in which debate had to be conducted before an audience of millions, untrained in discourse, unattuned to the codes and assumptions of an educated élite.[51]

In its first version the American Constitution contained no provision guaranteeing religious or intellectual liberty, except in debates of Congress.[52] Some of the states' delegates present at the making of the Constitution objected to the omission, but Hamilton defended it on the grounds that liberty was indefinable and depended on the stoutness of public opinion for its defence. But Virginia, New York and Rhode Island nonetheless embodied a statement of a right of expression in the course of their ratification of the federal constitution, and several states continued demanding an overtly stated federal right. At the first session of Congress a Bill of Rights was introduced (November 1791) which incorporated the First Amendment, which is now as much a part of the fundamental law of the United States as trial by jury. 'Congress shall make no law respecting an establishment of religion, or prohibiting the free exercise thereof; or abridging the freedom of speech or of the press; or the right of the people peaceably to assemble, and to petition the Government for a redress of grievances.' Those words, as Zechariah Chafee pointed out in examining the damaged state of press freedom in America in the aftermath of the First World War, represent 'a declaration of national policy in favour of the public discussion of all public questions';[53] they tend to halt the intrusion of government beyond a certain point. But that did not prevent in the United States fundamental discussions about the nature of press freedom and the rights of expression of individuals within a modern state (especially in regard to matters of national security).

The eighteenth-century press demonstrated clearly the prevailing notion that truth was something to be gleaned through argument by thinking men. In this the first great period of journalistic expansion a host of tiny papers sprang up, inspired (or paid for) by parties and individuals pursuing causes and opposing interests of various kinds. No ideology of journalism had yet been established; there was no distinction between news and comment. There was no implied guarantee of accuracy in what was presented.[54] In 1783 the Rev. George

37

Crabbe described the crowded and corrupt world of the newspaper:

> 'So idle dreams, the journals of the night,
> Are right and wrong by turns, and mingle wrong with
>   right.
> Some champions for the rights that prop the crown,
> Some sturdy patriots, sworn to pull them down;
> Some neutral powers, with secret forces fraught,
> Wishing for war, but willing to be bought:
> While some to every side and party go,
> Shift every friend, and join with every foe;
> Like sturdy rogues in privateers, they strike
> This side and that, the foes of both alike;
> A traitor-crew, who thrive in troubled times,
> Fear'd for their force, and courted for their crimes.'[55]

Crabbe and his contemporaries had a sense of the press being something quite new to city life. Although London and other European cities had enjoyed regular printed news since the middle of the previous century, the feeling of the imminent presence of a world of warring, squabbling newsmen was something which still had an air of novelty about it. Henry-Samson Woodfall, the proprietor of the *Public Advertiser*, gains a special mention in Crabbe's lengthy poem 'The Newspaper' because, alone of London newspaper-owners, he observed a policy of strict political impartiality: 'as many essays were admitted on the ministerial side of the question as on that of the opposition'.

> 'Oh! cruel Woodfall! when a patriot draws
> His gray-goose quill on his dear country's cause,
> To vex and maul a ministerial race,
> Can thy stern soul refuse the champion place?'[56]

It was when newspaper revenue began to come more from advertising than from party subsidy that a new ideology in journalism began to appear. The financial independence of journalism enabled it to gain a different perspective on its role in society. While it remained normal for newspapers to espouse a party interest, 'objective news' began to seem a viable and laudable ideal. Much later, the wire services conjured into being a race of neutral journalists in order that news could be sold to papers of differing political persuasions. As industrialisation grew, as newspapers involved an ever-larger investment of capital to bring them into existence, the press gained a greater and greater sense of itself as a kind of national resource; its ideology of truthfulness increased accordingly.[57] But the transition to the modern assembly-line journalism of the news-pages and the broadcast-newsrooms was a very slow one. The great newsmen of the nineteenth-century were concerned with their own scrupulousness and fairness. John Thaddeus Delane of *The Times* rejoiced in his own anonymity;[58] not until the First World War did journalism become a matter of personal publicity for the writer. There was a sternness of principle in the matter of newsgathering, but newspapers still regarded their greatest duty as that of arguing and espousing an important cause in an influential way. Newspapers were important political commodities, and editors began to see their interests (including their moral interests) as diverging from those of owners. While owners, properly, could direct and alter the policy of their papers, the professional journalist had to achieve and maintain a consistency of viewpoint within his own personality.[59] The newspaper was a commodity which could change hands. The editor was a 'professional' whose personal political consistency on public issues kept him apart from his medium. The intricate intermingling of politics and newspaper-ownership has tended to diminish; at the same time journalists have become far less involved in the rise and fall of political interests. They are today much more concerned with the management of the technical enterprises they command; they belong rather more to the machinery, but they are professional observers of government and have accepted a kind of generalised social responsibility.

In the United States the first generation of 'objective' journalism in the 1880s and 1890s came with the rise of the 'muckrakers', who while remaining politically and ideologically independent themselves discovered a mission in 'trouble-making'.[60] As the war approached they developed a more

39

purely radical streak. John Reed was to go to Russia in a fit of impulsive romanticism and describe the day-to-day events of the October Revolution. Upton Sinclair, of the same generation, denounced American newspapers as 'the servants of unscrupulous business interests'.[61] Both of them were masters of an art which would later come to be known as 'reportage', the detailed personal reporting of an important war or political crisis, which combined the talents of the newsman with the insight of the novelist in the cause of a higher truth. Mencken in the 1920s looked back on that world of changing values in American journalism with a nostalgic thrill: newspapers had grown so rich that they could at last afford to have principles. 'In almost every American city, large or small, some flabbergasted advertiser, his money in his hand, sweat pouring from him as if he had seen a ghost, was kicked out with spectacular ceremonies. All the principal papers, suddenly grown rich, began also to grow independent, virtuous, touchy, sniffish.'[62] Mencken spoke too of the new respect the journalist had gained for his own profession; 'he no longer sees it as a craft to be mastered in four days, and abandoned at the first sign of a better job. He begins to talk darkly of the long apprenticeship necessary to master its technic, of the wide information and sagacity needed to adorn it, of the high rewards that it offers – or may offer later on – to the man of true talent and devotion.... Now he thinks of himself as a fellow of weight and responsibility, a beginning publicist and a public man, sworn to the service of the born and unborn, heavy with duties to the Republic and to his profession.'[63] The growth in respectability was part of the trend towards accuracy and away from partisanship. 'Save in the South and the remote fastnesses of New England the old-time party organ has gone out of fashion. In the big cities the faithful hacks of the New York *Tribune* type have begun to vanish. With them has gone the old-time drunken reporter, and in his place is appearing a young fellow of better education, and generally finer metal.'[64]

What had happened was that journalism had become technicalised. The reporter had become a broker of information, exercising the specialised skill of journalistic writing: he occupied a new position in the relationship between government and the governed. He had to translate specialised jargons and specially coded knowledge (of government, the military, the scientists, the leaders of finance) into a language and a form of presentation which were understood by the new public which purchased newspapers.

Literacy greatly antedated the growth of public schooling and the development of the Northcliffian press. But the new homogenised reading public who understood the idiom of the post-Victorian journalism required, for the purposes of the state as well as its own well-being, to absorb the much more complex, technical and abundant information pouring forth from government.[65] The communicators of the new information needed the mass audience delivered to them as much as they to it. The new journalism was the machinery of brokerage between the two parties. The Code of professional responsibility spelt the end of the old role of journalism as an advocate of causes. The new mass society gave the journalist as an individual a new status and an entirely new role to play. He had all of his old roles available to him still, but his self-justification was that he was a professional communicator. His role forced him to adhere strongly to a new and difficult code; he had to collect information from other professionalised and mechanised sources and he had to preserve confidences and seek out uncontaminated information.[66] He was placed *between* the two ends of the communication process, with a professional responsibility to both. His skill lay in his ability to be readable, entertaining, a kind of showman; he had to deliver the audience, he had to sell newspapers on their 'entertainment value', but his product carried with it a series of social messages of far greater importance, expressed in popular language, and in the new photographic processes, in cartoon and cheesecake, in the blaring headline and the stereotype 'human' story. He had become one of the main agencies for cementing together the new societies.

Journalism thus became involved in the issue of *modernity*.[67] The new mass communicator had power over the machinery of social change as much as, if not more than, the politician. The issue of freedom of expression was severely modified because it mattered only if the message could be delivered into one or other of the technologies which controlled the pathway of access to the mass audience. The issue of freedom thus became, and remained throughout the period in which radio and television were developed, an issue concerning the ownership and control of media.

The propaganda of the First World War illustrated the abuse of the new resources. It left the intelligentsia, and many of the politicians, throughout the allied countries, realising, in a vision made powerful in the novels of Huxley and Wells, and made credible by the theorists of Behaviourist psychology, that powerful élites now possessed the power to intoxicate the broad masses into moods in which they could misuse their new political power. (In *Mein Kampf* Hitler was to write that he learned all his own propaganda techniques from British methods during the war.) In the newspaper barons of Fleet Street and New York they saw the process occurring. The new field of mass communication research was opened up for investigation; its lessons were rapidly absorbed by the advertising and public relations industries, anxious to base themselves on a more exact science than that hitherto available.[68]

In a series of writings Zechariah Chafee tried to bring the new discoveries into the canons of American law. After the Treaty of Versailles he published his classic work *Freedom of Speech*[69] which was partly designed to show that American constitutional law required positive efforts on the part of government to preserve the rights of the individual. The wartime Espionage Acts should not have been enacted, because 'the great interest in free speech should be sacrificed only when the interest in public safety is really impaired, and not, as most men believe, when it is barely conceivable that it might be slightly affected.'[70] The war had been a great watershed in the testing of assumptions about freedom of expression. Chafee believed that this right had in fact survived the ravages of war. He revised his work in the gloomy period following the outbreak of the Second World War;[71] arguing that the rise of Hitler would have been less likely if freedom of speech had not been so badly impaired after the previous war, as it had been in a series of judgements and enactments made during the thirties which interfered with materials carried in US Mails, shown on cinema screens and broadcast by radio. Like Canute imploring the waves to recede, Chafee continued to argue with an apparently unsympathetic American public that freedom of speech was as great a national interest as national security itself.[72] The instruments of radio, the talkies and television turned mass communication into a mechanism of vast psychological impact. The political and social messages were carried on the wings of a new instrument which commanded the entire resources of the culture in an untiring and highly specialised quest to maintain its links with the whole of the mass audience in a single moment.[73]

When broadcasting began it had to share the role of cultural 'brokerage' with the record industry, the cinema, the popular performing arts and to some extent the newspaper.[74] It inherited their problems too, the problems of how to address the audience, what image it should contain within itself of the single and simultaneous manifestation of the mass audience.[75] News was to be carried on the wings of song. There was a struggle throughout the twenties and thirties over the usurpation of the role of the newspapers fought very bitterly in America and by a process of slow but stealthy encroachment in England. Reith's solution and that of the Newspaper Proprietors' Association in London was that radio should merely offer, after the final editions of the evening papers had been sold out, a résumé of the wire services' reports of the day.[76] 'The public is well served by the Press in the matter of news, and we consider that any extension of the broadcasting of news should be carried out gradually, the effect of each extension being carefully watched. . . .'[77]

On both sides of the Atlantic the problem of 'freedom of speech' took the form of a debate about the precise proximity to government at which broadcasting should be placed. There seemed to be no intelligent alternative to making broadcasting draw its fundamental title from the state; the question was how to find a point of editorial control over the whole content which would satisfy the whole political spectrum of the nation (at least as far as that spectrum was represented in party terms in Parliament). It was taken for granted that broadcasting would be a further development of mass society, in that the instrument was thought to be not a means for developing or changing the shape of democracy but of containing it, fairly statically. The free and open discussion of ideas, the flow of communication between government and governed was subsumed under the rubric 'controversy'. Argument, by implication something slightly unsavoury and to be indulged in, like boxing, only under carefully controlled conditions in which it might not get out of hand, was the bowdlerised version of John Stuart Mill's libertarian theory. 'We are unable to lay down a precise line of policy or to assess the degree to which argument can be safely transmitted. In the absence of authoritative evidence such advice would be premature. But, speaking generally, we believe that if the material be of high quality, not too lengthy or insistent, and distributed with scrupulous fairness, licensees will desire a moderate amount of controversy. . . .'[78] Broadcasting has spent its history in an attempt to escape from that particular straitjacket.[79]

Essentially, broadcasting's in-built social vision is based upon that of politicians who saw themselves wrestling with a series of problems within a nation of which their own institutions were an accurate map. Broadcasting therefore absorbed and forever purveyed the impression that that was how society was, because, in its charters and licences and daily relationships with authority, that was how society had been in a sense defined. Henceforth the broadcasting institution had an interest in it remaining an accurate vision. 'The Post Office does not maintain any system of censorship of broadcast matter . . . while the Postmaster-General must remain the final arbiter when any question is raised as to what kind of matter may or may not be broadcast, we think it will be of great help to him to have a Broadcasting Board . . . who would advise him on such matters, and who would be free of any suspicion of political bias.'[80] Broadcasting thus developed a role as a kind of arbiter within the world of the politicians itself; this extra responsibility added to its power, its impact, and to the closer supervision which it incurred in response. Gradually it was to be obliged to take over more of the roles of the press, but it operated a national, governmentally-sponsored resource – the wavelength – and broadcasting therefore could never enjoy the spontaneity of newspapers. It had to be deliberate, calculated in all things. Monopoly was its privilege, its responsibility was never to initiate, always to reflect. 'It is agreed that the United States system of free and uncontrolled transmission and reception is unsuited to this country, and that Broadcasting must accordingly remain a monopoly – in other words that the whole organisation must be controlled by a single authority.'[81] Nonetheless the situation in America was gradually resolved in ways that made its deepest meanings and most long-term problems distinguished by their similarity to, not by their divergence from, those identified in the British system.[82]

Broadcasting helped to push back the directions in which press freedom had been driving; it helped the creation of the 'social responsibility' theory of the press, best expressed in the American Commission on the Freedom of the Press of 1947.[83] Society could no longer afford to be let down by the common carriers of ideas. Press freedom was a freedom to provide a certain kind of service to society, it retained no freedom to please itself. 'Today, this former legal privilege wears the aspect of social irresponsibility. The press must know that its faults and errors have ceased to be private vagaries and have become public dangers. Its inadequacies menace the balance of public opinion. It has lost the common and ancient liberty to be deficient in its function or to offer half-truth for the whole.'[84] Into broadcasting, its culture and institutions, was fed a picture of the modern audience, vast and simultaneous. That audience owned the medium. The broadcasters served it. The relationship was too highly charged with political tensions for the old Millian theory of free expression to survive. A cultural exchange could take place within the broadcasting institution, but not between it and the audience. The audience was too large, too diverse and therefore the medium was too powerful. Broadcasting challenged from its inception all the existing ideas about the nature of 'freedom of expression'.

III

There are two riddles coiled at the roots of radio and television broadcasting; in one sense they run through all political

45

discussion since the age of print began, but in broadcasting they have become inseparable, a double conundrum with a hundred answers, all of them unsatisfactory.

The first dilemma can be expressed thus: have I a pre-eminent duty to society to calculate in advance the possible effects of the information I intend to impart or do I in fact have a greater duty to the audience to tell them now and in a way I know they will enjoy exactly what they want to hear? It is embedded in every decision ever taken about broadcasting. To what extent to 'educate'? To what extent to 'entertain'? To what extent to water down the content of a programme in order to achieve a higher audience? Any decision taken in regard to the content of a *mass* medium is in one way political, in that the decision will tend to influence the nature of the information and attitudes contained in society and thus become willy-nilly part of the actual social environment in which we all have to live.

The second dilemma concerns freedom of expression: if there is only one soap-box available, or one megaphone or one printing press (or at best a limited number of them), to whom should they be given?—to the man who fights to the front of the queue, or to the man who in the opinion of some independent body has the most interesting things to say? When the means of communication were instantly available to a small number of people who in practice constituted Society the problem was easier to deal with; the privileged élite group of the articulate and the informed created a kind of intellectual free market among themselves. Today the context in which the decisions are being made is the mass enfranchised society. They can only speak through delegates and representatives. Should it be the prerogative of professional broadcasters – all of them half-way to being civil servants – to choose them?

Both these dilemmas were present in essence long before broadcasting had been invented. Indeed, it was 'invented' and developed in ways that were partly a response to them. In broadcasting the two, already closely interlinked, became fused into a single ever-vexing complex of problems.

Chapter Two

Building Citadels in the Air:
The Broadcasting Institution

'The BBC came to pass silently, invisibly; like a coral reef,
cells busily multiplying, until it was a vast structure, a
conglomeration of studios, offices, cool passages along which
many passed to and fro; a society, with its king and lords
and commoners, its laws and dossiers and revenue and easily
suppressed insurrection; where there was marriage and giving
in marriage, and where evil-doers and adulterers were
punished, and the faithful rewarded. As many little rivulets
empty themselves into a wide lake, all their motion lost in
its still expanse of water, so did every bubbling trend and
fashion empty themselves into the BBC.'

Malcolm Muggeridge, *The Thirties* (1940)

'We have adopted the best elements of every system of
broadcasting in the world and we have ended up with a
cartel, run by a clique.'

Israeli Member of Parliament, to the author (1972)

I

In the historical moment at which a new invention is being
pioneered it tends to take upon itself an aura of social salvation.
The research work is surrounded with exaggerated hopes. The
inventors are thought to be about to produce a solution to the
entire range of contemporary problems. It is only when the
new invention is firmly placed in its industrial and financial
context, surrounded by its own special bureaucracy, that its
limitations are identified.

In the case of instruments of communication, the technology
itself is only one part of the invention which depends upon a

complex of societal links. A railway engine was merely a curious metal monster until there were stations at locations between which people actually needed to travel at suitable speed and cost.[1] The telephone depended on a complex set of social circumstances and industrial organisations for its potential to be realised; in its earliest days it was often expected to become an instrument far more versatile and revolutionary than has in fact been the case. In the 1860s there were many attempts to use the technology of the telephone for a purpose analogous to broadcasting. In 1909 in San José Charles D. Herrold sent out regular scheduled programmes by telephone wire.[2] In 1875 a Hungarian, Theodore Puskás, who had worked with Edison, had the idea of linking all the telephone subscribers to a central point and sending out a service of news. In 1879 he actually did this in Paris while his brother ran a similar service in Budapest. In the mid-nineties, several thousand citizens of Budapest could receive his Telephone Newspaper which gave out a bulletin of news and stockprices, taken from the wire services, during the day and transmitted concerts in the evening.[3] The service survived as a curious spoken newspaper, until 1930, when it was overtaken by radio. Inventions take on a coloration from the existing social instruments which they replace or extend; they are institutionalised within the societies which develop them and they begin to appear far less revolutionary than in the moment of their conception. In the case of radio, it was the First World War which gave its development an enormous impetus and created a great industry of radio hams and 'experimenters' who continued to work in the field until the road ahead, in terms of manufacturing sales, social organisation and administrative control, was clearly visible. It then, very rapidly, became a medium of communication and, unlike the telephone system of the brothers Puskás, did not fall quietly by the wayside.

In 1916 the young David Sarnoff, an employee of the American Marconi Company, wrote a letter to the general manager suggesting a commercial formula for exploiting the new developments in radio-telephony on which the firm had been working. Sarnoff had achieved prominence within the Marconi organisation four years previously, when, as a radio operator demonstrating some of the firm's latest marvels in the Wanamaker store in New York, he had picked up messages from the sinking 'Titanic' liner. He had become commercial manager of US Marconi at the age of 25. Although there were already some transmitting stations sending out music and news to amateur radio operators in the United States, Sarnoff knitted together a series of ideas in a formula which showed that the mass consumer was in the forefront of his mind. 'I have in mind a plan of development which would make radio a "household utility" in the same sense as the piano or phonograph. The receiver can be designed in the form of a simple "radio Music Box" and arranged for several different wavelengths, which would be changeable with the throwing of a single switch or pressing of a single button. The "radio Music Box" can be supplied with amplifying tubes and a loudspeaking telephone, all of which can be neatly mounted in one box. The box can be placed in the parlour or living room, the switch set accordingly and the transmitted music received. . . . This proposition would be especially interesting to farmers and others living in outlying districts removed from cities. By the purchase of a "radio Music Box" they could enjoy concerts, lectures, music, recitals etc., which may be going on in the nearest city within their radius.'[4]

Sarnoff had mentally made a number of the necessary relationships of social phenomena which eventually brought a radio industry into existence. There was a certain view of the shape of society implied, a mental image of a manufacturing industry analogous to the phonograph industry, a vision of a technical potential, and a fundamental decision to separate that part of the equipment of a telephone which sent out messages from the part which received them. Sarnoff hit upon the idea at a moment when others were making the same connections and divisions within other societies with suitable technical facilities. No single person 'invented' radio; nor did any single society. The post-war world was in a number of partly indefinable ways 'ready' for a new piece of machinery which would disseminate the culture of mass society.

In the 1870s the financial and industrial infrastructures were not ready to turn the telephone into a medium of mass dissemination of news and music; fifty years later the soil was prepared and the plant shot up in a few years.

As the radio industry developed in the 1920s the institutions and cultural decisions fitted into the notions about the shape of society, its ideals, its economics that prevailed at that moment. The broadcasting organisations that sprang up in country after country were the institutional counterparts of technical, social, psychological, financial and political determinants. Each institution was an invention on the part of its originating society in much the same way that radio had been the 'invention' of David Sarnoff – it was a juxtaposition of a set of assumptions and dilemmas. 'The BBC is an invention in the sphere of social science no less remarkable than the invention of radio transmission in the sphere of natural science,'[5] wrote W. A. Robson, looking back on the first decade and a half of broadcasting in Britain. In America the institutional structures of radio were spread out geographically and financially with haphazard centralising efforts being made by government agencies and large conglomerates; in the first era of broadcasting the problem facing the industry was simply how to spread to every individual member of society the technical means for receiving the new messages.[6] Every society has to reinvent broadcasting in its own image, as a means for containing or suppressing the geographical, political, spiritual and social dilemmas which broadcasting entails.

The growth of the cinema had been far less problem-ridden than broadcasting. For one thing it seemed naturally to grow out of the theatre, because its relationship with its audience was almost identical rows of people who paid at the door. It did not, except perhaps in wartime, exploit a national resource. It did not in any sense depend on state patronage. It developed from the fairground stunt;[7] its first method of transmission to an audience, in 1894, was through a one-man-audience machine derived from the traditional peepshow. It spread with incredible speed in the first decade of the twentieth century and at the end of that decade had been forced into adopting codes and rituals to protect the young from exposure to immorality and anti-authority propaganda in a way which foreshadowed the methods by which radio and television broadcasting were to be made socially responsive instruments. In the case of the early cinema the film-maker had no difficulty in identifying his audience; he could go and look at the audience for himself twice nightly. The early film-makers were ordinary film-goers themselves.[8] The first generation of cinema-goers attended their cinemas weekly and represented a vast extension in social terms of the theatre audience and that of the music hall. But the products they saw were mass products manufactured for the entertainment of conglomerate audiences, groups of publics of different classes and ranks, and the same pressures for social accountability and control were set in motion as appeared twenty years later to demand the cultural policing of radio. The movie code of America obliged film-makers to ensure that 'no motion picture shall be produced which will lower the moral standards of those who see it'.[9] Worked out in extreme detail as to the manner in which prevailing institutions and beliefs could and could not be portrayed, the code is a decalogue of social propaganda: nothing was to be seen on the screen which might help to change the moral structure or assumptions of society.

Although the film-maker could observe his audience and even speak to them, his mass product was made inside an industrial enterprise. The film-maker takes with him to his studio as a writer to his study his mental image of his intended audience. His product is a kind of gamble between his creative imagination and his guesswork about what the audience will accept. The experience gathered with every new film enriches the creator's perceptions of the audience. Every mass media creator has the same problem but in broadcasting the time-scales are completely different, the audience can't be revisited and retested at a repeat performance in the same way. The television audience is believed to want the same product daily, the cinema audience was thought to want something different every week. In both cases the audience is not a unified concept but a set of impressions accumulated over time in the mind of the maker and embodied in the rhythms and patterns of the product. The codes and organisations on which the creator of the film or the radio or television channel depends tend to dominate his mental picture of the audience; their potential for

51

understanding, their potential to be *affected* by his product are ineluctable influences on his work. All programme-making work is conducted against a backdrop of the anticipated reaction of the invisible audience.

Broadcasting required a far more carefully worked out structure than the film because from the beginning it was seen to be a means of communicating a far wider range of content – it was not only an extension of theatre, it was a new technology which could carry into people's homes, beyond the neat control of the box office, a total range of cultural genres. Broadcasting brought to a head *all* the issues of cultural control, but it coded them in its own special terms.

The question of freedom of discussion is transmuted into decisions about the organisation of 'controversy' inside the BBC; the questions which Arnold pondered are turned into decisions about the levels of taste, especially in music. All of these decisions however are locked up inside the institutions; they are decisions over which the Director General of the BBC is given full control or matters which are deemed to belong, as a right, to the licensees of the hundreds of radio stations which sprang up in the American system.

Broadcasting, in Britain at any rate, did not have to confront any question of 'censorship' because there was only one centrally licensed 'publisher', the BBC. In a way broadcasting – with its wavelength problems – brought the issue of press control back into the Tudor age, where a scarce medium was placed under government licence. In the cinema censorship had grown up fairly quickly as a means to protect the domestic cinema industry from being the victim of foreign 'lewd' films dumped on British territory. The British Board of Film Censors came into existence just at the time when means had to be found to prevent French 'pornography' flooding the country's cinemas.[10] The mechanism of control has survived almost unchanged, although the set of social mores it upholds has been substantially transformed. Control of broadcasting content did not grow up analogously with the film because it was based upon a central organisation whose judgement was 'trusted' by authority. The film industry came under a kind of self-discipline and willingly acted, especially in time of war, as a propagandiser of its client audience. Broadcasting was born in Britain as an instrument of parliament, as a kind of embassy of the national culture and the national polity within the nation. The free exchange of ideas, the representation of the whole range of national issues of contention, was filtered through a stately organisation owning massive prestige; it implanted inevitably its own perspective of the world on the material which passed through its hands.

In the United States, the debate over the control of broadcasting – licensing and content – has been conducted in vastly dissimilar terms, but in response to the same problems of anticipated effect upon the audience. Americans have from the start distrusted the idea of a governmentally-financed central public broadcasting system, on the grounds that it would easily be captured by groups demanding excessively rapid social change.[11] The tradition of the First Amendment and the tradition of complete personal economic freedom meant that from the very beginning broadcasting was put into a myriad hands; hundreds of completely independent stations were licensed across the nation by a governmental agency with very little power of content supervision, the Federal Communications Commission. Broadcasting merely fell into the hands of local establishments, like-minded, commercially-motivated and heavily imbued with the same reactions to the problems of audience psychology. The message of cultural freedom contained in the First Amendment simply enabled market forces (against which broadcasting in Britain and elsewhere had been protected) to create institutions of broadcasting and process their products. In the very early years the American listener was identified as the purchaser of the receiving set. The listener was thus an extension of the phonograph purchaser and the revenue of radio was derived from sales of sets. Only later was the discovery made that broadcasting was the most powerful 'selling' instrument hitherto devised.[12] This transformation, which has become an automatic part of our thinking about broadcasting, meant that the broadcasting audience was to become the most heavily processed, the most subtly assailed, the costliest, and intellectually the most trivialised audience in the history of communication. Unlike Britain,

America possessed no element in its society powerful enough to protect the consumer against these forces at the moment when broadcasting was created. Herbert Schiller describes this point in American broadcasting history: 'Corporate complexes struggled for monopolistic control of the broadcasting medium while the public was considered first only as a consumer of equipment and later as a saleable audience.'[13] In fact the end product of American broadcasting (and of almost every other broadcasting system) is the audience itself. The industry grew up, after the initial period, as the most powerful instrument in history (except perhaps for the medieval Church) for delivering a complete social audience to a communicator.

The programmes help to get the audience the advertiser needs. John Kenneth Galbraith sees radio and television today as the prime instruments for the management of consumer demand: 'There is an insistent tendency among solemn social scientists to think of any institution which features rhymed and singing commercials, intense and lachrymose voices urging highly improbable enjoyment, caricatures of the human oesophagus in normal or impaired operation, and which hints implausibly at opportunities for antiseptic seduction, as inherently trivial. This is a great mistake. The industrial system is profoundly dependent on commercial television and could not exist in its present form without it.'[14] Galbraith argues that the effects of the system are upon the mass, not the individual. The individual remains free to buy or not to buy, to agree or not to agree, to accept the broadcasters' social priorities or to reject them, but the chances of sufficient people exercising their individual will on a scale sufficient to impair the working of the system as a whole is slight. Television on the American pattern not only controls demand and enables the management of the system to be smoother than otherwise; it also 'conducts a relentless propaganda on behalf of goods in general'.[15] Galbraith sees the mental conditioning of television as its main contribution to the economic system, rather than the propagation of any specific set of ideas. 'The process by which this management is accomplished, the iterated and reiterated emphasis on the real and assumed virtues of goods, is powerful propaganda for the values and goals of the system.'[16]

In a broadcast system in which points of editorial control are distributed in thousands, just as in one in which that control is heavily centralised in one or two sets of hands, broadcasting maintains the ideals of the society as a whole in the minds of the mass audience, it enforces the message of its institutional owners through a series of cultural products, it 'edits' the society's mental agenda, it absorbs the arguments going on around it, however radical they are in terms of the system, and predigests them as it sends them out again into the system. The broadcasting institution, whether it is concentrated in a single building or depends upon a thousand separate and competing wavelengths and transmitters, has been built up as a centrally licensed force and inevitably behaves like one. It is a gigantic sluice through which all the currents of a nation's culture and public affairs are fed; it diverts them in its own interests and purifies them according to its own formula.

There are thousands of individuals who work within this cultural-industrial enterprise and their minds are its cogs and wheels. Like the members of the mass audience they are individual people who accept in different measure the overall pattern in which they work, but they, like their audience, are homogenised during the hours of labour. The broadcasting institution, like any other within society, is made to fight hard for its own survival. It sits at a precarious point in the society, assailed by critics for encouraging violence or radicalism or escapism, berated for bias or for being anodyne, for overheating its audience and simultaneously for trivialising them; it picks a path cautiously through the cultural battlefields of history. The modern mass audience are the heirs of the drudges of the Victorian industrial cities released from total bondage by the 10 Hour Act, and provided with statutory leisure. As their leisure time has grown, so has their availability to be informed and to become the consumers of the products of the entertainment industry. But in one way broadcasting, especially in the United States, ensures that the viewing public are doing much of their most productive work not during the daylight hours but precisely in their hours of leisure. In the twenty-five-hour week which the average American spends watching television he is working to maintain his economic system, which depends upon his skilfully enhanced capacity to purchase the goods which he creates during his other working hours.

For the American, broadcasting is rooted therefore in economic control. For the British and European viewer it is rooted in social control. On both sides of the Atlantic societies spend about 1 per cent of their total national income on purchasing radio and television sets, and providing funds for the making and disseminating of programmes. Every society has thrown up a centralised method for policing if not actually running the programme-making institutions. Unlike the cinema, the theatre and the record industry, the content-control of broadcasting is ultimately in the same hands as those which control the physical means of distributing the message. In public corporation or private enterprise the licence ultimately depends upon government, which owns the initial wavelength, polices the message and presents the broadcasting institution, therefore, with a kind of permanent emergency.

II

'The BBC was formed as the expedient solution of a technical problem; it owes its existence solely to the scarcity of wavelengths.'[17] That was how the pioneer of radio, Captain Peter Eckersley, saw the origins of Britain's powerful broadcasting organisation. Half a century later it is hard to accept that wavelength shortage alone was responsible. The idea that broadcasting would have to be confined, technically and editorially, within a single *national* institution certainly stemmed from the problem of the wavelength. In the early 1920s America's wavelengths had become impossibly cluttered by a radiophonic anarchy in which radio operators almost overnight were allowed to grab wavelengths like early settlers staking claims on land. Thousands of stations sprang up trying to blast one another off the air. The news of this chaos spread across the Atlantic and fostered in Britain the creation of a highly disciplined system; Mr F. J. Brown of the British Post Office visited the United States in the very early months of 1922 when the BBC was scarcely conceived, and his report was a decisive influence.[18] A new kind of state monopoly was born.

Broadcasting began as an advanced technology of mass communication but with a series of doubts hanging over it concerning the manner of entertainment and education of a mass society; all the uncertainties were made the responsibility of a single organisation.

That broadcasting was locked and remained inside centrally controlled systems (in many countries within a single building) has been one of the most important and least-questioned decisions in media history. There were examples, even in the earliest days of broadcasting, of countries which developed systems partly analogous to publishing, where control of the wavelength and editorial control were in different hands, but these were very few.[19] Even in anarchic America it became rapidly necessary to set up a central licensing authority, the Federal Communications Commission (originally the Federal Radio Commission); the rapid development of great networks with their own codes, editorial and commercial needs and ideals helped to create a central ethos in American broadcasting. Nonetheless the United States presented a different picture from the rest of the world, especially from Europe where the central national authority (modelled in many cases on the BBC) rapidly came to seem inevitable.[20] America struggled against centralisation and has continued in part to do so to the present day.

In Britain the BBC's television monopoly was broken in the 1950s with the advent of commercially-based independent television. Although the whole idea underlying ITV in Britain was to place programme making in a number of separate organisations spread around the country, a series of forces gradually obliged the new system to display all the qualities of a second public national system, remarkably and increasingly similar to the BBC in its reactions to crises of policy and the 'balance' of its schedules. Sir Gerald Beadle chooses to describe the British television structure indeed as 'two state-owned networks'[21] one run by the BBC, the other by the ITA. Certainly the ITA came to share editorial control with the fourteen programme companies, of whom only five have emerged as major programme-makers. Television organisations are institutions whose power consists in their patronage; they distribute money and commissions to a large section of the articulate and the artistic and their influence transforms a section of the intelligentsia into their pensioners, in a manner parallel with the great salons of another epoch. But the salons of broadcasting are very few in number, and although their resources are immense, their security is scanty; periodically they must all undergo review by the state in order to achieve relicensing or rechartering – a process which shakes them to their foundations.

In Britain we have come to think of the BBC as rock-steady, as inexorable as the Church of England or Oxford University; within its walls, however, it conceals a number of permanent nagging fears. Its finance depends on the government of the day agreeing to put up the licence-fee paid by every viewer and listener; its whole existence depends on the government agreeing to renew its Charter on acceptable terms once every decade or so. From time to time a Royal Commission or special committee investigates it and the periods of scrutiny have a considerably sobering effect on all the internal decision-making over programmes. The result is that the organisation constructs its programme schedules in ways which will in effect harness the political support of various sections of the community. In the fifty years of its existence it has had to undergo at least twelve major pieces of external decision-making which could have affected, and indeed did affect, its vital interests in one way or another.

While the infant BBC was still working out its earliest policy on news and information, the General Strike of 1926 broke out, which placed its entire existence as an independent body in jeopardy; at that precise moment the Crawford Committee was sitting, which was making the crucial recommendations on the future of broadcasting in Britain. The programme-decisions were heavily influenced at that moment by the realisation that they would affect not merely the course of the strike and the history of the nation, but the possibility of the BBC existing at all in future. That was an archetypal instance; every similar crisis over what broadcasters should do in a given historical moment has been intensified by the knowledge that the whole central institution would be irrevocably damaged or sustained by the decision over the contents of a programme. The entire history of broadcasting is a history of these crises, each causing a wave of special caution, sometimes lasting for years, inside the organisation. In the thirties there were decisions pending on the future of the development of television and the form of content-control that was to be undertaken in the event of war.[22] After the war, when the prestige and political strength of the BBC were at their height, there was a slow smouldering national debate over the introduction of commercial television, over the work of the Beveridge Committee, and later of the Pilkington Committee. Sir Hugh Greene gives us a wry and amusing picture[23] of the campaign to 'win' the Pilkington battle in 1960 and of the efforts to ensure that no public row broke out over any programme during the waiting period. In the present decade the BBC is awaiting the results of the rechartering process which has been exercising a profound and sobering influence on all its internal policy-making. The broadcasting organisation is therefore constantly under threat of eviction; its programmes cannot be merely a bill of fare for the consumption of its viewers, even in commercial systems which also depend on official sanction for their existence. The story of broadcasting is in many ways a history of how broadcasting organisations set about the task of staying in business. The actual programmes reveal the institution's vital needs as much as the interests of the audience.

In 1971 the BBC earned and spent an income of approximately £100,000,000.[24] Commercial television in Britain enjoys a total income of similar proportions.[25] The vast majority of the funds of broadcasting are spent on fees and salaries. The BBC spends about 70 per cent of its total income in this way; of its actual operating costs 85 per cent goes in wages and salaries.[26] Well over £30,000,000[27] is given by the BBC to people outside its staff, for royalties, appearances, written work, musical performances etc. It is patronage on a scale unimaginable before the growth of this particular medium. In the United States the scale of the largesse is of staggering size. A single half-hour entertainment show on an American network at peak viewing hours can cost $80,000[28] to make (and can draw up to $150,000 in advertising revenue). Although American television spreads its enormous financial resources across a far narrower area of cultural life than European television does, it still supports an army of writers, actors and producers, and thereby influences more than any other single factor the way in which one section of the American intelligentsia earns its daily bread. (I use this term to cover all those whose normal work it is to make cultural products or distribute them.) In the year ending April 1971 the BBC produced on television 960 hours[29] of drama and light entertainment, and that does not include any of the religious or educational programmes which also involve a great quantity of dramatised material; on radio, excluding any of the regional programmes, it produced a further 1600 hours,[30] again excluding religion and education. The regions added to that 300–400 hours[31] of their own drama and light entertainment. In the sheer quantity of writing talent employed, and of actors and producers, the BBC is not only the largest commissioning agency that the world has known, it is actually responsible for a significant proportion of all the dramatic literature being produced in the English language at the present time. It is also responsible for the interpretation of the language's classic culture which most people receive. Although in the United States the central *mechanism* of broadcasting is different, the hegemonic power is remarkably similar.

In the field of music the BBC's pre-eminence is even greater; a large proportion of all the music produced within the United Kingdom is chosen, commissioned or performed within the organisation of the BBC. This cultural power is not potential, it is an actual influence wielded daily in the name of a set of widely acknowledged (and partly disputed) institutional ideals. The power to commission is by far the greatest source of influence there can be within a culture. In every section of the BBC's organisation the decisions are arrived at after extremely conscientious and prolonged consideration. The power is not exercised by the arbitrary whim of a single man or group of men. It is exercised by a corporation in the light of its proclaimed traditional ideals, its corporate conception of the nation's cultural needs, and its own corporate needs within that culture.

Although it is trying to reflect rather than itself create the trends of drama or entertainment (while seeking out 'the best' within every genre) sheer size forces it to perform the latter role, and in doing so it has to consider its own long-term interests. To encourage a group of dramatists whose work was considered socially dangerous or undesirable would be, after a certain point, politically and institutionally dangerous. The broadcasting institution has therefore to take constant readings of its society's political, moral and cultural state of mind. A major problem lies in the fact that the self-interest of the organisation in broadcasting is not necessarily identical with the needs of the culture. In 1972 the BBC commissioned a hotly-argued series of programmes about the history of the British Empire; they were very expensive to produce and the BBC entered into an alliance with Time-Life, the American journalistic enterprise, to share various aspects of the work and to participate in the financial rewards obtained by the eventual sales of the work outside Britain. The furore spread well outside the world of broadcasting, into Parliament and the press. The intellectual problems involved in such a series of programmes were immense and extremely subtle. How was the story of the Empire to be told and interpreted in the 1970s – as a story of national glory or of colonial oppression? The series appeared unable to decide and affronted an even wider spectrum of opinion than if it had taken a single clear and consistent line. One group of critics identified a danger that part of British history was being rewritten in the light of a certain kind of commercial bargaining between the BBC and the Time-Life Corporation. Other groups were angered by specific interpretations of areas of history, fearing that the programme's judgements would become the dominant judgements for decades to come. The production qualities of the programmes were probably overharshly judged in the course of the debate, which threw great light on the basic cultural dilemma inherent in broadcasting decisions taken within a large *national* institution. A judgement with important political side-effects was being made by people concerned primarily with efficient and viewable mass entertainment. At the same time this involved the question of whether the BBC possessed the right to participate in a debate of that scale in an 'editorial' capacity; yet how was it possible to do the task without exercising such a right? The identity of the BBC as a whole was felt somehow to be at stake in the controversy. It had misjudged the mind of its national audience, its powerful licensing clientele. The group of producers responsible for the programmes had created a mutually inconsistent set of historical judgements, but apparently the programme-makers' instinctive view of British imperial history was inconsistent with the interpretation which powerful forces within the community demanded the BBC should foster. In one sense the BBC was confronting an issue of intellectual freedom; but it involved at the same time a decision about precisely where the BBC stood in British society, in which generation, in which class, as a national organisation or a radical one. Was the BBC a kind of established church with a precise set of doctrines or a critical-journalistic entity speaking to a nation? Both roles were obligatory and both impossible.

Broadcasting in Germany has presented a number of classic examples of the political/cultural dilemma involved in the decisions of a national broadcasting system. German broadcasting was deliberately decentralised after the war and placed in the hands of the individual *Land* administrations, each of which created a separate and independent radio body, which was later given responsibility for television as well. In 1950 there were nine of these which formed themselves into a federal union, the Arbeitsgemeinschaft öffentlich-rechtlichen Rundfunkanstalten der Bundesrepublik Deutschland (Consortium of Chartered Broadcasting Companies of the Federal Republic of Germany – known as ARD) which made itself responsible for the networking of programmes. It was impossible for mass audience broadcasting of a comprehensive range to be achieved separately within each Land's small independent company. Nonetheless broadcasting had to be kept out of the hands of the national government at federal level. ARD was a successful and ingenious way of evading central control. Each Land however has a different political spectrum, and although most of the programmes transmitted within a given Land come from some other Land within the ARD consortium, each Land feels itself responsible for keeping the programmes it *transmits* within the bounds of local political reality.

In each Land a slightly different system exists for controlling the organisation and choosing its senior personnel. In North Rhine-Westphalia for instance there is a Broadcasting Council elected by the Land parliament which in turn chooses the *Verwaltungsrat*, or administrative committee, of the radio and television station; it also chooses the *Intendant*, or Controller, of the station who is in executive command of the programme-makers. The Broadcasting Council is composed of political figures in similar pattern to the political composition of the Land Parliament. In recent years there has been considerable debate and disquiet within German broadcasting as the '*proporz*' system by which jobs inside broadcasting are shared out according to the balance of political affiliations within the Land parliament has spread to more and more junior levels of the organisation. After many years of effort to model broadcasting in Germany on the BBC in London (whose one-time Director-General, Sir Hugh Greene, was sent to Germany immediately after the war to re-establish some of the shattered German radio stations) there has occurred an almost admitted failure to find a piece of national cultural territory on which to maintain broadcasting; there is simply no agreed point of neutrality within German society on which to balance broadcasting. There has been a general agreement to keep it out of the hands of the Federal Government in Bonn, but no regional point of neutrality has been found.

Nevertheless German broadcasting has built a central *code* by which it can guarantee itself some kind of national security. The ARD has a policy document of which the provisions act as a kind of central constitution on which case law can be based. The document speaks of the dignity of man, and the mutual respect of social groups, nations and cultures. The basis of the postwar German state must not be denigrated or brought into disrepute, nor may the institutions of marriage and the family. Religious conflict must not be raked up by television. The document is an attempt to find a social and cultural concordat between the Land-based programme-makers and German society.

When the moment came in the early 1960s to set up a second television channel a fearsome quarrel broke out. Chancellor Adenauer, feeling that ARD was too liberal a body, biased against him in its current affairs programmes, tried to set up a central commercial network at federal level. The company he inaugurated got as far as starting to record programmes when the Länder successfully challenged the legality of the enterprise on the grounds that the constitution of Germany made broadcasting a Land not a federal prerogative. The Länder, armed with this victory, then went and set up their own federal centralised (and commercial) body, Zweites Deutsches Fernsehen (ZDF) which was given the new channel, together with the ARD programme code and the responsibility of competing with the ARD network. The ZDF shares the viewers' licence fees with the ARD companies in the proportion of 70 per cent for them and 30 per cent for it; it is supervised by its own Television Council on which sit spokesmen for Federal as well as Land governments, as well as churches, trade unions, newspapers and numerous other organisations. It is a cumbersome body.[32]

Germany has ended up with two centralised bodies in practice responsible for the great majority of the programmes which the German mass audience actually sees. It has also ended up with a single programme ideology. Yet every stage of its history has been dictated by a desire to decentralise and to create a profession of independent democratic programme-makers. It has undoubtedly succeeded in the latter quest and has created within its awkward structure a group of television professionals who are jealous of their rights and responsibilities within the system. The intrusion of political control into the inner workings of the broadcasting companies is resisted stage by stage. At the same time it has become harder and harder for producers to get jobs carrying any weight unless they enjoy the sponsorship of a powerful political group within the Land. The '*proporz*' system has been spreading like cancer year by year from Intendant level down through editor and producer towards the researcher level.

An important debate broke out in German broadcasting in the autumn of 1970 triggered off by a programme about pornography. The form of the inter-institutional discussion was revealing of the real structure of German broadcasting. Herr Hammerschmidt, the Intendant of SWF, the broadcasting company of Baden-Baden, sent a paper to all his fellow Intendanten (which was later leaked and published) arguing that political 'balance' should be achieved in all programmes; a representation of all points of view should be given in all programmes, not merely in the general spread of programmes. Furthermore since it was the ordinary entertainment and documentary programmes, more than the overtly political ones, which contained political 'bias', these too should come under similar editorial scrutiny. Finally, he argued, it was impolitic and inadmissible within the law for programmes to be sent out through ARD which attacked the Basic Law of Federal Germany which was legally unalterable.

The Intendant of WDR at Cologne, Herr von Bismarck, replied spiritedly in a second paper which was soon being disseminated within the world of German broadcasting. A grand assembly of all the Intendanten was held, and later a second one. After many months the discussion disappeared into a series of compromises ingeniously drafted by Herr Schröder, the Intendant at NDR in Hamburg. The producers eyed the controversy with some wariness and some scorn. The Hammerschmidt proposal would have been impossible to observe in practice. It would have meant that the vocal and revolutionary students who came into prominence in 1968 would have been forbidden to appear on German television at all; the content of entertainment programmes could scarcely be policed for dangerous or inadvertent political 'weighting' without damaging the entertainment value of the programmes. The spectrum of political possibilities differed wildly from Land to Land and that which seemed 'fair' in Bavaria seemed extremely over-balanced to the right to people in Cologne or Hamburg. Nonetheless some company controllers were beginning to look suspiciously at programmes coming to them from one of the other Länder; there were one or two threats internally circulated that certain programmes might not be acceptable within the ARD consortium as a whole. The controversy died away after a year or so but lies uneasily below the surface.[33] It illustrates the tensions which exist in broadcasting which emanates from institutions dependent on politicians for their survival. The needs of the mass audience tend to place television in a slightly radical position; if it is to reflect all trends in society it is those that spring up on þhe far left which cause most controversy. It is the newest and most vocal elements in a political culture which have the greatest impact and are the most indigestible. They are also the ones which enter into the culture the most rapidly, into songs and satire, painting, cinema and teenage life. The contribution of radio and television to social and political opposition is among its most valuable gifts to society; licensing anxiety impels the broadcasting institution as a whole in the opposite direction, towards stasis.

The licence or charter to run a broadcasting enterprise is a licence to a kind of brokerage between communicators and audience. The broadcasting organisation acts as editor and supreme arbiter of what is said or performed or commissioned to be broadcast, but in another sense the organisation merely passes on the right to use broadcasting to a host of writers, musicians, politicians, creative people of all kinds who thereafter depend on its health as an organisation, its profitability or its political security, for the carrying out of their work. The organisation therefore opens up a huge opportunity of communication, a new and vast series of livelihood possibilities, but in exchange has to insist upon its own chances of survival remaining unimpaired. A playwright cannot be allowed to break the rules which the organisation has itself been obliged to adopt in exchange for its licence or charter. Nor can an organisation afford to stay in business if it neglects to reach its audience, in considerable numbers, without having some other source of financial or institutional security. The external needs of the organisation therefore tend to be fed into the community of broadcasters themselves as intellectual attitudes, as fears, as ideals, and a complete body of broadcasting doctrine tends to emerge from the relationship.

The organisation tends as a consequence of its own development to build up its own view of the identity of its audience, how that audience lives, what its needs are; that view of the audience is similarly filtered by the general attitudes which the organisation holds in order to ensure its own political survival. The organisation therefore in turn creates for itself a model of the audience that suits its own needs, and indeed a political model of the whole society it serves, to accompany it.[34] The struggle between these two forces – the view of the audience as it appears to the broadcaster and that view of the audience and the society in the name of which the organisation has been constructed – goes on inside the minds of the broadcasters, and that whole section of the culture-making community which depends or partly depends on broadcasting for its living. Purveying as it does a view of how the body politic operates, the broadcasting organisation opens the door to the creation of a source of political power outside the normal political process, but unlike the situation of the press this power is not diffused but concentrated in a single body licensed and controlled ultimately by government. This general picture applies in almost every system of government and every kind of broadcasting constitution. The central body responsible for broadcasting, whether by radio or television, has inevitably come to embody in its codes and in the organisation of its schedules its feelings of what the mass audience 'wants' or 'will take'; it selects the topics for discussion and the organisation of its own news priorities, the personalities who are to be developed through the medium of broadcasting, and emerges therefore as a separate single solidified source of power within society.

It was in the mid-thirties that the discovery was first made of the enormous latent political power of broadcasting. On both sides of the Atlantic politicians felt that they saw dangerous developments in certain early radio personalities. In the United States Father Coughlin and Huey Long in the years of the Depression both created huge followings by the demagogic use of radio and created fortunes for themselves at the same time;[35] they gave Americans a foretaste of fascism too. Coughlin was a kind of latter-day Populist who attacked the monetary system and all those who possessed large wealth and power. He had begun as a preacher trying to improve the standing of his small church near Detroit but he ended as a major national figure receiving each week a torrent of letters and money orders from his new nationwide radio-based flock. In Italy and

Germany fascism was developing through the figures of individual leaders with magnetic platform appeal; America began to see how the new instrument of radio could serve the purposes of unscrupulous freelance demagogues. At one point Coughlin's speeches were being relayed by 28 stations and were raking in about half a million dollars a year. Coughlin tried to pressure Roosevelt to adopt him; he set up in 1934 the National Union for Social Justice which many saw as the beginning of a fascist third-party movement. Coughlin organised a flood of 200,000 telegrams to Congress protesting against the decision of Roosevelt's administration to join the World Court, an intention which the administration soon abandoned. Simultaneously Huey Long's movement was enjoying a fantastic growth of popularity; the radio networks showered him with opportunities to spread his attacks on 'lyin' newspapers' and 'smartaleck' oligarchs; Long wanted the rich men of America to be forced to share their wealth. With Louisiana state in his pocket he amassed an enormous amount of personal power, subjecting all state appointments to his own personal whim. There was widespread fear that a merger of Coughlin's interests with Long's 'Share-Our-Wealth' movement would create an American mass movement analogous to the fascist movements of Europe. Long was assassinated and Coughlin made the tactical error of breaking altogether with Roosevelt and the New Deal. Although their threat gradually diminished in the later part of the decade, the broadcasting air of America was constantly trespassed by broadcasters who built up huge followings and then used them for demagogic purposes; the columnist Walter Winchell in the 1936–8 period created a similar set of fears.[36] The danger was built into the American broadcasting system which enabled the stations to pursue any programme or individual who could create a rapid following; the networks were involved in so exaggerated a struggle for the audience that they easily fell victim to the temptation of the 'overnight success', even when it contained dangerous political elements.

The political implications of broadcasting became apparent to all during the period of the growth of fascism in Europe. In Britain, Brigadier-General Spiers and other parliamentarians attacked the BBC in 1934 over a broadcast talk by Vernon Bartlett when Germany decided to leave the League of Nations;[37] the dispute which ensued in Parliament over the right of the BBC alone to decide the selection of political broadcasters gradually brought home to the political community that radio was creating an institutional focus for a political power which lay outside their immediate control. The government had retained the right in the BBC Licence to forbid any single broadcast but normally the Speaker of the House of Commons ruled out of order any Member's question concerning the internal decision-making of the BBC. Was it logical, MPs demanded (Robert Boothby in particular) to prevent discussion in the House of details of a matter over which a Minister did in fact possess reserve rights? From the moment of the Bartlett controversy the issue of broadcasting became an important political preoccupation in Britain.

The BBC meanwhile was trying to build on its still insecure foundations. It was regarded as the creation of the Conservative Party. But it was also the prototype of a form of public service enterprise in which the Labour Party too took great pride. The newspapers had wanted to exclude advertising from broadcasting to enhance their financial security and they too felt that the BBC was an admirable national compromise. The Post Office was used to dealing with monopolies in the other services with which it was concerned and it too, therefore, felt that the BBC system was a good and workable one. The intellectual community in general approved of the BBC which gave them a greater sense of hegemony over broadcasting than their counterparts in any other society of the time. The BBC therefore was well dug into British society, enjoying the support of both major parties, the bureaucracy, the other media and the educational élite.[38] A series of social changes was to oblige it to forsake that security in the decade following the Second World War, but its form and the professionalism it generated in the pre-war period were coloured visibly by the social forces which supported its protected and highly prized privileges.

Some of the men who created the BBC in the 1920s and wrote about it afterwards, reveal how insistently it concentrated on the task of protecting itself against its enemies,[39] who on the whole expressed their animosity towards the BBC in the language of anti-monopolists. The content of its programmes reflected the power struggle between the institution and the 'Establishment', between the broadcasters and the frequently hostile political community. 'I feel that the BBC overconcentrated upon securing its foundations', wrote Captain Peter Eckersley[40] (one of the most resourceful of the founders of the BBC with Reith). 'This prevented any clear conception of what was to be built upon them. Indeed this concentration has been so great and so prolonged that the BBC might be said to have disappeared underground; it has dug itself a deep shelter so as to be safe against any attack. Those who have dug for security have come to be as solid as the structure they have made.' (Eckersley was writing in 1941.) The BBC was not overly tempted to become a mere tool of government in its efforts to grant itself security of tenure over the airways. The political ingenuity behind broadcasting in Britain lay in the way in which the organisation was anchored to Parliament as a whole, by Royal Charter, under the technical supervision of the Post Office rather than the more thorough supervision it might have received if it had been attached, say, to the Board of Trade.[41] It was Reith who chose this device and exploited it. The BBC had to be responsive to the political community as a whole, not to any section of it. Any leaning to one side or another was a result of tactics rather than strategy. Its purpose was to 'dig itself in' to the overall socio-political structure of the country. It made itself a very close institution, with its own laws and traditions, codes and rituals; it acted as if broadcasting were the technology which would ensure the victory of Arnold's ideal 'to make sweetness and light prevail', but to do so involved a constant effort to justify its monopoly status by its cultural results. It developed for itself an image, greatly reinforced by its success during the war, of a group of men and women who were offering membership of an élite to the millions of listeners; the BBC spoke in terms which Arnold and Ruskin too would have accepted enthusiastically. 'There was to hand a mighty instrument to instruct and fashion public opionion; to banish ignorance and misery; to contribute richly and in many ways to the sum total of human wellbeing. The present concern of those to whom the stewardship had, by accident, been committed was that those basic ideals should be sealed and safeguarded, so that broadcasting might play its destined part. Marvellous. That was the way one had to talk in those days.'[42] That was how Reith summed up the Crawford Report; he argued too that it was 'the combination of public service motive, sense of moral obligation, assured finance, and the brute force of monopoly which enabled the BBC to make of broadcasting what no other country in the world has made of it – those four fundamentals.'[43]

As the BBC grew, firmly wedded to its ideals which were simultaneously the source of its rockhard security, in the struggle against people who wanted a commercial system, or a free political system or a government-controlled system or who simply disliked monopoly, it wove an entirely new cultural environment around the inhabitants of British mass society. The BBC discovered a different formula from other broadcasting organisations (or rather Britain discovered this formula in the BBC) for dealing with the classic historical enigmas of mass society. The idea of serving a public by forcing it to confront the frontiers of its own taste was a powerful one. It ensured the political success of the enterprise. 'Those were the austere days of Reith and their aftermath,' wrote Radio Doctor Hill looking back on the earliest broadcasts of his career,[44] 'and in every broadcast, major or minor, the BBC seemed to apply the criterion of public service. It tried to create some new appetites, to arouse new and hitherto unsuspected interests, rather than merely to give people what they wanted.' The inspiration of Reith's BBC coloured all the ways in which the organisation, in perpetuity, was to address the mass audience of Britain. In 1923, one year after the birth of the British Broadcasting Company and still three years before the creation of the Corporation we know today, C. A. Lewis could look back and recognise the moment at which the medium of radio became the tool of a powerful organisation rather than simply the property of the broadcasters. 'It was a democracy – short-lived, alas! A democracy of young pioneers, doomed like all the pioneering of youth to come up against the rigidity of age, discipline and experience; doomed to be swept quickly into the inexorable mills of civilisation and organisation – and forgotten.

We must content ourselves with the memory that once for a very short time it existed, that even in the heart of London, civilised and organised to death, there was a sudden flash – a gesture – made by a handful of silly young men who had, with the aid of a microphone, the ear of the world.'[45] But the real processes which institutionalised broadcasting were older than the BBC, were in fact firmly embedded in the whole notion of the wavelength as a natural resource in the custody of a modern national state. The broadcasting institution is an unelective power centre. It becomes an arbiter of the culture, a subtle patron of politics, an overt patron of entertainment in all its forms. Its most important problem is to engineer its own survival and to find some point at which it can make bargains of style and content with the civil power. Of its many products the most important is itself.

Chapter Three

News — The Ugly Mirror

'How shall I speak of thee, or thy power address,
Thou God of our idolatry, the Press?
By thee, religion, liberty and laws,
Exert their influence and advance their cause;
By thee, worse plagues than Pharaoh's land befell,
Diffused, make man the vestibule of hell;
Thou fountain, at which drink the good and wise;
Thou ever-bubbling spring of endless lies;
Like Eden's dread probationary tree,
Knowledge of good and evil is from thee!
No wild enthusiast ever yet could rest,
Till half mankind were like himself possess'd;
Philosophers, who darken and put out
Eternal truth by everlasting doubt;
Church quacks, with passions under no command,
Who fill the world with doctrines contraband,
Discoverers of they know not what, confined
Within no bounds—the blind that lead the blind;
To streams of popular opinion drawn,
Deposit in those shallows all their spawn.'

Cowper

'Journalism is an increasingly exacting profession, for the
journalist is becoming not just a collector of interesting
items that people want to hear about, he is becoming
increasingly a teacher in a world that has grown increasingly
complex to explain.'

Howard K. Smith, 1969

I

In the course of the Democratic Party Nominating Convention
of 1948 there occurred an incident in which the delegates from
the Southern States, roused to anger over a credentials dispute,

resolved to stage a walk-out. A team from the new Life-NBC television news unit was present, cameras whirring. Television news was new, at that time just beginning to explore its own potential; the director in charge had a sudden brainwave for dramatising the Southern walk-out and his viewers presently saw on their screens at home a close-up of a mounting pile of Democratic Party badges, which the Southern delegates were tearing from their lapels and flinging on to the table.[1] The television interviewers moved in and asked the Southerners the meaning of their action. They answered the questions, and the cameras moved to another scene. What the viewers didn't see was that immediately after the interview the Southerners picked up the badges and put them on again. The badge incident had been 'staged', the device of piling up the badges used to dramatise the emotion of the occasion. What the director from Life-NBC had discovered was that television involves the instantaneous mingling of theatre with the dissemination of actuality. The two facets of television are inseparable. The camera's presence makes people want to dramatise facts about themselves; even when the camera is live, television consists of representations of facts, not of facts themselves. The screen gives us *pictures* of events, even if those events are occurring simultaneously. The special power of television lies somewhere in the inextricable fusion of mimesis with factuality. Many contemporary critics of television have tried to isolate its technology from its social context and have looked for the source of television's power somewhere in its inherent nature. Television (and to some extent radio) news has in itself become a source of public controversy. The intrinsic nature of the medium is said to distort its subject matter in a number of ways; one writer has tried to group the distorting effects under three headings:

'1. The nature of sight-sound edited presentation in the medium heightens and accentuates the more surface visceral aspect of conflict and confrontation in our civilisation – the reporting of which, regrettably, is the *raison d'être* of journalism.

2. As the level of irrationality in an event rises, so television's record of it "heats up", and the camera begins to

exchange momentum, as it were, with the forces at work within the very situation it is supposed to be recording.

3. The medium undoubtedly tends to reward both personality and personability in those who are involved in and actually present the news.'[2]

Certainly, radio and television share special characteristics which cause them to charge the events they describe with a certain excitement; they also tend to neglect events which refuse to lend themselves, at a given moment, to high emotional interest. The question is to what extent the intrinsic nature of the technology of broadcasting, at the creative end or the reception end, causes this phenomenon and to what extent it can be attributed to the social purposes and organisational framework into which broadcasting has been built.

No department in any broadcasting organisation, however, is as carefully scrutinised and supervised as that which is responsible for news. It is the most vulnerable point in the broadcasting structure because it is the point at which the problem of making the actual product, programmes, overlaps with the security of the organisation itself. The decisions of the man in charge of news can damage the entire enterprise, by prejudicing it politically or financially. His work consists in making those programmes which are the most eagerly criticised parts of a station's output. His function is to tell society what is happening, especially in those areas of life inhabited by powerful people. News inevitably creates within an organisation a kind of model of the entire political environment in which the station is operating; the influences which shape that model are fed into the programmes which ensue. At the same time, news weaves a secondary environment around every one of us who receives it. News tends to lay out the order of 'priorities' among the issues which confront society; it creates some of the doubts and fosters the certainties of that society, placing them all in a context of its own. Yet in every single society which contains broadcasting on any scale, the news is under instruction to be 'objective'. Many wildly different renderings are given to the concept of objectivity; its meaning is in a state of constant evolution.

Newsmen everywhere share a similar ideology but their

values are shaped by the highly vulnerable organisations in which they work. The general attack has been directed, however, against their medium rather than the social and economic situations in which it is obliged to operate.

In recent years the argument about broadcasting has resolved itself, internationally, into an overall 'case'. The television camera, while encouraging greater credence than the press, gives it is said a false sense of reality; it is a contrivance which distorts the event it is observing. It forces peaceful crowds into riots and politicians into gladiatorial combats; it forces light out and heat in, wherever argument occurs; it is incurably sensational and trivial, by nature. It avoids whatever is normal and emphasises whatever is outlandish, extremist or unconventional. The charges are comprehensive and widespread. My contention is that the instruments of broadcasting do not, of their own nature, exhibit these characteristics. The distorting effects of radio and television news, if they occur at all in greater proportion than in other forms of reporting, do so as a result of the social and institutional framework in which broadcasting has grown. It is not 'television' that made the people of Watts burn their community to the ground, nor the Democratic Party supporters in Chicago conflict with Mayor Daley's police, but the relationship which the people of America have with their television sets, and which the journalists as a result have with their public. The roots of 'bias' lie very deep indeed.

II

That broadcasting would transform the world of entertainment, especially in music, was known from the very first moment that the radio receiver went into mass production; that it would become a major instrument of education and instruction was known and, if anything, exaggerated. That radio and later television would transform the relationship between the citizen and his environment by becoming dominant instruments of news collection and distribution was not predicted. The pioneers of broadcasting realised that their inventions could greatly enhance the possibilities for political indoctrination and that in the hands of dictators and demagogues broadcasting could become an appallingly effective medium, but they did not foresee that it would become the most powerful single instrument of journalism which the world had known. Broadcasting in both world wars had not created a journalistic profession dedicated exclusively to itself, although the Munich crisis had been chronicled moment by moment by the pioneering American broadcast reporters, H. V. Kaltenborn, Raymond Swing and Ed Murrow, who sent their reports live into the American networks.[3] But the idea of the reporter using an instrument of broadcasting, whether with sound or picture or both, as a reporter uses his pencil and notebook was not present in the minds of early broadcasters or executives.

So long as news remained in bulletin form a recital of 'facts' culled by news agencies and read straight into the microphone or camera with little or no background explanation or, in television, pictorial coverage, news failed to take off in either of the broadcasting media. Broadcasting needed both a further sophistication of its technology, and a new set of genres before news could become both a revenue raiser in its own right in commercial systems and a major new element in the new medium of mass entertainment. When that was achieved, the impact of news on institutions and their practices was considerable. It brought the very concept of news into the forefront of wide-ranging and sceptical discussion. It was when news reached its greatest dexterity and skill that people began asking whether what they saw was truth or merely a new kind of lying.

During the ten years from 1958 until 1968 the techniques of broadcast journalism were transformed together with the whole attitude of the audience towards news. The entire orientation of broadcasting was altered by the invention of a series of technical and creative methods which created a new interest in news which until that time, especially in television, had been little more than a solemn ritual. The creation of the thirty-minute news bulletin, on both sides of the Atlantic, and the development of the magazine format conspired to turn the news journalist on television into a major national figure. It seems, in retrospect, to have been an inevitable development, but it required for its realisation a number of institutional revolutions and the building up of a group of extremely powerful personalities to drive them through. News has always had to fight hard for its existence, not merely on television, and it seemed naturally to acquire among its supporters, everywhere, larger-than-life individuals who had the psychic energy to harry the various vested interests which were holding back the development of broadcast journalism; many risks were necessary to create the powerful news and public affairs departments which are the pride and terror of broadcasting organisations and political establishments in the present time. Donald Baverstock, in the BBC's 'Tonight' programme, Fred Friendly in CBS News, Pierre Desgraupes in ORTF's 'Cinq Colonnes à la Une' were among the individuals whose personal dynamism alone appeared to force their various parent organisations into a proper readiness to take the risks which enabled journalism to develop as a force within the world of broadcasting. The departments of television News ring with the legends of the Beowulfs of that time who simultaneously and with surprisingly little mutual inspiration fought a series of dragons whose presence had never been seriously challenged. They created news magazines where previously there had only been an announcer with a prepared bulletin or a sheaf of wire service tapes. They created the reporter with an individual style.[4] They created traditions of hard-hitting interviewing, confrontation with authority, deeply researched investigations of national and international scandals. They forced the technology onwards to serve their creative ends; they put 35 millimetre newsfilm into the lumber room after some years of experimentation with 'blown-up' 16 millimetre film. They forced the purchase of the 'Eclaire' camera and the more sophisticated versions of the traditional war-time Arriflex, modified to silence its own operating noise. They thumped desks and terrified film editors overturned the habits of generations. Laboratories were made to disgorge their film stock in hours instead of days. Rushes were no longer viewed by committees before technicians were allowed to start the process of editing. Reporters were taught to handle film crews and were made to shape their news reports around the film material available. The time-honoured perfectionism of the film world was jettisoned. Quite soon a film could be conceived, shot, developed, edited, its commentary written and the finished product transmitted within a day. Within the world of film-making and programme-making a revolution had been wrought, as great as the one which occurred in printed news when Caxton's converted wine-press was set aside after many centuries and the rotary press was adopted. Technological and organisational changes followed in the wake of the idea of a new kind of broadcast news. The new magazine formats attracted huge audiences and built up powerful individual figures. At the same time it put broadcast news into the front line.

There was a time in American broadcasting history when news was thought to be an expensive, cash-consuming activity indulged in either from a sense of public duty or to placate the Federal Communications Commission. By the end of the 1960s it was one of the most lucrative areas of television, responsible, in all probability, for about 40 per cent of the huge profits earned by the hundreds of local television stations in America, and responsible for making, in the early part of the period, the BBC television service competitive with the rival commercial system to broadcast a daily news programme, 'News at Ten', which became one of the great revenue-raisers of British broadcasting.

News programme-makers were searching throughout the period for a new technology, a compact piece of film-making apparatus which could be carried by two men at most, which could record sound synchronously without the necessity of a physical link between the camera and the microphone. As the years of news (and current affairs) expansion continued, the progressive miniaturisation of the electronic technology of television took place; the vidicon camera arrived, the satellite and the portable ground-station which enabled American news teams in particular to undertake prodigious feats of coverage in battles and revolutions, as well as great international sporting spectacles.

In 1958 the 'Tonight' production team at BBC's Lime Grove headquarters in the West of London were astonished at the discovery of Slim Hewitt, a pioneer of television journalist camerawork, that he could film an interview in a rowing-boat without any elaborate cranes or extra boats following behind;

within a few months he filmed an interview on top of a London bus, without the conductor realising what was happening (both men involved paid their bus fare as they slipped off the bus at the appropriate stop, stuffing their film into their pockets). By 1968 every major international news event was swarming with small television news teams, their equipment swinging round their necks on straps, their microphones connected by invisible radio links to their cameras; they covered riots, demonstrations and invasions. When Russian tanks rolled into Prague and the borders of Czechoslovakia were closed, small cars with hollowed out doors – normally used for smuggling contraband – moved cameras and film stock at night to couriers waiting across the border. As visa problems became more and more difficult, one American news crew arranged for a canvas bag to be hung from a tree on the Austrian side of the Czech border into which they could simply throw their tiny parcels of film from the Czech side of the frontier. In Biafra, Vietnam, and Paris news was being recorded and filmed in a profusion which would have been impossible even eight years before.

The first generation of managers in American television stations had very little idea what news was. They were men whose professionalism consisted in understanding the units of production cost, the whims of sponsors, Nielsenratings, 'adjacencies' and rate cards. Many of the senior executives in the early stations (and to this day) were former salesmen of radio 'time' and saw their tasks almost exclusively as revenue-raisers.[5] News was an obligation to be discharged between bouts of a wrestling match; it was normally collected by tearing the tape from an agency machine and reading it straight into a camera. The genre was dubbed 'rip-and-read' news and continues in many places to this day. News generally consisted of unpleasant information which was of little help to the commercial sponsors. News-readers tended to be out-of-work actors with suitably mature faces or advertisement readers who failed to measure up to the task. Nonetheless the news-readers competed among themselves for audience approval – they would project synthetic 'images' of themselves as typical khaki-clad war-heroes, or old family friends or favoured school-masters. The skills of news were trivial acting skills. They were attempting merely to render an obligatory task of news-reading as palatable as possible. The Federal Communications Commission had enjoined stations under the rubric of 'public interest, convenience, necessity'[6] to provide a service of news and this they did as inexpensively as possible. The only addition which television made to the existing armoury of news techniques was 'personality' and that, if anything, hindered rather than fostered its development. A few stations began to hire writers to inject a few good phrases into the bulletins, and some began to collect film of local news events.

In Britain, however, a totally different set of pressures was at work. The prevailing powers at Broadcasting House[7] believed that television was not intended by God to be a news medium at all. For many years the BBC's television service merely repeated, over a still picture of Big Ben or Tower Bridge, the news bulletin transmitted some hours previously on the main radio channel. It was several years before an individual was allowed to read the news visibly into a camera, and even then he was under instruction to inject no 'personality' into the task at all. A New Zealander, Tahu Hole, was in charge of the BBC's news service and the rigidity with which he governed his enterprise allowed none of the fresh potential of television to break through. 'The BBC does not have scoops', he was believed once to have said. When competition from commercial television's ITN (the Independent Television News unit which is paid for out of the revenue of the programme companies) forced the BBC to liberalise its oddly calvinistic attitude towards news-gathering, it was a completely different department in a different building which successfully undertook the task of creating a new 'Current Affairs' empire (and a new professionalism) outside the news division. It was in Lime Grove, the home of what was variously called 'Talks' or 'Current Affairs', that new forces were encouraged which transformed the techniques of news in British television; the whole relationship between the BBC and the British public changed partly as a result.

It was America however that was to create the market for the new technology on which all the developments depended. There could be no market for the new skills and the new equipment until there were sufficient regular programmes into which news material could be slotted. Until the end of the 1950s and in many cases for years later there were only brief 15-minute news programmes. The time would be divided into five minutes of general news, five of sport and five of weather. (Weather was something which television discovered at a very early stage that it could do better than radio.) Each of the three segments was read by a different man and the sponsors could choose to advertise in any of the three segments according to which 'personality' he thought the potential buyers of his goods would most readily respond.

In Britain the 'Tonight' programme and its early imitators (in the regional stations around Britain) had adopted the 'magazine' format, in which a group of skilled and experienced reporters (many of whom had come from the defunct picture magazine *Picture Post*) sent back to London day by day brief amusing and wittily written featurettes on various topics which took their and the editor's fancy; the quality of the writing and the dramatic impact of moving pictures which actually in themselves told a story created an enormous audience at a period in the evening when the BBC had traditionally observed the 'toddlers' truce' leaving the screens empty to enable parents to put their children to bed without cathode competition. The magazine format was devised to give families something to watch which didn't require extended concentration: they could attend to their domestic tasks while glancing at the screen from time to time, watching an item here and an item there but not necessarily the whole programme. The 'Tonight' team had an immediate impact and an astonishing flair for the job. They spread out in later years not merely in British television but in the cinema, journalism and the theatre and were a seminal influence in the regeneration of all the British entertainment media in the mid-sixties.

In America however the magazine format developed later, without the special circumstances of the 'toddlers' truce' to spur it on. It was News itself that was to discover the form. In 1961 Robert D. Wood, general manager of KNXT, a CBS-owned station in Los Angeles, created a remarkable success with 'The Big News', a 45-minute bulletin in which a team of reporters, with a studio-based 'anchorman', provided a glittering succession of on-the-spot reports on news events in the Los Angeles area. Los Angeles was and still is the most highly competitive television market in America. Wood transformed not merely the genre of news, but the economics. 'The Big News' employed an entertainment reporter, a political reporter, investigative, business, sports and weather experts. The profusion of faces on the screen, the flexibility in length of item, the sheer variety of texture, level of seriousness, and subject-matter made the programme an instant success.

In the old-style 15-minute bulletin a station would sell the entire programme to a sponsor whose name would appear throughout the programme; the sponsor would guarantee a certain stability of income to the programme by promising to retain his identity with it for a given number of weeks or months; in return he would receive twenty seconds of 'billboards' at the beginning and the close, as well as the right to refer to himself as 'the sponsor of the wxyz News Show' in his newspaper advertising. In the new magazine format, a station could simply sell 'spots' within the programme to members of a very long queue of advertisers. It is much more profitable to sell a few seconds of time as a single 'spot' instead of depending on a sponsor for the entire programme. When no single advertiser is identified with a programme, accusations of sponsor interference diminish, and the team working on a programme can develop its own ethos, and its own code of journalistic practice as a result of the new independence. Such was the economic background to the news explosion which occurred in the early years of the decade.[8] Robert D. Wood became president of the entire CBS Television Network division. KNXT's news programme achieved the fourth largest audience for any news programme in the United States, and only the early evening news programmes of the three networks exceeded it. At first KNXT's 45-minute programme was followed by a 15-minute national and international bulletin transmitted by CBS from New York. Within two years the former had expanded to one hour and the latter to thirty minutes. Spread throughout the United States the new market for news was of an extraordinary size. The new expensive equipment for collecting and transmitting news had discovered an economic basis, and was soon being copied and sold around the world. Each nation created a genre of news consistent with its own cultural and journalistic traditions; but the invention in essence was an American one. It made television into the dominant medium for distributing news. Five centuries earlier Gutenberg's new press was snatched up and copied throughout Europe, when it was discovered that the world contained many more intending readers and many more intending writers than reproduction of script by hand could cope with. There was a new hunger on the part of the audience; the technical means to satisfy it was seized upon as soon as it appeared in the world and it transformed the relationship between that audience and its world. So it was with the new electronic instruments of newsmaking in our own time.

III

In 1968 the US President's Task Force on Communications Policy started discussing the need for a detailed study of the new developments in broadcast journalism throughout the country; the National Association of Broadcasters proceeded to commission the Land Report, a study of the attitudes towards news of 329 commercial television stations throughout America.[9] (The NAB's interest in the project was mainly motivated by a desire to marshal the arguments against the concept of 'the wired city', the much discussed plan to develop the growth of cable television as the main national means of news distribution.) The Land Report showed that in the course of the preceding five years a considerable number of stations had doubled the amount of time they gave to news, or even tripled it. Of 297 stations which sent in details of their news operations, 228 were already doing 30-minute bulletins every day, 127 of them twice a day. Even in areas where there was no television competition (in the United States there are still places which for various accidents of geography only one, or in some cases no station at all can be received) viewers were able to receive a daily 30-minute news programme. In the big markets where there were six or more competing stations, the total volume of news was reaching 89 to 168 half-hours per week. In Los Angeles, where the boom had begun, viewers could receive 264 half-hours every week. One station told the Land Commission that in a single year it had devoted 115 man-years of effort to produce news and public affairs programmes. An instrument of entertainment which had grown up with the assumption that the audience would watch nothing but westerns, sporting events and soap opera was not only turning itself into an instrument of a totally different kind: it was inevitably changing the entire climate in which political events occurred; it was re-politicising the viewing public. A great deal of attention inevitably came to be given to the whole question of the effects of the new news coverage not merely on the audience but on the nature of the observed news events themselves.

In the fifties and sixties the late Elmo Roper and his son Burns Roper began collecting information on the development of public attitudes towards the various news media.[10] They showed over a long period how television was becoming the greatest single source of news for most people and was increasing its credibility over other media. In late 1959, 19 per cent of the public said that television was their exclusive source of news, in early 1971 it had increased by steady stages to 31 per cent. In 1959 29 per cent said that if they saw conflicting versions of a story in newspapers, radio, television and magazines they would be most inclined to believe the television version; by 1971 that had become 49 per cent, and the group which claimed greatest credibility in newspapers had dropped from 32 per cent at the beginning of the period to 20 per cent at the end. As many as 60 per cent thought in 1971 that most of their news came from television, nearly 10 per cent more than in 1959. The turning point at which television suddenly beat print as the major news medium was in 1968, the year in which the events of Prague, Paris and Chicago pushed most other events from the screen throughout the world. The newspapers never recovered their comparative prestige.

In creating a new genre specifically for television the newsmen were setting the seal on a new relationship between broadcasting and the mass audience. Through the clumsy mechanisms of the market they caught a new glimpse of the actual nature of

85

their vast public; in constructing the new genre, there were involved the making of a new type of reporter's personality, a different system for dividing up and arranging the facts of news, a reorganised concept of what constituted news, a new stance towards political interviewees (and hence towards authority) and a restatement of the inherited professional canons of journalism. The reporters and producers were impliedly working now for a completely new client.

In an apparatus of mass communication, the human, mechanical and institutional retooling necessary to create a new genre is so expensive to bring about that it can only occur when a new definition of the receiving audience is itself ready in the minds of the communicators. In other words a new sense of society always precedes a major step forwards in broadcasting, and that change involves a change in the mechanics of the medium itself.

David Howarth, the producer who helped Richard Dimbleby in 1938 and afterwards to produce a revolution in radio news of a kind comparable with the 1960s overhaul of television news, gives us an account[11] of how Dimbleby 'set about reforming the presentation of the news by starting a kind of underground movement, infecting people here and there among the staff with his own excitement at his own idea of radio news reporting'. The idea which animated him was the recorded or live on-the-spot report which required a reorganisation of existing personnel and equipment. It also required the BBC as a whole to realise that the audience wanted to hear not merely *about* the news but through the medium of radio to hear the news as it happened. While a newspaper account of a news event is second hand, a radio reading of an account is third hand; radio's 'true' mode of reporting was to have a man and some equipment at the place of the action. The war was to prove this beyond further doubt, but in the months preceding the war, Dimbleby and his closest colleagues at the BBC continued their preparations – these involved persuading the engineers to put some recording equipment into a motor-car. 'We even plotted to have the recording gear made in secret and put it in the back of my car and broadcast its discs without telling anyone how we had made them; but that fell through because neither of us could afford it. It sometimes seemed hopeless to move the BBC, and at one time we tried – or plotted – to sell ourselves and our ideas to Ed Murrow of CBS, whom Richard greatly admired.'[12] Murrow himself was in the midst of comparable problems with his own employers, and only the Munich crisis moved them to allow him to perform a series of remarkable technical and journalistic feats which enabled the American audience to hear the stages by which Europe gradually slipped into war. It is arguable that the reserves of public understanding which Murrow helped to build up in the last months of peace and the early months of war played a major part in bringing American opinion around to joining in the war a year or so later. Certainly, it took more than a boardroom squabble to bring about the changes in radio news which occurred in the last months before the war; it also took a new understanding of the audience. Murrow used to give the European-based reporters of CBS the following set of instructions at that time: 'Never sound excited. Imagine yourself at a dinner table back in the United States, with the local editor, a banker and a professor talking over the coffee. You try to tell what it was like, whilst the maid's boy friend, a truck driver, listens from the kitchen. Talk to be understood by the truck driver while not insulting the professor's intelligence.'[13] Of course, no such picture of the audience would any longer satisfy a mass communicator, but in its time it possessed a certain clarity and indeed a certain relevance to the prevailing relationships within society. Pictures of that kind give the newsman a place in his society.

On both sides of the Atlantic radio had suffered from a series of inhibitions about the whole business of news. Lord Riddell, Chairman of the Newspaper Proprietors Association, had conducted a long campaign in the 1920s to prevent radio in Britain doing any kind of news at all except for a 1200–2400-word bulletin written by the wire services and brought round to Broadcasting House towards the end of the day.[14] It was not to be read at all before 7 p.m., the time at which the newspaper owners deemed they had finished milking the newspaper-purchasing public for the day.[15] The BBC at first read the bulletin twice during the course of the evening's programmes. The press had developed an enormous prestige and power during the First World War[16] and this they exercised to advantage to threaten the straggly child of radio-telephony. The BBC was forbidden to collect any news itself, even racing results, on pain of the wire services cutting off the supply of news altogether. The Post Office, which itself derived considerable revenue from the wire services, and was party to all the negotiations, was hesitant to challenge the interests of the press. As the position of the press was gradually eroded in future negotiations by Reith and his colleagues, it became clear that the newspapers had thought of news only as something written and read as from a newspaper. They had objected to the growth of the habit of reporting live from an event itself, usually of a sporting or ceremonial nature, but the broadcasting of an event without a commentary was something that they had not seriously considered. It was explained to Riddell[17] that there was a plan to place the microphone simply in front of the speaker at a meeting. 'An occasional speech here and there is not a matter to worry about', was Riddell's reply. 'But no more!' Radio and newspapers it seemed were destined to be competitors and not cooperators. In his evidence to the Sykes Committee in May 1923 Riddell argued, 'If the edge is taken off the news by the dissemination through the broadcaster of all the important items immediately they occur, it is highly probable that the interest in newspapers will be seriously diminished and the circulation adversely affected.'[18] Broadcasting was not hampered merely by the proscription of controversy on the part of the Post Office, but by a parallel proscription of factual reporting as well. It seems difficult now to realise that at that moment in time the audience was thought to be capable of absorbing only a little information about the world around them and the events occurring within it day by day. The idea that the material was unlimited, that there was room for nearly all the existing newspapers and magazines, for a series of radio and television channels all to be competing to present slightly differing versions of the day's events and still to leave a general feeling that the news was being inadequately tackled, did not, unsurprisingly, occur.

The desirability of news to ordinary people was not apparent until a very late stage. Broadcasting was deliberately reduced as a news-provider to the position of a second-hand medium. Its initial inhibitions about collecting news itself, which was accompanied by a parallel tension between broadcasters and newspapers in the United States (until newspapers adopted the habit of acquiring lucrative radio stations themselves), left it very slowly and to this day broadcasting still tends to be cautious about breaking major news on its own initiative. It is of course no longer fearful merely of 'scooping' the press; its reporters see themselves as the direct competitors of their colleagues who work in print, and the feeling of rivalry is mutual, but broadcasting is fearful of becoming a causer of events rather than just a mirror of them. Ever since newspapers too found themselves seeking a mass readership they have realised and have seldom shrunk from the awesome responsibility, still less from the lucrative implications, of being an initiator of newsworthy events as well as a chronicler.

Newspapers will pursue causes, of course, while broadcasting cannot, on pain of being in breach of its own ground-rules, but print journalists will be far readier to publish documents of a secret and explosive nature, reveal information about public persons of a kind which will influence and will be calculated to influence the drift of political events; the neutrality of broadcasting, while no longer forcing it to abandon any of the principles and ambitions of journalism, does however make it fearful of being the first to report material likely to change the course of events.[19]

Of all the strands of culture which are fed into the world at present through broadcasting none has had to fight its way with such great difficulty into the processes of broadcasting as that of journalism. The press has always held that *disclosure* of facts was its main purpose. 'The duty of the Press is to speak; of the statesman to be silent', wrote John Thaddeus Delane, in one of his two famous replies to the complaints of Lord Derby against *The Times*.[20] 'If in these days', Lord Derby had said, 'the Press aspires to exercise the influence of statesmen, the Press should remember they are not free from the corresponding responsibilities of statesmen.' Delane saw his role precisely as a professional investigator and publiciser of the activities of statesmen *without* the concomitant responsibilities and inhibitions. 'The purposes of the two Powers are constantly separate, generally independent, sometimes diametrically opposite. ... To perform its duties with entire independence, and consequently with the utmost public advantage, the Press can enter into no close or binding alliance with the statesmen of the day, nor can it surrender its permanent interests to the convenience of the ephemeral power of any government.'[21] In the sphere of broadcasting, however, journalism confronts an unavoidable limitation on its powers; it cannot but take the Derby view rather than the Delane – it is not the interference of politicians which necessarily brings about the limitation but the exact nature of the role which broadcasting has been given to play, that of employing a nationally-owned wavelength in a mass society. Everyone who works in it uses the ethic of statesmanship rather than the ethic of disclosure, not because of fear of political reprisal but because of the inbuilt need to reach a *modus vivendi* with the invisible audience – an audience deemed to be coterminous with the entire society. The newsman working in television is obliged to make a far larger number of inclusion-and-exclusion judgements that the newspaperman (with many more individual items of news to insert) can take with lighter heart. The television producer and reporter must constantly refine and boil down their priorities to a few dominating ones,[22] and these must represent the issues which most dominate the society of the time. He cannot afford to be 'irrelevant', still less to ignore an issue which comes to be judged to be of major importance. The radio and television newsmen therefore are concerned with the top of a pyramid of information which has been constructed by the combined efforts of all the news media. They are gatekeepers among gatekeepers.[23] Their judgements are even more finely attuned to the pressures of society and to the needs of the enterprise which employs them. Because their judgement is more pervasive and yet narrower in scope, they feel the need to be all the better protected. News material issues forth from broadcasting like fine cream from a churn of milk, suffering from all the faults of the originating matter, but processed and supervised to a high degree.

It is often argued that the caution shown by broadcasters

is the result of the fact that they work in a more expensive medium and one that has a quasi-monopolistic status by virtue of the scarcity of its outlets. Newspapers are more free because there are more of them. The reverse is nearer the truth, for today the average citizen is offered more choice in broadcasting than in print. After March 1974 every major city in Britain will have access to 7 radio and 3 television channels – equal to the number of daily newspapers. In the United States the total number of radio and television channels is many times greater than the number of newspapers available in the average city. Nine metropolitan areas have twenty stations or more, and over 2000 towns and cities have a broadcasting originating system – radio or television – of their own. There are only 1750 daily newspapers in the whole of the country. While the average newspaper has to employ 200 men and women, the average radio station employs just 11. An American newspaper normally needs about 4 million dollars worth of buildings and equipment, the average radio station uses equipment costing only 160,000 dollars.[24] Nonetheless broadcasting everywhere gives the feeling of being a much more highly 'processed' medium, as if those providing it were holding back two-thirds of what they had to say and the impact of broadcasting is all the greater on account of this feeling. The knowledge on the part of the audience that what they see and hear is somehow public property is one of the causes of the enormous critical attention paid to broadcast journalism and of its enhanced impact.

IV

The history of news provision is the history of a series of human efforts to provide information more quickly and more directly on current events. The idea of the nature of news has developed alongside the struggle for improved techniques for collecting and distributing it. Even the earliest examples bear this out. In the 1640s, a new group of newsmen joined the small throng of newsbook-writers, who distributed their infrequent editions of European and home news in leather-bound volumes. It was not considered unhelpful when the editor of one of them, John Dillingham, who had graduated from tailoring to reporting, explained: 'Our Scout is returned very empty of newes this weeke, and that little that he brings is very uncertaine, he tells us that Gloucester hath been several times assaulted by the enemy, and that most furiously. . . . The Oxford Scout whispers up and downe that Gloucester is taken.'[25] Information was necessarily vague and its collection haphazardly organised. Nonetheless news from the very start was a commodity of international usefulness and the newsmen, variously known as coranteers, diurnalists, gazetteers and mercurists, quickly created an international and financially rewarding set of mechanisms for passing round their scanty and inaccurate information. In the 1620s the coranteers of Amsterdam, Antwerp, Frankfurt, Berlin and Hamburg had already set up a kind of man-powered wire service;[26] their papers have a line drawn across the centre of the page and a study of their considerable output shows that the news above the line was drawn from an international news circuit, that below the line from their own correspondents. The desire for profusion and accuracy was bringing about an organisational mechanism similar to the agencies of today. This in itself meant that news could not be wholly 'managed' by governments, even though many of them were working hard to suppress the new profession of newsmongering. It also meant that the need for accuracy was increasing. As far away as Warsaw the Poles were reading material taken from the Western European news network;[27] their monarchy was too weak to suppress the system and a lively Polish press came into existence, led by the *Polish Mercury* in the 1660s, basing itself upon its reliability in giving news. The chaotic affairs of seventeenth-century Europe made political and military news a valuable commodity. But it was slow in collection and slower still in distribution. A news item was almost a piece of history before it circulated.

Gutenberg's printing press, which printed one side of a page at a time, continued as the only method for nearly four centuries. It could achieve, in its most efficient versions, a quantity of about 600 impressions in a day.[28] Not until 1810 did any dramatic alteration occur, when finally the press was attached to a steam engine and was made to double its production. A 4-page paper would take 10 hours to put together, assuming it had no more than 500 subscribers. Its distribution would of course take considerably longer. It was *The Times* of London, much later, which transformed the printing scene by using one of Koenig's newly-invented rotary presses which increased production to 2,400 impressions an hour by using a cylindrical plate from which a lead casting was made; the printing could be done by using several duplicates. The rotary press printed on both sides of the paper at once. *The Times*, under its editor Thomas Barnes, could get itself printed in 50 minutes. Nonetheless the average daily paper to this day still requires about 10 hours to produce because of its increased size.[29]

The present century has produced further revolutions and potential revolutions in the various versions of offset printing which is already employed by most of the small American daily papers. Its value is not so much in the speed of printing as in the way it eases the process of type-setting. Within the last decade it has enabled type-setting to increase from 80 lines per minute to a potential of 20,000 lines per minute.[30] The development of electronics in the printing industry, although hardly yet fulfilling its potential, has in scientific terms caught up in speed and reliability with the medium of television. Both can transfer information at enormous speed across thousands of miles, while leaving some kind of stored record of the message for future reference. Gutenberg spent five years setting the letters of his Bible. The CBS-Mergenthaler Linotron can perform the same task in 27 minutes. Printing with a photographic plate eliminates the use of molten metal and photo-engraving. It abolishes the compositor and his cumbersome traditions and it changes the whole notion of what news is. Amidst the profusion of print made possible by the new techniques of printing, the idea of news as secret facts disclosed to an enthralled public has receded considerably. News consists mainly of public events. Facts are handed out in profusion. The journalist ceases to be a collector and begins to be a sifter of information. The listed virtues of journalism still contain physical bravado, insight, ruthless investigation, but the act of disclosure is more likely to take place in the office of an 'expert' who has spent decades studying one corner of a subject than in the noisy, ink-smelling newsroom, which for the most part has the task of reproducing in attractive form information available on handouts and on the wire services. The vast quantity of governmental information that is available passes through the judgements of the editors and journalists. The mental work involved in news collection and selection is a far more important part of the process than it was until even thirty years ago when the main effort was still towards revelation. The social organisation of Fleet Street, the pattern of work and relaxation, the selection and training of new journalists, the cultural milieu of newsmen, these are the factors which control the nature and flow of information.

In the sphere of broadcasting where the mental 'conditioning' of the newsmen is concentrated within one or two institutions where the process of publishing and of editing are fused, where the 'owner' in the form of the Chairman of the publicly licensed board, or the Director-General, is simultaneously the editor-in-chief, that is where the most important part of the news 'process' occurs. Television news is part of a composite enterprise concerned with mass entertainment; it retains only an important emotional link with Fleet Street.

The telegraph system was perfected in the 1830s by reporters from the Philadelphia *Public Ledger*.[31] It rapidly became indispensable to the industry of news gathering. By 1846 American presidents were sending out their official messages by wire and in 1848 the founding of the Associated Press meant that news was to become in part the product of a new technology, its nature influenced by the economic organisation entailed in that machinery. Newspapers throughout the world absorbed the messages of the wire services and used them as the raw material for further refinement. News had to develop a 'neutral' flavour in political and national terms so that it would be saleable to newspapers controlled by owners of various political persuasions and indeed of various political systems.[32] The wire services created a new kind of 'news' syntax, an adaptation of the journalistic language previously employed. At the same time the requirements of agency news helped to foster the code of objectivity in journalism generally. The technology of news-collecting helped the development of a professional brokerage role for journalism within the increasingly

94

complex societies of the last century but the new role was contained within the institutions and organisations which guarded the new technology itself.

After the development of the new presses and agencies, nineteenth-century journalists developed styles and professional techniques within the craft which helped to increase the speed and directness of news presentation. The development of the interview[33] for instance cut down the amount of time the journalist spent on a given job; the Philadelphia *Evening Bulletin* was one of the early pioneers of the genre of the interview and realised that it enabled its staff of reporters to fill the seven daily editions of the paper. The interview and the 'stop-press' column enabled a paper to change its appearance with each edition without too much hard work. The interview as a form offended an older generation of editors, of whom one complained that it was 'the most perfect contrivance yet devised to make journalism an offence, a thing of ill savour in all decent nostrils'.[34] It was of course to become an extremely important device in political journalism and a staple form in broadcast journalism. The increased flow of news meant an increase in the army of news-manipulators, public-relations-men, information officers and press conference organisers. The Presidential press conference which had begun as a private arrangement between Theodore Roosevelt and Lincoln Steffens of the *New York Times* (who used to discuss the political news of the day with the President while he was shaving) was turned into a major instrument of public communication by the later Roosevelt in the 1930s. Thirty years after that, in 1961, President Kennedy allowed the conference to be televised and this action symbolised the way in which the conference had been transformed from a device for the privileged prising of information from the chief executive into a means by which the chief executive presented high policy to the largest political audience in history, for the most part on his own terms. 'We Americans', says Daniel Boorstin,[35] 'have accommodated our eighteenth-century constitution to twentieth-century technology by multiplying pseudo-events and by developing professions which both help make pseudo-events and help us interpret them.' Within the world of news-gathering all the 'gatekeeping' processes have become and are becoming increasingly centralised. The development of chains of newspapers (159 chains own 828 or 47 per cent of all the newspapers in America; but 35 of these chains are responsible for 63 per cent of all the newspapers actually sold in a day),[36] the dwindling of competition between newspapers (1700 towns and cities have daily newspapers without competition), the interlocking ownership of broadcast enterprises and newspapers (28 per cent of all television stations are owned by newspapers), and the increased use of electronic apparatus to carry the news from the scene to the newsroom, are all processes which directly or indirectly help to concentrate the power of choice over subject and manner of presentation into fewer and fewer hands. It has been estimated that only 1700 individuals are responsible ultimately for the shaping of the news in print form for the entire population of the United States. There are even 73 towns in which all the newspapers, radio and television stations are owned by one person. In smaller countries the concentration is sometimes even greater.

More and more power lies in the hands of a tiny group within society to shape this new secondary environment in which we all live. As news arrives faster it arrives in a more processed form. In broadcasting, where news has the added impact of a 'realism' which is more apparent than real, news is highly compacted, emerging from a complex set of industrial processes, through an intellectually compressed news organisation and dependent on a number of electronic services which are centrally controlled by government or various corporate enterprises whose primary function is not the provision of news. Where once, in the days of the coranteers, news was suspect because its methods were crude and unreliable, today news has become suspect because it is increasingly the by-product of a business enterprise whose profits are mainly obtained elsewhere, sometimes in fields which are themselves the proper subject of journalistic scrutiny. The whole of the NBC network, for instance, is but a tiny fragment of the RCA giant, one of the big defence suppliers of the US Government.

News is also suspect, particularly in its broadcast form, because events themselves are known, or at least very widely believed, to be heavily influenced by the presence of the reporting machinery of radio and television. News, therefore, at the end of some centuries of increasing sophistication, and increasing concern with its own ethics, has ended up as a highly contentious commodity blamed for the disasters it records, and scorned for its alleged fearfulness and triviality. Yet under the banner of 'news' today comes the very process which politicises the individual and in a sense makes the world available to him; news-dissemination is the fountainhead of opinion and therefore the pump of democracy. That society has come to feel that its waters are polluted is a matter of profound concern.

V

In most countries the news department of a television organisation is placed in a form of protective custody by management; naturally, since news by television has such important political implications, no management can afford dangerous 'mistakes' by junior employees. Sealed from the rest of the broadcasting world, for good or ill, the news-collecting section pursues, even more relentlessly than the rest of the organisation, the doctrines of factuality. Even within communist countries, news reporters are concerned with the collection of 'facts', the selection and pre-digestion of information, the writing of descriptions of events. The problem lies in that 'facts' do not exist in isolation either from other facts or from wide-ranging sets of assumptions. The 'facts' of news come to us embedded inside the perspectives from which their selection proceeds.[37] There is a kind of Heisenberg principle which operates in news-collecting, which dictates that the editorial process for selecting the news stories (based on the traditional and collective 'news sense') itself alters the nature of the 'facts' it picks out. The British monarch has always spent his or her time launching ships and opening bridges and old people's homes; there was a time when the facts of these ceremonial visits were invariably reported as a first or second item on the BBC's news bulletins. The monarch continues to pursue the same duties, no doubt as frequently as in the 1940s and 1950s, but they are reported far less prominently and far less often. The 'news sense' of the editors, in broadcasting as well as in the press, has over the years altered the status of these occasions; for a BBC bulletin today to open with news of the Queen would be felt to be wrong, unless it was an event of exceptional importance. News is an internalisation of the broadcasting organisation's or the editorial office's sense of political realities. It expresses, it almost ritualises, the organisation's own picture of the society to which it is broadcasting.

In late 1968, when student discontent in many parts of the world had remained high in the headlines for an extremely long time, there was a widely expressed concern, in Europe and the United States especially, that the television coverage was *causing* the continuation of rioting. There was a great deal of pressure on the American networks, and on the BBC, to 'cool it', to find ways to defuse the situation by paying less attention to student unrest. There was, in a sense, a national *argument* about news values. Within a few months the subject felt 'boring'; the 'news sense' of broadcast news editors was beginning to tell them, in its mysterious way, that student unrest was no longer as important as it had been. Their 'news sense' was not misdirecting them; the phenomenon did indeed subside. It is of course impossible to unravel the complex chain of causes and effects, of pressures and internalisations of pressures, which resulted in the lowering of the news status of the student demonstration. 'News values' are a mesh of beliefs and priorities within a given news-making organism; they are shared in broad terms within a society. The 'facts' of news arrive as the encrustations of encrustations of beliefs. In broadcasting the beliefs are held by institutions,[38] as well as by individuals.

An individual critical of broadcast news is normally concerned at the failure of the reporter to produce a fact of which the critic is aware; it is difficult for him to produce evidence that the reporter is guilty of ideological distortion since distortion of a purely non-factual kind is subjective to the point of unverifiability. Protagonists on both sides of the argument are in any case concerned, in the case of news-reporting, not with an argument about the 'balance' of the news but with the viability of the reporter's news judgement or that of his editor.

People who charge news with prejudice cannot simultaneously demand factuality; facts do not 'balance' in the same way as opinions. There are therefore two arguments: first, that television or those in charge of it exercise an undesirable influence over facts and the description of facts; and secondly, that the prevailing news *judgements* operating in broadcasting institutions are placing in an invalid order of importance the events of the world which they are observing. The dispute over bias in news is in essence a dispute about newsworthiness, conducted between various social groups each of which feels its perspective to be valid though inconsistent with that of the other contending groups.

Miss Edith Efron[39] conducted a study after the Presidential Election of 1968 in which she transcribed 323,100 words of network newscasts of the election period. She selected thirteen topics, divided the list into those issues which by their nature supported Nixon and those which were helpful to Nixon's opposition. Every single report was then labelled 'pro'- or 'anti'-Nixon. She concludes from her arithmetic count that the networks were as a group against Nixon's Vietnam war policy, in favour of Black militancy, anxious to evade the issue of violence by the radical wing, and in general derogatory to Nixon. Her analysis, exhaustive and arithmetically precise, produced a flurry of statistical return fire. The defenders of network news set to work with a vengeance to fault her mathematics;[40] it was not a difficult task, since her choice of the 'issues' was extremely personal and could be disputed. Her calculations, however, were indisputably accurate. She found that the ABC network used 4,200 words in favour of Humphrey, 3,600 against; CBS had 2,400 for and 2,100 against. NBC had 1,900 for and 2,700 against. As for Wallace, Miss Efron counted 1,100 words on CBS for him, and 1,300 against; on NBC 1,000 for him and 1,800 against; on ABC 1,400 for and 3,400 against. It was over Nixon, however, that the networks found their 'bias' ran away with them: ABC had 900 words for him and 7,500 against; CBS 300 for him and 5,300 against; NCB 400 for and 4,200 against. Professor Paul Weaver[41] summarised her methodological errors: 'Most of her "issues" are not issues but political groups – liberals, conservatives, the white middle class, black militantism, the left, demonstrators, and violent radicals. One problem here is that the groups as defined are not mutually exclusive . . . they were not issues but symbols. To measure the fairness of coverage of symbols, one would have to identify the different symbols of left, center, right, etc. and then measure their relative incidence. Miss Efron's procedure does not do this.' Her book aroused a great deal of attention; it was impossible to ignore the fact that the critics of 'biased' news felt that at last something had been proved. The more reasoned the refutations put out by the networks, the more convinced Miss Efron's supporters became that she was right.

Professor Weaver, however, put forward a wholly different explanation for the 'bias' of the networks. He argues that it is vain to look for deliberate 'unfairness' on the part of the newsmen covering the 1968 Presidential election. They saw their job as a professional one; the bias against Nixon lay in the fact that the newsman uses a journalistic model of the political society, one that made him see the election as a series of events to be covered in narrative form in accordance with established professionalisms and definitions of 'news'. What Miss Efron discovered, Weaver argues, was not bias against Nixon, but 'bias against someone like Nixon for reasons of his journalistically-defined situation and identity'. Traditionally American journalism has seen American political life as a game played by individual politicians for personal advantage; this picture of politics, whether 'true' or not, gives American journalism its sense of realness, its no-nonsense flavour, a knowing air of world-weary wisdom. Against the background of traditional American journalistic practice the candidates are driven constantly to exaggerate their good qualities and minimise or explain away their failings. The electorate's ability to make sensible choices on the basis of judgement of the issues is severely reduced, as the reporters (especially in television where a small group of moral themes is restated again and again) concentrate on events and personalities, while the candidates concentrate on deceiving the electorate about the events and their personalities. Weaver sees the problem entirely in the inadequacy of the professional notion of news itself. 'Insofar as we rely on news in forming our mental picture of what is going on in the world, what we are receiving is not a neutral body of information, but rather information gathered and presented to illustrate certain ways of seeing the world, based on certain values and favorable to certain courses of action.'[42] Weaver poses a serious moral problem of legitimacy – what right do the newsmen have to force us to see the world, 'fair' though they may be in presenting it, through their own special lenses?

Weaver might be said to exaggerate the role of traditional journalistic assumptions within television news; in the United States, the newsman inherits the grand early twentieth-century tradition of muckraking.[43] Broadcasting, however, brings with it an additional ethic, that of its enforced 'fairness', its instinctive quest for the middle ground. The television reporter often sounds as if he resents any effort to render this territory intellectually implausible. The bias against Nixon can be interpreted as hostility towards a politician who appeared to affront the network of intellectual values within which broadcast news operates. Broadcasting tends to sell its neutrality, and to exaggerate divergences from liberal consensus, because these do not easily connect with the broadcaster's inherited model of the political world. Although many demagogues and many extremists have made their appeal through radio and television, broadcast news has always to foster liberalism, reasonableness, the view that all problems can be dealt with through discussion, and the evolution of practical solutions. The ideological centre of gravity has shifted considerably in the course of broadcasting history, but so has the general consensus of belief, especially within the West. From Jo McCarthy to Enoch Powell, from Winston Churchill to Spiro Agnew, those who have striven against the political consensus of their time have had a hard time with broadcasting; they have simultaneously all been felt as some kind of threat to the institutional well-being of broadcasting.

It is simply impossible for news values to exist at all without some general interpretation of the past and some general and accepted interpretation of the direction in which events and opinion are moving. The reason why in the decade of the 1960s broadcast news has been felt to be 'left-wing' (and in the writer's view has indeed been so) is that broadcasters have

101

accepted the view that that was the general drift of events. A revolutionary student was thought to be more plausible than a John Birchite student because he was felt not necessarily to be taking the correct view, but was probably taking the historically predictive position. News values in print and in broadcasting are two different intellectual traditions which have been fused in the period which has seen the rise of broadcast news. While it was possible in programmes of general culture and general entertainment for broadcasting to occupy a widely agreed neutral ground, it became exceedingly difficult to do that when news became the dominant form within broadcasting, and television the dominant medium in the culture. News values have to imply a direction as well as a shape in the configuration of the social phenomena which they illumine. The bias which was for instance noticed in the period prior to Nixon's election to the presidency was the result not of a personal or group political bias but of the situation of the entire phenomenon of broadcast news.

The question is whether news as a form is outmoded, in that society no longer sustains the consensus of values on which news depends. Broadcasting in general became the centre of a controversy because its news values came under fire. If society fails to re-adopt consensual values, it is unlikely that broadcasting – so long as it remains a means of news collecting and dissemination – will find shelter from the storm.

VI

Broadcasting absorbed the highest version of journalism's most sacred code – that of precision and factuality. In the West at least broadcasting built its news ethics around an extremely highly developed sense of pure truthfulness.[44] The growth of the power and quantity of broadcast news over that emanating from other media and its gradual growth in credibility over other media have tended to make people concentrate on the overall picture it provides of the content of any given society; that concentration of attention has produced a realisation, now fairly complete, that the factuality of news does not in itself lead to a satisfactory 'mirror-image' emerging. As social belief in the possibility or usefulness of 'objectivity' has declined the value of factuality in itself has accordingly declined.[45] If no individual person can be 'objective', can, that is, reproduce in words a description of 'reality' from a sufficiency of perspectives and angles to satisfy all his hearers that a truthful picture has been given, then reliability on fact in itself declines in value. Since no single large audience is satisfied with the 'fairness' of the picture presented, the defence that every word spoken is 'true' is simply not useful. The critic of news complains nonetheless against the practitioners rather than against the phenomenon of news in itself.

News is a genre, a literary 'kind', like drama, epic, the ode, the pamphlet, the novel, the documentary. It has its own *raison d'être*; it originated in the desire of people to have a suitable format in which to receive information about the world around them, information about events which they knew were occurring but which they were unable to see occur for themselves. The work of collecting news to fill this format, in whatever medium, implies a 'news judgement', exercised in the mind of an editor.

Men of letters discussed for many centuries the kind of historical event which was suitable for the epic form; for thousands of years poets have argued about the kind of emotions which were appropriate to various verse forms. Historians have argued about what facts constitute 'history'. To understand news one must try to delineate some of the elements which together compose the 'news judgement'. They function as an unconsciously held group of criteria which enable an editor to decide which facts and which methods of presentation are appropriate to the cultural form which he practises. News is not *supposed* to provide a pure view of 'reality'; it is not the same thing as historiography, nor is it a town crier, nor one of the mimetic 'kinds'. It has its own rules and criteria, each of which can appear to be equally a useful tool or a distorting element.

The first criterion operating within a 'news judgement' is one that insists upon the recency of an event. The newer the event the more probable that the editor will include it. Old facts are less useful than new ones, old events less interesting. In itself this criterion of news validity contains an inbuilt bias

103

against explaining the previous events which have led to a new development. News tends to underplay what it calls 'background'. The very fact of newness as an element in newsworthiness means that news events have a tendency to be presented as isolated phenomena, tips of unstated icebergs. The choice of which events to choose in order to present the full 'background' of a new event itself involves an extremely complex set of issues which are similar to the issues faced by historians. For instance, in the case of Northern Ireland, it is impossible to explain the full chain of events which have led to a given bombing or assassination. Every event in Irish history implies every other event along the wretched chain of circumstances which have resulted in the present.

The second criterion of news judgement is a geographical one; if the news form under preparation is destined for showing to the population of Birmingham only, then the events contained must have some validity in the minds of the people of Birmingham; the unemployment figures in Barnstaple are of little interest unless they are believed to act as some kind of heuristic device aiding comprehension of the situation in Birmingham. If the news is destined for a national audience, then the events described must carry some meaning for the nation involved. This fact tends to lead towards a bias on the side of authority, because government itself is the main centralised manifestation of the national audience, and the activities of government and its principal personalities naturally loom large in the mind of an editor of a national news bulletin; government will, in a sense, gain an 'unfair' advantage over other institutions and groups of individuals. The geographical criterion also gives an advantage in publicity to people and things already well known within the geographical area concerned; the divorce of a pop-singer whose songs are nationally sung will tend to be reported more fully than that of, say, a Welsh pop-singer who sings only in the vernacular, be he as famous a voice *in Wales* as Paul McCartney in Britain as a whole. The national criterion naturally provides a built-in bias against foreign stories, especially if they involve the internal politics of another nation. Domestic news also takes precedence over equal news from another country. The national criterion also tends to give news a special interest in the question of social order; events which tend to disrupt the very cohesion of a society (whether they are matters of scandal or of violence) will tend to provide the news editor with that sense of instant interest and audience involvement, which he is of course looking for in his material.

The third criterion can best be described as 'continuity'; an event will be covered, even if relatively unimportant, if it is part of a long-running story which the editor has been covering thoroughly all along. An explosion in Belfast will be reported because it provides some sort of guide to the intensity of conflict or of crisis within the Irish situation as that situation flows through the weeks and months. There is a converse force operating within the news imagination, which forces certain events into obscurity after a long-running story has become boring; thus, casualty figures in Vietnam have ceased to be stated daily on British news, although every murder and shooting in Ireland has continued to be.

Fourthly, there is a priority given to events which will tend to interest a 'mass' audience; there are stereotyped formulae for mass journalism, 'human' stories, stories of humble heroism, folksy sentimentality, stories which confirm or are felt to confirm stereotypical images which float about within mass society. These formula-stories have been part of the stock-in-trade of mass journalism for over a century but in broadcasting they are important tokens of the relationship between the news and the audience. They tend to leaven the concentration upon 'importance' in the events selected and they re-emphasise the relationships and values of the newsmakers towards the audience. They are part of news as a 'genre' precisely because they are unimportant. People who fall from high windows without hurting themselves, mothers who return from Australia after sixty-five years to meet their brothers and sisters, children who wander from home and are returned by strangers – their triviality combined with high interest value serve to confirm various of the assumptions which are contained within the relationship between audience and communicator in a mass medium.

Fifthly, there is a group of stories which gain prominence in any medium because they appeal to the technology of that particular medium. There are events which fit supremely into the needs of television, dramatic filmable rituals, processions, disasters, stories which involve grief-stricken faces, collapsing buildings, great fires and fiestas. These will inevitably gain some kind of imaginative precedence over stories which relate to finance or education and are much harder to realise in visual terms. The sixth criterion relates to the programme structure of the news itself; stories will be chosen which help to provide a pattern within the structure of a long news programme. In the course of thirty or more minutes there need to be high points of interest and low points, as in any other creative narrative exercise; the editor or producer of a given news programme will therefore include and order stories which will improve the 'feel' of the whole programme and turn it into an entertainment which will hold the interest of the audience. The need for radio and television to maintain a continuity of unbroken interest in the audience is of course greater than that of print.

Beyond the six which I emphasise, there are other criteria which tend to colour the judgement of news editing, in television especially. News reporters, for instance, cannot all be specialists, nor can specialists where they do exist always be sent to cover stories involving subjects with which they are familiar. News therefore contains a 'bias' towards the inter-disciplinary aspects of a subject; reporters will emphasise the more easily comprehensible aspects of a situation, as well as the 'human' elements and the non-technical. The believed public 'mood' of the moment will act as a powerful agent of choice of stories; if the public is thought to be bored with demonstrations or suffering from a surfeit of economic disaster then only the bigger demonstrations and the more disastrous of the economic events will fight their way to the front of the queue of events awaiting selection. The fact that any given news programme is in competition with other similar programmes for audience or for general critical approval means that all the criteria I have singled out will tend to gain in emphasis; editors will look for 'highlights' and highlights of highlights in the daily search for competitive advantage.

The final factor which tends to influence and to intensify all the other factors is the very speed with which news has to be prepared; a news editor internalises all the criteria because they have to operate within his mind by reflex. While other cultural disciplines can afford to take a serious and self-analytic interest in their own methodology, news must move along with the momentum of events and it is seldom that the news 'gate-keeper' can afford to examine his own motives for specific decisions, in the manner of an historian, say, or a sociologist.

News therefore contains within its own nature a series of characteristics which oblige it to give a 'news' view of the world rather than an 'objective-realistic' view. News is a cultural discipline, choosing it an intellectual skill, collecting it a profession. Within the confines of the broadcasting institution the news organisation absorbs the institution's picture of the society and inherits the professional assumptions and methods of newsmen in other media. News is only a single vessel in which broadcasting strives to catch reality. The answer to the problem of in-built 'distortion' of the disseminated picture of society is to create and to encourage other parallel disciplines for the broadcast representation of reality.

The BBC has for many years separated its 'current affairs' from its 'news', giving each of them a slightly different role and in the course of time the two have developed different ideas of what kind of event and what kind of treatment are most appropriate to their own nature.[46] The documentary, similarly, is an additional discipline and needs to be encouraged to grow separately. When all the various disciplines of factual programming are brought within the same organisational routines, either for the sake of administrative convenience or financial economy, the intellectual divergences of approach tend to be flattened. The result of necessity is that the criteria of news come to predominate; the programme unit with the most urgent needs has to be helped to reach them first. In any competition for attention or for resources news almost always has to win. Within small broadcasting organisations news can take up a huge and disproportionate section of the resources. In Israeli television for instance, with a tiny population to serve and an accordingly small budget, the news operation designed to fill a 30-minute daily bulletin absorbs well over a quarter of the total technical facilities (in camera crews, editing facilities, reporting personnel).[47] Inevitably the result is that the parallel disciplines within factual programme-making are relatively starved of resources. The capacity of news to exploit facilities is almost infinite, as near to infinity as events in the world. The social value derived from the predominance of this single genre needs to be critically examined. News everywhere has become the source of a remorseless daily competition, avidly pursued, for viewers; broadcasting organisations cannot allow themselves any longer to fail with their news operations if they are to succeed at all. Yet news has become the most contentious of all broadcast forms, the one which plays the greatest part in colouring the view of the world imparted to every citizen within it and the one which presents the greatest range of moral and political problems.

There have been many arguments advanced for the growth of a 'pluralism' within news. Miss Efron argues for the employment of Nixonite newsmen to ensure that the picture of American society and American politics is more fairly balanced.[48] There is a very attractive view advanced especially in the United States which argues apparently for a kind of democratisation of news. Professor Herbert Gans puts it this way:[49] 'In a heterogeneous society, in which no one version of the truth necessarily prevails, the most reasonable solution, it seems to me, is to have as much diversity and pluralism, both of viewpoints and of perspectives in reporting an event as possible. What I think we need is a pluralistic set of news media, which do not only reflect the predominantly middle-class values of the journalistic profession, but also report the viewpoints, the events and the perspectives of every cultural and political group in the society, be they rich or poor, young or old, left or right, black or white, educated or uneducated.' Even setting aside the problem of how Professor Gans proposes to reach this ideal condition, there remains a far more intractable conceptual problem involved in introducing 'pluralism' to broadcasting. Without its central *national* professional discipline, news becomes a different genre altogether; there is no need for a news 'programme', no need to bring together a series of heterogeneous reports of events which have allegedly taken place on a given day in various parts of the world. News based upon the idea of a homogeneous mass audience (in the sense that it has a common frame of reference for what constitutes a news 'event') listening to an account, as accurate as can be humanly ascertained, of actual daily events. The whole idea of news is that it is beyond a 'plurality of viewpoints'. The fact that the world has to a great extent ceased to believe in the intellectual possibility of such objective facts does not mean that one can quickly devise a new set of organisations in which new 'pluralistic facts' can be gathered and disseminated.

Ten separate news bulletins would not provide a more *accurate* picture even if we listened to all of them. A society which demanded its news from ten separate perspectives would not be receiving *news*. Ten views of reality do not between them add up to a new 'objectivity' to exchange for an old one. In the Middle East where conflict is so intense between adjacent population groups that they cannot each accept the other's 'true' account even of their battles, they tend to use the BBC's overseas broadcasts as a yardstick of reality. Even then they find a good deal to dispute. But their inability to find a mutual basis for credible news-reporting is an apt reflection on the total nature of the conflict. Credibility in the mind of the actual audience is the *sine qua non* of news. All else is either propaganda or entertainment.

There is therefore no easy recipe for solving what one might call the contemporary crisis in news credibility. Indeed, if one looks at the present conflict in a detached way one can see plenty of room for the traditional consensus of credibility to continue. Only over certain social and international problems – and they perhaps of a temporary nature – has the new disbelief arisen. What is more likely to happen in the medium term is that the news organisations will shift their centre of intellectual gravity to include some of the newly self-identifying forces which have been complaining of the 'bias' against them in news-reporting. For instance, in Britain the trade union movement has mounted a steady campaign against the news organisations which have allegedly failed to report industrial disputes from a standpoint which satisfies them as being truly neutral.[50] Strikes tend to be presented as the result of anti-social activity on the part of workers rather than, say, malice or incompetence on the part of employers. Some of the expositions of this point of view have been eloquently and effectively put.[51] It is probably true that among news reporters only a minority has hitherto been able to gain experience in the reporting of industrial disputes, and throughout the field of reporting work in the broadcast media, certainly in Britain, there has been a relative dearth of attention paid to 'working-class issues' prior to the outbreak of industrial disputes. It is likely – perhaps even predictable – that there will be in the near future a noticeable growth of thorough reporting of topics previously ignored or underplayed. Where some have been arguing for 'trade union time' on television during which reporters with a more familiar understanding of working-class politics can explain the issues, it is far more likely that the news will in the course of time simply mop up the areas of discontent, in order to regain credibility. Freedom of access to the air can be argued for in powerful and convincing terms, but not, I think, sufficiently for us to abandon the use of central news sources. What is more important is that the other genres which deal in factual reporting should be extended and encouraged. In that way we can preserve the social centrality of news without turning it into the instrument of a kind of socialising tyranny. There is plenty of scope for the fragmented presentation of reality in documentary programmes and special interview programmes and discussions. Indeed, there is a growing movement for reporting affairs through the eyes of a single person; there are many truths which are incomplete or observable only from single perspectives. It is unlikely that the phenomenon of news which has lived and struggled for so many centuries to be free from political interference will cease to exist in our time.

Chapter Four

Sharing the Labours of Statesmanship

'He who moulds public sentiment goes deeper than he who enacts statutes or pronounces decisions.'

Lincoln, 1858

'I have tamed that savage stenographic mystery. I make a respectable income by it. I am in high repute for my accomplishment in all pertaining to the art, and am joined with eleven others in reporting the debates in Parliament for a Morning Newspaper. Night after night I record predictions that never come to pass, professions that are never fulfilled, explanations that are only meant to mystify. I wallow in words.'

Charles Dickens, *David Copperfield*

'Gentlemen, when Jesus Christ wanted to found a religion, he had to be crucified, dead and buried, and to rise on the third day from the dead. If you want to convince mankind, go and do likewise.'

Talleyrand

When a modern politician considers his electorate he is contemplating a relationship vastly different from that which prevailed before the mass franchise. Disraeli and Gladstone were both conscious of the fact that they had to address themselves to a much greater body of voters in their latter days than in their earlier, but the distinction was, they felt, of number rather than kind. The audience of the politician, however, had changed in a manner similar to the audience of the journalist; the voters were now an undifferentiated mass in the mind of the political communicator, as they were in the mind of the new newspaper magnates. In fact, several of the latter, (Northcliffe, Rothermere, Beaverbrook) found it increasingly difficult to distinguish between their journalistic functions and their political aspirations. The politician found that the difference between his professional political audience and his electorate was growing; while he could speak to the former as in a drawing-room, the latter, increasingly, had to be reached through mechanical devices, through the filter of a mass press which imposed its own merchandising exigencies on the material which it fashioned for a purchasing public numbering millions.

The most important aspect of the new public (new in its political power) was its ignorance. It did not possess the quantity of information about the history of the society nor about the contemporary range of urgent issues which would have enabled the politician to speak to it on terms of greater equality. Nor could it be expected to respond in a homogeneous way to any single communication; it was an aggregate audience, consisting of a number of inconsistent but overlapping publics, which would read a given message in totally different ways. Yet all of these groups were equally important in that all of them collectively possessed power over the political life and death of a national leader. A speech which could be made in one place without raising a murmur could raise a riot if delivered in a different city or to an audience composed of members of a different class. Politicians had always been familiar with this problem; now, however, it was as if the politician had been given a single megaphone through which to reach all of them. He was unfamiliar with their attitudes and ways of life – all he knew was that in every pronouncement he played with dynamite.

Yet the new mass society continued to hold a picture of itself which was not markedly different from that held by the previous society. Although voting power had changed hands the electorate was still spoken to as if it sat in the same Victorian drawing-room as its predecessor. The role of the press was still thought of as a means by which ideas circulated, by which individuals received arguments and were influenced by them, by which facts about current issues were disseminated. In fact the press was becoming part of a complex process for manipulating large groups of people psychologically; politicians were becoming a group of highly organised professionals who were obliged to 'sell' to the public a product, which was themselves.

Within the new mass society there was present a traditional set of assumptions about the press, assumptions about the need for 'freedom of expression' which had been fashioned in quite different societies. The sentiments which people used about the press and which implied a certain model of the communication itself went back to Milton,[1] Hume,[2] Sheridan,[3] Mill and Palmerston,[4] and belonged to a discussion which was valid and wholly meaningful within a world of coterie politics, where discussion was on the basis of shared terms of reference. Even today we use the same terms as those employed in the treatises of the four who have been mentioned, and with the same emotional overtones, but the model of political communication in a mass society is utterly different. The modern politician has neither to inform his public nor to convince it; public opinion is moulded slowly (and scientifically) by processes which are psychological rather than logical. Opinion shifts in actuarial blocs. Most of the voting public votes according to slowly changing concepts of themselves and their personal identities within the massive blocs that constitute a modern society. The relationship between the politician and his public, in mass society, is befuddled by the fact that both sides imagine themselves to be in a completely different kind of relationship and behave as if this other relationship actually existed.

From the very beginning of mass society politicians have been increasingly concerned about their new psychological relationships; the politician, as for instance in Graham Wallas's eerily prophetic portrait,[5] looks out at his public as at a photographic plate on which he must imprint his picture slowly and forcefully: he must therefore at all costs be *consistent* so that the picture is not blurred 'as if a bird suddenly flew across the plate', he must acquire physical symbols by which he is popularly recognised, a case, a pipe, a moustache, a special kind of overcoat. The modern politician, especially in an age when the microphone and the camera have joined the popular newspaper as the means through which he has to operate, develops a second personality, a duplicate of himself, his 'image', which is something more than a static picture in the mind of third

113

parties, it is a picture of himself which inhabits his own mind and his own world. He lives the life of his image, as much as the life of his primary self; the two overlap and breed a special kind of self-consciousness.

Traditionally the politician has had to cope with the problem of the media of communication treating him with scepticism, hostility or derision. He has enjoyed traditional forms of protection against this, in libel laws, laws to prevent sedition, or by resorting to strong-arm methods. What he has not had to deal with until the present century is the force of a medium which proclaims its neutrality, and which is licensed to exist only by virtue of its neutrality. In a society with a free press, a politician can hope to win one section of it to his side; at least its traditional ethic will force the press to give the politician some kind of access to his public. But the broadcast journalist is free neither to express opinions nor to allow any other opinion to prevail. The whole art of advocacy is therefore lost on him; the broadcast journalist is a eunuch in the harem of ideas.

The politician is therefore torn between treating him as a journalist and treating him as a kind of mass telephone, a common carrier of messages. The politician finds he cannot treat the broadcasting organisation as a ministry, nor as a newspaper, nor as a public meeting. As an institution it lies outside the normal range of familiar arenas; as a set of skills it demands things of him which he may not be able to give. Yet the prominent politician increasingly depends on radio and television for his very existence. Politics within mass society is inextricable from the technology which provides contact between the few and the many. The periodic outbursts of fury and vengeance between the broadcasting organisations of the world and their respective political communities follow inevitably from the very existence of broadcasting.

'An Estate', wrote Benjamin Disraeli, 'is a political order invested with privilege for a public purpose. There are three Estates: the Lords Spiritual, the Lords Temporal and the Commons. . . . The House of Commons is not an Estate of the Realm, its members are only the proxies of an Estate.'[6] The world of broadcasting is in this technical sense an Estate; it is a political order in that it has a precise function within the management of the society, it exercises a privilege in that it is given exclusive control over a national asset and it has a public purpose of providing information for which that privilege has been granted. True, it exercises its privilege by proxy on behalf of the viewers and listeners, but then the House of Commons exists by proxy too. Like the Lords Spiritual it has access to every house and heart in the nation, like the Lords Temporal it works within a statutory system of rights and obligations, it exercises its influence by power over the air, almost as important in a modern state as power over the land. When Edmund Burke lifted his hand in a theatrical gesture towards the gallery of the House of Commons and shouted 'Yonder sits the Fourth Estate, more important than them all', he was expressing the feelings of a man who had just perceived the implications of the establishment in 1772 of the right of publishing Parliamentary debates. That right, like the right of franchise to broadcast about political and Parliamentary affairs, changed the relationships of the politicians with the people, relationships between politicians, as well as the personal identity of each individual politician. With the advent of mass society and mass media those relationships were transformed yet again. The broadcaster's particular addition to the armoury of journalistic tools, as far as politics is concerned, is to add the discipline of public theatre to the arena of politics.

The broadcast interview, the standard formula of political communication, is a fusion of a journalistic technique with a theatrical one. The politician is *seen* not to be the orchestrator of his own affairs, but merely one of the instruments. The struggle between the politicians and the broadcasters is a constant battle fought to prevent the usurpation of specific sets of functions which each lays claim to as of right. The politician needs privacy, the appearance of dignity, the right to time his actions and statements and the right to change his mind; he wants to address his public when it is in his own interests to do so. The broadcaster claims the rights of traditional journalism and employs additional tools; he demands the right of timing and scheduling, the right of constant publicity, together with the pretension that he represents the 'public' (which they both claim); the broadcaster wants the politician to appear when it is to the latter's disadvantage as well as when it is to his advantage. These claims are not of course in constant active conflict but they are always in latent conflict. To show how the peculiar functions of the broadcaster emerge as a source of actual political power if uncurbed by statute I shall take an example from the eastern world rather than the western where political television as it is practised in America, Germany, Scandinavia and Britain, for instance, is in its infancy.

One of the political changes which took place in Poland in the wake of the riots in Gdansk and the arrival in power of Edward Gierek was a decision to use television to communicate information about the far-reaching series of political changes directly to the people over the heads of the middle-rank party officials and party organs. Several senior members of the party appeared on a semi-regular series of programmes called 'Trybuna Obywatelsak' – 'The Citizens' Tribune' – in which a panel of interviewers put to them a series of questions, most of which had been sent in or telephoned in by viewers throughout Poland. In the earlier programmes the questioning was very stilted, all of it passing through the hands of a trusted senior official of Polish television. In the third of the series, however, the politician involved was Stefan Olszowski, later to become Foreign Secretary, although in this programme he addressed himself formally to the subject of education. Questions poured in, were sifted, and put to Olszowski who, unlike his predecessors in the series, discovered a skill for parrying difficult ones in a friendly fashion, answering some quite probing points with an openness and frankness that did him great credit, and evading others promptly and politely. Although he performed these tasks with neither the accumulated reserves of experience nor the dexterity of a senior western politician, he revealed an undoubted flair. The questions put to him were harder than those put to his predecessors and many of the Polish Communists Party's skeletons were paraded: a monk rang and complained of discrimination against religious people in the universities, farmers complained of lack of consultation on the fixing of annual targets, people rang wanting to know the fate of the recently deposed Party Secretary, Gomulka. The producer of the programme and the question-master Michal Szulczewski[7]

(Head of the Political Department of Polish Television) were creating deliberately for their guest certain tensions which they realised -- in a psychological and theatrical sense – would enable him to thrive. The unanticipated, the pressing supplementary question, the almost random selection of a topic, revealed that they too were exercising a form of political power which consisted in the power to 'test' Olszowski; had he failed to rise to the occasion his political personality would have suffered considerably as a result, even in a relatively closed political society like Poland. Because he coped extremely well with this novel political situation he gained considerably in national stature from the performance. It was his own personal political identity that was being moulded through the medium of television, through the peculiar fusion of the mimetic with the informational. He was becoming, to a small extent, a mass society politician; his public existence would to some extent be formalised, 'settled' for some time to come by his performance in a single programme. When he was asked questions about long-haired youth he took a fairly 'square' line, that which would have been shared by the older generation in his audience but he angled his answer towards a position of tolerance, arguing that a man's intelligence was not to be judged by the length of his hair and that the long-haired youth, misguided though they might be, should not be persecuted for their hair styles. He kept his audience clearly in mind throughout the performance and gave himself a credible role within that audience, keeping it consistent throughout the run of questions on quite disparate issues, but trying to broaden his appeal. The producers in the course of their work were gradually realising that an extraordinary power had suddenly devolved upon them, the power to orchestrate a political event. They were exercising an authority to which they had not been formally elected, which they realised emerged from their professional skills within this particular mass medium. Their judgements were *production* judgements, decisions about how to make the programme interesting for a mass audience, rather than overtly political ones, but the result was that they found themselves exercising a political power. They had started to become an 'Estate', in Disraeli's sense.[8]

It is virtually impossible to measure the direct influence of a televised political performance upon the voter; the influence consists to a great extent in the impact of broadcasting upon the identity of the politician, upon his status within the world of politicians. The impact of broadcasting on society is in the way it transforms the whole complex of these relationships. The mass audience does not sit and listen to arguments judging issues in a 'rational' manner, according to the classic view of political discussion. The individual member of the audience absorbs from the screen and the radio receiver that part of the message which reinforces his own sense of identity and bolsters his previously-held attitudes. The coterie world of politics will watch the performance of one of their number with perhaps the same set of attitudes as they do within the political drawing-room, although that too will be modified by the fact that they are watching him to see *how well he does on television*.

Broadcasting has thus emerged *in itself* as a special source of political power. That power is exercised always potentially and sometimes actually; the intense interest which politicians take in it demonstrates this permanent potentiality – that in itself is a factor in modern politics, even in societies in which there exists no leeway for an individual broadcaster to intrude into the political process. But the presence of broadcasting in every home brings about a much wider set of influences and pressures in society, a broader impact on the working of authority as a whole. Broadcasting is at present the *dominant* medium, and that means not only that it is the subject of the greatest amount of investigation and complaint but also that more forces are at any given moment competing to register its attention than that of the media. When the press was the dominant medium, all those seeking attention within society for political ends would behave in a manner which would achieve the most useful impact upon newspapers and those who wrote them. When radio became the dominant medium – albeit for a fairly short period – there was an adjustment of political styles to take account of its special needs. George Bernard Shaw was certain that radio would abolish humbug in politics, that it would profoundly alter the political style which made phrase-making the major technique of successful politicians. 'Already several front-bench celebrities,' he wrote in 1935,[9] 'unaware of the magic of Mike the Detective, have tried their rousing election speeches and their dollops of solemn post-prandial humbug on the millions of sober fireside listeners, only to be laughed at, slept through, or switched off. No corrupt control can neutralise a change of such subtlety.' He was being excessively optimistic. The arrival of television as the dominant medium, however, has brought about a greater pessimism; it has, allegedly, been responsible for the return to political life of a range of activities of which the common characteristic is that they are conspicuous visually. In the last decade we have seen the growth of major public demonstrations, hi-jackings of aircraft, dare-devil exploits at public gatherings such as the Munich Olympic Games which provide for those desiring to send out a political message a kind of world stage on which to perform. The styles of political speech have also changed to accommodate the greater intimacy of the studio and the camera. At one end political life has become more dramatic; at the other much more low-key, informal and unhistrionic.

To list the 'effects' of television on politics is to list a series of seemingly contradictory phenomena, a rag-bag of factors, all apparently self-evident but all simultaneously ascribable to other influences. Every effort to reveal a pure cause-and-effect relationship between a given political occasion and a given quantity of political coverage tends to disappear under the weight of the attendant issues which have to be taken into account. The messages which are fed into society turn up as political effects; but the intended and anticipated effects are fed into the messages in the first place. Would Ireland have erupted without television, or would it have erupted sooner and less violently had television paid attention to the situation a decade earlier? Would the Vietnam war have ended sooner without constant presence of cameras? or would it have been possible for the American government to fight the war more rapidly and victoriously if television cameras had stayed away? In an era which possesses the tool of television, its exclusion from a specific situation can only be deliberate and therefore in itself manipulative.

119

Was television responsible for the spread of the student rebellions of 1968 ? If it was, it didn't enable them to spread much more rapidly than those of 1848. Certainly a long list of other 'causes' can be made which could explain historically the outbreak of a student rebellion, widespread and extremely militant, without the attendance of television cameras; nonetheless it was impossible for a major movement of that kind to spring up without its being 'registered' on the television screens of the world; it was similarly impossible for it to exist without it attempting everywhere to capture the attention of the dominant medium of the time.

The whole problem involved in studying the political 'effects' of television is that of finding a suitable model of social 'influence'. For a very long time investigators concentrated on finding a cause-and-effect pattern within the political world; there were many studies conducted, some of them extremely complex and sensitively executed, which were done on an underlying assumption that the contents of a mass medium were injected into the body politic and into the individuals which composed it as serum through a hypodermic needle. As they began gradually to realise that the results were extremely meagre some concluded that television had little influence at all. Since few voters could be produced who had been 'converted' from voting one way to voting another by watching television, perhaps there lay no power in the Box after all. The fears which had affected so many in the 1920s about the effects of propaganda began to evaporate. Research studies piled up without isolating any major manipulative power in television.

People disturbed by the increase in reported acts of violence in recent years have conducted direct effects investigation, assuming that there *must* be a cause-and-effect connection between the enormous amount of violent acts portrayed on the screen at peak hours and the incidence of violence among the young. The codes on violence employed by the IBA and the BBC in Britain, and similar codes devised by the National Association of Broadcasters in America, have resulted from a proper sense of caution induced by fears that there might be a direct connection. Naturally, it is eminently sensible although extremely easy to equate a series of new social phenomena with a newly dominant medium; the decline of respect for authority, the increase in crimes of violence, the spread of moral laxity, the increased pursuit of consumer goods, the decline of religion, the trivialisation of politics, the growth in the power of the party leadership and the decline of the power of the back-benchers, all of these are variously ascribed to the influence of television. Certainly, they could not fail to be influenced by television. But every attempt to discover through research and the use of questionnaires the actual path by which the influence travelled from person to person has tended to become bogged down in its own methodology or else has come up with only trivial results.

In their celebrated study of the British General Election of 1959 Joseph Trenaman and Denis McQuail concluded that television merely increased voters' knowledge without altering voting intentions.[10] They could find no correlation between television-viewing and the alteration in party affiliations even of those who did actually change their affiliation during the course of the campaign. They spoke of a 'barrier between sources of communication and movements of attitude in the political field at the General Election'.[11] After the election of 1964 Martin Harrison studied the use of television in the campaign and wrote that 'Television . . . may inform or reinforce attitudes, but it rarely converts'.[12] That remained for some time the prevailing view. The publication of the study by Jay Blumler and Denis McQuail into the use of television in the 1964 election has helped to change the way we look at the problem of political effects;[13] it is an astonishingly elaborate and intuitive piece of work and examined television in relation to the actual circumstances of the election. Blumler and McQuail examined the motivation of the people who watched television most during the campaign in an effort to find out why they used the medium, what they looked at in particular and what they themselves therefore thought the influence of television consisted in. They conclude that television played an enormous part in the mental activity of those voters – quite a large group – who were rethinking their political position in the period leading up to polling day 1964. Television could naturally therefore play a major part in the lead-up to a *crucial* election, that is, one in which an important section of the population were thinking hard about politics, since we knew that television was a major source of fundamental impressions of the political leaders and of factual information about the issues at stake. In relating television to the actual circumstances of an election they were using a model of political persuasion that was far less stringently cause-and-effect, far less 'hypodermic'. In fact they see election broadcasting and political broadcasting in general as a kind of aerosol spray; one vital section of the electorate – namely those thinking of changing their minds – sniff harder than the rest, as it were, and therefore skilfully informative programmes can play not a trivial role, as had previously been imagined, but a major role in the result of an election.

Nonetheless one is left feeling that the impact of television must be greater than that implied in the Blumler–McQuail diagram; so much energy and skill is diverted into the process of inducing many millions of people night after night to pay attention to the political and other messages on their screens; so many phenomena in modern society are simply felt to be the *result* of television. There must be traceable another pattern of influence which will somehow amount to an explanation of what we instinctively feel to be the massive influence of television.

The most elaborate and systematic examination of the influence of television in general and the most advanced overall pattern at present offered us is that of Joseph Klapper. He has correlated all the hundreds of existing small studies and amalgamated their total range of discoveries into five simple laws.[14] He dismisses the traditional behaviouristic model which would have us accept that the individual member of the audience simply responds to a set of stimuli, and that his behaviour can be therefore influenced by a sufficiency of such stimuli accompanied by a sufficiency of promised 'rewards'. (With this theory a voter would be expected to change his opinion simply if he has been subjected to 'enough.' political messages and been tempted at the same time with 'enough' promises of a good life. Similarly a teenager could be turned into a criminal simply by 'injecting' him with enough screen murders accompanied by a promise that he could get away from the police.) Klapper explains that 'mass communication ordinarily does not serve as a necessary and sufficient cause of audience effects, but rather functions among and through a nexus of mediating factors and influences'. These influences, according to Klapper's second law, never act as a sole cause but only as one among a group of contributory factors. Klapper, thirdly, explains that when direct influence does occur, it does so only when for some reason all the other mediating factors have ceased to function or when they all impel the individual towards the same end. Fourthly, Klapper finds certain situations in which mass communication does produce direct effects – where in itself it fulfils some special psychophysical function. Then, fifthly, he identifies a number of characteristics of communication processes which enhance their efficacy, notably the fact that the media confer special 'status' on the issues and individuals they make prominent – 'if you matter you will be seen on television and if you are on television, then you must matter'. Klapper therefore leaves us with a highly enriched picture of the working of mass communication within society, but his is still only a version of the traditional picture. It is a long way from the Huxleyan vision of mass manipulation; it is even further from Orwell's *1984*.

A number of people who have studied the coverage of political events on television have changed the structure of the mental picture of television influence by emphasising how the technology of television itself, coupled with the professional attitudes of those in charge of it, has exercised a kind of tyranny over events. Kurt and Gladys Lang, on the basis of a series of minutely studied major events in the United States,[15] reached the conclusion that the television camera stage-manages reality, personalises politics (by forcing the viewers to concentrate on, say, the trustworthiness of the speaker rather than on his argument) and forces the unauthentic into being a kind of reality. We see a demonstration on the screen and believe that the people taking part are all actually motivated by the message of the demonstration; in fact, most of them have come to look at the crowd, attracted perhaps by the presence of television.

123

Their presence on the screen, however, is beyond doubt and the whole affair is registered in the viewer's mind as an important valid political event. The distorting power of television is profoundly undermined by its inherent capacity to reveal a scene live and direct; you believe what you see on the screen far more readily because the camera makes you believe you have observed the primary evidence for yourself; in reality the event has been distorted by a series of factors, many of them themselves the result of television. The Langs were the first to express and codify this argument which increased in forcefulness during the years of the greatest growth of television.

In 1968 television was blamed for distorting the nature of some of that year's many demonstrations, especially those which took place at the Chicago Convention of the Democratic Party.[16] It was also blamed for the fact that viewers, seeing the events on the screen, took action themselves of a political nature which they would not have taken had they realised that the screen events were being stage-managed by the cameras, or otherwise distorted. In the aftermath of the convention a considerable literature was generated which gradually helped to persuade perhaps a majority of people that this was an inherent and dangerous power in television, although the argument once absorbed produced its own self-erosion – the more people understand this inherent 'effect' of television, the less they are willing to believe what they see. The coil of self-repeating cause-and-effect thus begins to unwind of its own accord.

The case against television on the grounds that it causes the events it records is not merely confined to the machinery of television; it also embraces the people who use that machinery, in that the producers and reporters of news events are allegedly also induced because of the potentialities of their technology and the competitive (and ideological) pressures upon them to indulge in the practice of falsifying events. The FCC Inquiry into the coverage of the Chicago Convention put the allegations into very detailed terms. As well as listing all the letters of complaint received concerning bias in the reports against Mayor Daley of Chicago and his police, and bias against the Administration's Vietnam policy, the FCC investigated claims that NBC cameras and their producers had distorted the proceedings at the Convention, stimulated rumours, created controversy and gave undue coverage to minorities indulging in spectacular activities. Inevitably the uproar against the FCC's intrusion into such minute matters of political reporting was considerable, though not as great as the clamour against the networks' coverage of the events. The networks provided equally detailed replies to all the detailed accusations.[17] But a new dilemma henceforth hung over the whole business of political reporting and its alleged influence, the danger that the recurrence of public investigations into the decision-making of broadcasters would itself become a source of further distortion. As Howard Monderer, one of the lawyers retained by NBC, later put it:[18] 'Few spectres can be more frightening to a person concerned with the vitality of a free press than the vision of a television cameraman turning to one aspect of a public event rather than another because of a concern that a governmental agency might want him to do so, or fear government sanction if he did not.' One might go further than this and add that the entire structure of licensing and organisation within which the cameraman operates helps to decide the direction in which he points his camera. All the fears and the anticipated rewards which surround him, financially, institutionally, and politically, will shape his decisions. He will interpret the collectivity of these as 'news values', private processes of unconscious decision-making, but he will be responding to the pressures of an entire social system as these filter down into the processes of television-making.

Under the pressure of the events of the 1968 Presidential campaign, especially those which occurred during the nominating conventions, both the parties inevitably altered their own dispositions towards television. A party can alter the nature of its coverage by simply refusing to admit cameras to certain areas of the convention hall or certain hotels. The more skilful the televised become in manipulating their arrangements with the producers, the less powerful the built-in distorting effects of the technology and the more powerful the message-makers themselves become in the process. That, at least, is how one train of thought goes. There is however a further countervailing power in the viewer's awareness of all these processes. The reporters can inform the viewers of those things which are being kept from them and speculate on the nature of those things. The viewer, as he becomes increasingly sophisticated himself, can acquire the experience to accept or reject parts of what he sees or hears. The whole question of the influence of television on an event gradually disappears through a mesh of three inward-facing convex mirrors – the cameras, the observed event and the audience. All three are mutually dependent; they are resistant each of the other, and increasingly so; all three are locked in a situation of permanent ever-evolving interdependence. The producer is only trying to make the event 'interesting'; the viewer exercises his right of selection, perception and selective retention of the material offered him, resisting that which he doesn't 'like'; the observed politician constantly catches up with the skill and knowledge of the professional communicator in order to find more effective ways of getting his own message across and resisting those activities of the producer which might tend to diminish his credibility or despoil his image.

It is clear we need a different model of the communication process if we are going to be able to handle the mesh of issues which now arise in any investigation of the political 'effects' (or any other effects) of television.

The first characteristic of a useful model is that it should not try to isolate the individual act of communication, certainly not before the whole context of communication is clearer. The individual viewer is receiving impressions and images which are manufactured precisely to satisfy his own anticipated needs and beliefs and his supposed powers of comprehension; they may end up either by confirming them or disturbing them. Those images and impressions are being produced by a large and carefully supervised and licensed organisation which processes them heavily to ensure primarily that they do not disturb its political needs; in other words the broadcaster cannot place himself in permanent political jeopardy – but the terms in which he can rescue himself from this are profoundly related to the totality of the dominant beliefs of the society he is serving.

The viewer is therefore receiving a processed message, but one that he has himself as part of a mass society been involved in processing. Not only is every programme by implication an interpretation of some part of his special experience (constantly being confirmed or disturbed by other parts of his social experience) but the entire process of broadcasting is in itself a reflection of certain of the deepest meanings of his society. Every message in broadcasting has layers of meaning as impacted as the skins of an onion and every viewer possesses an astonishingly complex though unconsciously held code which enables him to strip the layers. Just as an advertiser cannot sell soap through the medium of television unless his audience has already, through a myriad of influences, developed a realisation of the importance of hygiene, so a politician cannot win the recognition of a society which has not acquired (or has lost) a belief in the necessity for order; the political messages of television therefore depend upon the totality of all other messages in the life of an individual if they are to have any validity or effect at all.

Finally our new model must take into account the fact that television provides such a minute fragment of material in all; the words in a news bulletin fill less than the front page of a newspaper, the number of individual news stories reflected in an entire day is but a minute portion of the total number of events in the life of a nation and a world. The events selected are chosen for their extreme significance, because their content has been chosen by all the processes of broadcasting as being of extreme importance – historical, symbolic or emotional – to the viewing society. It is almost irrelevant that the immediate selectors of those events feel a sense of randomness about their choice; for they too have been evolved and chosen by and must retain their positions within the complex system.

The communicators send out their heavily processed and finely selected messages to an audience which receives them, in a sense, twice over – once as individuals and once as a 'mass'. As individuals they observe, select what they need or what appeals to them in the light of their individual experiences; they build around the images of broadcasting and the information it provides a whole world of interpretations of their own.

127

As a mass audience they are receiving constantly symbolic messages embedded in the programme content, lessons about goods and wealth, power and social mores; at one section of the day they watch certain aspects of the battle for political power being argued out and at another time a different battle, in a way symbolic of the former, is being fought out in fiction, entertainment and drama – the categories within which daily serials, westerns and thrillers and the other characteristic forms of mass entertainment work out their themes encompass the same problems of authority and ways of life which are reflected more directly in the informational content of the screen.

In any process of communication the speaker first of all hears himself; he therefore objectifies himself and his interlocutor undergoes precisely the same process when he receives and recognises the nature of the message. 'The importance of what we term communication', writes George Herbert Mead, 'lies in the fact that it provides a form of behaviour in which the organism or the individual may become an object to himself . . . it is when he not only hears himself but responds to himself, talks and replies to himself as truly as the other person replies to him, that we have behaviour in which individuals become objects to themselves.'[19] What goes for the individual goes also for the mass. We communicate and are communicated with within mass audiences and in so doing recognise our mass nature in addition to our individual nature. We recognise the distinction between the products of mass culture and the products of individual culture and we realise too that variations of quality and purpose are possible within the former. We are no more susceptible to directly injected messages as masses than we are as individuals, that is to say, only sometimes. We digest and reject whole forms, and indeed whole media, resist or devour them, all the time conscious of our development as a mass audience. Soap operas and serials, formulae for news and entertainment arise and decline in response to our global mass taste as this itself is recognised by the professional makers.

The screen is not trying to enforce a set of rules or to undermine a set of rules or principles, it is trying to interpret a set of social principles already present in the society. The communicators are scanning the mass audience exactly as the electronic dot scans the cathode tube, registering light and darkness and returning again and again across the same electronic path in order to build up a picture. There are therefore two screens in television, the one on which the audience registers the communicators' messages and interpretations of its world, and the one at which the communicators look when they try to discern the features of their audience. The content of each screen reflects (and distorts through its imprecision) the content of the other. It seems to me impossible to consider the problem of direct 'effects' of broadcast content on an individual in the audience or upon the whole audience without recognising the pre-eminence of the two-way movements which are at the root of the mass communication process. Communicator and audience descry each other dimly through a compounded haze of stereotypes, constantly freshened by the efforts of organised audience research and by the ensuing efforts to create a pressurised and personalised single image of the audience.

The primary function of radio and television, as far as the political process is concerned, is to confer fame and status. Fame is itself a kind of coinage, a commodity used as the means of conducting transactions between the client politician and the broadcasters. Broadcasting depends upon the general or collective goodwill of the political community in every country; the politician depends upon the broadcasting instrument for not only enabling the smooth process of government to take place through the easy distribution of information, but also for publicising himself and his expanding or contracting potential as a statesman.

The great fear of politicians from the earliest moment when the political potential of broadcasting was first realised was that it would intrude into that part of the political world in which reputations are made and lost. Politics has its own methods for recognising rises and falls in the political fortunes of individuals. In Britain with its traditional subtlety and high skill in the management of political affairs it became necessary at an extremely early stage to devise methods for preventing broadcasting from usurping certain of these political functions.

Although Parliament had of course taken a permanent interest in all matters pertaining to broadcasting from the

1920s, the moment at which their attention became especially focussed on the news dissemination processes of broadcasting came a little later. The crisis of 1926 clearly registered radio as a medium of far-reaching political importance when, virtually overnight, it became almost the only national means of communication when the mass newspapers disappeared in the course of the General Strike. Nonetheless the debate about broadcast news, as we experience it today, only emerged in the course of the following decade. John Coatman, who was News Editor at the BBC in the early thirties[20] gives the turning point as October 1933 when a fierce debate broke out in Parliament over a broadcast talk by Vernon Bartlett, the BBC's international correspondent, at the time of Germany's leaving the League of Nations. It was the prototype of the rows between politicians and the BBC which have become staple in more recent times.[21] The BBC was accused of being pro-German and the cry went up for 'responsibility' to be shown by the BBC as the only alternative to censorship. The incident marks the point from which BBC News became a major focus of political attention and, in Coatman's view, the point at which it began to grow increasingly timid in the face of Parliament and Government. Naturally, the war acted as a great watershed in this relationship. The BBC grew enormously in stature. The style of politics in Britain was transformed. New pressures, notably concerning the growth of commercial broadcasting, preoccupied the politicians. The BBC began to be much more adventurous in the presentation of controversial issues; until 1928 the government used its power under the Licence to forbid any material of a controversial nature. After 1928 the regulation which forbade BBC editorialising was interpreted far more narrowly. Nonetheless the BBC always took good care that nothing it broadcast would be interpreted as government policy especially where matters under direct parliamentary scrutiny were concerned. The parties themselves made various efforts to ensure that they controlled the flow of invitations to Members of Parliament; the party leaderships were anxious to avoid a situation in which individual politicians could build themselves national personae outside the structure of their parties. The BBC never totally gave away the right to choose who would broadcast but it made various concessions; Winston Churchill for instance was prevented from broadcasting on areas of policy (India and Disarmament) which the Conservative Party found embarrassing when he became a party rebel. The BBC did not wish to offend the party as a whole and since the opposition parties did not feel inclined to nominate Churchill as their spokesman on either re-armament or India (the two issues which most concerned him) he was effectively silenced, although he made a number of broadcasts on other topics and was fully reported in the news.

This same fear of intervening in the internal processes of party management inhibited the BBC towards the end of the war when a number of politicians in the Coalition, seeing the imminent return of normal party warfare, wished to make controversial statements on matters under current parliamentary discussion. The leaders of both parties feared that the uncontrolled re-emergence of party controversy would undermine their own plans for ending the Coalition, and the BBC, after much discussion, introduced a rule, which seems curious and even outrageous to us today, by which no issue due to be discussed in Parliament within fourteen days would be discussed on the air. In vestigial form the Fourteen Day rule remained in force as late as 1956.[22] The rule had been introduced originally as a kind of self-denying ordinance which would enable the BBC to ration airtime for senior ministers without appearing to be ordering them about or restricting them. It became in the course of time a great weapon in the hands of party managers, a weapon of internal party patronage and of internal discipline. For some years after the war the ordinance was applied spontaneously but gradually the BBC developed an antagonism to the rule on professional grounds. The party leaders, however, resisted any change and eventually the BBC was forced to ask the Postmaster-General to issue it with a formal instruction to enforce the rule because it was no longer suitable to apply it voluntarily. 'I hereby require' begins the Order which then ensued, '(a) that the Corporation shall not, on any issue, arrange discussions or ex-parte statements which are to be broadcast during a period of a fortnight before the issue is debated in either House or while it is being so debated; (b) that when legislation is introduced in Parliament on any subject, the Corporation shall not, on such subject, arrange broadcasts by any Member of Parliament which are to be made during the period between the introduction of the legislation and the time when it either receives the Royal Assent or is previously withdrawn or dropped.'[23] It reads today as an extraordinary, indeed impertinent statement, which no broadcasting organisation outside a totalitarian political system could countenance. Nonetheless it seemed a plausible and proper measure in its time. Among the parties only the Liberals opposed it. The Beveridge Committee had called for its revocation.[24] Winston Churchill thought it would prevent broadcasting eroding the centrality of the Houses of Parliament as the national forum of political debate.[25] In February 1956, after a period during which opposition to the Fourteen Day rule had been mounting in the press and among certain groups of Parliamentarians, the House of Commons set up a Select Committee to discuss the question; the Committee, after hearing a wide range of views, decided not to support the BBC's and the ITA's request to drop the rule but to recommend instead merely reducing the period to seven days.[26] A free vote in the House of Commons on 30 November 1955 voted 2:1 in favour of keeping the rule. By the end of the year, however, further pressure and public discussion persuaded the Government to drop it for an experimental period after which it disappeared altogether.

A similar issue arose over a programme called 'In the News' in the early fifties in which a group of prominent backbench MP's would discuss one or more issues in a provocative and polemical manner. The party leaders complained vigorously at the fact that the BBC was turning certain non-orthodox party members into national celebrities. 'They firmly demanded that we should use mainly reliable party politicians even at the cost of less attractive broadcasting', writes Lord Simon of Wythenshawe of the incident.[27] 'On the whole I think our critics were right and we were wrong; the BBC gave way to the protests and thereafter chose more representative speakers.' Michael Foot, Robert Boothby and the others whose presence in the programme had caused the trouble were soon booked by one of the new ITV companies for a similar programme entitled 'Free

Speech'. Even today there continues a constant although normally gentle pressure between the party managers and the broadcasters and executives of the BBC over the choice of speakers. At election times, the party managers still formally have a great deal of power, at least to recommend speakers, although the BBC jealously guards the privilege of issuing invitations; there is no fixed line between the two sides, not a line, that is, which the parliamentary Whips in practice recognise as fixed. Of course, in the party political broadcasts (programmes which are wholly given over to the parties for use as unpaid propaganda time) the parties make all the decisions, although the BBC retains ultimate editorial authority. The fear that the broadcasters will choose speakers who by their presence will tend to manipulate the distribution of privilege within their parties has found it hard to die.

The history of the rule, however, illustrates the permanent fear that nags politicians – the fear that their own functions will be usurped by the broadcasting media and the functions of their own institutions. They are of course quite right. Broadcasting inevitably alters the structure of discussion, it helps to build up or to undermine politicians who, left to the career-making mechanisms of their party organisations and those of Parliament, would develop in different ways. Politicians who are able to 'use' television are undoubtedly aided in their political careers. Those who are involved in issues which give themselves to television coverage are more likely than others to be seen on the screen and become known to the public.

In the use of the party political broadcasts organised by the BBC and the ITA, in the way that television has expanded the annual party conferences into annual national institutions, in the frequency with which ministers and shadow ministers appear on the screen arguing the details of their white papers, green papers and bills with one another and with the public, it is clear that television and radio have both entered the political world and equally that the latter has absorbed and digested the changes which electronic publicity has imposed upon it. The politicians however still fear the usurpation of their freedom. In Britain they have found a way to transfer the drawing-rooms of politics to the screen; the political discussion on British television, although extensive compared with many other countries, is nonetheless 'coterie' television – it helps to carry on the general debates of politics, but it is doubtful whether it has helped to extend very greatly the actual world of those actively interested in the details of politics.

The relationship between the political community and the broadcasting authority is the most crucial aspect of broadcasting organisation in almost every country. Perhaps the United States is the only place in which the broadcasters can feel that their interests could survive even major buffetings by the political world. (The American Civil Liberties Union, however, has documented a process which it describes as 'the engineering of restraint' throughout the American media as a result of a major assault by the Nixon administration.)[28] In Germany the public structures which were created to safeguard freedom of expression and the institutional independence of every broadcasting organisation administered by the Länder have been put under very great strain in the era of saturation television; in many of the Länder the argument for control, formal or informal, by a single ruling group within the Land administration has become overwhelming. Strangely enough, in countries where the ruling political community has gained the upper hand (France, Germany, Israel, Italy, for example) the actual conflict between broadcasters and politicians has not diminished, in many cases it has increased. Israel attempted to construct a governing body for her television organisation, which only began in the wake of the Six Day War of 1967, in a manner which would exclude partisan influences; the controlling authority was designed to be representative of a number of communities within the nation – economic, trade union, educational, academic, theatrical, etc. – yet within a matter of months the posts, while still being held by the post-holders designated in the law, have been in fact given to people with a party allegiance. The Chairman, a government appointee, is a member of the same party fraction as the Prime Minister. The Plenum of the broadcasting authority has thirty-one members; one of them has to be a representative of the Jewish Agency, and the other thirty are 'members of the public recommended by the Government after consultation with the representative organisations of writers, teachers and artists in Israel, the institutions of higher learning and the Hebrew Language Academy, and other public bodies concerned with broadcasting affairs, provided that not more than four of the members be State employees'.[29] Yet the vast majority of the Plenum in fact are staunch members of one party or another. The entire atmosphere of Israeli television is bedevilled by politicking; the employees are themselves far from blameless for the gradual erosion of confidence between Parliament and broadcasting organisation. In microcosm Israel affords an example of what can happen in any democratic system in which the broadcasting body is neither strong nor independent. The group most disappointed by the results are the politicians themselves who feel, naturally, that they still fail to extract from the broadcasters the degree of coverage which their political hold on the organisation should provide. Six directors of television were despatched within three years of the new statute being enacted. The politician, used to pulling the levers of power, finds that when he grasps the levers of broadcasting and pulls them, the intended result often fails to transpire. He blames the personalities of the broadcasting world, or the techniques of journalism, or bias, or untrammelled trivialisation; he fails to find within the broadcasting organisation anyone who 'understands' his point of view. Politicians tend to be guilty of a kind of categorical fallacy when they look at broadcasting organisations; they find it hard to understand an organisation which is wholly owned by the public but which eludes the grasp of the politician. They fail to understand the full range of pressures which play upon the broadcasters, of which they are only a single one, and indeed one which the broadcaster's atavistic journalistic ethic obliges him to feel it is his duty to thwart.

The relationship between the broadcaster and his society is a powerful and complex bond; he tends to reflect the cynicism or boredom of the viewer with politics. He may wholly misinterpret it but nonetheless it weighs upon his mind and he feels that scepticism is often a valid general attitude to hold towards all politics. The broadcaster's own position of enforced neutrality tends to make him withdraw from political involvement, to see the political world as a 'game' played between

135

equal sides. Endemic in broadcasting is the thought that, to keep the attention of the mass audience, politics must be displayed as an entertainment, or at least as a competitive sport; there has developed a kind of 'testing-game' between the television interviewer and politician in which the former tries to be as challenging as he dares; certainly, the broadcasting community tends, quite wrongly, to measure the success of the political coverage of a programme in terms of its 'daring' rather than its information. Increasingly the 'modern' politician who has grasped the pressures and processes of broadcasting connives at the playing of this game.

Television is an international medium and, like journalism, has developed a set of widely agreed standards of excellence of its own. Journalists and broadcasters thus tend to use the same standards for judging one another's work, even across social systems. Lucien Pye, in his study[30] *Communications and Political Development*, remarks on the widespread nature of 'the assumption that objective and unbiased reporting of events is possible and desirable and that the sphere of politics in any society can best be observed from a neutral and non-partisan perspective. . . . The emergence of professionalised communications is thus related to the development of an objective, analytical and non-partisan view of politics.' The audience in a society which has developed such professionalised communications is therefore likely to be influenced to believe that neutral positions are possible and desirable in politics, possible too that neutral institutions are similarly desirable. Television imposes its nature upon all that it touches – that is one of its direct effects – and the phenomenon which it is most likely to influence is the medium of politics itself.

The paradox goes even further. The course of the protracted efforts of politicians and broadcasters to come to terms with their new relationship is simultaneously the history of the development of television as a means of government. The press, too, struggled for many years for its independence before discovering that it had become equally a tool of government and a means of scrutiny of government. In the United States the 1950s saw the rapid development of television as a reporting tool; its live cameras transformed the whole nature of the nominating conventions. President Eisenhower ordered 'no more long boring speeches'; tiresome procedural elements were removed to off-peak hours; unpalatable speakers were persuaded to stand down; the organisers ensured that the content of the convention was comprehensible, entertaining and bereft of anything that might offend. The cameras came to show the people what actually happened in an important but private meeting at which Presidential candidates were chosen; after the first major attempt they came to show the American people what actually happened inside a convention when it was televised. The same process of change occurred in the British annual party conferences from 1960 onwards, when the Labour Party finally agreed to allow television full access. There was a decade during which politicians came to understand that certain of their regular rituals had to be made into public spectacles in the name of electronic democracy; there was much grumbling as they were persuaded to cooperate. A new generation arrived in the world of politics who understood instinctively that large areas of their lives had to be henceforth lived in a kind of arc light. But then television became far more flexible an instrument, and political activity for a time moved into the streets; a second confrontation took place between the two sides, which reached its climax at the Chicago Democratic Convention of 1968 and the ensuing post-mortem. The forces of law and order, despatched by Mayor Daley to preserve outward calm at all costs, used methods which were unacceptable in societies which now conducted much of their political business in the open; police clubbed down dozens of reporters and cameramen, as well as demonstrators, all in broad daylight. In vain did Mayor Daley protest that the cameras failed to reveal the provocations which had been inflicted on his police. Although Daley was proved to be factually correct in a large number of respects, it was evident that no longer could the political demonstrator and the policeman be allowed to clash at public gatherings before so large an audience. The blood-letting at Chicago proved to be a turning point in the new broadcasting situation, and the lessons of Chicago were learned throughout the world, not least in Britain, where intense public interest in a vast public demonstration on

27 October of the same year outside the American Embassy was rendered almost totally peaceful by the sheer quantity of publicity which had preceded the occasion and had helped to defuse and almost ritualise it. Henceforth both sides had as much to lose from a violent clash with the police, street politician and administration. The de-escalation of passion towards the end of 1968 helped to make television once again a neutral ground. The politics of protest gave way – not entirely of course – to the politics of participation. Television after a time became more discursive, more thoughtful, offering its facilities to a far wider section of the politically-interested community than previously. New demands were made for wider spread in the political coverage of television – on both sides of the Atlantic.

Television may be on the way to turning into a new kind of political forum. Different types of people involved in new types of consumer politics and grass-roots activity are beginning to want to use the screen and are discovering the way in which television forces them to groom themselves, modify their messages to suit a mass audience, to use low-key persuasive argument and be conscious of their overall 'image'. Television too is learning to admit them. In Britain the most important single group are perhaps the trade unionists who, after many years of deliberate withdrawal from and hostility towards electronic and other media, are demanding better-informed treatment of trade union affairs on the screen. At the same same time the public has had to adjust itself to new kinds of argument on an adjusted range of issues; which involve wages, working ameni- ties, fair practices, issues which they were formerly used to hearing about only from the lips of formal party spokesmen.

To say that television is developing as a new kind of political forum does not alter the fact that the same tiny group of people issue all the tickets, and that admission remains by ticket only. It means only that the producers and institutions are just beginning to realise that there is a public interested in more than the traditional gladiatorial display between the distinguished interviewer and the prominent statesman. In Britain we can expect the decline of the dramatic protest following a pro- gramme attempting to prise from a politician something more about his personality or his policies than he was otherwise prepared to vouchsafe. The public is felt to have ceased to sympathise either with the injured Goliaths of the networks or the would-be Davids in the political world. Nonetheless the new terms of reference – more open, more catholic, based on a wider interpretation of the meaning of politics – depend upon the willingness of the broadcasting institution to recognise them. That too will depend on the central institution's perception of a newly identified set of audience needs. The wider the demands for broadcast time, the more crucial become the internal processes of the broadcasting institution.

Chapter Five

Broadcasting Autonomy Under Threat

'This purpose you undertake is dangerous; the friends you
have named uncertain; the time itself unsorted; and your
whole plot too light for the counterpoise of so great an
opposition.'

Henry IV, II: iii

The right to broadcast and the physical opportunity to do so are
granted only by the state. A few pirate stations have managed,
briefly and in great discomfort, to operate free of all constraints,
free of all governmental permission. Pirate broadcasting suffers
from the disadvantage that it cuts itself off from the open supply
of its own raw material. It is at best a flimsy and temporary
method of broadcasting, more useful as a form of protest against
some lacuna in a nation's broadcasting arrangements than a
viable means of carrying on with the tasks of mass dissemination of entertainment and information. No matter how popular
his programmes, the broadcaster has to obtain and retain
official approval and protection if he wishes to carry on the
business of broadcasting. The central dialogue in the life of
broadcasting is a dialogue with the state; whatever the relationships with the public, radio and television are both engaged in
an eternal quest (publicly or privately conducted) to safeguard
their autonomy within the state. All broadcasting begins with a
franchise granted by government and depends for its continual
existence on periodical renewal.

The autonomy of a broadcasting institution is a delicate
flower, nervously planted, tenderly nurtured and easily plucked
up by the roots.

A broadcasting organisation to gain credibility must be seen

140

to be under the actual control of the people who in title are its managers; the programmes have to be believed to be the responsibility of the men who are seen and heard presenting them. A society which is obliged to watch broadcasting of however high a technical quality which emanates from a manipulated or state-managed set of professionals rapidly comes to distrust the information with which it is being fed. A mass medium bereft of credibility becomes a colossal albatross around the neck of its audience.

In Britain, a society which has produced broadcasting institutions that have retained a relatively high reputation for reliability and truthfulness, there has of course been a long tradition of independent media. The principles by which the worlds of journalism, theatre and education operate free of state intervention were laid down decades or even centuries ago. Radio and television benefit from the fact that they obtain their material from groups of people trained in Fleet Street, the theatre, the cinema, and so on, but the overall control of these two media of dissemination is only kept apart from the state by dint of vigilant and constant effort. There is a delicate set of balances which separate the broadcasting institutions from the apparatus of state, and an equally delicate set which govern the relationship between the Governors (chosen by the government) and the senior staff of the BBC. From the earliest days John Reith began to work out a viable system, a set of ritualised rights which separated his powers, as the senior executive, from those of the Governors. The harmonious operation of that system made all those involved in broadcasting develop a sense of their independence. At any moment there was nothing to stop any reigning government from simply walking into the building and taking over the control of the programme-making. In fact in 1926 Winston Churchill, Minister of Information at the time of the General Strike, wanted to take over the BBC and run it, during the prevailing national emergency, under his direct ministerial control.[1] It would have become, like the temporary government newspaper set up in the days of the strike, a straight organ of propaganda and the BBC would probably never again have regained the national belief in its durability and independence.

In 1956 during the attempted Suez invasion there was a plan devised by the Prime Minister, Anthony Eden, to take over the running of the BBC. The BBC resisted this threatened measure and continued to operate its traditional system by which the Leader of the Opposition is allowed to reply to Prime Ministerial statements. This meant that the BBC continued to reflect something of the national controversy over the Suez adventure under its own set of rules the formal ritual of which was rigidly stuck to (to the fury of the impatient Leader of the Opposition).[2] These two episodes and others which have cropped up from time to time have left in their wake a powerful internal mythology which has bolstered the BBC's sense of independence. Autonomy feeds upon pride.

The relationship between the organisation and the government is therefore the most crucial of all the relationships which bind a broadcasting organisation to its society. Ministers often find it difficult to separate the channels which enable them to communicate legitimately with broadcasters from those which would enable but not entitle them to interfere. After all, any member of the public has the right to suggest and complain to the chief executive and the programme-makers. Why should I, the Minister of X and Y, be deprived of the same basic citizen right? The political coverage of broadcasting is the minefield on which the constitutional life of the organisation and the actual programme content overlap. A minister may have some excellent editorial copy in his mind, but if he chooses to offer it in certain ways he may be guilty or be thought to be guilty of trying to intrude a government view into a programme. The BBC makes arrangements for ministerial broadcasts and counter-ministerial replies to be made whenever some major piece of governmental policy needs to be publicly presented. The ministerial broadcasts, like the party political broadcasts which occur during and between election campaigns on a carefully rationed basis, are not thought to be greatly enjoyed by the audience. They tend to interrupt the flow of programming; they are clearly interposed 'messages' not presented in a context of critical exposition. Nonetheless they provide a safety valve for the political community – a valuable cushion against pressures which might otherwise become overwhelming, rather than a Trojan horse threatening autonomy.

Far more important than the relationship with government is that with opposition.

The freedom with which the broadcasters contact, invite and discuss questions with the opposition is the touchstone of broadcasting independence. If that can be guaranteed, then government too will succeed in conducting its dialogue credibly with its society. That crucial freedom however depends on the structure which enables a state-appointed functionary – in Britain the Chairman of the Board of Governors – to supervise his organisation in the general public interest while allowing it to make its own judgements and dispositions about what it actually transmits. It is impossible to lay down what the rights and duties of the Chairman actually are, but if he oversteps his function in either direction, he certainly jeopardises the autonomy of the entire enterprise, or alternatively the rights of the public.

In 1931, with the appointment of J. H. Whitley to the BBC Chairmanship, the British Postmaster-General started the practice of sending to every new Governor on appointment a copy of a document (drafted by Whitley with the approval of Reith) which spelt out the proper relationships between the Board of Governors, the BBC executive chiefs and the British public. Relations between Reith and Whitley's predecessor, Lord Clarendon, had been bad; henceforth the divisions of responsibilities were laid down: 'With the Director-General they discuss and then decide upon major matters of policy and finance, but they leave the execution of that policy and the general administration of the Service in all its branches to the Director-General and his competent officers. The Governors should be able to judge of the general effect of the Service upon the public, and, subject as before-mentioned, are of course finally responsible for the conduct of it.'[3] Many have found this set of definitions too subtle for easy practice. Lord Simon rejected the formula when he came to look back on his own period of chairmanship, on the grounds that it prevented 'individual Governors from taking an active interest in any special aspect of the BBC'.[4] The relationship, while difficult to live up to in its delicate separation of overlapping rights, never-theless contained a set of broadcasting rights which served the public as a whole. The Whitley document was a kind of Magna Carta. In the Governors the public enjoyed a form of representation, certainly no right of choosing or removing them, but nonetheless there was within the structure of broadcasting a group of powerful people who were looking not to the im-mediate advantage of the BBC but to a set of national interests. The vagueness and inadequacy of the arrangement are easy to perceive. Nonetheless it was better than a system in which the public had no visible stake in the internal affairs of broad-casting. There has been carefully spelt out a territory between broadcasters and government, which the public could regard as its own. When that ground was lost, a major conflict between government, public and broadcasters was almost inevitable.

When commercial competition came to Britain, the Gover-nors found that they were sitting eyeball-to-eyeball with another set of Governors in charge of another rival broadcasting system, one that after initial setbacks started to compete fiercely and endanger the stability of the BBC. Inevitably an element of protectiveness crept into their attitude towards the BBC. Increasingly they felt that they were part of the BBC as well as public scrutineers of it. Different chairmen and different directors-general of course came and went and built up different relationships. The crucial distinctions of function remained, however, and the most crucial element, that of the executive supremacy of the professional chief, the 'DG', most promi-nently remained. Sir Hugh Greene, Director-General for most of the decade of the sixties, maintained his supremacy within and over the system.[5] His relationship with the chairmen with whom he had at first to deal (Lord Normanbrook, a former chief of the Civil Service, reigned for most of the early period) was peaceful and cooperative. The BBC adopted courses which caused enormous public controversy. The Greene method of leadership was to take a considerable personal interest in crucial individual programmes, leave the rest alone, and gradually to lead the BBC into a culturally 'vanguard' position.[6] In the context of British society at the time this was an immensely successful role for the BBC; its daring built for

144

it an international reputation as the pacemaker among broadcasters.

It was the decision of Harold Wilson, on becoming Prime Minister, to 'curb' the BBC by putting Lord Hill (until then chairman of the ITA) into the chairmanship of the Board of Governors which undermined the traditional system. Lord Hill made himself the chief executive of the entire organisation.[7] He lived for much of the time in the building. He came into frequent conflict with Greene. Eventually Greene departed and was replaced by Charles Curran who arrived in the job at a time when Hill had established himself firmly at the helm; he had no choice but to continue as a kind of number 2. Lord Normanbrook had at times asserted his right, as a chairman, to have the final say on programme content[8] but Hill interpreted this reserve right as the basis of a permanent practice. Within the organisation the change occurred imperceptibly but over a period of years the entire balance of editorial power had clearly shifted.

The rise of the chairman to the position of senior executive meant that his role as public guardian was no longer simultaneously credible. True, Hill was merely taking a stage further a process which had been occurring, by fits and starts, over a very long period. Nonetheless he made explicit the new role of the chairman at a moment when television was becoming a highly contentious medium. The crunch occurred over a programme, transmitted in June 1971, entitled 'Yesterday's Men'. It was a light-hearted, at moments extremely cynical, look at the senior members of the erstwhile Labour administration, one year after their ousting at the General Election of June 1970. The programme produced an enormous furore. It became a basic text in all subsequent disquisition and analysis of the evils of broadcasting. The crucial element in the affair however was that on the insistence of the Chairman, the Board of Governors had scrutinised the film on the day of the transmission, and, setting aside vigorous protests from Harold Wilson, decided to transmit it, with one sentence deleted. When the transmission brought about a further and increased bout of fury in the press, Parliament and the postbag of the BBC, an inquiry was held by the Board of Governors who in the

145

light of meticulously culled evidence[9] decided that the programme had been compiled in a proper fashion, apart from the title and the attendant title song, which had not been communicated to the participants during the making of the programme. The programme-makers were criticised for this, but defended on a further series of charges made by Wilson and Richard Crossman.[10] The report of the Board of Governors' inquiry was treated contemptuously by a great section of public opinion, both in the press and in Parliament. The Governors had put themselves in the position of acting as judge and jury as well as investigators into a decision for which they themselves had been responsible. The public found itself therefore, in 1972, finally bereft of any instrument within the structure of broadcasting which it could in any way regard as its representatives. The Board of Governors of the BBC was now a purely executive Board running a busy national enterprise in a competitive way.

The pressure for some new form of public scrutiny of broadcasting which would investigate complaints and lay down journalistic standards grew rapidly and considerably. It gained support among people who wanted to curtail the freedom of broadcasters as well as among groups who wanted to reduce the independence of the BBC in the interests of various forms of 'democratisation'. Mr Julian Critchley MP argued that 'the setting up of an impartial body for the investigation of grievances would be of some reassurance to the outraged, and would, over a period of time, build up a code of practice. Its sanctions would be indirect; but it is unlikely that a public corporation like the BBC would choose to ignore its findings, and the television companies, whose franchises are at risk, would take care not to offend'.[11]

The BBC's response to the pressures and the protests which grew up in the wake of 'Yesterday's Men' was to set up a Complaints Commission, specially housed and salaried by the BBC itself, to whom complainants would be referred if they rejected as unsatisfactory the replies they received to complaints which had been sent directly to the BBC. The Commission consisted of three retired public servants of great distinction, one of them a former Ombudsman, one a former Speaker, and one a former Lord Chief Justice (who died within the first year). The cases they received in the first year were very few in number.[12] Their very existence tended to do little to assuage those demanding a full-scale Broadcasting Council outside the BBC and the ITA and governing the standards of both. The judgements they handed down were treated with some scorn within the broadcasting world, because they revealed the investigators' lack of knowledge of the way in which programmes were put together and because their investigations were held in secrecy and at the expense of the BBC itself. The complaints dealt with were treated as complaints against the BBC as a whole. The individual professionals called in for investigation had, in effect, the status of witnesses in a legal action against the BBC. (The complaints were referred to the Commission only if the BBC's own prior machinery was exhausted without satisfying the complainant.) It seemed that once the original machinery for representing the interests of the public had ceased to function (with the redefinition of the role of the Governors) there was no separation of power within the structure. The future opened up the possibility of an infinite regression of new layers of public bodies replacing and supervising other public bodies. The task of separating broadcasting from the direct interference of government or Parliament became much more difficult. 'The setting up of the Commission does not affect the constitutional functions of the Governors, the programme responsibility of the executive, or the role of the General Advisory Council as the principal advisory body to the Governors' was the BBC's insistent defence of the new structure.[13] Nonetheless its judgements could do nothing but begin to change the canons of practice within which the broadcasters operated. Either those judgements carried weight or they did not; when a court makes bad judgements, there must either be new and better judges or new laws. British broadcasting was being governed by a court which had no laws and appeared to be making bad judgements. There was no viable source of new and more credible law. In the Complaints Commission, the viewing public did not gain a source of accountability. Shortly before the replacement of Lord Hill as Chairman of the BBC (at the expiry of his term of office) by Professor Sir Michael

Swann, Sir Hugh Greene, former Director-General, attacked the Commission in scathing terms in a public speech in London. It is possible that in the post-Hill era the whole policy of the BBC towards public accountability will be thought out again.

There is a case to be made for increasing pluralism within the national system of broadcasting, whereby more elements within the society can obtain a chance to broadcast or alternatively a chance to participate in controlling broadcasting. There is only a much weaker case for an 'internal' body which seemed to weaken or confuse internal lines of control while continuing to exclude the public from any positive rights within the workings of the broadcasting system.

No broadcasting system can escape from being the possession ultimately of government. The Legal Adviser to RTB of Belgium, Monsieur A. Namurois, aptly summarised the impossibility of guaranteeing 'freedom of speech' through broadcasting within a system which is licensed by the state: 'A Government supervision of the pin-prick kind; in skilful or overskilful use of air time under cover of a legal provision regarding official announcements, and intolerable moral constraints on the director-general designed to make him a mere creature of the Executive, would seriously impair the necessary autonomy of the broadcasting institutions in news or programmes.'[14]

Since pressure or advice cannot be channelled through government to the broadcasters without endangering the sensitive relationship which exists between the two, various plans have been considered and urged in a number of countries for institutions which would interpose themselves between government and broadcasting institution, and which, with varying degrees of advisory or statutory authority, can act as a buffer, representing a 'public interest' without acting as an agency of official pressure. The aim in all of these proposals is to pre-empt or evade direct government intervention in the editorial processes.

The first post-war plan for a council of this kind came in 1947 in the recommendations of the Commission on the Freedom of the Press under the chairmanship of Robert M. Hutchins of Chicago University.[15] The Hutchins Commission wanted: 'the establishment of a new and independent agency to appraise and report annually upon the performance of the press.' The problems to which it was intended that the commission should address itself were those of setting up and supervising professional journalistic standards, observing processes of concentration of ownership, encouraging the growth of professional training in journalism, and investigating complaints of inaccuracy and misrepresentation. During the Home Secretaryship of J. Chuter Ede a British Royal Commission on the Press was set up and was active between 1947 and 1949; it too recommended that the press set up its own General Council which would 'consciously foster those tendencies which make for integrity and for a sense of responsibility to the public'.[16] The aim was to oblige the British popular press to take note of public disquiet over its vexatious faults and set its own house in order. In Britain the proposal was adopted and a Press Council, later given an independent chairman and some non-journalist members, but consisting largely of editors of newspapers, supervises Fleet Street, apportioning blame after considering specific complaints sent in by aggrieved members of the public. The press, however, consists of a number of privately-owned agencies which perform an important social function. They have chosen to surrender albeit under public pressure internal functions to a common supervisory body in order to demonstrate that, though still privately owned, they have a collective spirit of public responsibility.

All broadcasting is publicly controlled from its inception. The problem has always been to make it live and be seen to live outside the purview of the executive. Those who support the various proposals for a Broadcasting Council argue that they want it to have functions similar to Fleet Street's Press Council. Those who oppose the plans fear that a Broadcasting Council would merely duplicate the intended functions of the existing Boards of Governors but in a form which might simply develop as a gigantic inhibitory pressure. Lord Aylestone, Chairman of the Independent Broadcasting (formerly Television) Authority, said to the Select Committee on Nationalised Industries, when pressed on this point: 'I have always felt the Broadcasting Council idea is simply imposing above the Authority or the BBC Board of Governors another body doing precisely the same sort of thing.'[17] In a letter to the same committee, the Managing Director of the small ITV Company, Channel Television, points out that the dividing line between censorship and responsible control, as regards the Authority's relationship with the companies, is a narrow one. 'It does at least indicate that there could be no justification for a Broadcasting Council as far as ITV is concerned, as the Authority itself, not being a programme producer, adequately fulfils that position.'[18]

Nonetheless although the Authority, in the ITV system, has not in fact ever made its own programmes, it has the right to do so and has the prerogative of *sharing* editorial control with the programme companies which it supervises. Its position is no different from that of the BBC. Both systems contain a delicate tracery of constitutional arrangements which enable them to represent the public interest while being responsible for programme-making. Only when the confidence of either of the parties who are impliedly represented within this arrangement (i.e. the programme-makers and the public) is broken down does the need arise for some additional supervisory body, or court of last resort.

One of the more interesting attempts to introduce a measure of pluralism to the broadcasting system by means of a Broadcasting Council is that of Sweden, where an unconventional mixture of private finance and public control is made to cope with public complaints through an open forum of argument and adjudication. Swedish Radio is a private company, of which 20 per cent is owned by the manufacturing industry of radio and television, 40 per cent by the press, and 40 per cent by a range of national organisations and public movements. Although the Government own none of the stock it has the right to appoint the Director-General and five members of the Board, who between them can outvote the five members who represent the interest of the stock-owners. The Company is financed by a combination of licence fees and advertising, and the annual dividend is fixed at five per cent. The Government, however, owns the transmitters outright.[19] In some ways the structure resembles that of the old British Broadcasting Company which preceded the present Corporation between 1922 and 1926.

The Swedish organisation has been restructured on a number of occasions, the principal ones being in 1959 when a new agreement and new regulations were made to take cognisance of the changed conditions of the television era,[20] and in 1967 when preparations were made for a new second television channel. The Agreement between Swedish Radio and the Government which was approved in May 1959 spells out in some detail the general code of practice according to which the system should operate. It emphasises the need for cultural diversity and for political impartiality. The Agreement gives broadcasting a central national role and contains elements which might strike an outsider as 'manipulative' in nature. For instance Clause 1 states that the Corporation is required to 'disseminate, in objective, impartial and suitable form, information on current events and to orient the general public towards more important cultural and social issues, as well as to encourage debate on such issues'. In the 1960s a more detailed Code of Broadcasting Practice[21] was drawn up, which continues to emphasise not only the need for the strictest impartiality in all programmes but also contains a positive instruction to observe a scientific objectivity. Nonetheless Swedish Radio is obliged to create platforms for controversial and minority opinions and to undertake that all of these are adequately put and cogently contradicted by other views. The existence of a published and fixed code of journalistic conduct and programme practice means that the public can judge (or at least conjecture) whether a given programme has infringed the organisation's rules.

Sweden has also a Broadcasting Council which since 1967 has consisted of seven independent individuals appointed by government, and drawn from the ranks of professional, managerial and intellectual groups.[22] The function of the Council is to judge whether, in individual cases brought before it by members of the public, Swedish Radio has infringed the Agreement of 1959 made with the Government. The Government, under the law, has no right of prior censorship or prior supervision of programme content; the Council has no right to interfere in the making of programmes, but only to judge whether, after the event, they were consistent with the basic

151

law. The Council cannot judge, nor even approach an individual producer. Like the BBC's Complaints Commission, it can address itself only to the Corporation as a whole.

In the first three years of its existence the Broadcasting Council (unlike the BBC's Complaints Commission) held 64 meetings and received 626 complaints.[23] It ignored 91 complaints as being outside its jurisdiction and dismissed 399. It decided that 45 of the complaints were justified and of these there were 14 violations of the Agreement which it felt involved issues of principle of sufficient importance to be detailed in its annual report.

It decided, for instance, that a children's programme entitled 'Why do we have a King?' was over-simplified in its treatment of the constitution, betrayed the presenter's personal prejudice but was not in basic breach of the Agreement.[24] It received a complaint that the record by Jane Birkin, 'Je t'aime, moi non plus' (famous for its heavy breathing as much as its melody) was being unconstitutionally discriminated against in being omitted from a 'Top of the Pops' record programme even though it figured very prominently in the charts which officially registered the popularity of records. The Council argued in its judgement that 'the non-playing of a single record – irrespective of its quality – would not be regarded as a breach of the Corporation's duty to provide good quality amusement and entertainment, while paying attention to the complete range of the audience's taste.' Swedish Radio is enjoined to provide material to satisfy all cultural predilections, but the Council decided that 'the normal selection procedures could not be held binding so as to make a single departure from them a violation of the Agreement.'[25]

However, the Council has shown its teeth on a number of tougher political issues. A programme on Berlin, 'The Dying City',[26] was judged to have been unbalanced. In it building projects in East Berlin had been described as if they were already in existence. The programme had exploded as false a report that a certain youth had been wounded by East Berlin guards when trying to escape to the West; but the programme had not explained that such incidents did actually occur, even though this particular incident had been fraudulently reported in

152

the West. The programme had held up the views of one German student who disliked West Berlin as if he were representative of all students in the Western part of the city; this student did not refer to the fact that there was any lack of personal liberty in East Berlin.

A classic and highly contentious issue arose over a series of programmes entitled 'From Socialism to Increased Equality'[27] which gave a Marxist interpretation of the history of the Swedish labour movement. The Commission decided that this series was biased and factually distorted, although two members of the Council dissented, saying that 'This series cannot be regarded as fulfilling in a completely acceptable manner the expectations of impartiality and objectivity.' The Council had been obliged to listen to several days of testimony from a group of independent historians, while Swedish Radio and the producers of the programme provided their own expert witnesses as to their historical validity.

The existence of a legal machinery for investigating breaches and non-breaches of a law enforcing 'objectivity' has a curious effect within any culture. While in the Anglo-Saxon tradition the broadcaster makes an effort at impartiality in a spirit of honest endeavour, the Swedish system has transformed it into a theology. Professor Jörgen Westerstähl, who has conducted several investigations on behalf of the Broadcasting Council into programmes concerning Vietnam and the coverage of the election of 1968, insists[28] that there are definite yardsticks by which 'objectivity' can be established, both in practice and in the breach. 'Truthfulness, relevance, balance and neutral presentation' are the four basic requirements of objectivity, Westerstähl asserts, and all of them are verifiable according to logical standards and standards of taste. He argues that subjective reporting is a bad new tendency which is creeping into broadcast journalism, a tendency which 'could lead away from the democratic idea which guarantees each citizen objective information'.

If broadcasting is to be used as a tool for intelligent exchange of cultural products, political information and controversial disquisition, it needs to be left flexible and left alone. Its independence has to be guaranteed, together with the autonomy

153

of any organisation which is empowered, under whatever institutional arrangements, to conduct the business of broadcasting. To make it publicly accountable to super-bodies with power to investigate the details of the intellectual work of individuals must surely be spiritually destructive of any serious broadcasting industry and destructive of the very 'democratic idea' which Professor Westerstähl wishes to preserve. If the dilemma of power inherent in the act of broadcasting is to be resolved only by the creation of legalistic norms of 'impartiality' to be mechanistically determined by public trial, then it is unlikely that broadcasting will flourish creatively while remaining impartial. The danger inherent in the new forms of Broadcasting Council is that they will further internalise in the minds of broadcasters a set of strictures which have more to do with the politics of institutions than the health of broadcasting. Something has to be interposed between the state and the actual organisations which conduct and organise broadcasting, but a pseudo-judiciary is not likely to be an answer that will satisfy in the long run the needs of those demanding it, still less those who are concerned to increase the quality and vitality of the broadcasting product. The dilemma is almost unresolvable within the present technology and structure of broadcasting. It is a pain we have to learn to live with rather than one for which we should seek cheap placebos.

Chapter Six

France and the ORTF: Personal Power plus Television Monopoly Equals Gaullism

'Being a journalist working for the ORTF is not like being a journalist elsewhere. Whether you like it or not, ORTF is the voice of France. You who write the news must always keep in mind that you are not talking for yourself, you are the voice of your country and your government.'

President Pompidou

'The connecting line of execution extends downwards uninterrupted from the minister to the individual subject, transmitting the law and orders from the government unto the last ramification of the social order, with the speed of electric fluid.'

M. Chaptal, a minister in the government of Napoleon Bonaparte

'The dread of disturbance and the love of well-being insensibly lead democratic nations to increase the functions of central government as the only power which appears to be intrinsically sufficiently strong, enlightened and secure to protect them from anarchy.'

De Tocqueville

Two weeks before the 'événements' of May 1968, M. Gorse, the French Minister of Information, made a speech in which he spoke scathingly of the political pressures which were formerly, in the dark days of the Fourth Republic, allowed to interfere with the work of French radio and television. M. Gorse was severe with his predecessors: 'Every new Minister of Information

155

would receive as his first commission on taking office an instruction to take a serious look at radio and television.'[1] Within a fortnight of making the speech M. Gorse himself was swept away in a vast crisis of French society, one aspect of which was the distrust of a broadcasting system believed to be nothing more than a tool of the Gaullist administration.

France has created the most unstable set of broadcasting institutions in Europe, if not the world. They have suffered crisis after crisis since the beginning of radio in 1924 in an endless and fruitless search for a point of equilibrium; no one can say with confidence that even now any enduring principle has been established in structure or programme content. It is uncertain whether the French will finally settle for private or public institutions, commercial or non-commercial ones, government-controlled or independent. Nor has any combination of any of these proved hitherto sufficiently reliable to endure. Although for many years the aim has been to set up some form of 'public service' it is never clear, when the phrase is used on French lips, whether it implies a cultural aim or an administrative instrument. But the issue on which many of the individuals have risen and fallen has tended to be the same: the extent to which the instrument of broadcasting should be placed at the disposal of the prevailing political group.

Although every new set of institutions which have been set up to house broadcasting in France has resulted from a fresh effort by government to make broadcasting (especially television) politically responsive, it is certainly possible to view the fifty years of upheaval as merely a series of accidents, the product of administrative resourcefulness rather than sinister chicanery.

In the 1920s France's radio stations were run either by departments of national and local government, or specially licensed private bodies, under a law of November 1923.[2] Revenue was provided by government and through advertising, under the supervision of the PTT, the Administration of Posts and Telegraphs. By 1933 there were 24 stations altogether broadcasting from French soil, and it was decided to levy a licence fee on each receiver in order to improve the revenue. All the political groups in France had been using radio for propaganda and discussion purposes and in the election of

1936 the PTT arranged for every contending party to share broadcasting time. After the election new regulations were enacted forbidding all local station controllers to touch news or politics, which henceforth was concentrated in the Paris station. Throughout the period prior to the outbreak of war the local stations though state-owned were all under the control of locally elected management committees, chosen by all the radio licence-holders in a given community. With the arrival of advertising, however, their existence became of doubtful, or at least complex, legality, since they had been set up under a law governing only non-profit-making enterprises. Finally, when war came broadcasting control was centralised completely and the local committees were all sent home; the PTT Minister handed over control to the ministers responsible for waging war. In the areas under the Vichy Government, however, things went a step further and the government removed all the permissions for local stations to broadcast at all; their facilities were taken over for direct military use. By a series of haphazard processes in the period of social emergency, broadcasting in France moved into government control, although on the basis of no permanent plan. Then radio was finally silenced altogether in the dark days of the Occupation.[3]

It was in Britain, in the studios of the BBC, that a new system of French broadcasting was born. Brigadier de Gaulle made his historic broadcasts to the people of Occupied France from British soil. It is uncertain whether many people heard him, certainly in the early months when millions were fleeing from their homes and the Germans had attempted to confiscate every single radio receiver in the northern part of France. Nonetheless the political personality of de Gaulle, which was decades later to be the foundation stone of the broadcasting structure, was created at that moment by the transmitters of the BBC. It was at that time that he first realised, more powerfully and more skilfully than any other world leader, the political potential of broadcasting and its particular applicability to the chaotic conditions of the French nation. As M. Raymond Aron later wrote of this period: 'Radio London was a more powerful political reality in France than the official Vichy government, or the German radio.'[4]

Under the law of October 1941, enacted by de Gaulle's exiled government, an organisation called the RTF (Radiodiffusion-Television Française) was created. It automatically operated as a monopoly and was the employer of all broadcasting workers on French soil. It existed under the direct supervision of the Prime Minister and the Cabinet. This system prevailed when de Gaulle returned to France, at which point all the existing stations went off the air. (Some of their operators were later imprisoned for acts of collaboration with the Germans.) The problem of the 1940s was an appalling scarcity of all means for disseminating information in print, by wire and through broadcasting. The state monopoly of 1945 was a result not of policy but of scarcity. Furthermore it confirmed a situation which had emerged step by step during the war. When, later, de Gaulle was accused of interfering with broadcasting he was able to blame not his own Fifth Republic, but the Fourth for having initiated the vicious circle of political interference and declining credibility.

We can detect five separate factors which led to the monopolisation of broadcasting in France.[5] Firstly, there was the tradition of government control of the telegraph initiated in the middle of the nineteenth century because of fear of its use by enemies of the régime. Secondly, there was no real debate within France over who was to control broadcasting; it had grown very slowly (television in particular) and continued to grow slowly until de Gaulle arrived again in 1958. State control was a convenience rather than the result of a firm policy. Thirdly, the newspapers seeing that radio elsewhere, and later of course television, was potentially a usurper of advertising revenue became staunch supporters of a system by which the state would guarantee the financial viability of a French system of broadcasting. Fourthly, broadcasting was seen as a primary instrument of the traditional French policy of cultural diffusion. In private hands, as in the United States, broadcasting automatically became an instrument of low culture; the French, with their deeply-held feeling that France had been and should remain the chief receptacle of European civilisation, saw that centralised control of broadcasting was the only guarantee that the instrument would be employed to ensure that high culture would prevail. (Matthew Arnold might well have agreed.) Finally, there has been throughout the century an anxiety in many sections of French society that their state lacked coherence and a centre of gravity; there were fears constantly that French society might crack up altogether and the knowledge that broadcasting was centralised and in public hands made society as a whole that much more secure.

This combination of factors certainly ensured that all who controlled broadcasting in France would realise that it was no mere toy that lay in their grasp. The French government ended up running broadcasting because no one else was available uncontentiously to do so. Conditions in France had not made it possible for the growth of instruments of public control outside government as occurred in the Anglo-Saxon countries. There could be no 'gentlemen's agreements' between outside public bodies and the French state or government; in the years that followed the Second World War the instruments of broadcasting in France fell foul, inevitably, of that besetting vice of all authority: interference.

The underlying problem with French broadcasting, especially in the television age, was that it found no administrative resting place; although in the hands of the state, broadcasting went through a series of convulsions, no suitable administrative system emerging. Between 1948 and 1964 television gradually became a major force, and for the whole of that period before and during the years of de Gaulle, the universe of French broadcasting remained a bureaucratic one, its mental picture of the audience that of a patient with the hypodermic needle of French high culture pointed at him. The problems of broadcasting in this period, at the end of which a new broadcasting organisation (the ORTF) emerged with a guaranteed statutory identity, bear witness not to a French dilemma about the role of broadcasting so much as a French dilemma about the nature of social administration itself. The Fifth Republic found an interim solution to the problem of administration because in concentrating power completely in the centre it was able to depoliticise the problem of broadcasting, together with other social problems. Philip Williams and Martin Harrison have aptly described the bureaucracy of Gaullism; they refer to 'the growing army of specialists dispatched to run the nationalised industries and the vast penumbra of parapublic bodies, to keep the ORTF docile, or to serve in ministerial cabinets or the influential entourages of Matignon and Elysée. .... Thus the Fifth Republic, with its belief in hierarchy and depoliticisation, its indifference to meaningful consultation, and its elimination of so many of the former constraints and interferences, has given many of its technocrats exceptional opportunities.'[6] Broadcasting passed from the hands of amateur and uncaring bureaucrats in the 1950s into the hands of experts. Nonetheless each fresh reorganisation left it with an unsolved problem of 'interference' from one quarter or another.

In the 1940s radio in France had settled down to a pattern of four channels, two of them the National Programme and the string of FM stations concentrating on serious music, talks and discussion of cultural questions of a fairly highbrow nature, and the other two – France Inter and the Parisian network – concerned largely with popular music and light entertainment. From the chaos of war an organised listening public grew up; by 1960 it owned 10 million receivers on each of which a tax was paid.

Television, however, was struggling. Before the war there had been about 400 sets in all France and although various forms of experimentation continued during the war years, television was reinstated on a regular basis only in 1948, when for a few hours a week a privileged group of 3000 Frenchmen (confined to only 30 per cent of the geographical area of France) were able to receive programmes. By 1960, when television had come of age in most other countries and was on the verge of reaching saturation level in almost every country of the West, still only a million sets had been sold in France. Television had remained an exclusive luxury. It was broadcast on 819 lines, a unique system which could not be connected to any other television system in the world and which enabled the manufacturers of receivers in France to have *de facto* a highly protected market. But there were still only fifty hours of television programmes per week being transmitted at the end of the 1950s.

The administration of the RTF was inseparable from that of the PTT. Its budgeting was not independent, nor was its central organisation. Bureaucrats came and went and imposed their age-old office methods upon an industry which was bursting to gain some form of structural independence within which it could feel its own limbs. Television news was so retarded that when disasters of world scale occurred, wars, earthquakes, plane crashes, it took days, sometimes weeks, for the necessary high-level policy and budgetary decisions to be made to enable a cameraman to fly to the scene to provide news coverage. An infant medium was suffering from organisational sclerosis. The principal ministries involved were those of Finance and Information and their policy was to run television for cultural purposes, providing the French with a glimpse through television of their own cultural greatness. Broadcasting in France at this time was nevertheless of high quality and many of the men and women who worked in it look on those pioneering days with nostalgia. One of the entertainers of the 1950s on French television has written: 'On pratiquait le direct – le trapèze volant – qui vous mettait en présence du public et qui vous donnait l'impression de vous adresser vraiment au spectateur. Tout ce qu'on faisait prenait valeur d'essai et l'on n'avait pas peur du risque.'[7]

Television in France was not reaching a mass audience; it had not yet entered the era of synthetic mass-produced entertainment.

Nor had it entered the age of political fears and pressures. The main news 'Journal Télévisé' was until very late in the 1950s a ramshackle affair, its general direction dictated by the government of the day. M. Delaunay, the Director-General from 1957 to 1958, presided over a reorganisation which involved the separation of the Information division from the rest of television; the new department was kept under careful scrutiny; M. Delaunay protested in vain against the changes he was obliged to make. Nonetheless a wide spectrum of political standpoints found expression on French television. Politicians were in general totally apathetic toward the power of this slowly growing instrument. The intelligentsia treated it as a toy for the stupid. The manipulation of French television by the civil servants who ran it was not a source of protest. Jacques Fauvet wrote in *Le Monde* as de Gaulle approached power: 'La IV

République a succombé pour bien des raisons dont l'une est d'avoir trop souvent célé la vérité au nom d'un conformisme qui s'abritait dans les grandes circonstances sous les raisons d'état.'[8]

Many of the officials of the RTF were pressing for some kind of formal charter under which they could operate with some elbow-room of their own. The domination of bureaucrats was making the system unworkable even in its own terms. As Jacques Thibau remarks,[9] 'RTF had become a synonym for disorder and muddle.' There were frequent strikes, partial or total. At the very moment when programmes were being prepared for public holidays bureaucracy would decide to impose its heavy hand. Christmas 1957 was reduced to chaos because of a strike.

In 1959 the two Ministries worked out a plan whereby the RTF would be allowed to operate under a new administrative instrument, as an independent commercial organisation with a certain amount of budgetary autonomy. Not until 1964 was this system given statutory status; until then it had the force only of an administrative decree but nonetheless the standing of broadcasting was greatly enhanced by the change.

Parliament would vote the licence fee each year, and advertising continued to be banned. Nonetheless the financial arrangements of the ORTF were inextricably tied up with the general budget of the Ministry of Finance. The Minister of Information continued to exercise total control over broadcasting *a priori*. The RTF was renamed L'Office de la Radiodiffusion et Télévision Française ('l'Office' popularly). The Assembly would frequently hold debates on the problems of freedom and control at the ORTF under the guise of budgetary debates. The Senate was able to hold periodic commissions of inquiry into the workings of L'Office, such as the one led by Senator André Diligent which revealed in 1968 many of the working arrangements between the government and French broadcasting. The 1959 and 1964 changes thus enabled the issue of broadcasting to be brought out into the open in France.

The Minister of Information had three buzzers on his desk (until M. Peyrefitte, coming into the job in 1962, in a liberalising clean sweep had them removed): one for the Director-General of the ORTF, one for the editor of the news section, and one for the editor in charge of radio. In the early 1960s a new information system was created to rationalise the whole of the government's press information establishments. The Service de Liaison Interministeriel pour l'Information (SLII) met daily in the office of the Ministry to discuss the news situation. SLII consisted of representatives of the Ministry and the ORTF and became the butt of much of the complaints of the ORTF staff concerning censorship. Peyrefitte always denied that censorship was any part of the committee's purpose, but it was nevertheless widely believed to be so. Jacques Thibau, Peyrefitte's assistant at the time, has subsequently said that the censorship occurred on a 'direct, personal level' and was not channelled through the committee at all.[10] In the course of the troubles of 1968 opposition among the public to the SLII arrangement grew enormously and the committee was abolished. When Pompidou came to power he abolished the Ministry of Information altogether, hoping by this action to shed the unpopular image of censorship which surrounded it.

Between the State and the ORTF there existed an important intermediary body which was conjured into existence in the course of the law-making of 1964, the Administrative Council. It consisted of eight civil servants, one representative of the viewers' organisation, one pressman, two delegates from the staff of the ORTF and four people chosen directly by the government. Its functions, according to the Law of 27 June 1964 (64:621 p. 5637), were to 'establish general lines of action. It deliberates and controls the execution of the budget. It evaluates the quality and morality of the programmes. It watches over the objectivity and the exactitude of the news which is broadcast by l'Office. It certifies that the principal tendencies of thought and the most important mainstreams of opinion can express themselves on the air.' In practice this amounted to very little.

On the budgetary side, Giscard d'Estaing, the Minister of Finance at the time the new law was enacted, refused to allow control of the budget to go outside his ministry. The Director-General of l'Office (who was an appointee in any case not of the Administrative Council but, together with his two assistants, of the Council of Ministers) thus had no direct day-to-day control of his own finances. Nor did the Administrative Council, which in practice could only take irregular long-range glances at them. While the Council was attempting to examine the objectivity of the news, the Government itself took an ever-increasing interest in the content of the ORTF News division, as the number of television sets in France increased from 1 million in 1959 to 10 million in 1968. French politicians in the sixties suddenly woke up to the importance of television; they decided, many of them, to *use* it. Regional television was introduced as a measure of pluralisation of news, and the more news that was available the greater the active curiosity of the great and would-be great. The Gaullists in particular saw television as a means to circumvent the bias in the French press against them. The Council therefore tended in practice to act as an intermediary body between government and television workers. The government controlled half of its members in any case and could *give orders to* and remove from office the most senior staff in the ORTF. The great measure of 'liberalisation' therefore did not amount to much. It certainly did not amount to the creation of a public body as independent as the British Broadcasting Corporation and as subtly oriented towards a generalised public interest instead of a sectional governmental interest. But this was what the Gaullists often claimed. Until 1968 the ORTF was described in legal terms as being autonomous but financially under the 'authority' of the Ministry of Finance;[11] after the further reforms of 1968 its status changed to one of 'protection'. There was a gradual process by which government tried to withdraw from immediate editorial control while retaining the essential lines of influence. The history of the period of the 1960s indicates how this policy finally came unstuck.

In any case, as far as news was concerned, it remained firmly in Gaullist hands whatever the formal and legal arrangements. The head of television and the head of the news department were both acknowledged Gaullists. The total number of people viewing French television news every day is estimated at 25,000,000; the total number of newspaper readers is 22,000,000.

The employees of the news department of the ORTF were

divided into a specially privileged group of 'staffmen' and an under-privileged group of contract employees who could be dismissed at any time. No one has made an accurate measurement of their political sympathies at this period, but it is frequently alleged that the most senior and most secure jobs went to those with Gaullist loyalties and the rest were distributed to supporters of other political factions. Communists were employed as technicians but not as journalists.

From the late 1950s French television had achieved a great international reputation for a series of magazine programmes which dealt with political topics in a remarkably frank and detailed manner and with admirable professional skill. They came outside the jurisdiction of the News department and employed contract producers. M. Pierre Desgraupes (later to become head of news on Channel One) was one of the principal figures associated with 'Cinq Colonnes à la Une', which dealt largely with foreign affairs. In later years 'Face à Face', 'Panorama', 'Zoom' joined the list of these exciting and distinguished television programmes. An analysis of the total content of 'Cinq Colonnes à la Une' for 1965 shows that only three of the fifty-six subjects it tackled dealt with French political issues, even indirectly. 'Panorama', in the same year, the year of a Presidential election, managed to touch on domestic affairs in similar proportion. These programmes between them covered every major world trouble spot; their highly imaginative producers and dauntless film crews were to be seen at every invasion, revolution and assassination in the world. But the issues which dominated France were almost totally ignored. André Harris, one of the producers of 'Zoom', has described the process of self-denial which brought about this curious gap in the screen coverage of current affairs as a set of 'collective taboos, a sort of unconscious censorship'.[12]

The dilemma posed for the French government by television was that it created a popular force for a cultural product which might or which did interfere with the running of the administration. It was a novel problem for France with its traditionally highly centralised administration. It is extremely difficult to pull the levers of power and control the outpouring product of the television screen; it cannot be achieved by a group of civil servants without any understanding of the nature of entertainment. Television brought show-business into government in France, albeit a little later than elsewhere, and French officials discovered at a moment when television had already become a major instrument (instead of at the moment of its inception) all the forces of a social and political nature which are generated from the domestic screen. While administrators thought they were merely dealing directly with a group of professionals in various forms of contractual relationship with them, they were in reality dealing with the entire civil population of France through these professionals. The perceptions of the audience's needs and interests which the professionals experienced could not be altered at the dictate of civil servants whose previous knowledge of the public had been confined to running sewage systems, railways and colonies. One of the most popular programmes in France was 'La Caméra explore le Temps', produced by Stellio Lorenzi, one of the rare communists in a production job at the ORTF. This programme used to take an episode of history, and present an extremely entertaining and skilful account of it. One edition, transmitted at the height of this programme's popularity, was called 'L'Affaire Ledru', and concerned a highly principled lawyer who is duped and forced into retirement by court officials; he is presented as a good man caught in the coils of bureaucracy. This particular edition ended with a reminder to the audience of the universality of the theme. The series was taken off the air abruptly with no reason given.[13] Four months later 'Tele-7 Jours' conducted a poll to discover the most popular programme on French television; 'La Caméra explore le Temps', defunct but vivid still in the minds of its former viewers, was still being placed at Number One.

There was no effective buffer between producers and bureaucrats, nothing absorbing the shifts of public taste, no dialogue between media and government, in short no *institution* of broadcasting in France. Director after director came and went. There was no central point of loyalty to the medium itself, still less to the ORTF. Some kind of clash was inevitable.

A gigantic internal convulsion in the ORTF was on its way. Before one can set the scene, however, for the great revolt which occurred in the course of the May events in 1968, there are two further factors which must be described. First is the fact that television in France was rapidly developing along the pattern recognised in every other mass society in the world. It was becoming a means of mass entertainment. For a decade and more television had been dismissed as 'La boîte à concierge', the servant's means of entertainment; but the ORTF was receiving 200,000 new licences per month as the phenomenon of television spread rapidly in the period of economic boom of the mid-sixties and was therefore well on the way to becoming the second richest television organisation in Europe. (Every licence cost an annual sum which increased gradually over the years to approximately £15 in 1972.) A second network was inaugurated in April 1964 and while it provided programmes for only 25 hours a week, the first channel had meanwhile increased to over 70 hours. The new channel covered 70 per cent of French territory within a year and a half and was dedicated to a set of ideals in which the task of sheer entertainment had finally triumphed. 'The Public of the Second Network wants a happier television, a rosier one, more relaxed viewing.' That was part of the new channel's opening pronouncement on its first day. The programme controllers at the ORTF also discovered the benefits of proper scheduling, which kept to the pattern of mass work and leisure. Although 50 per cent of all programming was still of an informational nature, the proportion of light entertainment increased and serious drama decreased considerably; French television became known for its violence, its triviality. It had joined the world family of mass entertainment media.

The second important factor which affected the attitude of ordinary French people towards the phenomenon of broadcasting was the existence of a chain of commercial radio stations on the fringes of French soil, broadcasting throughout the day in French to French listeners. They provide news and entertainment and grew rapidly in popularity during the period in which French administration had been devising new and subtler tools for safeguarding the content of the ORTF channels while granting l'Office an appearance of greater autonomy. Radio Tele-Luxembourg (RTL), Europe No. 1, Sud-Radio,

Radio Monte-Carlo are known as 'les radios périphériques' because their transmitters are actually outside French territory although their studios are in Paris. They run commercials. They are not under daily governmental control. However, through SOFIRAD (La Société Financière de Radiodiffusion) the French government had controlled since 1947 the majority of the shares in Sud-Radio and Radio Monte-Carlo. It has minority holdings in RTL and Europe No. 1; but only in 1965 did the French government officially admit the extent of the connection;[14] at that moment it made an attempt to increase its holdings of RTL stock to the consternation of the directors of the firm. The Grand Duchy made an official protest to the French government because although the station is under Luxembourgeois supervision it is not controlled as to its content by anyone except its owners, a group of French businessmen. The French government stock-holding is through Havas, an advertising agency which it owns, and the government tried to increase the holding by purchasing stock in the Compagnie Sans Fil (CSF). After the protests the French desisted from the purchase. For several years RTL had been stealing listeners in large numbers from France Inter while developing its news and information programming very considerably by putting out three major news programmes a day. On one occasion in 1960 the French government cut the connection between RTL's studio and the transmitter because it disapproved of the station's coverage of the Algerian war; two years later it threatened to do the same thing again when Jacques Duhamel (a member of the opposition in the Assemblée) was elected president of RTL's Administrative Council.[15]

The chief influence on broadcasting between 1959 and 1968 was of course the personality of de Gaulle himself. As we have seen, he was the first politician of world status to discover the political possibilities of broadcasting. He knew that the instrument of radio had created a second de Gaulle, his *doppelgänger*, whose identity needed to be protected and proclaimed; it existed outside the physical personality of Charles de Gaulle, but it was this second man through whom the first would govern France.

'I made this discovery at Douala, which was my first contact with the French people after my call to resistance. I landed there after the expedition to Dakar had failed. There were thousands of people and they began to shout "de Gaulle! de Gaulle!" I was taken aback. Until then, in London, my contacts had all been personal and individual, with ministers, soldiers, attachés. . . . From that day on I knew I would have to reckon with this man, this General de Gaulle. I became almost his prisoner. Before I made a speech or reached a major decision I had to ask myself "Will de Gaulle approve of this?" '[16]

Despite the fact that he had been 'made' by radio, de Gaulle was not allowed to make a broadcast for eleven years. In 1947 M. Paul Ramadier, the Prime Minister, declared that the General would not be allowed to broadcast again.[17] Until he returned to create the Fifth Republic he remained electronically invisible. Then he made television the instrument of personal power, the means by which he emerged over the head of squabbling politicians to become a symbol of the French nation, in monologue with it. He presided over a series of magisterial press conferences, the questions 'arranged' in advance. In every crisis de Gaulle appeared alone speaking directly into the camera. He spoke in archaic syntax a series of speeches which kept alive the de Gaulle he had discovered in Douala. In some of them he announced policy which had only just been communicated to the Prime Minister and the Cabinet, sometimes it turned out to be news for them as well (as, for instance, when he announced his policy for a compromise peace, 'une paix des braves', for Algeria). The news programmes on French television would emphasise his activities; he would be seen moving about the country and the world, shaking hands, making speeches, on occasions which on their sheer news interest might not have warranted mention at all. During the gathering crisis of May 1968 he was seen endlessly moving through the various stages of a state visit to Roumania, as if issuing a silent and implied comment to the French people on the strikes (unfilmed by the ORTF) which were already paralysing France.

In the Presidential election of 1962 a brief period of television time (seven minutes) was allotted to every party contending the election. De Gaulle, of course, had enjoyed the benefit of continuous exposure for several years, while the opposition politicians had been presented fleetingly only on the news, their lips moving silently while an announcer explained the main points of their speeches. Although the time was distributed with a greater degree of fairness during the period of the actual campaign, the opposition parties had the appearance of being squabbling, self-seeking 'politicians', hopelessly upstaged by the General. In the next Presidential election, in 1965, M. Alexandre Parodi was chosen to head a National Control Commission which would supervise the conduct of the election as far as the media were concerned. The principle of equality was to be respected as regards the distribution of time for advocacy and in the news programmes too.[18] There were two elections, a primary and a final, in which the winning candidate had to receive more than half of the votes. Each of the six candidates was given two hours; de Gaulle however chose to use only thirty minutes of his share, hoping, his critics alleged, to make his opponents appear garrulous, complaining trouble-makers, drowning themselves in their own speech.

Nonetheless the election brought television politics for the first time to France, and M. Lecanuet emerged as a kind of Kennedy-figure, handsome, enthusiastic, basing his surprisingly large share of the poll on his skill in the use of the medium of television itself rather than on purely intellectual appeal. Lecanuet was thrust into the world limelight for several months with his attractive centrist politics before the arc lights were switched off and he returned to relative obscurity. Miterand was a technical failure, too wooden to adapt himself to the needs of the medium, but he achieved $7\frac{1}{2}$ million votes to de Gaulle's $10\frac{1}{2}$. The General was obliged to quit the race or face a second run-off election. He chose the latter and entered into the fight with a far greater determination to engage all his forces, to capture the very large bloc of voters who had remained undecided in the previous round. He also decided not to fight alone but as the leader of a party. His staff used all the resources available, at meetings and dinners, issuing posters and booklets and making full use of the peripheral radio stations. De Gaulle decided to use television this time not for another national fireside chat but for an interview. Michel Droit, a journalist, was chosen to do the questioning, not sycophantically, but clearly and frankly raising issues; no one expected a gladiatorial affray, but those who expected a superficial line of questioning and the appearance of a 'rigged' interview were surprised. The election took place on 17 December and de Gaulle received 12,645,315 votes to Miterand's 10,557,480. De Gaulle had become leader of his people for the first time as the result of their directly choosing him for himself rather than an equally available alternative. At the same time he had learned the lesson of competitive politics: that one is more powerful as a result of using modern techniques of electioneering straightforwardly and winning, than by manipulating them while remaining aloof.

This, then, was French television on the eve of the great convulsion of 1968: it was a medium that had belatedly discovered the equations of mass society; it was in the hands of men who understood the need for autonomy but who were prepared to provide it with only a sham version of autonomy; it contained professionals whose international experience had whetted their appetite to explore the full potential of the instrument in their hands, which means the full potential for touching the nerve-ends of whatever is socially possible; yet television has become the principal and most reliable instrument of the personal rule, not of a man ignorant of television's essence, but profoundly skilled and resourceful in its use. The professionals always are the key to television, but de Gaulle too was a professional.

In the events of May 1968 many of the dammed streams of French life broke their dykes, in education, industry, the media and politics. All the various issues were interconnected and it is difficult to describe merely those aspects of the cataclysm which affected television without giving the impression that television was the central strand of the discontent which boiled over. Nonetheless it was in itself an extremely important element. Spring 1968 saw the setting up of one of the many Senate commissions into television. The report which bears the name of André Diligent which finally appeared in May 1968 was eagerly awaited by the professionals and the politicians

171

who had been discussing heatedly for many months the already intolerable situation in the ORTF. The Diligent Report[19] was all the more devastating because of its timing.

The French government's contribution to the debate about broadcasting of that year[20] was a decision to increase the quantity of advertising on French television. 'Why should all the extra advertising revenue just go to the peripheral stations?' Pompidou argued in his speech to the Assemblée. The government survived, narrowly, a censure motion on the question of television advertising, the first of a series of censure motions of that year.[21] M. Diligent criticised the ORTF for its biased handling of news and a group started up appointed by Henri Fréville in the National Assembly, calling itself Progress and Modern Democracy, and demanding a Committee of Wise Men to ensure greater fairness in news presentation.

The strike of ORTF workers which broke out in May and continued for eleven weeks was not a strike of sympathy with the students; it was not inspired by the example of students, nor of the workers of France. It was initiated by a group of men at the very highest level of French television reporting, men and women who were household names in France: Desgraupes, Dumayet, Igor Barrère, Roger Benamou, Alain de Sédouy, André Harris, Philippe Labro, Henri de Turenne. The touchstone of the revolt was the interference of the authorities in the work of reporting the crisis which was breaking out throughout French society. While the peripheral radio stations were providing detailed news and information on the conduct of events, the ORTF workers felt themselves frozen in attitudes of sycophantic news suppression which in the context of the events occurring became intolerable to the reporters.[22] De Gaulle was later to complain that the television workers had waited until he was on his knees before stabbing him in the back.[23]

The instrument of the dispute was in an edition of 'Panorama' which had been the object of interference by the Ministry of Information. The programme, which was to contain an account of the student strike in the Sorbonne, had been subjected in any case to various humiliating difficulties; several of the participants had dropped out (including François Mauriac and Jacques Monod) declaring that they distrusted the programme's intentions. The film crew had been insulted and threatened in the street while working. On the day of the transmission, at 7.45 in the evening, two officials of the Ministries of Education and Information came to Rue Cognac-Jay, the headquarters of the ORTF, and gave orders for the programme not to be shown. In the same week two discussion programmes on the *événements* were cancelled on similar orders. On 15 May a group of senior editors announced that they would withdraw their programmes ('Zoom', 'Cinq Colonnes', 'Caméra III') if any further acts of interference occurred.[24] A week after that the Intersyndicale ordered a general strike throughout the ORTF but excluded journalists and technicians involved in news programmes. The General went on the air and announced a referendum; and on 24 May a programme which was to have discussed this plan was suddenly cancelled, and the newsmen held a meeting of protest at which nearly one hundred of the ORTF's journalists decided to join the strike. A group of 23 others voted against this measure and continued working throughout the strike preparing news bulletins. The fact that these 23 were able to carry on and provide a fairly full news programme during the many weeks of the strike was one of the factors in the decision, taken much later, to 'compress' the staff of the ORTF news department and sack 59 newsmen.

It was a curious kind of industrial action. The workers of the ORTF, 13,000 staff people and 35,000 on various forms of freelance contract, constituted an enormously wide range of political persuasions. Roger Louis[25] describes how carpenters who supported the OAS, Poujadist engineers, Trotskyist drivers, make-up artists who supported Lecanuet, assistant producers who were 'Chinese' and producers who were conventional communists somehow managed to join together with a host of other groupings extending as far as the 'barbouzes' to decide to hold a strike in the pursuit, not of higher wages, but of 'professional honour'. Some of the ORTF employees wanted to take over the organisation and run it themselves with the help of student guards on the building, but some of the engineers pointed out that the students would have to stand guard on the Eiffel Tower as well in order to keep the transmitter going; nonetheless the

173

newsreaders wanted to continue their bulletins while refusing to accept orders from 'above' as to content. They were voted down in favour of a total shut-down.

At a moment when the fabric of French society was coming apart, the whole apparatus of subtle government control through carefully selected placemen in key positions, thousands of creative staff on loose contracts, and a network of unofficial lines of contact between the government and the ORTF suddenly ceased to function. All the revolutionaries of 1968 were people carefully selected for their jobs under a Gaullist administration. What had happened was that the manipulated machinery of information had cloaked the social realities from the eyes of government rather more than from the eyes of the viewers and listeners. Miterand in the course of May stated that he would fire all the ORTF's journalists if he became president of France in the elections. The journalists were therefore in a completely exposed position; they had long lost the respect of their colleagues in the written press for their connivance at news suppression and their involvement in government controlled news. Their shame bubbled up together with a simple fear for their future – only a substantial gesture of a collective kind would indicate both to the world of journalism and to the possible incoming post-Gaullist administration that the errors of the past had been forced upon them.

Although the strike was fought in the cause of 'honest news' and 'objectivity' many of the strikers gave the impression that what they wanted was the right to perform their work freely according to their own persuasion. M. de Closets, one of the striker leaders, wrote in *Le Monde* in the last moments of the strike; 'Once each home had its television set, we saw our civilisation was no longer the same. From then on, citizen and society had a means of direct contact which could be used to initiate action as much as to diffuse information. The Fourth Estate was born. . . . ORTF can only fulfil this mission if it is truly recognised as an essential element of the fourth estate and not as the fourth instrument of government after the administration, the army and the police.'[26] In other words, the ORTF strikers had stumbled across the central dilemmas of broadcasting and were demanding, in the name of freedom (and sometimes demanding in the name of what they imagined was the policy of 'free' broadcasting organisation such as the BBC) a right which no broadcaster has ever really achieved – the right to be an individual member of a Fourth Estate. Decades in which the state had insinuated its interests into broadcasting had failed unsurprisingly to teach the French broadcasting fraternity that broadcasting operates under *national* constraints everywhere; in most other parts of the Western world these restraints are automatically imposed and normally internalised in the minds of the professionals. The strikers were drawing upon reserves of traditional French liberal thought. In broadcasting, however, the professionals are never 'free' even when broadcasting is 'free' – they are, even in the most admired systems, guardians of a machinery which allows for certain free discussion. They are brokers and megaphones, not politicians and speechmakers.

M. Edouard Sablier, the editor-in-chief of ORTF News, argued in *Le Monde*, 'Censorship has never existed. Not unless you consider censorship to be the legitimate right of an editor-in-chief to judge all subjects before they are shown. For my part, I side with the principle governing the BBC: the producers in charge of particular programmes are not authorised to say, exactly, everything that comes into their heads because we believe that beyond certain limits liberty is no longer tolerable.'[27] The problem with all broadcasting is that the decisions of the editor-in-chief disappear into the higher politics of the institution. In the case of the ORTF those decisions disappeared into the higher politics of the Gaullist state. Many of the men who have held senior posts in the ORTF (including Jean d'Arcy who was chief director in the 1950s and Jacques de Bresson who became Director-General after the strike) have always argued that television under their care has been free, held back only by a few fundamental, totally reasonable and widely accepted limitations.[28] In the case of the May events television in any system would have had to cope with the problem that its own coverage would have influenced the course of events themselves. No mass society has ever been able yet to resolve the problems of media coverage imposed during the course of a social cataclysm without resorting to controls, if not outright censorship.

The striking ORTF workers held rallies in various parts of France to raise money for their cause. Twenty-five such rallies were held and thousands of pounds poured in. The ratings of the news show, transmitted by blacklegs, went down from 65 per cent to 50 per cent; a daily newspaper poll indicated that the public were very largely on the side of the strikers.[29]

The ORTF management offered certain concessions; the Administrative Council was enlarged to include among others a larger number of ORTF personnel from 16 to 22 members. Strike pay was agreed. A new body within the Administrative Council would supervise the vexed problem of 'objectivity'. Parliament would give the ORTF a new constitution. There would be no sanctions against strikers. The union agreed on a return to work on 25 June without consulting the strikers. Eight hundred journalists, however, refused to return until a greater concession was made on the question of objectivity. The strikers' request for a compromise whereby a Committee of Wise Men would supervise fairness in programme content was turned down. The primary national election took place and de Gaulle was clearly the winner. The public was getting used to the news in the form produced by the 23 non-strikers. On 11 July the strikers gave in. They received notices telling them to go home and await instructions about future duties.

When the new shape of the news organisation became known, it was seen that 100 journalists were excluded, about 40 of them moved to the provinces and 59 sacked. M. de Bresson has ever since continued to argue that the changes were administrative and did not constitute special sanctions against militants. He has not been widely believed. There was little doubt in the minds of the strikers, however, that their position was going to be extremely difficult in the months and years to come, whether they remained on the payroll or not. Claude Darget, one of the sacked journalists, sued the ORTF management for wrongful dismissal and was awarded a sum of £12,000; after the case he commented wryly, 'The TV tax which the public pays in order to see us is now being paid to us so that the public should not have to see us any more.'

The old ORTF system never really returned. SLII was abolished. So were all the programmes whose producers had complained most bitterly about it: 'Cinq Colonnes', 'Zoom', 'Caméra III'. 'Panorama', however, made a comeback under M. Olivier Todd whose broadcasting experience had been mainly at the BBC in London. M. Pierre Desgraupes (who struck) was appointed to the sensitive post as head of news on the first channel and Mlle Jacqueline Baudrier (who did not strike) was appointed to the equally sensitive post as his counterpart on the second channel. In the further reorganisation of September 1969 they were given separate budgets and told to compete with each other; they acquired each his own set of reporters, film crews, cutting rooms, administrations, and their rivalry spread around the globe, to the perplexity of foreign professional colleagues who watched French reporters and cameramen tearing each other to pieces in a frantic scramble to prove the superiority of M. Desgraupes' organisation or Mlle Baudrier's. The new structure which was created personally by M. Pierre Chaban-Delmas, the Prime Minister, in the teeth of open criticism within his own party represented undoubted progress and speculation continued only about how long it would last. Unable to find a central institutional pivot on which all the work of broadcasting in France could rest, the managers of the ORTF chose the logical but unconventional path of setting up two systems, one more 'loyalist' to the régime than the other. In the spectrum of political affiliation among the new employees the 'leftest' individual was Olivier Todd, political editor of *Nouvel Observateur*. After eight months an incident arose over the banning by M. Desgraupes of an extract from the film 'Battle for Algiers' which M. Todd wanted to use in a discussion on 'Panorama' which was investigating the reasons for the decision to ban the film in French cinemas; Todd walked out that night claiming that the decision had been made as a result of pressure from the Matignon. Allegations of pressure and political control continued to be made, although the period from 1969 until 1972 was on the whole one of consolidation and a kind of growing optimism, in certain sections of French opinion and the ORTF itself.

The ORTF decided to move much further towards entertaining the new television public (the French term '*distraction*' makes the point more clearly). Colour had been introduced shortly before the crisis;[31] its progress was now accelerated. The cost of a television licence fee was reduced from 4,500 francs to 3,500. However, the quality of the information programmes declined considerably; the professionals concentrated on manner and spectacle rather than explanatory comment. It has been argued (by M. Thibau)[32] that de Gaulle's failed referendum of 27 April 1970 was one of the casualties of a poorly organised information service in French broadcasting after the troubles of May 1968; government simply descended upon the people from on high – there was no argument about social needs. No one dared to explain frequently and clearly the arguments for or against the proposals for regional reform which were the subject of the referendum and became the cause of the General's departure from office. Television returned to a preoccupation with high culture and with 'divertissement' of the masses. While de Sédouy and André Harris were not permitted to return from the exiled ranks of the 59, Guy Lux and Pierre Bellemare returned to help with the new policy of light entertainment.

Information programmes were completely separated from the general programme production and programme planning of both channels. For instance, M. Cazeneuve, the controller of the second channel, had to operate a policy of competing with the first channel without having access to the content of the crucial peak hour 7.30 to 8.30. That period took the brunt of all the anxieties and new emphases of the ORTF. It was professionalised; the hour was made to pass slickly and efficiently. Politicians scrutinised it jealously and complainingly. The concentration on the personality of de Gaulle gave way to a concentration on the new leaders – Pompidou and Chaban-Delmas. (M. Thibau draws attention to the way that ORTF news took on many of the characteristics of 'Anglo-Saxon' news bulletins.)[33] The prevailing ideology of the régime of Pompidou invaded every moment of the screen while the actual credibility of the information was high. The real problem of television news – that of expression – was evaded. The professional is to television, M. Thibau remarks, as the technocrat is to the state: both worship the cult of competence. But that is all.

The process by which the wavelength extends its power of patronage throughout society had however now emerged as an important force in French society as a whole. In fact one of the many levels of the crisis of May was that television had become a major issue in French society, not merely one issue in a list but one which dramatically affected all other issues. The debate about broadcasting had entered into the general debate about the future of France. That fact reflects the way in which mass society had finally arrived and the way in which broadcasting had created its own cadre of professionals. The issue of what kind of public control France required became increasingly important because traditionally public control meant a régime of professional civil servants; in other parts of Europe public control meant that power would be placed into the hands of a group of respected citizens whose overall composition would keep broadcasting an uncontentious issue. In Britain the composition of the Board of Governors reflects the major blocs of power in British society – the unions, business, the universities and so on; it is so informally constituted that any newly emergent group can be rapidly represented without changing any basic law. In France, however, the government representation on the Administrative Council, and its influence throughout the organisation was top-heavy with representatives of the state administration.

The task of those wanting to alter television and radio in France was therefore complicated; they had to open up the broadcasting institution, they had to divide the idea of public control from the idea of bureaucratic control. Two further questions were revealed as inevitable concomitants, those of worker participation and of private ownership. In a society which could not find a neutral position for broadcasting to occupy within its public life but outside its formal bureaucracy, pressure would automatically be generated from within the organisation of the ORTF and within commercial life for the creation of private enterprise broadcasting. That is exactly what occurred.

The Paye Commission which reported in June 1970 examined the question of a third network in the context of a general administrative overhaul. After examining the entire range of alternatives offered by France's European neighbours (especially Britain with its mixed private and public systems), Paye opted for state control through the ORTF of all three networks; the ORTF, however, would become a 'holding Company' for its many enterprises, and an important admixture of regionalism was to modify the structure of the new channel. Despite considerable pressure from advertisers and the press, the Paye proposals met with some favour and the ORTF prepared to turn itself into a unique world institution, a state authority with three channels under its control. The Director-General, M. de Bresson, set up his own internal reorganisation inquiry (the Riou Commission) which enabled him to decentralise, democratise and diversify without turning the ORTF into the skeletal command system desired by M. Paye. The 'professionals' put up little objection; no issue of principle seemed to be involved any longer, after the ORTF had since 1968 increased its own dependence on advertising. Pierre Desgraupes said in *L'Express*,[34] 'Je ne vois aucun inconvénient à l'apparition d'une troisième chaîne privée ou nationale ... parce que je crois aux vertus de la concurrence. Je crois que plus le marche de la télévision sera large, moins les hommes de la télévision dépendront d'un seul employeur, plus ils y trouveront leur affaire. Donc, il me semble, raisonnablement, qu'un homme de télévision devrait se réjouir de voir apparaître 2, 3, 4, 10 chaînes. Qu'elles sont privées ou pas privées, cela m'est égal ...'

By early 1971 France had increased its licence-payers to 12 million, its audience to 35 million. Altogether there were 5,000 hours of television every year, 3,000 of them produced directly by the staff of the ORTF.[35] A huge industry of free-lance television programme-making organisations had sprung up depending on the ORTF channel-controllers for their livelihood, but employing producers who had no fundamental loyalties to the organisation of the ORTF; their careers did not depend on the managers of the ORTF. Some of them developed reputations of an international character. Their interests were represented to the ORTF largely by the trade unions which themselves had undergone a major internal ideological transformation. The unions, since 1968 and 1969, had put the questions of organisation and control at the top of their list of concerns; wages and conditions tended now to take second place.

Despite the Paye recommendations, despite the reforms of

1969 and 1970, despite the improvement in the quality of the entertainment, despite the growing self-confidence of the professionals, none of the deep-seated problems had been resolved. The ORTF and the French public had become fascinated by the problems of their broadcasting service. So had prominent members of the Assemblée and the Senate. A new series of convulsions was still to come in an effort by some to break the last controlling links between the régime of personal power in the Fifth Republic and the instrument of broadcasting, and in an effort by others to keep the ORTF on a steady though compromised course set by the 1969 reforms.

Wracked by periodic strikes, the ORTF was divided into a series of warring baronial fiefs; top-heavy administratively, it was described by one writer[36] as a 'collective struggle for influence tempered by general immobilisation'. Certainly a subtle combination of inertia and anarchy coloured the atmosphere of Rue Cognac-Jay; to attempt to collaborate with French broadcasting at this time was to court days or weeks of frustration unsurpassed by any other broadcasting body, with the possible exception of that of the Soviet Union.

Yet the ORTF was in hot pursuit of the viewers. The size of audience dominated its thinking; whereas once the ORTF emphasised the way it dignified its audience's interests by providing large quantities of high culture, of interest only to small groups at a time, it now went all out to obtain the whole of the audience the whole of the time.

During the course of 1971 a new set of internal arrangements, labelled 'structural reforms', were set in motion; these meant that a layer of administrative men would oversee the work of the producers. At every stage of their work, 'responsibility' for finance and organisation would be taken from their shoulders and placed on the backs of professional organisation-men.[37] The unions kept up a steady barrage of complaint, and turned down the new contracts offered by the management until the producers had obtained some greater degree of control over their work.

The atmosphere within and around French broadcasting towards the end of 1971 was ready for a new crisis; it needed only a match to cause a major flare-up, but in fact what occurred was the inauguration of two slowly smouldering bonfires. The first was a matter of censorship and the second an important financial scandal.

One of the new post-1969 programmes to earn a great deal of praise was 'Armes Egales', a weekly discussion programme in which each of two main protagonists would present his side of an argument with the help of a filmed essay, in which he was enabled to build up his case in any way he wished. When the two essays had been presented the two main speakers would conduct a debate which could last for up to two hours. It was a show-piece of public affairs work, reached 36 editions and provided a wide variety of political platforms. It became deservedly famous, even though, by the slicker standards of Anglo-Saxon broadcasting, it was hopelessly long-winded. On 13 December 1971, Maurice Clavel, journalist, dramatist and some would say professional self-publicist, was to take part in an edition of 'Armes Egales' with Jean Royer, a Gaullist deputy of an independent turn of mind, on the subject of the permissive society. While the programme was on the air Clavel noticed that a word had been omitted from the sound-track of his filmed essay; in it he had paraphrased the text of an interview given by Pompidou to a French journalist in which Pompidou had said he was tired of hearing stories about the French Resistance – Clavel had said in his film that Pompidou treated the Resistance with 'l'aversion et l'agacement' and the word 'aversion' was the one that the producers had deleted. Clavel rose from his chair as the lights went up after the transmission of the film segment, bowed, called out, 'Messieurs les censeurs, bonsoir!' and walked out, leaving the producers with ninety minutes of television time to fill with only one participant. The affair caused an enormous furore and the French press took sides heatedly, some supporting Clavel and listing other cases of 'censorship' in the recent past of the ORTF, others declaring that he, by walking out, had 'censored' the programme. The usual range of confusions concerning what constitutes freedom of expression in the context of broadcasting was duly registered in a series of shrill editorials. In vain did the producers issue an open declaration a week later explaining that Clavel had been told in advance that the word had been ex-

182

cised.[38] The critical press wanted to denounce censorship in the
ORTF and censorship they denounced. 'La liberté ne se divise
pas', exclaimed *Le Monde*.[39] 'A bad excuse', said *Figaro*.[40]
L'Humanité filled a page with a long saga of ORTF excisions and
suppressions since 1969.[41]

The second bonfire was more serious and was ignited on
November 29 by Senator André Diligent from Northern
France, who had for some years made it his business to speak
out on broadcasting affairs, against commercialism and against
censorship, in favour of liberalisation and the depoliticisation
of the ORTF. Officially he holds the post of chairman of the
finance commission on information. He came to deliver his
annual report to the Senate and as he reached the end of his
speech dealing with the financial affairs of a variety of enterprises, including the ORTF, he lowered his voice and declared,
'L'Office doit défendre son integrité, c'est-à-dire, sa liberté
matérielle et morale'.[42] He went on to reveal a scandal in the
ranks of the ORTF which led, necessarily, yet again to its dis-
mantling and total reconstruction. 'Under the protection of
advertising agencies and public relations firms methodical and
scientific corruption is being organised inside the ORTF.'
Diligent described a system by which a particular advertising
agency (later revealed as none other than Havas, owned by the
French government and holding company for the government's
shares in some of the peripheral radio stations) was paying
large sums to employees of the ORTF to advertise 'clandestinely'
in its programmes, cars, entertainers, aviation companies and
other firms and products. The sports programmes were singled
out in particular.

Diligent's carefully argued and undeclamatory speech was
decisive in its accusations and bit very deep into the pride of
the ORTF administration. 'On ne peut pas ne pas constater que
l'abaissement du niveau des programmes s'accompagne paral-
lèlement d'un envahissement systématique de la publicité,
qu'elle soit officielle ou clandestine. C'est la raison pour
laquelle votre commission a décidé de s'afforcer de limiter l'une
et d'empêcher l'autre de faire de cet irremplaçable instrument
de détente, de culture et d'information, un terrain de choix
pour le mercantilisme, l'affairisme et la vénalité.'[43]

As the scandal began to develop, a new twist occurred when a burglary took place at the offices of Havas, where, as well as a few pieces of property, there disappeared an enormous file of papers – the papers later turned up on the desk of M. de Bresson, the Director-General of the ORTF, without any explanation publicly offered. Two men were arrested by the police for the crime of burglary, but their names withheld. A few weeks later (17 December) the Senate empowered a group of its members under the leadership of M. Diligent to hold a full-scale inquiry. Meanwhile the affairs of the ORTF were put under the scrutiny of a Control Commission, composed of eleven members of the Assemblée who were charged with the task of reporting back, within four months, on a new charter and reorganisation of the ORTF. Viewers of French television began to watch their programmes with enhanced attention, as they watched the cameras engage in multiple contortions in efforts to avoid the brand names of vehicles, and the tyre posters at races and matches.

Meanwhile de Bresson set an inquiry of his own in motion which reported in March; the complex and insidious corruption was exposed and the guilty party named: M. Roland Pozzo di Borgo, the chief of Havas, who denied it all. About twenty employees of the ORTF were fired, reprimanded or moved to different departments. The virtue of a corruption scandal is that everyone with a special point of view of his own can, after the culprits are dealt with, explain how the underlying and long-standing causes of the rottenness are such as to prove his own exclusive recipe for curing the disease. M. Thibau found his way rapidly into print: 'Le scandale de l'ORTF n'est pas, pour l'essentiel, dans le pot de vin touché par X ou par Y. Il est dans le fait qu'un organisme national, lourd de responsabilités de réflexion, de libération et de joie, crée un univers où la sottise et l'ennui le disputent à l'insignificance (qui entraine à la suîte l'affairisme et la vénalité).[44] For Thibau, and indeed for many others, the issue was whether the new policy of out-and-out entertainment was a proper course for a public television channel to pursue; 'affairisme and vénalité' (Diligent's phrase originally) flowed naturally from a socially corrupt information policy. The problems however were not answered: Should

France adopt a system of mixed competing networks, private and public? Should there be two or three competing public systems? Should broadcasting be somehow separated from the state and if so, how should that be achieved in a state as centralised, bureaucratised and politically divided as France? Finally, how can autonomy or independence be granted to any enterprise in the Fifth Republic constituted as it is on the principle of personal power?

By June of 1972 the ORTF had been given its new statute, which continued to beg or ignore all the central issues. A new Director-General replaced the sacked de Bresson; Arthur Conte, a Gaullist who had once been a socialist. He was at once pilloried with his own phrase 'the strength of joy and entertainment' which reminded the French of an older German slogan. Desgraupes was removed, and left to do some medical programmes;[45] his assistant, Joseph Pasteur, joint architect of the liberated professionalism of Information Première, went off to the motor-car industry. About thirty of their colleagues were due to be declared redundant in a new streamlined news and information schedule. In their place there started arriving a trickle of Gaullists. The new third channel was put in the control of Jean-Louis Guillaud who had once been Pompidou's press officer and who had come to that job from the ORTF in 1968 where he had helped to draw up the list of the men who had led the strike and were to be sacked. The most interesting of the new appointments was that of M. Jean-Pierre Angrémy in a new post, Head of Programme Harmonisation. M. Conte introduced him to the staff of the ORTF without shedding too much light on his intended role in a special personal message.[46] In it he spoke of the need to maintain the monopoly of broadcasting in the teeth of continuing opposition. 'La bataille du monopole est devenue la mienne; il ne peut pas y avoir d'équivoque là-dessus. Vous ne serez, tous et toutes, avec vos familles, protégés, que si tous ensemble nous sauvons sauver, avec le monopole, l'unité de cette Maison.'

Conte understood the nature of popular journalism; the new ORTF chief once worked on *Paris-Match*, spent twenty-five years of his life as the mayor of a small southern town, and won a prize at the Monte Carlo television festival for a

185

documentary on the Conference at Yalta. He is not cast in the mould of the career civil servants who had traditionally run broadcasting in France. As an ardent supporter of Pompidou he had been brought back to Paris when Pompidou entered the Elysée. In November M. Conte had warned that one-sided coverage of national news at the ORTF had 'reached the limits of prudence.'[47] It was therefore felt inevitable that Desgraupes would be removed as soon as Conte arrived. He continued to promise, in every public communication, that his changes would be organisational only, that his policy would guarantee the accuracy and liberty of information.

The policy of autonomous units dealing with information was abandoned and Mlle Baudrier moved to a job on the first channel. The unions gave notice of a strike, of indefinite duration, awaiting elucidation of the mysterious role of the Programme Harmoniser.

The new programme chiefs had hardly entered their offices before a new scandal broke upon France, that launched by M. Aranda who went into hiding announcing that he possessed a huge pile of documents of a scandalous nature which would incriminate a series of prominent French citizens in acts of the profoundest corruption. He did not exclude leading figures of the world of French broadcasting. The unions announced that they possessed some hundreds of documents which would show systematically how the leading politicians of the Republic had been leaning on the ORTF to distort the flow of news, and manipulate public opinion. French broadcasting in half a century had found no neutral ground, no neutral institutions, and no neutral men.

It felt perhaps like the approaching crescendo of an old and familiar symphony: the theme was authoritarianism and the variations were chaos.

Chapter Seven

America: The People's Air

'Radio is not to be considered merely as a business carried on for private gain, for private advertisement, or for the entertainment of the curious. It is to be considered as a public concern, impressed with a public trust, and to be considered primarily from the standpoint of public interest.'
Herbert Hoover, Fourth National Radio Conference, November 1925

'If I could control the medium of the American motion picture, I would need nothing else in order to convert the entire world to Communism.'
Joseph Stalin

Every week 400,000,000 people around the world watch the American western 'Bonanza'.[1] NBC, the American network, whose overseas sales include 'Bonanza', is active in nearly 90 countries and provides material for 300 stations outside America.[2] CBS sells its programmes to 100 nations.[3] ABC's subsidiary *Worldvision* has major holdings in 64 television and 30 radio stations outside America.[4] American television is the best known in the world. The Peruvian peasant is united with the Egyptian fellahin and the Polish dockworker through the medium of American television. 'American television has made the development of a Canadian cultural identity almost impossible,'[5] cries an anguished Canadian, terrified of the hungry cultural Leviathan lying along his frontier. American television invades the screens of half of the world; the enormous concentration of skill and capital which creates an endless flow of thousands of hours of expertly manufactured entertainment programmes, westerns and serials is the basic fodder of a kind of televised world culture.

187

When most people are watching the television screen they are seeing something which has emerged from an alien culture, the product of a colossal American industry which no single person has ever planned or can even fully understand. Nonetheless it emerges from a single economic mechanism, coupled with a specific response to the problem of how to reach and hold the American mass audience, and it produces the range of styles and themes which fill the screens of the world. The software of the world's television is to a very great extent manufactured by a communications complex which emanates from an American economy and American mythology; it is not fully accountable even to its own people, still less to the countless millions whose minds are filled with its imagery and presumably its values. America's domestic cultural condition is thus linked to the world's network of communications, especially that part of it which provides entertainment within the third world. All the messages of television, highly processed by the institutions and public control systems of the United States, radiate into nations for which they were not at first designed.

The enormous and diverse system of American television is based on an extreme version of the ideal of cultural freedom, but provides for the overwhelming mass of American viewers and listeners a stultifying sameness which appears to be far more the victim of a kind of censorship than the product of other television systems which are more overtly controlled by public authorities.

American television provides the spectacle of a bewildering myriad of conflicting sectional initiatives, thousands upon thousands of independent stations (all possessing the capacity to originate programmes), a brace of networks, independent and competing for the attention of a vast audience, scores of independent programme-making organisations with limitless capital, fabulous quantities of writing talent, and no state officials to coerce them, a loose system of public control which encourages more and more groups of people to get their hands on newly created stations. Yet the end-product betrays the signs of an appalling cultural tyranny. It is impossible to grasp the nature of the broadcasting dilemma, as it has been described in the preceding chapters, without discovering how this machinery actually works. In the complex web of relationships, it is possible to identify five separate elements which together constitute the American television industry.[6]

It is necessary first to look at the relationship between the individual stations and the great networks. Secondly there is a group of pressures which exist to link the stations and the networks to the advertising agencies and the sponsors. Thirdly one has to measure the impact of the FCC, the chief regulatory agency on the whole industry. Only then does it become possible to see how the fourth relationship works, that between the creative individual, the writer and the system. Lastly there is a series of questions concerning censorship – external, internal and anticipatory – which bear upon the total model. This is the machine which conjured 'Bonanza' into existence, and makes the western a dominating cultural genre of the twentieth century. This is the machinery with which Vice-President Agnew attempted to grapple. This is the source of the dominating world image of America and American society which is influencing the course of world political history.

The model I describe in this chapter applies only to the commanding heights of American broadcasting – prime time network television. There are other elements in the American television industry, there is public broadcasting, and the beginnings of cable and cassette television. There is also a large movement seeking to change the system radically from within, which is already beginning to exercise various forms of countervailing power to challenge the rigidity and supremacy of the underlying structure. These are the subject of the following chapter. They are all reactions to the leviathan strife of the three major networks whose peculiar impact upon American and world culture is the result of the coercive operation of this central mechanism, deeply rooted in American society.

The American system takes an extreme, indeed distorted, Millian view of the central dilemmas of broadcasting; it takes the purest and most abstract conceptions of freedom of expression and places them inside a high-pressured commercial tyranny.

The American system, founded on the strictest application of the doctrine of personal cultural freedom, has found itself so nervous of initiating new formulae lest these cause irreparable damage to the sale of advertising time (which in 1970 totalled 3,336,600,000 dollars[7]) that a single programme series can run for years. ABC has been showing 'Bewitched' for seven years, NBC has given its viewers the 'Dean Martin Show' for six years, the 'World of Disney' for ten and 'Bonanza' for twelve. CBS has been churning out 'Mission Impossible' for five years, 'My Three Sons' for eleven, 'Gunsmoke' for sixteen, and 'Lucille Ball' (under various titles) for no less than twenty years.[8] The collective financial and social pressures which operate within the system cause a stultifying contraction of all creative thinking into mechanistically contrived 'strands' outside which all risks are too great financially to run. A shift in the average ratings for a single network throughout the season of 0.1 per cent can cause it to make or lose 1.8 million dollars.[9] It is hardly surprising that the system runs on formulae which once successful can be guaranteed to continue capturing audiences virtually for generations. To effect any substantial change in the network's perception of the nature and needs of the audience or in the networks' willingness to broaden their creative access would involve a major shift in the economic and administrative structure in which they operate. To change an important television series is as difficult as to change the design of a motor-car, and almost as much is at stake financially. American television is a more industrialised process than the television of any other society; it operates under a cultural ethic but it is a manufacturing industry, with tiers of middle-men through whose processed judgement the material passes from creator to market.

I

The ultimate responsibility for broadcasting in the United States devolves upon the management of the small local station, licensed by the Federal Communications Commission to serve a given community with programmes which conform to 'public interest, convenience, necessity'. During the main hours of television viewing, however, 95 per cent of all the programmes actually being seen emanate from the studios of a national

190

network, based in New York.[10] Legally the station manager in each of the 686 stations which are affiliated to the networks has to carry the can; in fact this, as one critic of American television has said, is rather like making the newspaper-hawker juridically responsible for the content of the papers which he sells. The network is not in practice trying to serve the individual station's local clientele; it is trying to reach for the largest possible section of the huge national American audience. Between 7.30 and 8.00 p.m., 75 million viewers are watching in the average minute; in the next 30-minute period the figure rises to 80 million and after that to 81 before starting a slow decline until 10.30 p.m. when only 57 million people are watching during the average minute. The networks' quest for audience is more subtle than a mere scramble for total figures. The most important section of the audience is the section with most money to spend, that aged between 18 and 49. At 7.30 only 36 per cent of the audience is within that age range; at 10 in the evening, when the audience reaches only 63 million per average minute, the percentage of those viewing who are aged between 18 and 49 rises to 50 per cent, as children and old people retire for the night. It is this lucrative pasture which enabled the networks alone to gather in a total of 1,144,600,000 dollars from advertising revenue in 1970, and to make in that year between them a profit of 50 million dollars on their network sales. Far more lucrative, however, are those stations which the networks own themselves (they are allowed to own no more than five VHF television stations each) in the major cities of America; these stations in 1970 gathered in 312,600,000 dollars in advertising, but left a total profit of 117,300,000 dollars.[11] The function of the individual station in practice is to provide an audience for the network to entertain; the local links and local roots of the individual station enable it to create a certain viewer loyalty and it is this which the local station sells to the network at so many dollars per thousand viewers. The end-product of the broadcasting industry is the audience. The station sells it to the network and the network sells it to the advertiser.

The value of each station affiliated to a network is assessed at regular intervals by one or other of the research organisations, Nielsen, Trendex, Hooper, Sindlinger, Simmons, TvQ, ARB;

191

of these, Nielsen is the biggest and provides the complex data on how many viewers watch which station throughout the country. It is an expensive process to collect viewing 'diaries' from hundreds of families and to maintain the 1,200 monitoring devices attached to specially selected sets in various parts of the country; it is only because Nielsen is large enough to run this whole service at a loss that it is possible to keep the information reliable and up-to-date. Nielsen considers its status within the television industry important enough to run the service entirely for the sake of its public image among the advertisers.[12]

The advertiser purchases his viewers at anything between $2\frac{1}{2}$ dollars per thousand unassorted to 8 dollars a thousand if they can be refined down to particular valuable categories[13] like middle-aged men, young women, etc., who can be more valuable in that form to sellers of specific products. The biggest advertisers, however, are manufacturers of foodstuffs which are sold to the vast middle-class 18–49 age range.

One of the problems that have increasingly troubled both networks and advertisers since about 1965 is the decreasing value in actual commercial results of every minute purchased on television. Studies of viewing habits which used to reveal a loss of about 20 per cent of all viewers during the commercial breaks have tended in recent years to increase that figure to anything up to 50 per cent.[14] An advertiser therefore finds that he has to spend a great deal more money to reach the same number of eyes and ears. One of the results of this has been a splitting of the commercials into tiny segments of twenty or thirty seconds, an advertiser devising very brief messages which are repeated over and over again during the day. A viewer in America is therefore exposed to an ever-increasing number of messages, sometimes up to twenty in an hour's television.

One of the reasons for this change is that the traditional sponsor has almost disappeared. Where once in the 1920s and 1930s a programme was introduced by an announcement to the effect that the listener or viewer owed the ensuing thirty minutes of entertainment to the manufacturer of a given product of which the virtues would be briefly extolled, today the programme, no longer belonging to any particular manufacturer, is merely a vehicle for a large number of advertising slots purchased by a succession of unconnected commercial firms, none of them concerned with the content itself.

Where in the 1930s Paley of CBS told an investigating committee that less than 1 per cent of all his broadcasting time was used by advertising, in 1966 the percentage (as measured by students at the Columbia University Graduate School of Journalism) was over 17 per cent on the three wholly-owned network stations in New York in the course of an 18-hour day. During the daytime hours the percentage rose to 24 per cent, including the period set aside for news broadcasts.[15]

Every station affiliated to a network may receive or reject any programme which the network sends out. If the station refuses to accept programmes on a scale which the network deems reasonable and profitable, then the station runs the risk of disaffiliation. This would leave it having to fill its prime hours by buying very old re-runs – or making its own programmes. The network gets an assessment of the individual station's audience rating several times a year, sometimes monthly. Each station works out a rate-card according to which it sells its advertising time. In a large city a station which can reach, say, 10 per cent of the available audience in an average evening (giving it a station rating of 10) will charge 2,000 dollars for every minute of advertising. Out of this about a quarter is given away to the advertising agency and to the station's own time-seller. When the station takes a programme from the network it receives compensation of about one-eighth of its own advertising during the period of the transmission – this is of course far less than it would cost the station to make its own programme. The network thus purchases its right to send out its product (and the attendant advertising) to a 10 rating, and the station receives cash without having to make its own programme for that segment of time.[16] At the same time the station's rating is only kept up to the mark because it is relied upon by its audience to provide certain popular network programmes. The networks, incidentally, have to pay large sums to their own fifteen wholly-owned VHF stations which amount to over 4 million a year each.

When a station takes a programme from the network it loses the right, of course, to sell the advertising time within the programme, apart from one segment normally of two minutes which the network allows it to retain to sell locally. In a normal one-hour programme, six minutes of time are sold, in three blocks. The network pre-sells four of these minutes, and can usually, in prime time, raise 50–60,000 dollars for each minute.

If a local station decides to take the bulk of its programmes from the network it enjoys the additional advantage of being able to cut down on its overheads; it can avoid the expense of an elaborate studio, performers and writers. It has a good guaranteed income, so long as the network holds up its standards of attractiveness to the viewers. American television is extremely profitable at almost every level. A station which cost a million dollars to create in the 1950s, which was the period in which most of the available VHF wavelengths were given away, is worth at least 12 million dollars by the 1960s. The special stations owned by the networks themselves, which are all situated in cities like New York, Washington, Los Angeles, Chicago, are worth breath-taking sums of money. They are virtually priceless; the total capital equipment involved in each of them need not be more than a few million dollars. The NBC station in Kansas City, for instance, which cost 150,000 dollars to put on the air was sold in the late 1960s for 7.6 million.[17] It is the franchise granted by the FCC which is the source of their value, a socially-owned right given away to a private company and virtually irretrievable thereafter.

The primacy of the local station is the key to the American system. It appealed originally to the democratic instinct of Americans to distribute the valuable and extremely powerful agency of broadcasting to the community leaders around the nation. The boards of directors of the local stations are made up of local 'bigwigs', prominent figures in industry, education and administration. Any controversy stirred up by the station within its community neighbourhood is immediately apparent to them. The pressures against cultural vanguardism (which need not mean very much) are rapidly visited upon the owners of the local stations who are the gatekeepers of the entire content of the broadcast system.

One quarter of all the television stations in the United States are owned by newspapers. In the twenty-five most lucrative television markets (which contain most of the population of America) 35 per cent of all the television stations are owned by newspapers.[18] It need not be stressed that newspapers in America, as elsewhere, have undergone in the post-war period a period of growth of concentration into powerful groups and an absolute decline in numbers. In the press, as in television, the underlying motivation for a system in which the dissemination of information was placed in the widest possible control is being frustrated by processes of centralisation which are increasingly leaving whole informational and cultural industries in ever fewer hands.

II

In examining the television networks and their place in the broadcasting system one must emphasise first their huge size and vast profits, and secondly the fact that they are but small excrescences on the bodies of much larger enterprises. NBC, which has existed as an important radio and television network since the 1920s, represents just 2 per cent of the total turnover of its owner, the Radio Corporation of America.[19] RCA sells household appliances and aerospace systems. It owns the Random House publishing company (and other smaller publishing houses), Arnold Palmer Enterprises, the Hertz car-rental enterprise, the Hoffman-La Roche drug company, and RCA Victor records. It has a vast array of overseas investments and is active in nearly 100 countries. It is an important supplier of the American department of defence. It is difficult to imagine a major item of world news in which the RCA does not have a direct financial involvement.

CBS owns a publishing house (Holt, Rinehart & Winston), film studios, The Fender Musical Instrument Company and a series of magazines. Until 1973 it owned the New York Yankees baseball team. It has subsidiaries in 18 countries. It has a block of shares in the credit affiliates of General Motors, Ford and Chrysler, and has a major subsidiary which fulfils contracts in aerospace and defence.

The third major network, ABC, which was originally formed when NBC was forced in 1940 by the FCC to divest itself of one of

195

two networks of radio stations which it controlled, is similarly diversified. There was a point at which it was about to merge with IT & T but this was stymied by FCC intervention in 1967. It owns four hundred cinemas, a dozen overseas subsidiaries, record companies, magazine publishing houses, and a series of tourist resorts. The merger would have allowed IT & T to take over 17 radio and television stations, wholly owned by ABC.

Three-quarters of the total revenues of the networks arise from activities outside broadcasting, and some of them are in certain respects actually deleterious to the interests of broadcasting.[20] It is of direct pecuniary interest to all three networks that defence spending should remain high, to promote certain authors whom they publish, as well as specific sports in which they have a stake (mainly golf and baseball) and music based upon electronic instruments. They must at times be tempted to further the interests of the films they make. A series of foreign governments might be thought to be heavily involved in the extra-mural activities of the networks; the disappearance of certain régimes in Africa and Asia would deal a financial blow to the network owners. Yet the networks, responsible as they are for the content of most of the television seen by most of the people of America, are free of government licensing. It is the stations who are under the scrutiny of the FCC, lax and trivial though that itself may be.

When a network starts a new series of programmes a major risk investment is involved. Hundreds of thousands of dollars are spent on pilots and try-outs. A distant visitor unfamiliar with the culture of American television might not be able to discern easily the differences between the successes and the failures, but these are acutely visible to the network chiefs who are engaged in an extremely fierce competitive struggle to maintain and increase each network's share of the American audience.

Take an example of a 30-minute series which, when it is in full spate, will cost 80,000 dollars for each episode. The network can rake in up to 180,000 dollars[21] for the three advertising minutes which it will contain, but it has to pay every station which takes the programme the agreed compensation rate (of about one-eighth of the station's own times rates). If, however, the network repeats the programme the costs will probably drop to 20,000 dollars and the advertising for the three minutes will drop only to 120,000 dollars. The network will therefore benefit to a very similar extent from an old programme as from a new one. This is one of the pressures which help to make American television not merely bland but highly repetitive.

Even in peak viewing hours repeats or 'reruns' have reached an extremely high proportion. The FCC has been attempting to find legal devices for limiting reruns to 25 per cent of prime time, hitherto without success. In the autumn of 1972 reruns reached 50 per cent of total network peak-hour broadcasting time.[22] The Screen Actors Guild in the course of the 1972 election campaign made the problem of unemployment an issue of some political importance, blaming reruns for the increasing rate of worklessness among actors and producers. President Nixon found it necessary to make a public statement denouncing the extent of the practice and endorsing a proposal which would force the proportion back to 25 per cent. At one time the networks would run new programmes for 39 weeks of the year and spend the whole of the 'off-season' of 13 weeks repeating some of the most popular programmes. That season then gradually shrank to 26 weeks, then to 24. The unions in Hollywood were trying to restrict the repeat period to 13 weeks through FCC intervention. The industry's reply was that this would merely restrict the growth of a new spirit of adventurousness which was in fact beginning to creep into the schedule of the networks. Instead of running 39 new episodes in each series the networks might still confine themselves to 13 and fill in the rest of the time with sports and foreign productions. President Nixon's pressure was exerted at the precise moment when, under the influence of some short series purchased from the BBC, American television was beginning to show a glimmer of interest in adaptations of classic novels. It had scheduled a series of 200 'culturals' which the networks had acquired for the 1972–3 season.

The cost of launching a programme and the fear of having to restart a series or replace it obliges the network chiefs to find programmes which will last for long periods of time. The same central character, or group of characters, the same arrangement of plots will repeat endlessly and mindlessly for years. If the network is offered a European product, say, the BBC's 'War and Peace', its concern is not merely with the attractiveness of the programmes to its viewers, which may be as successful in America as in Europe, but with the problems involved in replacing 'War and Peace' when it is finished. The network can lose large sums simply by having to start introducing the audience to a new programme. The temptation is to run 'War and Peace' and then some kind of endless continuation of it, in which the characters, once launched, will continue their lives week by week in a creatively impoverished but financially effective, eternal domestic drama. The family serial is born of pressures of this kind; it means that the viewer's habits are never broken. And it is the viewer's decision to watch his screen for a given period of time which is itself the end-product of the whole broadcasting industry.

At an earlier period in American broadcasting most advertising was created through a 'sponsor' who owned the programme in which he advertised; he had a stake in it and it was in his interest to make the programme as enjoyable as possible and render the advertising as unirritating as possible. At the same time the sponsor had total editorial rights over the programme. Today that system has eroded away to a very great extent, certainly in peak hour time, where the normal procedure is for the network to create the programme and sell time within it in short segments of one minute or a half-minute.

There is, however, discernible at present the growth of a new system whereby an advertiser will create and produce his own programme and pay its entire production cost himself, taking one or two segments of internal advertising for his own use, and allowing any station willing to take the programme to do so; inside the programme he leaves two minutes free for the station to sell at pure profit to itself. The attraction of this system is that the advertiser can dispose of the programme exactly in those markets in which he wishes to sell his goods at any moment; the advertiser is also freed from the obligation to purchase advertising time because his advertisements come packaged into the programme which he is distributing.

The networks have so much at stake in every change they

might be tempted to make in the style and choice of their programmes that, apart from political pressure which has to be exerted with very great force, only the fear of a sudden and dramatic change in popular taste will induce them to alter their set patterns. For a network to try to change its own ways involves a considerable financial risk, one which is normally institutionally impracticable; no network chief could survive professionally the corporate losses resulting from a bad risk taken solely on cultural grounds.[23] The attempt by the ABC network to improve the quality of the cinema films it was due to present in the 1972–3 season provides an interesting example of the problem.

For many years the networks had been obliged to purchase old cinema films (extremely important in terms of their revenue) in bulk; in order to keep the average price of a network showing (plus one repeat) down to 800,000 dollars the networks would be forced to buy a group of extremely third-rate films in a package with the good ones. When in the summer of 1971 the ABC network, which had been for some years lagging behind the other two in the annual race for supremacy, decided to make a major bid to draw even with its rivals, the broadcasting world was startled to discover that ABC appeared to be in the midst of an amazing buying spree.[24] Before NBC and CBS fully realised what was happening ABC purchased a group of films in the course of five days at enormous prices. *Love Story, Lawrence of Arabia, Funny Girl, Ten Commandments, Odd Couple, Patton,* and seven James Bond films were snapped up; knowledgeable observers estimated that 50 million dollars had changed hands, putting the average price of each film many times the normal average for a prime time showing. ABC's tactic was to make its season's offerings so attractive to the viewer that it could show them more often than was normal and could attract a higher advertising rate. Five million dollars was known to have been paid for *Lawrence of Arabia* alone, for the right to show the film five times over the course of several years, and to divide it into two parts. *Love Story,* which cost three million dollars, was to be shown four times. General Motors agreed to buy advertising time on one of the films, *Patton,* for no less than 150,000 dollars per minute, nearly three times the normal rate. ABC's

199

extraordinarily hard-fought struggle to inch itself ahead left it extremely exposed to financial disaster. The effort to improve 'quality', however, left the American viewer with an even higher proportion of repeated material than normal, albeit spread over a number of years. A successful cinema film can be extremely important to a network's ratings because a single film fills two hours of prime time; if the film wins the network race for those two hours then the entire evening's programmes will win. A single two-hour film can alter the averages for a whole week by 1.5 rating points.[25]

III

American television presents the spectacle of a series of helpless giants; no single agency is in control of the system; no one knows all that is happening at any moment; no one possesses simultaneously the right and the actual opportunity to intervene. In the 1920s the Supreme Court ruled that no one, not even the President, had the right to distribute or withhold licences.[26] The air-waves chaos which resulted rapidly changed the position and a Federal Radio Commission was set up to regulate the distribution of franchises. Licences were to last for three years only. When Herbert Hoover pleaded for freedom for radio he meant freedom for the public, not for the individual station-owner. When radio was first regulated under the acts of 1927 and 1934 (when the present Federal Communications Commission was set up) it was intended that the air would continue to belong to the people, though lent for given periods of time to individuals.[27] It was never intended that privately-owned industrial empires would be constructed upon publicly-owned airways. It was never intended that the actual programmes would be made, not by the companies to whom licences had been given, but by vast conglomerate corporations whose activities lie outside the jurisdiction of any official agency.

It was inimical to the Federal Constitution for any governmental agency to have the power to intervene in an editorial process, and so the FCC was deprived of any power other than of regulating the wavelengths themselves, apart from the fact that under the 1934 Act the phrase 'public interest, convenience, necessity' was inserted, which has in the course of time given the FCC a lever to interfere occasionally with the content of the wavelengths it controls. It made sporadic efforts to assert a kind of creative supremacy, but most of these have failed dismally. In 1946 the FCC issued The Blue Book, a carefully argued document (drafted originally by Charles Siepmann who had held prominent posts in Reith's BBC) which was designed to force, and to state its right to force, the stations to pay far greater attention to public affairs and to a sense of their own social responsibility, on pain of losing their licences. The Blue Book created a huge stir among the broadcasters (i.e. the station-owners) and a succession of expensive legal cases gradually whittled away the editorial power which the FCC had acquired in its one giant step. Of course, it was not seeking to 'edit' actual programmes, but merely to ensure that the total content of the radio stations contained more news and public affairs material than had been the case in the 1930s and early 1940s. The FCC never repudiated The Blue Book, but merely let it slide, through juridical exhaustion, into disuse.

It has long been thought that broadcasting should have been given some form of 'common carrier' status, like the railways, the truck services, the telephone and the telegraph, but it was decided that since the broadcasting stations were concerned not merely with operating a transmitting service but actually making programmes themselves, broadcasting was not a 'common carrier' of public goods or services, but a means of expression. If the stations had, or could be made to acquire 'common carrier' status, they would be obliged to allow themselves to be used for the discussion of public issues.[28] In fact, with the domination of the networks over the programmes carried for large parts of the day over most of the system, pressures are now being exerted once again to transform the status of broadcasters to that of 'common carriers'.[29] As it is, broadcasters can operate as private companies, with very little obligation to disclose their profits, programming policies or operating records to public scrutiny. Yet when their right to operate so privately is questioned they have simultaneously the further right to plead that the First Amendment which guarantees freedom of speech and of publication covers their right to exact the greatest possible profit out of their licence to use the public air. They have their cake and they eat it.

It is believed that nearly one quarter of all the members of Congress have personal pecuniary involvement in radio or television.[30] It has been extremely difficult to build up in America a powerful regulatory body at the centre of the system, even though the FCC could have theoretically built upon its scanty powers and turned itself into something more closely resembling the British Independent Broadcasting Authority. In fact the seven members of the FCC have, over their forty years' existence, had every temptation to leave the system relatively unpoliced. Many of them have, on retirement, been offered extremely lucrative jobs within the industry which they were appointed to keep under scrutiny.[31] John F. Kennedy commissioned a study of the FCC from James Landis before his inauguration and was told that 'no other organisation had been more subject to pressures, more subservient to industry, and more in need of reform than the FCC'.[32]

The FCC's task is basically to handle nearly one million applications for broadcasting licences every year, and for their renewal. Most of the licences are for private two-way radios in use by industry or public authorities. (24 out of the 30 million channel miles of communications circuitry in America are owned by the Department of Defence.)[33] When Newton Minow resigned as Chairman of the FCC under Kennedy (a job he had taken on with the intention of putting teeth into the broadcast regulation system) he suggested separating the functions of the FCC, so that a new agency would have exclusive concern with broadcast administration.[34] The suggestion has never been adopted. The FCC continues to act as a kind of court, judging disputes between rival powers, but also trying at times to make the laws which the various parties involved in broadcasting are expected to keep; it also has to act as a general administrator of the broadcasting system. Newton Minow in his letter of resignation told Kennedy: 'I do not believe it is possible to be a good judge on Monday and Tuesday, a good legislator on Wednesday and Thursday, and a good administrator on Friday.'[35]

An applicant for a broadcast licence has to fill in a number of official forms. If it is a lucrative franchise there will be a number of willing contenders, some of whom will have amalgamated into large conglomerate groups before the actual hearings at the FCC begin. In the case of a television station, the case will cost all the applicants hundreds of thousands of dollars. A staggering amount of official activity is involved on the part of the government agency also. Hearings are held on a public record before a trained examiner, appeals and further arguments can then be made to the FCC and before the courts. The transcripts run to thousands of pages. Cases can last for a decade or more. In one of the very rare cases in which an existing broadcaster was ousted from his licence, when Boston Broadcasters Inc. took over the Boston station previously held by WHDH, owned principally by the Boston *Herald Traveller*, there were seventeen years of litigation before the new station holders took over their franchise in March 1972.[36] The complete 40,000 pages of testimony and exhibits would make a tower twenty feet high. It is impossible for a Commissioner at the FCC to cope with the mountainous paperwork involved. It is hardly surprising that the work of supervising the stations which actually exist is discharged perfunctorily. The stations must supply complete logs of their broadcasting activities when applying for relicensing after three years, but stations tend to be relicensed wholesale, virtually without inspection or even consideration of their record. Only in the very rare cases when franchises are challenged does the FCC actually have to confront the record in creative programme terms of the station involved.[37] If the station is one of the six to seven hundred network affiliates, it will hardly in any case be the right agency at which to complain of the quality of most of the actual programmes broadcast during the three years under review. Newton Minow described the work of the FCC as that of 'the responsiblity to award television channels, to decide who shall possess this unobstructed, no-speed-limit, multilane superhighway to men's minds. The FCC must determine who speaks to America; this means denial of the claims of all others scrambling fiercely for this same priceless privilege.'[38]

Since Minow lambasted the networks for a few fruitless years in the early 1960s, a great industry of pressure upon the FCC has built up, some of it from inside that bastion of apparently ineffective overwork. Much of it has been able to build itself upon an important tradition within FCC doctrine, which had been well established already – the tradition of the 'fairness doctrine'.

The doctrine emerged through the years after a number of licence renewal cases had brought up the question of editorialising. At one point, after a long struggle for the right to editorialise, the FCC, in turning down an application by the Mayflower Broadcasting Company for the franchise of WAAB in Boston, used the station's record of editorialising as part of the case for its disqualification, thereby inhibiting the practice of station editorials throughout the United States.[39] Later cases gradually reversed this inhibition, until in June 1949 the Commission issued a detailed report[40] on the obligations of broadcast licensees in regard to 'news, commentary and opinion'. The FCC argued now that since a broadcasting station should not be deemed a common carrier, it was the station which had the public responsibility of deciding what percentage of a broadcasting day should be devoted to public issues and what voices should be heard on such public issues. It was therefore necessary for every licensee to determine in what way the 'public interest, convenience and necessity' which it was already enjoined under the Act of 1934 to promote, would apply to its obligation to provide facilities for a number of voices to be heard on important public questions. 'Licensee editorialisation is but one aspect of freedom of expression by means of radio. Only insofar as it is exercised in conformity with the paramount right of the public to hear a reasonably balanced presentation of all responsible viewpoints on particular issues can such editorialisation be considered to be consistent with the licensee's duty to operate in the public interest.'[41] Out of this set of considerations was the 'fairness doctrine' born, which henceforth forced every station to provide time for contrary viewpoints to be presented on any issues on which a partisan position had been expressed.

Successive interpretations of the doctrine laid down more precisely the methods which had to be employed to ensure that fair opportunities were provided for response to be made to personal attacks and partisan editorials. Throughout the years of development of television the FCC gradually codified its new rules, sometimes hardening them, sometimes softening them.[42] An enormous amount of public effort was devoted to achieving reforms of the entire broadcasting system by building upon the doctrine. In the next chapter we shall examine some of the efforts to undermine the whole commercial basis of American broadcasting, by successive accretions of case law which have attempted to spread the doctrine to cover the content of commercials as well as programmes.

It was a slender basis upon which to try to create an editorial centre at the heart of American broadcasting without infringing the even more precious founding doctrine of pure freedom of expression and publication. The more powerful and intrusive the doctrine became, the greater the pressure against it. Together with a parallel doctrine, that of 'access' which has been gaining ground in many pieces of case law over the last decade, the whole involvement of the FCC in the business of laying down standards of content has attracted hostility and repugnance as fast as it has gained in clarity and in its general spread. Thus Dr Clay T. Whitehead, who was appointed by Nixon to preside over the White House Office of Telecommunications Policy, declared that 'Big Brother himself could not have conceived a more disarming newspeak name for a system of governmental programme control than the fairness doctrine'.[43] Whitehead's job has been to supervise the electronic media for the Nixon administration and although the doctrine is now firmly established in the industry it is clear that it is beginning to interfere with commercial as well as editorial freedom and is gathering very powerful enemies.[44]

One of the effects of the Agnew speech of November 1969 was to strengthen the stations in their warfare with the networks. It was the three networks who earned the Vice-President's eloquent jibes of 'effete snobbery', the 'tiny enclosed fraternity of privileged men', and it was the stations who by implication were allowed to appear relatively innocent. Pressure increased in the aftermath of Des Moines for the stations to be given greater responsibility for broadcasting, and for the power of the networks to be reduced. By a strange irony many stations had not shown the Agnew speech in the evening prime time at which the networks unanimously agreed to pump it out; it happened to be the week during which a large number of stations were to be assessed for their rating, and the station managers, thinking that the Vice-President's long address might well cause the viewing figures to drop, unilaterally decided to defer the speech for several days until a less crucial viewing time.

For some years a new rule had been fighting its way through the machinery of the FCC,[45] a rule which would forbid the networks to supply more than three of the four prime viewing hours in an average evening, instead of the three and a half hours of programmes which the stations normally took from them. The new rule is known variously as the Westinghouse Rule and the Prime Time Access Rule. The effect of the Des Moines speech of Agnew was to speed the rule on its way; the FCC adopted it and henceforth every station was obliged to find its own programme for that extra thirty minutes of prime time. The intention was that the stations would do their own local news programmes and thereby water down the enormous centralised political power of the networks as regards news and public affairs. The FCC however has no power to instruct the stations to spend the time on news, merely to forbid them to take a network programme for that period of time.

The rule was due to come into force on 1 September 1971, and many thought that it would be rescinded before its date of commencement. The networks (CBS and NBC) had vowed to challenge the rule as an unconstitutional infringement of their freedom of expression. The chairman of the FCC thought that, within a few months, the political complexion of his colleagues on the commission would alter through expiration of tenure,[46] at least enough to obtain a reversal of their decision. But very great pressure was building up to maintain the new rule. A powerfully persuasive weapon was placed in the hands of its supporters when the Justice Department wrote to Dean Burch, the FCC Chairman, informing him that its Antitrust Division would be taking a friendly interest in the progress of this attempt to decrease the power of the networks.[47] (The Prime Time Access Rule also forbade the networks from syndicating programmes as well as networking them.) The FCC's reaction was to reaffirm the rule and to delay it by one month.

The rule, when it finally came into force, simply mocked the energy which had been consumed in the struggle for its enactment. The stations used the extra half-hour as an excuse for an extra quiz programme and/or an extra celebrity talk-show to fill the empty slot. The syndicators of 30-minute programmes discovered a new guaranteed market for fifth reruns of 'I Love Lucy', for 'rested' material, for tryout programmes of sufficiently popular appeal to increase local advertising revenue without adding anything to the general informational or cultural level of the total programming.

The FCC found the rule almost impossible to administer. It decided to waive the rule altogether in the case of the network decision to run 'The Six Wives of Henry VIII', purchased from the BBC, on the grounds that it was 'distinctive and meritorious'; 'Wild Kingdom' was similarly given special dispensation but 'Lassie' was refused. Old films which had not been shown within a particular station's area for two years were exempted, but in the top fifty television 'markets' the networks were banned from showing films during the 'access' half-hour. The FCC then found itself in a muddle over whether a film which had been made for television in the first instance, although two hours long, was permissible in circumstances when a similar film, which had been made primarily for theatrical showing, was not. The system quickly became arbitrary, confused and dictatorial. *Variety* magazine was able to run a headline 'US Government in TV Programming'.[48] That was not what the fathers of the Constitution desired at all, nor the authors of the Prime Time Access Rule.

It seemed that every effort to use the existing machinery as a means of policing the system in the interests of improved quality collapsed in the face of the structural realities of American broadcasting. Each effort seemed to undermine its own intention, or to become excessively intrusive of important public doctrine.

IV

In looking at the actual process of programme-making within network broadcasting, the first vital and surprising

207

statement to be made is that the networks make virtually none of the programmes. Although the network exists with all the trappings and paraphernalia of an editorial body, the manufacturer of a cultural product of vast significance, it prefers, outside its news division, to act as impresario and commissioner of work, not as a direct employer of writers, producers and actors. The networks, residing in New York, in expensive magnificence, stand at the top of a very deep well from which they extract such talent as they feel will be conducive to the winning of the ratings battle at a given moment in time. They do not nurture and protect budding writers. They select goods, package them and advertise them and cast them away when the audience ceases to want them in sufficiently large numbers to sustain the network's position in the ratings war.

Much of the programme-making goes on in Hollywood, three thousand miles away from the headquarters of the three networks. It is concentrated in a variety of organisations, many of them owned by writers and producers themselves. The creative worker is thus turned into businessman competing with other businessmen. Scripts are hawked around production companies and network offices. The world of American television was born into that of a fading film industry and the patterns of work were based to a considerable extent on those of the cinema of the 1940s. Whereas in Britain much of the pressure to build into television a tradition of new quality writing has come from writers themselves, in America the writer, although for a time he did exert great pressure upon the system, has been turned into part of the machinery. American television produced an important dramatic flowering in the early post-war period but recent years have seen both the degradation of the writer within the system and the elevation of the writer as another entrepreneur within the economy of mass entertainment goods. Whereas in some systems the writer is the voice at least of some real section of the public whose experience is expressed or reflected on the screen, the system of the United States tends to sever the writer altogether from his public and make him virtually a (very wealthy) proletarian in an industry. The American public thus is doubly disenfranchised, both by the sequestration of its airtime by private companies remote from public supervision, and by the shutting off of the strands of creativity which should bind the community of the creative to their society.

V

Two great blows struck the world of American television at the very point at which the new medium was ready to develop in its own right and was causing considerable disruption to both cinema and radio. The first was the wave of McCarthyism which spread throughout the media; writers were sacked together with producers and technicians; a tight net of silent persecution caused the destruction of many careers, especially of individuals with a record of spirited and critical work.[49] Then came the quiz scandals, when it was revealed that the most successful of all the programmes on the burgeoning new medium of television, programmes which were earning the networks revenues beyond their dreams, had been totally 'rigged', the brilliant question-answerers being fed with the answers in order to improve the spectacle.[50] Both episodes caused a wave of nausea throughout the United States which tended to separate the 'serious-minded' from television; the very group whose talents, if applied to the task of criticising television and contributing to it, might have forced the medium to serve its public better, turned away from the medium altogether, and stayed away.

The group which called itself 'Aware Inc.', formed in 1953 and led by Vincent W. Hartnett who had contributed to the notorious 'Red Channels', started compiling dossiers on writers, actors and directors working in television. It issued bulletins containing details of its 'suspects', who were instantly removed from the employment lists of radio and television companies. The harassment drove a new school of dramatists completely out of television into the cinema. Paddy Chayevsky (whose play 'Marty' was first written for the television 'Anthology' series) together with Ted Allen, Rod Serling and a small group of highly talented colleagues moved from television never to return.[51] Sponsors had in any case complained that the portrayal of American characters leading fulfilled lives in low financial status inhibited the purchase of goods. A period began in which the commercial structure of television shaped not merely the timings and forms but the essential ideology and content of the screen.

It was in the world of news that this brand of 'censorship' was first challenged professionally. Fred Friendly[52] and Ed Murrow at CBS began building up a style of television news presentation which brought about the development of documentary and journalistic techniques of an investigatory and 'trouble-making' kind. They had a healthy tradition of muckraking American journalism to inspire them. The series 'See It Now' was instrumental in the breaking of the power of McCarthy. Gradually the commercial pressures encircled and strangled Friendly's movement; he walked out of the presidency of CBS News in 1965 after the last of many conflicts over the extent of news coverage; the Vietnam war had greatly increased public interest in the coverage of major events, and the development of television techniques made possible a presentation of the war and the political background to it which frightened many politicians and ultimately invoked the controversy over the role and nature of television which we find ourselves in the midst of at the present time. Friendly's quarrel with the CBS management[53] was over whether one set of committee hearings on Vietnam should be allowed to replace scheduled peak-hour programmes. The loss of revenue involved in televising the hearings would have been on a scale which CBS was not prepared to tolerate. Network profits had continued rising dramatically throughout the decade. But the three managements were locked in a mortal conflict which enabled none of them – so it appeared to them – to relax their commercial efforts for an evening. The total quantity of news on peak-hour television gradually decreased between 1965 and 1970 to an average of 2 per cent.[54]

The underlying problem was that a large number of network affiliated stations were beginning to find that they could make more money by selling advertising in their own local programmes than by taking network offerings. The networks were therefore having to provide ever-more attractive offerings to keep the loyalties of the stations in prime time.

From 1 January 1971, cigarette advertising on television in America was banned. At a stroke the income of the networks was cut by a sizeable percentage; ABC and CBS complained they had lost no less than 50 per cent of their total income compared with the same quarter the previous year.[55] Pressure began to mount to reduce or cease advertising altogether in children's programmes. The general economic outlook began in any case to decline. The pressure to decrease the amount spent on news and documentary work began accordingly to increase. CBS dropped its regular news polls. The size of all network news rooms was cut. The revenue from the fifteen owned and operated stations of the three networks dropped from 323.2 million dollars to 312.5 million, the first drop for many years.[56] Live news coverage decreased everywhere. CBS cut back by 15 per cent in all departments. The networks cancelled their airplanes for news work. ABC fired 35 people, including the head of their public affairs unit. News, which had been the chief element offsetting the declining standards of television in the early fifties and had created new political awareness in American society in the period of the Vietnam war, was being eclipsed, by the sudden jolt which the balance sheets of network broadcasting were experiencing. News had grown phenomenally between 1960 and 1968 in budgets and staff. The financial problems came simultaneously with the attacks from Agnew and from the Nixon administration in general. The American Civil Liberties Union issued a report 'The Engineering of Restraint'[57] in which they warned of the growing manipulation of all America's newsmaking media by the White House.

After the Agnew attack Dean Burch, Chairman of the FCC, asked all the networks to send him transcripts of their programmes dealing with the subject 'basically for information'. Meanwhile Herb Klein, head of the new Office of Communications in the White House, was given the job of centralising all the government's information agencies; throughout the world of American news reporting the new office was thought to be sinister and dangerously hampering to the freedom of reporters attempting to observe the activities of the administration.

Federal investigators subpoenaed the files of *Time* and *Life* and *Newsweek* magazines in the course of their investigations into the Weathermen.[58] CBS in January 1970 was similarly served with a subpoena for all the 'off-cuts' of a film it had made on the Black Panthers (CBS complied).[59] Justice Department officials approached the CBS correspondent Mike Wallace in an effort to make him testify in the trial of some of the Black Panthers.[60] A black reporter on the *New York Times* was held in contempt for refusing to testify in the trial of David Hilliard, one of the Panthers.[61] Throughout America there was a 'chilling effect' on journalism. Fred Powledge of the ACLU reported that the whole relationship between journalism and government had been deteriorating. 'The federal government has sought to change the rules of the old game. Attacks on the press by the officers of government have become so widespread and all-pervasive that they constitute a massive federal-level attempt to subvert the letter and spirit of the First Amendment.'[62]

It was, however, in Nixon's second term that the pressure against recalcitrant network news men really began to mount. Within weeks of his re-election, the White House inaugurated a new stick-and-carrots policy in an attempt to bring the news making organisations to heel. For some time, in the wake of the movement to challenge the renewal of station licences around the country, prominent licence-holders had been demanding a five-year renewal period, instead of the traditional three-year period. The stations were now beginning to feel vulnerable and there was pressure within the industry for the title of existing stations to be made judicially more secure. Dr Clay T. Whitehead at the Office of Telecommunication Policy promised new legislation to provide five-year licences so long as stations 'served the needs of their communities'; there would be no hard or precise requirements about how that responsibility should be fulfilled. In return for this easier enfranchisement Whitehead demanded that the stations 'jump on the networks' to ensure 'fairer news'. Stations which merely re-broadcast network news without questioning its 'fairness' or inquiring into 'ideological plugola' would conceivably find themselves having to answer for their neglect at renewal time. This kind of leverage against the powerful networks through their affiliates had been attempted in the past (and was faintly implied in Agnew's very first outburst) but no threat of such an explicit nature had ever been made before Whitehead's speeches which followed Nixon's re-election. The new strategy augured, however, a new round of pressure and counter-pressure between the administration and the broadcasting industry. Whitehead and the President were not likely to enjoy a once-for-all walkover victory.

The commercial mechanism by which American broadcasting is controlled operates according to a series of sudden paradoxes. While one aspect of radio and television was undergoing a sudden 'chill', other quite opposite side-effects were discernible. In 1972 a wave of liberalisation swept through the networks. The coverage of sexual themes suddenly became fashionable in television programmes. *Variety* magazine listed the newly available themes 'sex, bigotry, divorce, homosexuality, race consciousness and a trace of anti-establishment'.[63] There were traceable three quite separate causes of the liberalisation. In one sense the change was a reflection of the times; social mores had changed and television, however careful it had to be in a commercial system not to offend any section of opinion, had at some point to reflect the transformation. Then there was the fact that the networks were trying to find some new way to attract younger viewers who tended to eschew television and who were now desperately needed recruits to the ratings to restore fading revenues. The liberalisation was therefore in this way a reflection of the increasing, not decreasing grip of the commercial system over the culture of broadcasting. The third and most powerful reason for the change was that widespread concern over the growth of violence on the television screens of America had become effective in bringing about a deliberate reduction of crimes of violence portrayed on the screen and violent scenes in general. The networks were in search of new themes which would maintain the sensational nature of the regular series and this hunger rather than a deliberate mood of enlightenment lay behind the changes.

It meant that American viewers were able to see on ABC a drama which dealt explicitly with male adult homosexuality ('That Certain Summer') and NBC presented a medical drama dealing with lesbianism. A new CBS situation comedy 'Mash' adopted themes which involved mocking the military, attacking authority, and referring explicitly to sexual matters. Yet only

213

a few years previously television had censored divorce as a suitable theme. In the mid-sixties there had been a fashion for comedy series which centred upon children with a single parent, but the children always had to be orphans since no screen hero or heroine could be a divorcee. The same commercial pressures which had previously made certain themes taboo were now bringing them onto the screen. In response, in various parts of America, citizen groups were starting to spring up dedicated to stopping 'immorality on TV'. Mrs Mary Whitehouse, leader of the British campaign for 'moral standards' on television, the National Viewers' and Listeners' Association, was invited to go on a lecture tour.

The search for 'one big audience' which was the shaping characteristic of the system and the programme content had reached and perhaps passed its peak. It was no longer possible for the financial system to survive its own quest for audience maximisation. The very processes which had led America into the appallingly anodyne television of mass viewing was now forcing the break-up of the vast moral consensus on which it depended. The financially viable audiences were beginning to be sectional audiences and the internalised pressures dictated new kinds of programme content. In order to obtain young viewers, now necessary to the networks, a new style had to be introduced, together with new themes. It bore the mask of liberalisation but was basically a shift in the needs of the corporations whose mutual conflict is the central core of American broadcasting.

Although this chapter has concentrated only on the central core, there is a good deal else in the sheer profusion of American television. Prime time network broadcasting is the commanding height of American television. The other elements in American broadcasting exist as modifications of and alternatives to that mechanism. Throughout the period of greatest domination of the networks over the system, there were growing pressures for change and for additional sources of television altogether. These are the subject of the next chapter.

Chapter Eight

American Viewers in Revolt: Talking Back to the Networks

'Give me the making of
the songs of a nation,
and I care not who
makes its laws.'

Andrew Fletcher 1703

'So they came to Jerusalem, and he went into the temple
and began driving out those who bought and sold in the
temple. He upset the tables of the money-changers and the
seats of the dealers in pigeons; and he would not allow
anyone to use the temple court as a thoroughfare for
carrying goods. Then he began to teach them, and said,
"Does not Scripture say: My house shall be called a house
of prayer for all the nations? But you have made it a
robbers' cave." The chief priests and the doctors of the law
heard of this and sought some means of making away with
him; for they were afraid of him, because the whole crowd
was spellbound by his teaching. And when evening came he
went out of the city.'

St Mark 11: 15–19

I

The central mechanism by which the three major networks of
America shape the contents of American broadcasting, especially that of television, has been firmly established now for
several decades; it appears to be overwhelmingly powerful. The
average American child watches television for six hours per day,
and the adult for two and a half.[1] Nicholas Johnson, the
maverick FCC commissioner, is fond of quoting the statistic that
the average American watches three years of television before

215

he reaches his teens – he also sees between a quarter of a million and half a million commercials. The grip of television over the lives of the American nation appears unassailable, and unreformable. As the competing corporations struggle harder and harder for the attention of the viewer, the most powerful nation on earth, it seems, is caught inside a downward spiral of cultural degradation; the American nation's economic growth and its own sense of cultural health are pulling in opposite directions. There is however a different side to the picture, a complex of influences and countervailing powers which promise in the future, perhaps quite soon, a new shape to American broadcasting, and new sources of editorial power.

There are individuals and groups who are trying to create additional elements within the system of American broadcasting, the most important being the phenomenon of public television, which grew out of the chain of educational television stations licensed in the 1950s. Although only about 1 per cent of the public in America are regular viewers of their public stations the last few years has seen a checkered growth of activity, itself countered by deliberate attempts from the White House to restrict and divert the development of a fourth non-commercial network. Nonetheless the movement has made great headway.

Secondly there have sprouted up several small but energetic citizen groups determined to alter the balance of power within their communities, between the controllers and owners of local stations and the community itself; these have been campaigning for freer 'access' to television for local groups, as of right and free of payment.

Thirdly there have been, at national level, the activities of a small group of people led and inspired by Nicholas Johnson, the one FCC commissioner who has campaigned tirelessly to alter root and branch the existing system. He and his immediate colleagues have made the quality of American television a national issue (though not yet an electoral one) and have helped to generate the local groups who have sprung up to agitate about the state of American broadcast culture.

Fourthly, there has been a growth of activity at the FCC level, in which some of these groups have come together to challenge the licences of local stations at renewal time (every three years), which has helped to start to turn the FCC itself into a more vigilant body and which has created a certain turmoil within the management of the networks. This movement most importantly has brought about an increase in public knowledge of how the broadcasting system actually works in America. It has also helped to show the public how powerful grass-roots effort can be in the matter of reform.

Fifthly, there are attempts to undermine the financial basis of the networks by forcing though the courts a number of decisions which have the effect of bringing television commercials within the compass of the Fairness Doctrine. If this movement succeeds, future stations would have to give free time to citizen groups who wish to disseminate material to counteract the harm contained within commercials. This has not unnaturally led some of the officials in network broadcasting to start up a movement of counter-pressure, indeed of opposition, to the Fairness Doctrine altogether.

Finally there is the rapidly growing development of television distribution by cable, which, coming as it does when these other criticisms are beginning to play upon the system as a whole, could lead to important changes in the structure of broadcasting as a whole in America. The cable, with its capacity largely to increase the number of channels, can bring to the viewer far more than an increase in the number of programmes with better reception; it ushers in the possibility of a wholly new broadcasting culture; it could also become the means for making television an instrument for local and national political dialogue.

The overall effect of all these movements has not yet been to alter the content of broadcasting in any other than trivial ways, but it serves to indicate the extent to which an undercurrent of discontent with the standards of American television is bringing about the development of actual activity directed at altering the structural basis of the medium.

II

Throughout the history of broadcasting in America, there has been the development, parallel to the mainstream growth of

217

the networks, of stations of a totally non-commercial nature. Among the earliest experimenters in radio there were many universities and in the early years of radio a great number of them continued to run stations for internal campus purposes. In 1924 there were no fewer than 151 educational stations on the air. When the relicensing of all stations took place with the establishment of the Federal Radio Bureau in 1927, many of these stations were removed, never to return. Some were ordered to share their wavelength with commercial stations. Others which survived were reduced to very low level diffusion and still others fell by the wayside as it became impossible for them to purchase new and advanced technical equipment without the advertising income earned by rival commercial stations.[2]

Nonetheless a straggling tradition lingered on, even after the Act of 1934 dealt a further blow to the educational broadcasting movement by deciding to allocate no special section of the waveband for educational stations, on the grounds that the existing commercial stations would themselves make time available for educational purposes. Such hopes were quickly dashed. With the development of the FM waveband in the thirties about twenty frequencies were set aside, however, for educational users, and this served to keep the movement alive until the use of television brought about demands for its expansion.

The real basis for educational broadcasting was laid in the period of the Korean War when, for a period of four years, the granting of all television franchises was halted; the FCC, daunted by the sudden flood of applications for stations on the VHF band, decided to hold its hand, work out a new general policy towards the new UHF band, and then re-expand the television industry in a planned way.[3] The temporary freeze would enable the electronics industry to concentrate on the war effort. In fact, the pause did irreparable damage to the development of competition within American television, because it meant that in the great early growth period of television the new wavebands were omitted from sets; attempted legislation to force manufacturers to make available to their customers the new wave spectrum failed because at that time there were very few stations actually operating on it. When the UHF band was later allocated, the great majority of Americans had purchased sets; and the second generation of stations have as a result never developed the competitive potential of the VHF stations – relatively few of them have been courted by the networks to become affiliates. However, when the new band was allocated in 1952, 242 stations were reserved for educational broadcasting, at the vigorous insistence of FCC commissioner Frieda B. Hennock.[4]

Throughout the fifties these relatively low-powered and low-financed stations spread out across the country. They drew their finance from a number of different sources. They were joined by over 500 non-commercial radio stations. Of the television stations 62 were licensed to universities, 59 to non-profit local community organisations, 68 to municipal authorities, and 23 to school systems. Between them they reach 74 per cent of the American population. (The educational radio stations reach roughly the same proportion.)[5]

At the end of twenty years of existence the new stations were drawing a total income of over 100,000,000 dollars. 30 per cent of the sum came from state governments and boards of education and 20 per cent from local sources. The Ford Foundation spent nearly 9 million dollars a year on support for special institutions and projects at federal level. The average budget for one of these stations was 650,000 dollars a year. A good deal of money was contributed by the three networks as a gift; in New York the educational station benefited considerably from the generosity of its commercial rivals.[6] Nonetheless in comparison with the costs incurred by professional commercial stations, educational television in America was impoverished. So long as its role was merely instructional, a kind of teaching aid to fill the gaps in the local education system, this perhaps did not matter greatly. But as a rival system of general broadcasting, the non-commercial stations were hopelessly ill-equipped financially. Mary Mannes once called them 'the seedy beggars with the cultured voice'.[7]

Every community in America which possessed three commercial stations had been allotted an educational channel by the FCC. This meant that when a movement started up to provide some leaven to the increasingly unacceptable though commercially profitable mainstream television, there was an ample set of wavelengths available. Around these stations a controversy developed as to the proper role of publicly financed broadcasting within a commercial system. How did the new and growing force break into the Big Audience? Should it remain on the sidelines only? Anyone actually discontented with the networks was free to turn to educational broadcasting. But for the reformers, that was not the point. To try to improve the general quality of American broadcasting involved interfering with established patterns of popular choice, even when these were eloquently expressed in the profit margins of the networks and the commercial stations. To turn educational television into a cultural ghetto only helped to entrench the existing system in that it enabled the network chiefs to argue that (partly due to their generosity) there was now a source of 'highbrow' broadcasting, leaving them even less responsibility to cater for that band of taste. There appeared to be no way for the public television movement actually to intrude into the inner workings of the system which, increasingly, was felt to be 'polluting' the air of America. In vain did the non-commercial stations import material of high quality from the BBC and show it on their screens; it increased the frustration of the crusaders for quality but failed to tempt the network chiefs. Only in 1970 and 1971 did a small breakthrough occur, when the BBC's successful 'Forsyte Saga' enabled non-commercial television for the first time to make a dent in the commercial ratings, and helped to create a mood of interest in the networks to start purchasing some of the BBC's best dramatic work themselves. For the most part the pressures delineated in the previous chapter which were bringing about an increasing struggle to maintain high audiences continued to work themselves out in a downward spiral of dreariness and audience exploitation.

One of the main problems of educational television was that, modelled as it was on commercial broadcasting in the broad geographical distribution of stations, it had no central caucus which could actually cause programmes of high quality to be made. American broadcasting, born into a highly federal system, had spread that system to non-commercial broad-casting also. There was no centralised network of public television. There was no central body either, only a wide spread of small stations among whom any money available was dissipated in small sums.

In 1962 the Federal Government amended the 1934 Communications Act to allow federal funds to be used to help the development of truly educational (i.e. instructional) television. The ETV Facilities Act of 1962[8] provided just over 30 million dollars a year for the purpose, with the proviso that no single grant was to exceed 1 million dollars. The money was made available through the US Office of Education only to strictly educational bodies trying to improve the provision of instructional broadcasting. The money was for building rather than programme-making purposes. The importance of the development was that it placed for the first time a responsibility at national level for improving the quality of broadcasting.

The Ford Foundation had from 1953 been spending large sums on the making of programmes for circulation within the educational stations. Altogether the Foundation spent 200 million dollars between 1953 and 1971, much of which went to a body called National Educational Television which made programmes,[9] and financed the making of programmes by individual stations. Through NET a movement started up to widen the definition of educational broadcasting, and to provide a style of programming which matched the notion of public service broadcasting used by the BBC. NET was not a network, but merely a programme-making body, a kind of syndication agency, which the customers did not have to pay. When the moment came for it to attempt to expand its public service role further it was hampered by the fact that it was not a representative body; it could not help to mould the hundreds of small stations[10] into a network, because it had no status among them other than as the bringer of free gifts; it had no governing body nor advisory council with any standing outside the Foundation itself.

When Fred Friendly in 1965 resigned from the presidency of CBS News in the dispute over the coverage of the Vietnam investigations by the Senate Foreign Relations Committee, he was taken into the Ford Foundation to help develop its

221

broadcasting work. He produced a blueprint for an idea for funding the new burgeoning public broadcasting movement by exploiting the satellite system which was coming into use.[11]

The commercial networks are linked together by a complex of lines and line-of-sight microwave relays owned by AT & T which by 1967 was drawing nearly 85 million dollars a year in rentals for its service. The networks had to pay 1.15 dollars per mile of connection in order to circulate their programmes around the affiliates and wholly-owned stations. The costs rose annually. Even the infant NET was forced to spend one-sixth of its entire income on the copying of tapes; it sends them by train and plane on long journeys around the educational stations. (NET was not a network and therefore rarely had occasion to use the AT & T linking facility.) From 1965, however, the problem of networking was in the process of being revolutionised with the arrival of the new stationary satellites which could provide non-stop networking facilities. The new satellites were able to 'spray' programmes across America to be picked up by individual stations. Even at the very beginning the new satellites were able to provide the required service at about a third of the amount charged by AT & T. Friendly's idea was that the new service should be placed in the hands of public television, which would henceforth enjoy a trouble-free income destined to expand considerably over the years.[12] Without depriving the networks of an existing source of income, public television could have the chance of growing up alongside its commercial rivals with an income which in due course might even come to equal theirs. It would not interfere with the traditional American misgivings about financing journalism and entertainment from a government source, for the satellites were not government property. It seemed that America had discovered a source of funding television that would give it the same kind of neutral national but non-governmental basis that the licence fee gave to broadcasting in Britain. McGeorge Bundy, the new President of the Ford Foundation, incorporated the proposal in a formal submission to the FCC's Chairman, Rosel H. Hyde, urging it to study the scheme. 'This is not magic, or sleight-of-hand. It is a people's dividend, earned by the American nation from its enormous investment in space.'[13]

While the FCC was considering the proposal, a new element came into the discussion. The Carnegie Commission on Public Television published a Programme for Action,[14] prepared under the leadership of James R. Killian and the moral support of President Lyndon Johnson. The much awaited commission proposed a completely new structure, a central corporation for Public Broadcasting to be financed through a levy on the sale of television receivers. The new Corporation would encourage the growth of a number of programme-making centres including the Ford-backed NET, and with the help of the Department of Health, Education and Welfare would increase the provision for the individual stations. The discussion about broadening the scope and strength of non-commercial television thus took a giant step forwards; in a message to Congress of February 1967 Johnson backed the proposals in substance,[15] recommending the passing of a Public Television Act which provided some short-term financing for a new CPB system – on Carnegie lines. His message promised further action at a later date to provide long-term finance, and it was this omission that was to cause in the Nixon era a major setback to the whole movement.

The Public Broadcasting Act of 1967[16] was an attempt to create in America a broadcasting system which was national but free from the political interference which had always been predicted in any but a purely commercial free enterprise system. The new Corporation was authorised to 'facilitate the full development of educational broadcasting in which programs of high quality, obtained from diverse sources, will be made available to non-commercial educational television or radio broadcast stations, with strict adherence to objectivity and balance in all programs or series of programs of a controversial nature'.[17]

Seven programme-production centres grew up, by far the main one being the older NET based in New York. Alongside CPB, whose duty it was to receive and disburse the funds available, there was created a Public Broadcasting Service which was, in a sense, the 'network' of public broadcasting: PBS selects, schedules and promotes the programmes which are to be distributed nationally, though produces none of its own. For several years the system, wracked by an extraordinary series of internal rivalries and convulsions, continued to grow and in certain areas actually flourished.

Several expensive names from public affairs television were brought into a new programme-making centre in Washington, the National Public Affairs Centre for Television (NPACT) which became the epicentre of minor political storms every time it attempted to deal with any important area of public controversy. Sander Vanocur (at 85,000 dollars a year) and Robert MacNeil (at 65,000 dollars) earned among the most highly publicised salaries in the United States; Congressmen constantly[18] harped on the public nature of the source of public television's finance, as they complained of the 'lack of balance' in the programmes of NPACT. Public television in America was born into a system which provided for the maximum of internal tensions among hundreds of small sovereign units, each working under its own series of local political pressures and each responsible for the totality of its programme content. Above these under-financed and squabbling stations there was a superstructure of public and privately-financed organisations each of which had its own history, its own internal problems and was jealous of its own status within the system. Above the entire system sat the President (no longer the charitable Johnson, father of the project, but Richard Milhous Nixon, suspicious of eastern intellectual snobbery, and hostile to any centralised aggregations of editorial power) who through his new White House appointee Dr Clay T. Whitehead, Head of the Office of Telecommunications Policy, decided to make the funding of public television as difficult as he could.

Johnson had intended that soon after its inception a form of long-term funding should be worked out by which Congress would vote a considerable sum, up to 60 million dollars a year, guaranteed for some years ahead. In this way public television could carry on its work without having to worry each year about the source and size of the following year's finance. Every effort to pass a bill was blocked at White House level. After a year of wrangling, during which time CPB's cash trickled through at a level which could barely maintain the existing programming, still less improve it, an appropriation was finally passed, but in a form which dealt a crippling blow to the business of centralised programme-making. Public television, in the era of Nixon at least, was not to be allowed to pursue the 'one big audience' of commercial television. The money was to be distributed in small sums to the local educational stations; a giant question mark hung over the work of NPACT and over the possibility of public affairs programming within public television as a whole. Dr Whitehead: 'There is a real question as to whether public television, particularly the national federally-funded part of it, should be carrying public affairs and news commentary, and that kind of thing, for several reasons. One is the fact that the commercial networks, by and large, do, I think, quite a good job in that area. . . .'[19] In the summer of 1972, as the future of public television became gloomily clearer, many of the members of the CPB board resigned, to be immediately replaced by Nixon appointees.[20] As the election of November 1972 drew nearer, Nixon made a kind of peace with the commercial networks; he made speeches supporting the protesting out-of-work television actors in Hollywood and praising the efforts of commercial television to provide America with quality entertainment.[21] Public television ended up with about 35 million dollars on which to conduct its activities, and a lease of life, financially, of a single year. Commissioner Johnson, observing the flurry of resignations, commented, 'I have watched with growing dismay and outrage as President Nixon, acting through his Office of Telecommunications Policy, the Vice-President and others, has tried at every turn to frustrate the development of public broadcasting, to limit its growth and potential, and to turn its program content to its own political ends.'[22] It seemed to many that November 1972 would mark the end of an important chapter in the attempt to create within the United States a new broadcasting culture which would grow to compete with and change the nature of American commercial broadcasting. One of the resigning members of the CPB board drew attention to a statement in the Carnegie Report on which so many hopes had been based: 'If we were to sum up our proposal with all the brevity at our command, we would say that what we recommend is freedom.

225

We seek freedom from the constraints, however necessary in their context, of commercial television. We seek for educational television freedom from the pressure of inadequate funds. We seek for the artist, the technician, the journalist, the scholar, and the public servant freedom to create, freedom to innovate, freedom to be heard in this most far-reaching medium. We seek for the citizen freedom to view, to see programs that the present system, by its incompleteness, denies him.'[23]

The Carnegie Commission had been an attempt to bring broadcasting into the centrality of the cultural and intellectual work of America. It failed. Its supporters failed to recognise the slender basis for the apparent victories of the Johnson era. They achieved an advance into the territory of the media which simply gave a small niche for the intelligentsia and in doing so made that small community as conspicuous in its control as the business community in commercial television. They underestimated the extent to which they would be opposed by all those who opposed centralism in American life and all those who opposed intellectualism or apparent intellectualism. One influential attack on the 1967 Act was couched in these terms: 'The Public Broadcasting Act of 1967 is unnecessary, inefficient, inequitable, and subject to dangerous political influences. But perhaps I do not mention its worst feature. It is a striking example of what is coming to be a common situation, in which the educational community sets itself apart from the rest of humanity. They claim special privileges and by political action attempt to secure them.'[24] Educational television had expanded up to the point at which it began to be a threat to the major networks, and at which it began to be a regular source of journalistic material of a kind which scrutinised sceptically the work of government. At that point, it was held back from reaching out toward the 'one big audience', and the rug was pulled from beneath its feet.

What the protagonists saw as the development of diversity in broadcasting the opponents saw as narrow and sectionalist. Public television in America achieved a great deal of success, however, in certain areas. It has transformed children's television in the wake of 'Sesame Street' which, in providing a programme of extremely high quality for children, helped to

226

open up all the issues affecting children's broadcasting –
namely advertising within children's programmes and the level
of violence in them. The children's programming wing of
public television (The Children's Television Workshop)
helped force mainstream stations to think again about the nature
of their work. But children's programming is not prime time
programming.

A group of documentaries by NET provided cause for a considerable agitation in the minds of politicians. 'Banks and the
Poor' emphasised the role of banking institutions in perpetua-
ting slum conditions, 'Who Invited Us?' was a study of im-
perialism; there was a report by Ralph Nader on Mobil Oil
commercials, and an item in an extremely successful magazine
programme 'The Great American Dream Machine', which
dealt with the work of FBI informers in American society. These
were some of the most controversial documentaries which
produced public reactions. Certain local stations were placed
under pressure by local representatives of the interests which
were being pilloried, not to transmit the programmes at all.
Mobil Oil contributed 1 million dollars to the funds of public
television at an opportune moment and this appeared miracu-
lously to coincide with a decision not to go ahead with the Nader
report on oil commercials'.[25] Under considerable pressure PBS
cut out the segment of the programme on FBI informers. All in
all, public television lost its credibility for journalistic independence. The White House was the source of a Washington
campaign against 'left-leaning' tendencies in NPACT. Dr
Whitehead argued publicly that public television should stay
out of public affairs anyway. The Vice-President attacked
Sander Vanocur for being left wing. The Corporation for Public
Broadcasting, which was supposed to be the funding body only,
without a right of editorial supervision, agreed after further
pressure to ensure that it would ascertain that 'balance' was
being maintained in the programming produced by public
funds. The legislation of 1967 was ill-starred. America did not
produce a form of television that was independent and publicly
financed. Nor did it find, among its programme-makers, an
area of detached but sceptical curiosity on which to build a
viable school of public television journalism; its documentary

makers derived from traditional American journalism – they seemed to go out to challenge vested interests and those interests fought back with all available tools. When America attempted to move from purely educational broadcasting to *public* broadcasting it failed to create either among the political community (on which the system depended financially) or among the programme-makers a professional *ideology* of neutrality. It found little ground in which to plant sturdy roots.

III

Despite the relatively inactive role of the FCC in matters of programming policy, the FCC's history contains many precedents for an active role in altering patterns of ownership within the broadcasting industry. In 1940 NCB was forced to divest itself of a whole chain of radio stations which were later formed into ABC.[26] A number of other stations had been divested of ownership on grounds of misdemeanour within the terms of the 1934 Act. Although the FCC is entitled to levy fines, the fines have always been merely fractions of the sums of money culled from the misdemeanour; its only real sanction therefore has been total dispossession.[27] In recent times there has been a row of zealous attempts by public and community organisations to oppose the renewal of their local stations' licences on the grounds that its programming failed to meet the needs of the community in some way. A long legal battle was fought by the Public Information Office of the United Church of Christ against a certain station, WLBT in Jackson, Mississippi, which was inadequately covering the affairs of the black community; after a successful effort to create a precedent for ordinary citizen groups to be represented at FCC hearings, the United Church managed to oust the holders of the station altogether.[28]

Apart from the untypical example of WHDH in Boston, Massachusetts, which was dispossessed on extremely complicated grounds, partly as a result of the fact that it held only a temporary franchise, there have been virtually no cases of a station franchise being taken from one local group and placed in the hands of another. The idea of regular open competition as in Britain has never gained ground. So long as the permission of the FCC is gained stations-owners may 'traffic' in licences at the prevailing market rates.

Although the FCC in its public statements since its inception in 1934 have proclaimed that the licence to run a station has depended upon a willingness on the part of the franchise holders to provide a balanced service, the FCC seldom took any active steps to supervise stations in this regard. When granting licences the FCC has been mainly concerned to ensure that the applicant has sufficient funds to keep the station going rather than to see whether he has valid professional qualifications or the relevant programming intentions. The FCC has acquired various codes relating to fairness, equal time and access and it has undertaken to police these and to take up complaints which have been directed at alleged breaches, but for nearly thirty years it took virtually no steps to examine the broad spectrum of programming undertaken by stations, either at the time of granting the licence or when reconsidering them at renewal time.

In 1960, however, the FCC issued a statement indicating that its future policy would be to scrutinise applications and re-applications.[29] Two years later it held public hearings on the performances of two stations in Chicago and Omaha, before agreeing to renew their licences. In 1965, however, frustrated at the amount of work involved, the FCC, without abandoning the 1960 policy, instructed its staff to desist from collecting the type of information upon which scrutiny of this kind could be based. It returned to its traditional practice of ritual renewal of licences. Stations are renewed in batches at a time. Deficiencies in engineering matters, or finance, or, it is alleged, poor form-filling, can result in delay; deficiencies in programming are not treated as matters of substance. Since the FCC is supposed not to have editorial power, and since it cannot process the broadcasting records of the stations, it cannot acquire any useful criteria on which to base its judgements.

One of the issues which arose generally in America in the latter part of the 1960s was the need to restore or invigorate local democracy. The media became a suitable focus for social action. After all the whole American system of broadcasting was in essence local rather than national. The role of the media in each community was vital to any plan to encourage and improve keen local citizen participation in government. The reason for making American broadcasting local in nature in the first place had been that it was believed to be a medium which could bind communities together, could act as a kind of cement for the heterogeneous elements of which American society is composed.

The issues of bad programming and lack of attention to specific local communities or to local affairs in general began to be raised in certain areas. But the question of intermedia ownership dominated all others. At the FCC, Nicholas Johnson and Kenneth A. Cox made a determined effort to challenge the renewal of various groups of licences, partly to draw attention to the laxity of the FCC in its renewal policy and partly to draw attention to the need for activity around the country in neighbourhood after neighbourhood as the only appropriate way to challenge the problems of American broadcasting at their originating source, or at that point at which the law left some of the responsibility.[30]

In June 1968 Cox and Johnson decided to focus attention on a group of stations in Oklahoma,[31] selected at random, whose licence renewal they decided to question. They called for an examination of the record of the stations and made it public. They concluded as a result of their own investigation that as far as Oklahoma was concerned 'the concept of local service is largely a myth. With a few exceptions Oklahoma stations provide almost literally no programming that can meaningfully be described as "local expression".'[32] Of the ten stations under consideration, which drew in all 16 million dollars in gross advertising revenue annually, only one station provided two hours a week of programmes dealing with local public affairs. Six stations provided less than one hour, and one station none at all, yet the stations each transmitted between 105 and 134 hours a week.

The two commissioners examined the state of media ownership in the state and found that while 73 firms controlled various parts of broadcasting in Oklahoma, 4 firms accounted for 88 per cent of the total income. The largest of the four was a complex of interests centred upon a single family which also owns the two main newspapers in the state capital, as well as four further television stations in other areas. Virtually any state in the Union could have been singled out, with fairly similar results.

One of the by-products of this new mood of scrutiny which was emerging, albeit from a minority group at the FCC, was a growing interest on the part of citizens in various parts of the country who were keen to find a way to improve American television; it was part of America's small but growing 'consumer' movement which is deeply concerned about techniques of marketing and advertising. Many of these had started fighting the networks over the level of violence in children's programmes and various aspects of 'fairness' in regard to commercials, but the most dynamic group started studying the problems involved in challenging licences wholesale.

The experience of Dr Everett Parker of the United Church of Christ in his effective challenge of the licence of WLBT in Jackson was invaluable to newcomers to the art of licence-challenging. He fought for five years to persuade the FCC to recognise his right to be heard formally by them and finally he used that right to overturn the station ownership. In the wake of his victory 150 other challenges were issued to the FCC within two years.[33] The rate at which they poured in increased from 4 in 1969 to 80 in 1970, even though the work involved in a challenge is formidable, and the expense equally so. Of the 18 stations in Rochester, where activity was particularly fierce, no fewer than 14 were under siege.

The grounds for challenge varied considerably. In San Antonio, El Paso, Odessa, Texas and Albuquerque, groups of Mexican-Americans petitioned for a denial of renewal to stations belonging to the Doubleday Broadcasting Company on the grounds that Mexican newsmen were not being employed. The petitions were withdrawn when Doubleday changed its hiring policy. Similar victories were won in Memphis, Mobile, Chicago, Denver, Los Angeles and San Francisco. An organisation called Community Coalition on Broadcasting announced that it would challenge renewal of all 28 radio and television stations in Atlanta, in April 1970. Within weeks the local stations promised to train blacks for jobs in broadcasting, provide scholarships for black student journalists and to produce programmes on black history.

The new challengers also worked against media conglomerates. In Washington, the Citizens' Communication Center, under the leadership of the lawyer Al Kramer, challenged the right of the Walter Annenberg group to sell nine stations for 147 million dollars to Capitol Cities Broadcasting; before they were persuaded to desist from the challenge, the purchasing company agreed to spend a million dollars on minority programming on three of the stations in Philadelphia, New Haven and Fresno.

Perhaps the most intricate and effective challenge of all was Kramer's lawsuit to prevent the deal negotiated between McGraw-Hill and Time-Life by which the former would purchase from the latter five television stations for a little under 70 million dollars. Kramer helped nine Spanish-speaking groups together with a black group from Denver to challenge the agreement of the FCC to this arrangement on the grounds that the promised programming by McGraw-Hill ignored minority needs, and also that the conglomerate ownership proposed was socially undesirable. McGraw-Hill gave in on the programming question but not on the transfer of ownership. The FCC, with the opposition of two of its members, agreed to let the deal stand. The challengers, however, decided to continue the fight over the head of the FCC through the courts; as a compromise offer McGraw-Hill agreed to set up citizens advisory committees in each of four of the cities concerned, dropped one station from the deal completely, and agreed to employ 15 per cent of station staff from among blacks and chicanos. With that set of victories the licence challengers emerged as a fully fledged movement. They had discovered the most sensitive nerve in the whole broadcasting system and were making it hurt.[34]

A further breakthrough occurred when the challengers found that they could obtain the necessary legal help free; it costs an enormous sum and requires considerable expertise in communication law to fight FCC cases at all. The United Church of Christ and the Citizens' Communication Center had the help of full-time legal teams which they were able to make available to help others. The Stern Community Law Firm's Washington office, operated by Tracy Westen, formerly a legal aide at the FCC itself, was provided with funds by the Los Angeles based Stern family, which wished to use its foundation funds for the purpose of encouraging local democracy. The Ford Foundation also considered providing financial assistance for fighting licence renewals. The broadcasting industry became, not surprisingly, extremely worried by the new developments, especially as these were coupled with a further spate of legal action concerned with challenges under the fairness doctrine, and on grounds of advertising accuracy. Dr Whitehead began advocating the institution of a longer period prior to licence renewal and called for the abolition of the fairness doctrine on the provisions of which most of the challenges were based. Some of the challengers were making reimbursement by the station one of the clauses of the challenge; a group of citizens in Texarkana, after long appeals, were granted reimbursement of the legal costs incurred while challenging the licence of a local station KTAL and this decision promised to make the whole licence-challenging movement financially self-sustaining and therefore infinitely more dangerous to the interests of commercial broadcasting.

FCC officials began to fear that their new caseload would disrupt the system.[35] The renewal staff had to be doubled in numbers during the course of 1971. Dean Burch, the chairman of the FCC, however, made a formal announcement to the effect that the commission 'welcomes the participation of responsible community groups in the licensing process';[36] he ordered a study of methods for overhauling the complicated renewal procedures. Licence-challenging not only introduced a new element into grass-roots politics in the United States. It provided for the first time an important tool in the hands of those wanting to change the basic rules of commercial broadcasting.

IV

Throughout the United States there are about two dozen separate citizen groups wholly or mainly concerned with struggle over television quality; they range from *Black Efforts*

233

for Soul in Television to the *Institute of American Democracy* and the *American Council for Better Broadcasts*; most of them have offices in Washington and are concerned with the processes of lobbying and litigation, designed to exploit the existing provisions within communications law which can be made to help minorities or to change programme content.[37] Apart from the efforts to improve the quality of children's programmes throughout American television which have resulted in a growing professionalisation in this area of work, and the concomitant efforts to reduce the sheer quantity of violence portrayed on the screen, most of the efforts are devoted to creating opportunities within programmes and within broadcasting employment for minority groups. The activity has been local in focus, scattered and uncoordinated. In 1970 the Citizens' Communication Center in Washington offered to provide rudimentary legal and strategic advice to the groups working in this field. It provides research information and working manuals on the issues relating to citizen rights, on access to the media and on the complex procedures of the FCC. Without becoming in itself the basis of an organised movement at national level it has been able to provide a certain general reserve of experience and political know-how.[38]

The Stern Concern is much more involved, through legal work, in dramatising the issues which are being discovered and fought out by the small citizen groups. Its programme of litigation is a publicist's daydream. It is trying to force stations to sell time for 'anti-commercials' which proclaim the deficiencies of goods advertised on the screen; it has for instance attempted to gain publicity for the fact that aspirins are identical whatever their brand name, and it has tried to make stations, under the 'Fairness Doctrine', publicise the damage done to the environment by the gasoline advertised in their ordinary commercials. It is concerned with what it calls 'attention-getting' projects, although these tend to be of a legal nature also. As with many of the citizen groups, the Stern Concern adopts an underlying radical critique (anti-business, anti-military) of American society and works this out in reference to broadcasting. Its efforts, for instance, to exploit the fairness doctrine through station commercials inevitably point toward

234

the goal of a television system without advertising; by trying to establish a legal obligation on the part of stations to carry commercials (free under the obligations of the fairness doctrine) which contradict openly their normal commercials, their efforts tend towards breaking down the central core of American broadcasting. It is hardly surprising that, fearful of the possible long-term logical extension of the Stern Concern's efforts, spokesmen for the broadcasting industry, in addition to Dr Whitehead, have been calling for a complete overhaul of the fairness doctrine, and even its abandonment. Their great weapon has of course been the First Amendment which they can use as a tool to aid their business interests, as much as others can use it to try and force the broadcasters into the position of being 'common carriers'.

The First Amendment forbids any state intrusion into the untrammelled right of anyone in America to speak and write whatever he wishes; the commercial broadcaster therefore can claim that the efforts of the FCC to force him to transmit news is an infringement of his constitutional rights, even though the FCC (and those who are trying to reform broadcasting through lawsuits) can claim that it is not interfering with *what* the broadcaster says, but to coerce him into providing coverage of public affairs. The reformers claim that the station-owners have an obligation to allow their wavelengths to be used for the purposes of free speech by others; the station-owners claim that the airtime is their own. The First Amendment can be used to stretch the rights of either party. The question is whether the next few years are going to see the broadcasters becoming 'common carriers' in law rather than free exploiters of the public resource of the wavelength.

A movement toward common carrier status (which is the logical corollary of the present wave of radical activity) would tend to deal a heavy blow to the commercial broadcaster, in that it would divest him of much of his control over the content of his programme schedules. The pressure in the United States is therefore of extreme importance in that it points towards a situation in which broadcasting might be obliged to separate the unity of editorial control and control over the resource of the wavelength. If a station manager is no longer able to decide the content of his airtime, but has to share that control with citizen groups, or has to open up his airtime for messages of whatever nature, then he is likely to be driven back to being a kind of local public servant; he is cut off from his overriding network links.

In such a situation America could see the break-up of the 'one big audience' strategy, and the whole broadcasting culture which has resulted from the efforts of a few major business interests to grasp the full-time attention of the entire middle range of the public. The societal implications therefore of the media radicals is far greater than their size or their existing achievements might suggest. Although their present concrete achievements in programme matters amount to a few local advertising spots changing their nature, and a few local programmes beginning to pay attention to the interests of social minorities, and although they have not to any important extent challenged the grip of the networks upon the system, nonetheless the long-term logical extension of their efforts in the legal field suggests a fairly powerful intrusion into the infrastructure of the American system of broadcasting.

Within the field of those pressing for change the most important dominant personality is without doubt that of Nicholas Johnson. John Kenneth Galbraith described him as 'the citizen's least frightened friend in Washington'.[39] As one of the FCC's seven commissioners (his term of office expires in 1973) he presents the inspiring spectacle of a man of great intellect and eloquence who challenges day after day, in speeches, lectures and books, the basis for the commercial system of broadcasting. He has acquired an extraordinary skill as a self-publicist – he bicycles around Washington, he writes pop songs, he advocates a return to the simple life, taking camping holidays, and campaigning against the entire range of 'phony values' purveyed by the broadcasting medium.[40] The broadcasting industry tends to exaggerate his eccentricities and treats him as a dangerous animal let loose in their large and valuable store. His eccentricities and radical epigrammatic style conceal or rather assist a powerful legal intellect, trained in his earlier years in the shipping industry when (to the concerted protests of that industry) he was made Maritime Administrator. President

Johnson summoned him to the FCC to continue that body's thin tradition of radical figures. Nicholas Johnson makes no secret of the fact that the direction of his efforts is to attack the commercial broadcasting system root and branch. Without someone filling his position at the highest level of American broadcasting the movement for reforming broadcasting through citizen action would not have reached the pitch of organisation which it has. He had occupied a comparable role in the media to that filled by Ralph Nader in the consumer field.

V

While there has been a small amount of effective action to dislocate the pattern of national network broadcasting, most hopes for change in America are pinned on the new technologies of broadcasting, which would increase the range of choice and therefore produce improvement through competition. The greatest hopes are being placed in the developments which are presently under way in the field of cable television, by which dozens of channels can be made available to a household by pumping them not through the air, but through a pencil-thin coaxial cable. Distribution of radio and television by wire is an extremely old technology; there is a great deal of wire broadcasting, for instance, in Switzerland and in the Soviet Union.[41] In Britain before the war there was a considerable development of wired radio until legal problems arose over the editorial rights entailed in transmitting by wire programmes made by the BBC for distribution over the air.

In the United States the cable began when viewers in Palm Springs decided they wanted to see the programmes transmitted in distant Hollywood; a local entrepreneur had the sensible idea of erecting an extremely powerful aerial on his own territory and feeding a wire from it to the home of any Palm Springs resident who wanted to watch the programmes from Los Angeles and Hollywood,[42] charging a monthly fee for the service. The idea of the Community Antenna spread rapidly through areas in which there were few television signals available because of geographical problems; CATV thus was introduced in the early years of television in those parts of the

United States which were remote and sparsely populated. The cable was used to bring 'distant signals' into the homes of station-starved communities.

The FCC, however, decided to forbid the bringing of distant signals into any of the hundred largest television markets in America which are jointly responsible for 87 per cent of all viewers. The CATV movement was thus stopped dead in its tracks; it had earned the bitter hostility of the broadcasting industry wherever it was used to enable viewers to receive stations not intended primarily for them.

The roots of the present dilemma over how to introduce cable television to the majority of the United States population lies in a previous dilemma over the exploitation of the UHF band of wavelengths. When after the Korean War most of the VHF wavelengths were used up, critics of the poor quality of the network programming which fed these stations turned to the new UHF band hoping that its exploitation would increase the range of choice for the average viewer. Most medium and large cities would receive three or four VHF stations, one of which was occasionally an educational station. The distribution of UHF stations could increase that number to eight or nine in most places. But the networks had completed their pattern of affiliation, and the programmes of greatest appeal were accounted for on those stations which obtained the vast majority of the audience. Those UHF stations which started up seldom if ever obtained a network affiliation; they failed to entice viewers to purchase the new aerials and equipment necessary. The stations on the UHF band therefore failed to get enough viewers to sustain a level of advertising revenue which would have enabled them to make programmes themselves of any quality. There seemed no way out of the vicious circle which kept most viewers watching skilled low-quality programming on one band, while the UHF channel remained unavailable to any but the most determined viewers who had undergone some considerable expense in purchasing special converters for their sets. At first the FCC tried to force the network affiliates onto the UHF band by simply changing their wavelengths, but fierce local lobbying soon put a stop to the policy – neither the advertisers nor the networks would countenance such acts of dispossession.

There was a period of great embarrassment at the FCC when a number of UHF franchise-holders returned their certificates to the FCC, with some contumely. The UHF stations which remained were able to keep going only by running extreme minority services, such as stock market reports, or by showing fifth and sixth reruns of previously popular programmes.

The prospects of a sudden spread of cable television in the late fifties and early sixties cast great gloom over the commissioners. CATV's were spreading rapidly (640 by 1960)[43] and their arrival in the major markets was imminent; they would enable the mass of American viewers to receive dozens of peripheral stations (broadcasting originally on the VHF band) and the chances of developing additional signals through UHF would be doomed for ever.

The early cable enthusiasts were local businessmen who saw the chance to earn enormous incomes very quickly and with no work; five dollars a month would be collected from every viewer who joined the system in return for giving him stations which were already there; cable was a device for improving the quality of reception for the average viewer, not the range or quality of his programmes. No royalties of any kind were payable by the cable firms. The networks argued that cable (and pay-television) would destroy the traditional system by which Americans received their broadcasting free, in exchange for watching the commercials. Liberal Commissioners (like Kenneth Cox) who were to vote on the question of licensing cable franchises in 1966, saw cable as the enemy of VHF; non-Liberal Commissioners saw it as the enemy of the networks and the wealthy VHF stations whose interests they seldom tried to subvert. Together they designed a system by which cable entrepreneurs were forbidden from importing distant signals into the major markets; they waited for some years and saw that UHF still did not begin to flourish and they redoubled their measures against cable by deciding that the retransmission of such over-the-air stations represented a breach in the laws of copyright. The real problem besetting UHF, however, was that VHF station-owners could always outbid UHF station-owners for any popular programme; without at least a modicum of high-audience programmes the new stations would never raise by advertising alone the revenue necessary to provide the viewer with any additional competitive programming.

In 1971 the FCC began to relent in its hostility towards cable broadcasting. It reduced the number of markets into which the carrying of distant signals was forbidden to fifty. In the medium-sized cities therefore cable firms would now begin to increase the number of available stations. In the largest cities they could lay their cables only to the existing over-the-air stations within the receiving area. The sheer potential profitability of cable was pushing the movement slowly forward. Even while developing under severe restriction, it had turned itself into an industry worth 300 million dollars nationally in a year.[44] It had acquired 6 million subscribers. It looked forward to multiplying its subscribers by five within a brief period. The FCC decided to impose upon all new cable franchises the responsibility of adding new programmes to the total amount they transmitted; they are now obliged to find a few hours of new programmes every week, but this in itself has been enough to inject a certain new life into the independent programme-makers of America who see in the burgeoning cable market a chance to relay television programmes to an important but small audience which will support high quality television. One prediction is that cable will create 800,000 new jobs in America by 1980.

But the cable is more than a new method for distributing an old culture in broadcasting. The multi-channelled cable can bring many kinds of message into the office and the home other than those contained within the existing over-the-air stations. It can, for one thing, bring new sources of programming, from the middle of the transmitting community. It can bring specialist services of information and sales. It can become the basis for pay-television and for specialist programmes. It has also, potentially, the possibility of being used for the video-phone system of the future. New developments in the cathode tube now make it feasible for printed material to be sent along the cable channels to be torn off the tube at the receiving end, so that newspapers would no longer need to be hauled around the streets early in the morning. The cable can be used by shops for advertising and with the help of the telephone actually used for the sale of goods. Most important of all, in the view of some, is the fact that the cable can become the connecting device for new machinery which would transform the idea of the business office – it would enable people to speak to one another and write to one another on specially closed circuits instead of travelling to meet in the same building every day. The cable is more than a means for distributing entertainment. It is connected at almost every level with some kind of hoped-for social revolution, which may, like all the other communications inventions of this century, be used either for good or ill.

The real question involved currently in the field of cable television is that of the spread of ownership and access. At present, more than half of the existing installations (nearly 5000 of them) are owned by other American media interests. Mainstream political interests in most communities are not tending to support moves to make the basis of ownership a group of interests within a given community, although radical groups within the media world are trying to bring about a pattern of ownership which is community based. Established political interests naturally fear that locally-based cable would become a megaphone for the voices of radical minority but well-organised political interests. Nonetheless there are various figures within the cable world who are trying to persuade local organisations to attempt to obtain cable franchises: there exist at present two manuals designed to help 'citizen action' in the cable field.[45] The Cypress Communications Corporation which owns a number of installations mainly in Ohio (which have now been sold to Warner Brothers) produced an impressive scheme for cabling the city of Dayton, Ohio, in a way which would allow joint ownership of the cable system between Cypress and a local citizens' organisation: the 2-million dollar installation would be shared by the Citizens' Cable Corporation which consists of the local leaders of a predominantly black community.[46]

The most important document to change the climate of thinking on the question of the cable was the Report of the Sloan Commission,[47] which was published in 1971 and promised enthusiastically that the cable would transform social

241

communications in the late twentieth century in the way that
printing had changed communications in the late fifteenth.
The Sloan Commission recommended the abolition of the
fairness doctrine and the equal time provision in programming
disseminated by cable.[48] It recommended that the owners of
cable installations should be protected by law from responsibility for libel, obscenity, incitement to riot etc., in communications disseminated by outsiders through their cables.[49] The
commission recommended a large measure of democratisation
in the business of cable enfranchisement.[50] It wanted intermedia ownership to be prevented and local community interests
to participate in or even become principal owners of local cable
franchises. It made an exception of public television stations,
which by owning local cable franchises would discover a source
of revenue for financing the making of programmes without
recourse to advertising.[51] It predicted that by the end of the
seventies more than half of the homes in the United States
would be 'on the cable' and would be able to receive at least
twenty and possibly forty channels.[52] While many cable enthusiasts have been encouraging the belief that very advanced
uses for the cable would become widespread quite quickly,
including the electronic transmission of newspapers and inter-
office written material, the Sloan Commission took a modest
view of these possibilities. Dr Peter C. Goldmark, who served
on a committee of the National Academy of Engineering, has
become one of the most vocal spokesmen for a highly futuristic
view of the cable, which holds that the rapid and complex
spread of cabling could even enable the population to be more
rationally distributed and could, by reducing the necessity for
people to travel to their offices and back home again every day,
solve the problems of traffic and transport in the modern city.[53]
The Sloan Commission took the view that his kind of development would be too expensive to be considered realistic in the
short term. In doing so, the commission kept its general tenor
one of convincing pragmatism and optimism. The report
played an enormous part in making the media world feel that
the cable revolution had indeed begun and would become the
long-awaited means for transforming the nature of television
communication in the United States.

The virtue of the cable is that, especially when attached to small domestic video-recording equipment, it can transform the nature of the audience. No longer does the broadcast audience (if that is the correct term to describe the recipients of a communication which is no longer, in the literal sense, *broadcast*) have to be simultaneous. Nor does it have to be only a passive audience: the cable works almost as easily in reverse and can enable the viewer to participate in the production of the message, in a manner similar to a telephone. Because the audience pays a rental there becomes a source of broadcast revenue which is not entirely based on advertising. The entire mechanism of the broadcast system therefore changes. A programme can become financially feasible even if it is required only by a very small audience, numbering thousands rather than millions. (Certain strands of a cable can be shut off and supplied only to specific homes in a neighbourhood, so that, for instance, doctors could subscribe to a special service of medical information which would be receivable only on special sets.) The cable audience does not have to be homogeneous. The programmes do not have to be continuous. All the structures and assumptions which have appeared to be inevitable in the era of broadcasting become redundant in the era of the cable.

There is, however, no inevitability that cable will become a means for transforming the broadcasting situation for the better in the United States. For one thing a cable franchise, once it starts attracting high revenue, becomes an immensely valuable capital asset and when changing hands can command an extremely high price. The carrying of minority messages can therefore again become excessively 'expensive', if they are to return revenue as a percentage of the capital value. There could be a shortage of channels extremely quickly, if it becomes normal for every large local store to rent its own cable channel for several hours a day in order to sell goods. (It is very easy to attach a device to the apparatus which enables a viewer to reserve an item of goods after seeing it on the screen, projected from the local store.) The great optimism generated at the present time among those who see the cable as a source of high quality minority programming could rapidly be dissipated.

If American broadcasting is to be transformed in the era of

the cable, it will require far more than a mere technical revolution to bring this about. The nature of broadcast content is profoundly influenced by the idea of the audience which the communicator has in his head. The fashioning of the audience image is partly a product of economics and the structure of media ownership and control. A genuine revolution in American broadcasting could well be at hand, but it will depend as much on the political and administrative decisions which are taken during the decade of the seventies as on the technological possibilities which are being opened up. At present it is as likely that America will have the chance of seeing a choice of twelve westerns and soap operas, plus an array of department stores, as it is that the twenty or forty channels in every home will carry an abundance of plays, documentaries, information and discussion of a type to satisfy the more optimistic apostles of the technology.

What is important in the period of the expansion of the cable is the immediate impact on the central mechanism of American broadcasting. The networks can foresee a time, not far hence, when they will disintegrate in their present form. The immediate future could well, however, bring with it a tightening of the competitive pressures as the major groups contend for the last drop of revenue extractable by playing the traditional game, before the rules are changed. Nonetheless the professional can now begin to see television as a source of a more complex relationship with the audience; he can begin to think about the tasks of making programmes which are not part of a 'one big audience' strategy and which will help to mould all the internal thinking and decision-making about programme content.

What the networks most fear is that the ability of a cable enfranchisee to alter the times of day at which the network programmes are shown (which he can easily do by video-recording and rescheduling every signal he picks out of the air) will change the nature of prime time, around which all the decision-making of American broadcasting has revolved. Almost certainly cable television holders will find themselves further than any television station of the present time along the road toward being 'common carriers'; at least some cable channels will be reserved for community groups or for anyone at all to send out programmes within small areas, or to use time for political campaigning on neighbourhood and national issues. The fusion of channel control and editorial control must then surely come to an end, and with it so many of the practices and attitudes of commercial television.

The importance of these imminent changes in American broadcasting is that the products of this powerful and volatile system travel around the world and become the dominant broadcasting culture of so many other nations. If American broadcasting can produce a new culture, as a result not only of the cable but of all the other strands of pressure and development described in this chapter, then we can all look forward indeed to a very different shadow on the wall of our cave.

Chapter Nine

Japan: The Television of Hard-Training

'If there is ever to be an amelioration of the condition of mankind, philosophers, theologians, legislators, politicians and moralists will find that the regulation of the press is the most difficult, dangerous and important problem they have to resolve. Mankind cannot now be governed without it, nor at present with it.'
John Adams, 11 February 1815

'How can one govern without television?'
André Malraux

The Japanese broadcasting system, more than any other, bears witness to a national effort to deal with the problem of freedom of expression in a mass society. The Japanese have borrowed ideas and institutions from the West and have transformed them in the light of a characteristically Japanese sense of perfection, but have ended up, despite their amazing technological prowess and heated concern to preserve a quasi-Reithian set of broadcasting ideals, with exactly the same series of dilemmas which besets broadcasting everywhere else.

The Japanese have built a 'free' system inside a set of powerful, politically independent, institutions, and have found that a public broadcasting system has still to compete for viewers against a commercial system. They have attempted to use television as an instrument of mass 'improvement', and then they have been obliged conscientiously to 'debase' it in order to keep its share of the viewing public at realistic proportions. In the name of freedom they have allowed a series of commercial stations to come into existence and then shuddered at the results. After twenty years of experience with their most carefully constructed set of broadcasting constitutions they are in the midst of a national debate about vulgarity, violence, disrespect for authority and the portrayal of sexuality which exactly mirrors, perhaps in an even more intense form, the debate under way in the West.[1] In fact every event which takes place in the American networks or the BBC or German television is avidly seized upon and studied for its possible implications for Japanese broadcasting. A resignation in Fifth Avenue, an angry intervention in Parliament after a particularly adroit edition of 'Panorama', a protest by Mrs Mary Whitehouse, a new appointment to high office in the ORTF, and someone at the Research Institute of the Nippon Hoso Kyokai will prepare a detailed report on the event for discussion throughout the television worlds of Tokyo and Osaka. In the early 1950s a new word passed into the Japanese language: *masu comi*; it is a nipponed version of 'mass communication' and is now the generally used verb. To see the ways in which the long debate in the West over the problem of freedom and mass entertainment has influenced the development of *masu comi* in Japan, we have to look back into the very roots of modern Japanese journalism, even before western ideas began to take root.

It was not until 1870 that Japan produced a regular daily newspaper – the *Yokohama Mainichi*[2] – which was at first read only by the upper crust of society, the small class of ex-samurai who inhabited the towns. At first the government encouraged the growth of the press which gradually spread its clientele to the new and growing commercial middle-class before reaching the population generally. But gradually various forms of police control were enacted in a series of Press Laws after 1875, as authority began to fear the influence of the new source of power, and the growing public pressure for reform. The Press Law of 1909 made provision that: 'The Home Minister may prohibit the sale or distribution of or if necessary seize a newspaper when it is deemed that articles disturbing to the peace and order or injurious to public morals are contained therein . . .'[3]

As circulation grew from a total of 53,000 a day in 1875 to 6¼ million in 1924, authority went through a series of phases in its relations with the newspapers; the Press Law was liberalised, but rapidly followed by direct control, then a further period of total freedom ensued, relieved by attempts to introduce a government point of view into the press through processes of subtle insinuation.

Japanese newspapers were vehicles for political opinion, usually opposition opinion in the days of the *Yokohama Mainichi*. They were written in the heavy literary language, not the colloquial one, and contained very little in the way of straight information. In Osaka however, boulevard papers developed in the 1880s, full of popular love stories, which were sold in the restaurants and geisha houses. The beginnings of government pressure and legislation to restrict the free operation of the press caused a sudden carnage of newspapers in the 1880s in which fifty dailies were suppressed and those that remained were free of direct party control, although they continued to be concerned with political debate and were addressed to the growing politically conscious public of Tokyo.

At the end of the century a new journalism appeared in Osaka, in the pages of the *Asahi* which combined entertainment with politics and general news. It was the Northcliffe revolution, Japanese style, and had arisen partly as a result of the new liberalised constitution of 1889 which permitted a certain measure of free discussion, but as a result, too, of rapidly spreading literacy.

Despite the movement towards social freedom which had been gradually coming into existence since the 1870s with the aid of political ideas imported from France and America, the situation of journalism was extremely precarious. The Jiru Minken Windo (the Freedom and Popular Rights Movement) had used the newspapers for its agitation and already in 1876 thirty journalists had been put in jail, three newspapers banned and 400 prominent radicals banished. In the years which followed the new constitution things were scarcely any easier, and the government suppressed for instance all mention in the press of the Rice Riots which followed the Russo-Japanese war of 1905.

The 1920s were years of great press freedom and press expansion in Japan. Universal male suffrage arrived in 1925 partly as a result of press agitation. It was a period too in which

Marxist ideas were spreading among the new Japanese proletariat and, despite liberalisation, a new source of discipline, the Special Higher Police, was created to ensure that open political discussion did not go too far. The problem of the new constitution was that it allowed various forms of legislation to be left in the hands of the executive branch of government, so that the Ministry of Communications or Education or Home Affairs could in effect pass laws at their own behest. The Peace Preservation Law of 1925 updated an old statute which allowed the police to suppress anything which interfered with civil order in the nation. The pattern of government–press relations had thus, for the whole period of the existence of newspapers in Japan until the early 1930s, been like a concertina, blowing loud and soft according to the political needs of the government.[4]

When it was clear that radiotelephony was going to spread to Japan, its government, in 1924,[5] before any actual stations started up, extended the existing Press Law to include broadcasting. A year later a directive of the Ministry of Communications (which had been created to run telegraph and telephone services) forbade the transmission by radio of any political speeches or any political discussion. Within a few years a new Wireless Telegraph Act specifically empowered the Communications Ministry to stop any broadcast which might spread disorder or damage national morale in any way.

Despite these enactments radio was growing in Japan. Three stations were created in 1925 and merged after a time into the NHK,[6] the forerunner of today's Japan Broadcasting Corporation. As with Reith's BBC (created simultaneously on the other side of the world), the NHK was a strange amalgam of public and private enterprise. It was not a government-run institution and has technically never been government-run, even during the years of Japanese wartime fascism. It was begun and has remained a body set up under the Civil Code as a 'private juridical person'. Its function has been to bring about the most rapid feasible spread of broadcasting throughout the country and to ensure that every part of Japan was made accessible to its programmes.

In 1931 the Manchurian Incident triggered off a fifteen-year war with China, which brought about a major cataclysm in Japanese politics and society. Party politics was brought to an end. All liberal opinion was prevented from expressing itself. The power of the army in civil affairs grew continuously as the pressures of war bit deeper and deeper. Writers and scholars were persecuted, the social democrats were harassed, and all other groups of citizens who opposed the war with China. In 1936 a group of rightist officers staged a revolt which was bloodily suppressed in a countermove in which radio played a prominent part. Three million radio licences had been issued in the first decade of broadcasting in Japan.

Until the officers' revolt the Japanese government had supervised broadcasting but had not employed it for direct propaganda of its own. In the late thirties, however, this was done with a vengeance. All communications media were gradually invaded by government. The cinema was provided with a system of pre-production censorship which ensured that all films, from their inception, were conceived as part of the national effort. The newspapers were intimidated into submission. A Broadcast Programme Compilation Group decided the policy of the NHK; it consisted of the Ministers of Communications, Education and Home Affairs plus half a dozen 'learned and experienced men'. Later, as the war turned into a world conflagration, a new Information Bureau was created which simply took over all newspapers, magazines, publishing houses and cinema enterprises and which was dominated by the military.

Under the General Mobilisation Law of 1937 all journalists were forced to collaborate with government and obliged to spread the message of personal heroism. The National Spiritual Mobilisation Movement injected a spirit of xenophobia into the Japanese. A central national news agency, the *Domei Tsushin*, was created to supply war news. The Prime Minister explained at the meeting at which the Movement was founded that a modern state should be 'a community having a definite cultural mission' and that every citizen should be 'not a profit-seeking materialistic entity but a spiritual entity whose purpose is to make certain contributions to humanity through the structure of a Nation-state'.[7] That was to be the path leading to National Spiritual Mobilisation. It was strewn with suppressed newspapers. Representatives of the Government and the Police joined the board of the Society of Japanese Newspapers to ensure that the press followed the official line in war-reporting; the supply of newsprint was centrally controlled and various forms of journalistic 'self-discipline' were encouraged.

At the end of the war the Japanese heard the voice of their Emperor for the first time in their long history; he read over the air the message of capitulation which was to be the starting point of an effort to reconstruct Japanese society from its foundations. The GHQ of the American occupation for five years was the supreme civil authority, above the government itself. It set about creating a total programme of democratisation; it tried to refashion Japan in the image of the United States and the mutual impact of the two cultures brought about some surprising results.[8]

GHQ was determined to create complete freedom of speech in Japan, but to do so involved direct participation by the occupying power in all aspects of social life. Freedom was being imposed. In previous periods of liberalisation the sovereignty of the Emperor had in fact never been impaired. Now creating democracy involved a degree of interference as far as the media were concerned which would have been intolerable in the democracies of the West. To indicate how the guiding philosophies of broadcasting were re-created it is necessary to identify certain features which developed in or were retained in the Japanese newspapers.

It was and is forbidden for anyone to own stock in a newspaper unless he is an employee.[9] This was to prevent the holders of concentrated wealth from getting a foothold in the press. Banks therefore had to supply the bulk of the capital for restarting the press in Japan, and in fact are responsible for about 70 per cent of it. The banks may not participate in editorial control. Advertising, unlike the West, provides only 40 per cent of the income of the major newspapers of Japan, of which there are fifteen. (Three of them at present – the *Asahi*, the *Mainichi* and the *Yomiuri* – have over half the total newspaper sales of the country.) The fact that actual sales are responsible for so large a proportion of newspaper revenue has meant that competition between newspapers is extremely fierce; this has brought in its wake a tendency to sensationalism and scandal-mongering of a marked kind. Every newspaper is responsible for its own distribution throughout the nation. An army of salesmen go from door to door, each of them distributing a single mass-produced national paper, and inevitably the reports on readers' reactions of the sales departments with their web of salesmen are extremely influential in the editorial offices. The distribution system is simultaneously a means of reader-research and market-analysis of a very sensitive kind.[10] The salesman becomes very well-informed on what will sell and the journalists are tempted to follow his prescription. Japanese newspapers therefore tend to underplay politics; they breed an apathy and ignorance of political matters which cause much criticism in political circles. Newspapers try to run after the prejudices of their readers and tend to exaggerate each shift in public opinion in their content in order to be one step ahead of their rivals in the competition for circulation.

One of the provisions of the new constitution imposed by GHQ and the early post-war administration is that all journalism in Japanese is to be 'objective' and newspapers are supposed not to be politically controlled. All editorials are consciously moderate in tone despite the fact that they shift with every current of opinion. Majority opinions are emphasised and minority opinions are reflected far less than elsewhere in the Western world's press.

The exclusion of personally-held capital from the press at the end of the war meant that the pressure for commercial broadcasting rapidly gained ground. It was widely assumed that commercial radio would be permitted on the American pattern, and within a few months of the surrender applications were handed in to GHQ for permission to start private radio stations. GHQ however had other ideas. A complex and tortuous war-dance started up between the occupying force and the new Japanese government which was not resolved until the very last hours of the American presence in the early 1950s. It reflects a good deal about American thinking about broadcasting, as much in fact as about Japanese broadcasting ideas

252

and it is worth recording in some detail. The shape of modern Japanese broadcasting was determined partly by the ideas held by General MacArthur and his staff on how to 'create' a free broadcasting system, which would stand the test of time and prevent the resurgence of those forces in Japanese society which had been responsible for the war.

Of the nations which conquered Japan, Britain, China and the Soviet Union all agreed that the defeated nation should have a single broadcasting monopoly, as in the past. Only the Japanese government wanted to restart broadcasting on competitive lines, the Americans favouring a public system controlled by a kind of FCC. The Japanese government, thinking that commercialism was imminent, encouraged local interests to keep their applications in hand, but GHQ continued producing statements about the new principles of free speech and failed to pronounce finally on whether private stations would be allowed. NHK was separated from government control. The new Constitution adopted in 1947 stated in Article 21, 'Freedom of assembly and association as well as speech, press and all other forms of expression are guaranteed. No censorship shall be maintained, nor shall the secrecy of any means of communication be violated.' But the Allied Occupation set up a monitoring system to discover any communication which criticised the occupation. Several years went by and the Japanese government was still unable to discover GHQ's ultimate intentions on independent radio or to agree on the basis of the new structure for the NHK.

The government produced a plan which would have made the NHK a 'private juridical person' as before the war, but separated from official supervision; the plan was leaked to the press in order, it was said, to test GHQ's reaction. It was hostile. GHQ really was aiming at a system by which the government was deprived of any power, even a reserve power, over broadcasting after the occupation had been dismantled. American Far Eastern policy was gradually shifting towards the idea of a peace treaty and normalisation of relations between the two countries and was keen to leave behind a system which no Japanese government could again dominate. The Japanese retorted that the plan proposed by GHQ was meaningful only in a country which had an American-style constitution based on the separation of powers; in a society based upon a system of responsible cabinet government it was not possible to create an agency over which the government could never in any circumstances exert influence or direct power. A compromise proposal which involved a two-tier structure for the NHK – a public supervisory body governing a separate editorial authority, with a third element, a Radio Wave Agency simply policing the wavelengths – was put forward but produced only a further series of disputes. Eventually the Japanese government demanded that General MacArthur issue a formal public directive instructing them on the form of instrument they should use to set up a new NHK, since there could be no agreement. A strike broke out among the broadcasting staff. General MacArthur refused to issue the directive.

After some weeks the Japanese government received a letter from the General stating once again GHQ's plans. The government decided at once to treat this as the directive they had demanded and went ahead to draw up the legislation. As the Diet's various bodies processed the new bill, amendments were added which restored the government scheme for unitary control; the Americans then objected on the grounds that this was a violation of the MacArthur letter, and the amendments were withdrawn. In the meantime the Japanese press had fanned the flames of an agitation in favour of independent commercial broadcasting, and a poll indicated that 75 per cent of the population favoured the idea. Only the parties of the far left opposed it. The bill went through, but as soon as the peace treaty was in force in 1952 new measures were adopted which enabled commercial radio to begin.

The Act which finally ended the quarrel with GHQ on 26 April 1950 was in three parts. First there was to be a Radio Regulatory Commission modelled on the FCC in Washington. It was a non-governmental agency but was absorbed after the American departure into the Ministry of Postal Services. Secondly the NHK was given a new start as a special corporation under a Board of Governors, rather like the BBC. It was dedicated to democratic ideals and obliged to provide the widest possible coverage geographically and culturally in its programming.

The Board is appointed by the Prime Minister with the consent of Parliament and is intended, as in the case of the BBC, to represent the Japanese people as a whole; it can appoint and fire its own President and has to agree the senior appointments on the staff of the NHK. The third enactment was that independent broadcasting could be commenced under licence from the Radio Regulatory Commission.

The growth of broadcasting in Japan in the period immediately following the legislation was phenomenal. By 1956 there were 63 stations owned by 40 different companies. The American 525-line system had been adopted. By 1956 the medium wave had been used up. By the late 1960s there were 1300 television stations in all in Japan, nearly a half of them commercial, and 450 radio stations, a third of them commercial. Well over 80 per cent of all households had television sets. Their licence fees, amounting to £104 million per annum, make the NHK the richest public television network in the world, able to compete in technique and content with any system of broadcasting on earth.[11]

Perhaps the most interesting feature of the Japanese system is the method by which the NHK acquires its vast annual income.[12] The whole tradition of the NHK as a 'private juridical person' has persuaded it that money is best provided directly by the customer rather than through government. Although in its organisation and its cultural ideals it has consciously and quite proudly used the BBC as its model, it has distrusted a system by which the annual licence fee paid on the set and collected by the Post Office in Britain leaves the broadcasting body at the mercy of government. It is the government, in the European systems, which hands over the cash to the organisation, even though the cash comes directly from the viewer, and it is the government which decides when and by how much to raise the fee, as inflation gradually wipes out the value of the regular income. The NHK collects the annual fee itself, with its own cohorts of collectors who, as in the case of the Japanese newspapers (whose methods of distributing their products are the model used by the NHK), provide an expert and regular audience survey service at the same time.

The system by which each viewer pays the man from the

255

NHK £6 to £7 a year for the right to own a set has very shaky constitutional foundations. The system is based upon honour, honesty and the persuasive powers of the collector. No major test case has ever been brought in a Japanese court to determine whether the NHK has the right to oblige every owner of a set to pay his fee. The relationship between the two parties is that of an unwritten contract, in which, by the purchase or renting of a receiving set, the viewer enters into a solemn commitment to pay the NHK for its programmes, even if he chooses to watch none of them and prefers to stick to the commercial stations who demand nothing from him, other than that he watches their advertisements.

NHK is considered legally as a kind of cooperative friendly society of which the viewers are all constituent members; the broadcasting facilities are their common properties, of which they have technically the right to dispose. None of the money vested in the NHK comes from the government; when it was set up it merely consolidated the funds which had accumulated in previous years from the surplus of past licence fees. The fee is nowadays therefore the contribution paid annually and equally among all members to the costs of running the system. The non-existent contract, therefore, is a kind of internal arrangement of the cooperative organisation. It is a strange system by world standards. But it makes the NHK the securest and wealthiest single broadcaster on earth.

The government, under the Broadcast Act of 1950, is empowered to inspect the finances of the NHK annually and in detail; it also contributes to them an extra sum to cover the costs of broadcasting overseas which the NHK is also obliged to undertake (exactly as with the BBC).

There are various provisions in the law covering the impartiality of programme content in the NHK but there are no sanctions or penalties if it disobeys them. It exists virtually entirely outside government, although accusations are made from time to time, as in all systems, that the programmes have come under some subtle form of authoritarian influence. There is no legal recognition of a government right to any kind of broadcast. Nor is there any government right to withdraw or order to be withdrawn any communication, as in the British system. There is no body outside the NHK to which an aggrieved citizen may bring any accusation of ill-treatment or bias. The whole system is a neat Japanese device, perfected from a European model, for creating an independent broadcasting system, based on the ideals of democracy.[13]

The system by which a country organises its broadcasting system contains to the outside observer a strange coded version of that country's entire political culture. This is certainly the case with Japan. The whole basis of the modern state was the extirpation of militaristic authoritarianism, and in the organisation of television the pursuit of a Japanese pluralism has resulted in a situation in which television mirrors the contemporary preoccupations of the nation. Commercial broadcasting in Japan is as profitable, as tough-minded, as determined and as competitive as Japanese industry. The purchaser of advertising time in the Japanese system pays a sum of money for the 'time charge' (calculated according to the length of the advertisement and the desirability of the time slot concerned) plus the cost of making the programme into which the advertisement fits.[14] There is no haggling over the former part of the payment, because the time slots are graded and command viewing audiences the size of which are generally agreed. The only variable in the system is the cost of making the programme and so under the Japanese method there is enormous pressure to make the programme as cheaply as possible, greater pressure than in other commercial systems. The advertiser, although he doesn't 'sponsor' a programme on the American pattern, nonetheless has an interest in the programme being as cheap as possible. When you consider that there is thought to be insufficient demand for advertising at present to support the large number of commercial stations in the major cities, you realise why, in programme terms, the results are so bad. Unlike almost any other television system, the Japanese has been unable to develop a group of free-lance producers or production companies. The advertisements are superimposed on the programmes themselves, avoiding time-consuming 'commercial breaks'. Advertisements use up to one-sixth of the total transmission time in hours of peak viewing.

Although newspaper control was deliberately worked out to

257

exclude ownership by interests not belonging exclusively to the journalistic world, the same provisions were not built into the commercial broadcasting system. Fuji Television is run by the head of a paper mill, Mizuno Shigeo, who is also President of Bunku Broadcasting. One of the key figures in a prosperous steel company is the senior figure in Nippon TV. Adach Tadashi, the President of Radio Tokyo, is also President of the Japanese Chamber of Commerce. It is frequently complained that commercial television in Japan has developed a rightist slant, despite the fact that it is supposed to maintain the same impartiality enjoined upon broadcasters almost everywhere. As in the case of the newspapers, the efforts to build 'freedom' into the broadcasting system have led to a mood of conformism in broadcast content which veers slightly to the right and sometimes to the left with the shifts of public mood and the political situation in general. In the furore over the Security Pact of 1960 the press of Japan opposed the Kishi government and favoured the opposition stand; immediately after the issue died down, however, the entire press rapidly slid back into a midway position in which the policy of one paper cannot be greatly distinguished from another. The efforts to create a democratic exchange of opinion in Japan after the war have in practice led press and broadcasting towards a shifting neutrality based on the self-interest of the media institutions themselves rather than on actual currents of intellectual or political opinion. Professor Kumata of Michigan State University, in trying to discern the kind of force that television has become in the political world, has summed up his picture in a paragraph which reveals the weight of his Japanese experience: 'It is desirable, but highly unlikely, that broadcasting will function as a critic of the social scene. More likely, broadcasting will become institutionalized as part of the formal power apparatus of society. This means that the output will have more emphasis on maintenance functions and less emphasis on deliberate social change. This need not necessarily be so, but broadcasting as a system will avoid placing itself into a marginal position.'[15] Were the point made in less professional sociological language, it might have been couched in more cynical phrases.

The average Japanese spends eight hours per day asleep,

five working, one and a half eating and three and a half watching television or listening to the radio. It is not the world record for media obsession but it is not far short of it. Within a decade of the inauguration of television, the Japanese were the second nation in the world after America for the number of television sets owned.[16] Nearly 90 per cent of urban homes and 70 per cent of rural ones contain sets. It is more than twice the number of people who own refrigerators; in Japan the purchase of a television set appears to have been a more urgent consumer decision than the purchase of any other piece of electric domestic equipment. Throughout the decade of the sixties, the growth of the television habit was the largest factor in the phenomenal development of the Japanese electronics industry. Only at the end of that period did the advance of the computer push the television receiver aside. The industrial implications of the spread of television have been of some importance in modern Japan. The creation of a market for the television set was an important element in the rise of the industry and the development of its export potential. The Japanese electronics industry became the second largest in the world towards the end of the decade, although still a good way behind the American in bulk of production.

It was the transistor which suddenly in the middle of the fifties put the electronics industry on its feet in Japan and focussed world attention on it. Exports started growing immediately, mainly of radios, and by 1959 the manufacture of radio and television receivers was responsible for nearly half the total electronics industry just at the point at which that industry was surpassing the West German, British and French. For the next ten years the manufacture of broadcasting receiving equipment grew at a staggering rate, the exported section alone increasing from 7,000 million yen in 1957 to 160,000 million yen in ten years. By the end of the sixties it had doubled again. At the end of the decade the export of radio and television sets exceeded that of motor cars, about 40 per cent of all Japanese exports.[17] At the same time the Japanese government decreed that all television broadcasting would be gradually changed to the UHF band over the course of a decade beginning in 1968. Immediately the manufacturers started adding UHF tuners

259

to the vast majority of the sets made and this helped to keep the expansion boom going. The government had ensured that a huge demand would be stimulated not only for receiving sets but for all the renewed broadcasting equipment that the change would necessitate in the broadcasting organisations. The latter did not welcome the promised change but the manufacturers were highly pleased, and retooled their equipment almost overnight. Through the intensity with which the Japanese watch television they aid the growth of their country's export prowess. While spending their leisure time idly at home, they have been working hard for the economy.

In many ways the Japanese system looks like a parody of the British one. Indeed, it has started from a number of similar premises and principles. First it began with a public institution whose name was made synonymous with broadcasting itself and whose ideal was to spread a certain view of civilised culture and western democratic standards. Then, in order to create the further profusion which democracy in a mass society appeared to demand, it opened the doors to a particularly voracious commercial system which competed greedily for audiences and little else. The result of the pressure between the two halves of the system is that the NHK has to turn out a certain proportion of programmes which will obtain for it the share of the audience it requires, not for the sake of profit, but simply to maintain its privileged status, in other words to survive institutionally. Without a 'realistic' share of the audience, NHK feels that it would not be able to keep up the argument for maintaining the system in which it collects a fee from every viewer in the country. By collecting its own fee it is freer than the BBC from the pressures of government, but in another sense it is all the more vulnerable.

NHK manages to win hands down in the ratings games from dawn, when the programmes begin, until dusk when the evening peak viewing begins; it is watched by over thirty million when it begins the day with a news bulletin and its daytime programmes are statistically the most effective. In the evenings the commercial stations, however, get well over half of the audience. Japan therefore has developed a strange quirk unknown elsewhere in world television – an extra peak hour at dawn.

It is an odd but predictable fact that in defining the basic elements of a national broadcasting structure one can almost automatically define the style of the programmes themselves, the attitudes and emphases. NHK, like the BBC, has developed an extremely large, skilled and well-financed news division, with twenty-four bureaux around the world, and a vast team of superbly trained cameramen and journalists. News is one field in which a national broadcasting organisation must excel if it is to be seen to fulfil its national function. The NHK News division, in fact, is larger than that either of the BBC or the CBS. The emphasis on news was of course inevitable, given the fundamental purposes which broadcasting was created to serve in the early post-war period.

It is not only the luxurious situation of the television news collectors of the NHK which arouse the envy of television workers around the world. The extraordinary degree to which the entire organisation of NHK has been automated is something of a legend in world television. The studio operation is run by four men and a computer; all the programmes, recorded and stored on tapes, are fed automatically to the transmitters; the complex operations of the studio side of the news bulletins are similarly automated, with virtually no opportunity for human error, as each of the dozens of news items is slotted into the flow of the bulletins at the instigation of the TOPICS computer, which is now storing information on the entire NHK library of archive film for instant retrieval by producers. All the booking of studio time and the innumerable pieces of expensive and scarce gadgetry is handled in a matter of moments by TOPICS, instead of the hours or days which the organisation of these resources can involve in most broadcasting bodies.

Similarly the discussion on broadcasting effects, on screen violence and teenage crime, on voting and election coverage, on the problems of learning through television, is lavishly illustrated in Japan by surveys and research work of an exhaustive kind. Although research into the effects of television in society seems to have run into very much the same set of dead ends which it has reached elsewhere, the discussion in Japan has been extremely well informed as a result partly of the work published by the NHK's own research institute. The NHK affects the same lordly disregard of viewing figures as other public service broadcasting bodies and the same simultaneous zealous concern to get good and up-to-date statistics on viewers' likes and dislikes. The NHK is obliged, under its charter, to undertake sociological research as well as collecting the normal statistical data on the audience.

Although Japanese culture is strikingly different in its traditional content from that of any western country the genres of television have somehow found a way to impose their nature and needs upon it. Japan thus has developed samurai westerns which can be virtually manufactured on a kind of assembly line in the same way that American westerns are. NHK's westerns, however, try to be a cut above the others, they have a moral purpose, and they try to instil a respect for the traditions of the culture. Soap opera and variety are further genres which have sprung up inside Japanese culture, although fashioned for the domestic screen. The 'kinds' of television are international even though the mythology belongs to the originating nation. One of the most characteristically Japanese types of programme are the 'hard-training' dramas, in which the characters are all frantically concerned to reach a certain goal: there are hard-training dramas about schoolboys trying to win a football match, or businessmen trying to succeed with a product, or students zealously cudgelling their brains to pass an examination. The theme in these plays is always dedication to something that is almost but not quite impossible. It is strikingly symbolic of Japanese broadcasting as a whole, certainly of Japan as a whole. John Reith would not necessarily have felt the theme out of place in his broadcasting system.

The broadcasting culture of Japan breeds psychological intensity and reflects the traditions of extreme self-control and self-impulsion which are ancient Japanese characteristics. The democratic freedoms, tenaciously built into the structure and ideology of Japanese broadcasting and post-war Japanese society, have landed the Japanese with precisely the same set of social issues puzzling other societies with highly developed mass entertainment industries. The Japanese are cudgelling their brains over the same problems of screen violence and delinquency, of free political discussion and the need to maintain respect for authority, of mass edification versus trivialisation. The desired objectives of democratised culture and citizenship are jeopardised precisely by the mass nature of the broadcasting technology and its institutions.

Chapter Ten

The Dutch System: The Pillars of Hilversum, the Issue of 'Access'

'Radio must be changed from being a means of distribution to a means of communication. Radio could be the most wonderful means of communication imaginable in public life—a huge linked system, if it were capable not only of transmitting but of receiving, of allowing the listener not only to hear but to speak, ceased to isolate him but brought him in touch.'

Bertolt Brecht: *Radiotherie*, 1932
Gesammelte Werke, Band VIII, p. 129.

' "There's no sort of use in knocking" said the Footman, "and that for two reasons. First, because I am on the same side of the door as you are; secondly, because they're making such a noise inside, no one could possibly hear you." And certainly there was a most extraordinary noise going on within—a constant howling and sneezing, and every now and then a great crash.'

Lewis Carroll: *Alice in Wonderland*

Inevitably the concentration of power in broadcasting has created demands for 'democratisation' in various forms. From the earliest days there have been trails of discontent arising from a disbelief in the impartiality or objectivity of the professionals responsible for making programmes and distributing invitations to broadcast. For many decades, in Britain especially, it was possible to fight off attacks of this kind with the argument that since they came from all sides of the community and were fairly randomly distributed, the overall performance of the broadcasting institution must after all be successfully impartial.[1] Recent years have brought a more intensified assault and the demand that by giving direct 'access' to the wavelength to relevant groups and interests an equitable and democratic element could be introduced into the broadcasting of political and social issues. The demands for access have not come merely from small radical or fringe organisations which feel themselves ignored in the media of national discussion; they have come equally from major interests – unions, management, government itself – which have felt themselves deprived of the means to speak to the mass public in their own terms. In a number of countries, senior politicians have complained of the way in which lack of the facility to explain major policies directly to the electorate is, allegedly, actually preventing the proper functioning of government.[2]

In the United States the speeches of Vice-President Agnew were the principal focus of this argument. In Britain Anthony Wedgwood Benn has repeatedly returned to this theme,[3] emphasising that 'the present combination of corporate or commercial control theoretically answerable to politically appointed Boards of Governors is not in any sense a democratic enough procedure to control the power the broadcasters have'. Benn advances the ingenious argument that by democratising the production units within broadcasting, by allowing them openly to discuss their output and afterwards label it (even within the existing formal structures) the public would simultaneously be gaining a measure of accountability, in that every member of the production team would be forced to accept public responsibility for the output of his unit. It is a development which seems unlikely to occur except in a period in which workers' control in general gained greater support than it hitherto has. If society as a whole were to move in this direction, broadcasting would be unlikely to lag behind.

Benn argues that a second road to democracy in broadcasting would be through a system by which organised groups could be granted broadcasting time. Broadcasting institutions would adopt a publishing function rather than a purely editorial one. It is an attractive idea, at least on the surface. New issues and new groups have tended to have to fight their way onto the screens in the past. It can be argued that the wave of violence in political demonstrations which occurred in the late sixties

265

in various parts of the world was the result of an inability on the part of various groups to express themselves clearly before the same large audience which was available to well-established interests in society. The result was that by advocating activities of a news-making nature the issues could be forced onto the screen, although even then in a distorted and perhaps over-heated form. Benn argues, and many with him, that access to the screen at an early stage would have enabled the radical movements of that time to participate in general discussion and obtain the social 'feedback' essential to correct social problems before damage occurs.

In January 1971 a group of trade unionists in Britain under-took an intensive period of scrutiny of every reference to trade union issues on the television screen. Their report 'One Week'[4] concluded that 'industrial affairs are covered in a superficial and haphazard fashion; that the BBC in particular scandalously failed to maintain impartiality in dealing with three issues during the week monitored. . . .' Their grievance was a demand for 'access' also, but of a slightly different kind. The trade unions were complaining that their reasoning and motives were not understood adequately by the people who were responsible for shaping the content of news bulletins; the kind of access they required therefore (in addition to the right to their own opportunities for outright advocacy) was a right to be understood in their own terms, a right to upgrade their own status in the minds of broadcasters.[5]

That definition of the access problem complicates and limits the value of the Benn approach. The most that can be hoped of television is that globally it presents an accurate portrait of the society, whatever means are adopted for controlling it. It is the choices made by the people who man the institutions which make or mar this portrait; if the existing professionalisms are inadequate to guarantee that the task is well done (and the very existence of widespread discontent is almost in itself evidence enough to prove this) it is unlikely that in an institution which simply had the task of distributing airtime the quarrel would be at an end.

Benn lists three main groups who would automatically, by a 'self-selecting' process, identify themselves as groups worthy of the regular right to broadcast. He names Parliament, the trade union movement and industry, then the professions, and regional authorities.[6] He is therefore re-creating a model of access which gives predominance to the existing major interests. 'Then there are the thousands of pressure groups representing racial minorities, special interests and a host of other concerns that at present depend solely on the possibility that they may be invited to contribute a speaker to a discussion that has been set up by a producer to fill a slot in his schedule.' Already a model begins to appear within the system which Benn advocates that tends to reproduce something of the existing problem – large interests remain large interests, and have greatest access to the audience, while other groups, labelled 'minority', appear later as 'thousands of pressure groups'. The problem of access which has hitherto been contained within the professionalism of the producer is transferred to another point in the social chain of command over broadcasting.

It is undoubtedly quite practical for broadcasting to undertake a simple publishing function, which it has traditionally in most countries eschewed.[7] The problem of the mass audience however remains, the problem of ensuring that by using television in this way it remains the same mass medium to which the complainants wish to enjoy access. By allowing innumerable interests to take part in a competition for airtime, competing partly on the basis of their existing power and partly in editorial terms (on the basis of their intrinsic interest), it is possible that the audience will disappear, that television will cease to be the skilled mechansim for delivering a vast audience. If broadcasting becomes mainly a means of self-expression for frustrated individuals and groups, it cannot remain as overwhelmingly powerful as it has been as the supreme deliverer of a massive audience to a communicator. That may be a very good thing indeed, but is it what the advocates of 'access' are really wanting? The problem has arisen in the first place because television delivers its vast audience to too narrow a spectrum of communicating interests. Reform could make it broaden the spectrum but narrow the audience, perhaps to the point at which it ceases to be the audience which is being sought.

Many argue that there is room for a series of compromises,

that mass entertainment can still remain the backbone of a more democratically oriented system. Is it possible for the audience created by the products of the entertainment industry to switch itself into a frame of mind in which it becomes the political public of John Stuart Mill? Broadcasting was born with an undifferentiated audience – it grows remote, hidden from its audience because of that underlying relationship. What happens when that audience is handed to groups of propagandists, when the communication consensus is shattered?

There is one nation which has tried to build its television system on the basis of religious and political pluralism: Holland. It has done so because of the deep-rooted historical requirement for certain forms of cultural pluralism as the sole basis for a viable Dutch society. Television in Holland is based on total freedom of access almost as the broadcast counterpart of a politico-religious tradition. Its system is however often held up as a model to the rest of the world.

In the United States, as we have seen, the issue of access is a simple extension of the political tradition of the First Amendment.[8] In Europe freedom of expression has always been seen as a relative rather than an absolute value. There are different versions of cultural freedom, different versions of the issue of access – they arise from the varying ways in which peoples interpret their cultures rather than the ways in which they label their rights. While for one nation free access is felt to be a road towards anarchy[9] (France, for instance), for another it is merely a way to break the editorial monopoly of a single broadcasting institution[10] (Britain); for Holland it is a way to express its own ancient pluralist traditions in a new medium and in the context of a new politics.

Few countries can claim that their broadcasting system has aroused crisis and passion on the scale of the Dutch, and yet, apart from Britain, scarcely any country is more boastful of the system of organisation and control it has evolved, in many ways justly so. On 27 February 1965 the coalition cabinet, headed by Marijnen, found itself so divided over legislation, already under discussion for two years, which would reorganise and expand the Dutch broadcasting system that the government was forced to resign: it was the first government in history to fall as a result of a row over broadcasting. The Cals cabinet which followed – the 'Radio Cabinet' – succeeded in laying down a structure for a new system which enables the Dutch to lay claim to having the most open, free and liberal system in existence, but whether it really solves any of the riddles of broadcasting as these exist outside Holland is a matter for some dispute. The new Dutch system is an updated version of that inaugurated in the 1920s.[11] Holland began a regular broadcasting service well before anybody else, and from the beginning has enabled the listeners and viewers to exercise a very considerable degree of authority over the content of broadcasting.

On 5 November 1919 the *Nieuwe Rotterdamse Courant* published a notice announcing the inauguration at eight the following morning of a regular daily radio service; the founder was a young engineer Hanso Idzerta,[12] who continued for many months to entertain and inform listeners with a regular and prolonged set of broadcasts. His efforts aroused the interest of radio amateurs everywhere in Europe; his station call sign was PCGG, and although its claim to be the first regular broadcast is disputed, especially by Pittsburgh's KDKA station,[13] Idzerta was certainly several months if not years ahead of most of Europe's pioneers in the field. In England *Wireless World* appealed for funds to help him carry on with his service. The *Daily Mail* commended his efforts to its readers. There were other pioneers in Holland, however, who started very early in the business of broadcasting. The Amsterdam Stock Exchange installed a transmitter to provide financial news to a list of subscribers; later one of the Dutch news agencies created a radio network to link the newsrooms of fifty Dutch provincial papers.[14] The listeners themselves, and the manufacturers, were in advance of the authorities in their thinking and planning. In the mid-1920s the Hilversumche Draadloze Omroep (HDO), a kind of broadcasting foundation, was set up jointly by the main radio manufacturers and a group of enthusiastic listeners; it quickly produced the desired effect of creating a manufacturing boom and providing listeners with something to make purchasing a receiving apparatus worth while. It meant, however, that the very roots of the Dutch broadcasting service were planted among the users of radio rather than among parliamentarians intent on designing convenient institutions.

Despite the relatively calm atmosphere of Dutch society, despite its ability to maintain domestic order and national unity in an atmosphere of unruffled calm, there is and has always been considerable religious rivalry. The main religious groups have learned to live together by dividing various spheres of interest between them; to this day Protestant and Catholic factions control large sections of Dutch political, business and trade union life. When radio began, especially when listener organisation became the point of control, it seemed natural that religious organisations should set up their own organisations to control mutually agreed areas of the programme output. Dutch educational and cultural life is heavily oriented towards divisions along confessional lines. In the course of the last fifty years a system which was born to preserve the interests of various churches has been extended to preserve the interests of an ever-expanding series of groupings based upon beliefs or causes of one kind or another.

Until 1927 there was only one transmitter in Holland, at Hilversum. It was shared by five organisations each of them with a religious affiliation. The HDO was succeeded, as owner of the transmitter, by the Algemeene Vereeniging Radio Omroep (AVRO – the General Broadcasting Association) which was neutral and governed by private commercial law. There was the Catholic Broadcasting Foundation (KRO), The Netherlands Christian Radio Society (NCRV), which was an organisation of Orthodox Protestants, the Liberal Protestant Broadcasting Association and the Workers' Radio Amateurs Society (VARA), which broadcast with a socialist tinge. Broadcasting was thus born inside a private world, not a governmental one, with a series of companies, all administered under ordinary commercial law, yet dedicated to public broadcasting. When a second transmitter arrived, at Huizen, in 1927, KRO and NRCV divided the spoils between them. VARA considered it had an inadequate share of the time available on the first transmitter.

A year later the government stepped in with legislation which set up a Broadcasting Council (Radio raad) under official regulation, to organise the distribution of time. The rules were fairly simple: there was to be no advertising and nothing was to be broadcast which interfered with security, public order or morality. Later a company was set up, 60 per cent owned by the government, the remaining 40 per cent shared among the broadcasting organisations, with the responsibility of setting up and operating transmitters throughout the country.

The organisations were financed through their members. They retained the right (and still do) to exclusive powers to publish papers giving the content of programmes and this remains an enduring source of finance. Through the programme publications the companies and associations raise the money to make the programmes. In the 1920s, they also paid for studio-construction and equipment. Each organisation purchased its own equipment, and hired its own staff. There was no licence fee as in other parts of Europe.

At the outbreak of war the system was abruptly ended; the German army of occupation confiscated the entire set-up, and created a centralised system based upon the listeners' licence fee. When the Germans left, the title of the original broadcasting organisations was restored, after a transition period. By arrangement with them, the government created the Stichting Radio Unie (NRU – Netherlands Broadcasting Foundation)[15] which absorbed all the capital property of all the organisations; they gave up their studios, libraries and all forms of equipment. The Minister then arranged a timetable for the sharing of broadcasting hours. Although everyday operations continued as before the war it had become a closed system; there was no machinery by which newcomers could join. For the moment, there were no more organisations knocking on the door, but nonetheless 'the Pillars of Hilversum', as the organisations came to be nicknamed, earned a great deal of opprobrium for their static and socially divisive nature. In various parts of the country the cry was going up for the creation of a unified system, modelled on the BBC; but the quality for which this new organisation was needed was that of openness – the confessional groupings had earned for themselves a reputation for exclusiveness of outlook, something totally alien to their original ideal.

After the immediate post-war period of reconstruction, the Dutch government set up a Television Foundation on the same lines as NRU for radio; the five companies were each licensed to transmit a given number of hours per week, and the government provided most of the money. After the 1956 Television Decree, viewers had to pay a licence fee, a Crown appointee was placed in the chairmanship of the NTS, with a further three government appointees on its board. The companies between them supplied ten members to the board. Unlike the radio set-up, Dutch television had central editorial power in that the NTS itself retained 40 per cent of the broadcasting time, which it deployed on news programmes and on the purchase of foreign material, extremely important in a small country which cannot afford, in the television age, to make a complete comprehensive range of programmes by itself. Like the NRU system, the NTS was not allowed to expand its membership. Holland thus developed a static confessionally-based system, in place of something which had traditionally been open, and even within the five-member system, television had brought about an element of official participation, and a strong element of centralised editorial direction.

As the sixties arrived, Holland found itself under ether-attack from pirate broadcasters, both in radio and television. Although most politicians continued to feel that the standards of the established organisations were still high enough to command respect and continuing official support, the cry was heard within Parliament for the opening of the system to all outside groups who wanted to participate in the national broadcasting system, even if they were not able to reach the same standards of professionalism as their older rivals.

The Marijnen coalition government prepared some legislation which would have liberalised the system, opened it up to new organisations and allowed a degree of advertising. It was in the course of the attempts to pass this legislative package that the government fell, its constituent party groupings irrevocably split. The Cals government which succeeded had committed itself to laying the foundations of a new system of broadcasting. In the conditions of the political crisis of 1965 the Cals cabinet moved gingerly forwards and set up a transitional experimental system in December 1965 with a brief to retain the politico-religious basis of broadcasting but within a central cooperative organisation. The transitional system became the basis for a further major reform in 1969 and this system is now the source of great national pride among Dutch broadcasters.[16]

Out of the political crisis of 1965 was born a system which clearly reveals the period to which it belongs. The 1960s were years of widespread political activity and a time in which 'fringe' politics and popular culture became closely interconnected. It was a time of spectacular and original growth of forms of participation in public life by small groups. The Netherlands system of broadcasting is very much a child of its age, and bears close resemblance to its parentage. It is extremely Dutch and extremely up-to-date. It enshrines the grass-roots political aspirations of its time in a way which gives them a status in national life in Holland which they do not yet possess elsewhere. It enabled every group of discontented or inspired individuals to propagate its beliefs on its own terms. In providing this facility as of right (a right unrecognised in any other broadcasting system) it tried to bring by implication all the movements of the time out of the shadows, out of a kind of cathode outlawdom, and into the forefront of public life. It enabled broadcasting to be used as a primary instrument of advocacy by people who belonged to no established and powerful pressure group or party. It tried to make broadcasting as flexible and available an instrument as printing. Whether it has succeeded in dealing with the problem of open access to national wavelengths is another matter. It is doubtful whether, in the neat antithesis of Brecht, it has in fact turned broadcasting into a means of communication rather than a means of distribution.

The NTS and the NRU were merged into a single supervisory body, the NOS,[17] (Nederlandse Omroep Stichting) which took over their facilities and their right to between 25 per cent and 40 per cent of broadcasting time. The idea is that these programmes should become a 'meeting place' for different kinds of people. NOS was also given responsibility for an expansion of regional programming, except in one province, Limburg, where this was organised separately.

273

The Minister of Cultural Affairs is the responsible government member who must ensure that the provisions of the law are being observed throughout the system. The government is supposed to be excluded from all forms of editorial control, but the reserve power in the hands of the Minister of Culture gives him a right of retrospective censorship,[18] in that he can ultimately withdraw the right to broadcast from any of the licensed organisations if they commit a breach of the laws concerning security or social order.[19]

The chairman of NOS is an official appointment, as are six of the twenty-four members of the Board of Management. Six more are chosen by various national cultural organisations, and twelve by the broadcasting organisations.[20] The NOS owns a group of orchestras, choirs, libraries, studios, archives, tape and record collections, laboratories and other centralised sources of programming. A 30-hectare site at Hilversum was set aside for constructing a complex of buildings to house the central facilities while each major organisation has a building of its own.

The licence fee was set at just over £9. Since 1967 there has been a certain amount of advertising permitted in the 'block' form, familiar in Europe, in which four short periods are set aside during the evening, before and after each of the two main news bulletins. The two channels thus have a total of 180 minutes per week of advertisements (24 minutes in radio). Once the periods of block advertising are finished there is no more. 40 per cent of the advertising is given to the newspapers in compensation for an assumed loss of revenue. That sum is now being progressively reduced. Under supervision of a government appointee, the total revenue from licence fee and advertising is divided up among the broadcasters according to an agreed and extremely complex scale.[21]

From the beginning of the transitional period all groups demanding to become broadcasting organisations were divided into three sections, those with a membership of over 400,000, those of over 250,000 and those of over 100,000. The time available is divided on the formula 5:3:1, with the proviso that the smallest groups must have at least $2\frac{1}{2}$ hours a week each. If an organisation cannot supply proof that it has the requisite number of members to qualify for a particular group, it is given a full year to attempt to regain its members, and then is allowed to qualify for its time retrospectively.[22] Of the five founders of Dutch broadcasting all except VPRO qualified for the first category. VPRO could only muster members sufficient for category C. But soon after the transitional period began a new applicant appeared on the scene: TROS, a pirate station from the North Sea which decided to try to come in from the cold. It joined as a 'C' member but gradually upgraded itself to 'B'. It is conservative in tone, with a small 'c', having no overt political affiliation. The only other major change was the arrival of the Evangelical Union (EO) with candidate membership for category 'C'.[23]

To qualify to compete at all, an organisation must prove that its principal reason for existence is to broadcast. It must also indicate that its membership reflects a cultural or spiritual or religious identification of some kind. It must have corporate status but be non-profit-making. It must collect membership fees and be prepared to open its membership lists to the minister. The membership fee must be at least 5 guilders per annum or 13 guilders if it includes the annual subscription to one of the programme magazines which played so important a role in the life of Dutch broadcasting at an earlier period.[24]

After the experimentation of the early transitional period, it was realised that many intending broadcasting organisations were not able to muster a membership of 100,000 paying viewers. It was decided that any group that could reach 15,000 could have the status of a candidate member,[25] and in the final legislation (which was passed in February 1967) such groups were awarded one hour per week on television and three on radio, provided that they could produce a 'fully comprehensive' set of programme plans.

In addition to these the system was further opened to allow a series of organisations to have programme time even though they are not attempting a 'fully comprehensive' programme and don't have memberships according to the rules governing the major organisations. A number of religious organisations decided they wanted to broadcast, as well as the Humanist Movement, Moral Rearmament, The Sexual Reform Society and a number of political parties represented in the Second Chamber of Parliament. In all, thirty separate organisations share time within the system, although the vast majority of them only occupy tiny and infrequent segments of it. (The Sexual Reformers, for instance, have twenty minutes once a fortnight, the Humanists ten minutes a week on radio and ten minutes a month on television.)

The Dutch are prouder, however, of their system than their programmes. An air of earnest dullness surrounds the entire output. It lacks dynamism. It lacks the air of unpredictability. The impact – that supreme quality of television – has somehow been reduced. Nothing seems to *happen* on the screen, now that the system has been, in so enlightened a manner, opened so freely.[26] VARA imports 'Z Cars' and 'Coronation Street' from Britain, AVRO (sometimes called the channel of the silent majority) takes 'Peyton Place', while NCRV buys 'Softly, Softly' and the Catholic KRO 'Bonanza'. The content of the screens is therefore for much of the time identical with that of every other network in the world; Dutch television, as much as any other, has to deal with the problem of creating large audiences, reaching after an ever-larger section of the mass audience. It takes the same homogenised view of the audience that is taken by television in other similar countries. In order to reach its audience each of the major groups must send out its message of religious or political material to an audience that has switched to a particular channel for some other purpose.

The broadcasting time is distributed, most of it, to organisa-tions which technically possess large memberships, but the affiliations they draw on mean no more to the individual who pays his dues than similar allegiances today involve elsewhere in the world. Although Holland is a more religious country than most, even today, it is still hardly likely that for the bulk of the people their membership of a Catholic broadcasting body or an Orthodox Protestant one is a matter of deep personal importance. The confessional groupings therefore do not represent in all probability the things that most trouble or involve the audience. The Dutch system therefore creates a kind of pluralism within the class of activists and professional communicators, but does not fundamentally change the role that television plays in the lives of the inhabitants of Holland. By taking from television the voice of supreme media authority which its supposed impartiality helps to bestow upon it elsewhere, television in Holland has less rather than more impact. Foreign material is required to a very great degree, to provide the really high-audience entertainment on which the system depends for advertising and for delivering an audience of useful size to the propagandist programmes.

The Dutch system therefore does not solve the historic problem of the mass audience; even though it is a unique and laudable effort to do something utterly different from anywhere else, it is left with the problem of freedom still unsolved. Recognised, labelled and overtly defined intellectual groupings can express themselves to an audience, but that audience has already segmented itself, in the terms of the system, and, in effect, 'switched off'. Part of the great impact of great broadcasting is the result of the fact that the broadcaster faces a mysterious audience of whose identity he is unaware.

In Holland television is still divided into segmented slots of time, into which a specially fixed and regular set of genres is fed. The forms of television have not changed with the organisational structure. The big companies are in competition, not for a unique kind of dialogue with its audience, but to chase statistical phenomena in the same way as any other competing television companies in any other system. Increasingly, in any case, NOS itself provides some of the most expensive foreign programmes.

The programme companies hold annual meetings with the rank and file of their membership; they collect suggestions and criticisms.[27] The producers and broadcasters meet their members as professional communicators meeting laymen anywhere else – the non-professional speaks an 'unrealistic' and useless language, unschooled by 'the facts of life'. The dialogue is like the dialogue of a parent–teacher association or of a grand meeting of doctors and their patients, not the dialogue of a community in which both sides expect any mutually enriching communication to take place. Without redefining the relationship between the professional in television and the audience (even the active and involved section of the audience), indeed without redefining the role of the professional altogether (in whose skills and working methods the audience itself is delineated) there can be no real advance towards a solution of the problem of 'access'.

Nonetheless the Dutch system is one that must command the respect and attention of anyone concerned to find ways to make television as available a medium for general discourse as the press. The faults in the Dutch system are of creeping centralisation, as well as of uninvolving programmes. The role of the NOS, the central agency, is growing because it succeeds in getting more programmes into the Dutch Top Ten than any of the companies. It is NOS that broadcasts the moonwalks and the big sporting events; it is NOS that collects a great deal of the satellite material which in recent years has commanded some of of the greatest audiences in television history. There is a danger that in the course of time the social, statistical and financial pressures which affect broadcasting elsewhere in Europe will corrode Hilversum's broadcasting, leaving the thirty private stations to wither slowly as a result of their inability to hold on to the mass audience. The pillars of Hilversum may be crushed by the harsh cultural realities of mass society in the long run. Nonetheless the Dutch experience shows that programme diversity can be achieved without monopoly in broadcasting, that a modern society can survive without 'objectivity' in all its broadcasting and that *editional* power can be successfully devolved within a determinedly pluralistic nation.

Chapter Eleven

The Last Resource of Freedom

> Day unto day uttereth speech, and night unto night
> sheweth knowledge.
> There is no speech nor language, where their voice is
> not heard.
> Their line is gone out through all the earth, and their
> words to the end of the world. In them hath he set a
> tabernacle for the sun . . .
>
> Psalm 19

I have tried to show that there are several unargued assumptions buried inside both media of broadcasting. There is an assumption that radio and television must necessarily, of their nature, provide a means of expression and self-expression for a tiny group addressing a vast multitude. That assumption is no longer technically valid, and it is doubtful whether it ever really was. Broadcasting was placed inside vast increasingly-powerful institutions and instructed to find a way to aggregate all the audiences of a single society into one. All the political problems arose with the realisation that the contours of society did not, or did no longer, follow the contours around which the broadcasting institutions had been built. The hierarchy of taste enshrined once in British radio (and still partly surviving in British television) entailed a false vision of society. In America the effort to escape from this formal strait-jacket led to a broadcasting culture which systematically degraded taste in the attempt to discover the true denominator of the vast audience. Both systems claimed and claim that they are serving the whole of their audience; both have evolved some way from their original schema. Both are nevertheless saddled with an inbuilt belief that there is a 'minority' audience and a 'majority' audience; every night a senseless competition takes place between rival and highly financed concentrations of professional talent. Each team is fighting for its institutional and financial life. Each team behaves as if it 'owns' the wavelengths which it exploits, and is managed by men whose duty it is to filter all the messages which pass through the air. Saddled with the duty to attract a simultaneous audience coterminous with the entire population, they are obliged to behave as if they were national governesses presiding over a vast nursery. The entire apparatus of their power, and the fantastic political patronage which flows from it, is based ultimately upon a no longer valid belief that the resources of broadcasting are scarce.

The French nation is one of a number which have failed to find a suitable point of intellectual and political balance on which to build the powerful machinery of broadcasting. As I have shown, every effort to build a broadcasting institution has collapsed for lack of underlying consent between politicians and broadcasters as to what should constitute a suitable political balance. Canada has been similarly wracked by indecision as to exactly where in society the power of broadcasting should find its fulcrum. The French dilemma is an extreme example of a universal broadcasting dilemma.

The United States pursued an ideal of diversity which turned into a crippling conformity; its choice of a fulcrum was the business community in whose untrammelled power radio and television became as deadening as they are lucrative, and as tyrannical as any totalitarian system. The products of the American system, however, spread out across the world and have become the fodder by which the vast audience is nurtured not only in the West but regrettably in large areas of the Third World who receive in their homes rations of a fifth-hand American pseudo-culture like donations of cast-off clothing. A broadcasting system which creates its basic audience in this way finds it increasingly difficult to escape.

The Dutch have tried to escape by building their own unique system upon a wholly different idea of cultural freedom. They too have probably failed, but with more glory. In dividing broadcasting time among rival propagandist groups they dealt with the problem of 'objectivity' with which the alleged scarcity of wavelengths had saddled broadcasting everywhere, but they confronted then the problems of their own small size. It has not proved possible to build a truly effective *Dutch* broadcasting system because so many of the programmes have to be purchased elsewhere. In effect the Dutch system is grafted onto a kind of motley internationalised system. The messages of Holland's multi-confessionalism are carried on the wings of exported Anglo-Saxon entertainment. In the case of Japan, another of my major examples, we have a system which evolved alone while attempting to imitate the best in the broadcasting institutions of the West. Yet, by wrestling as they have with the same underlying problems of the wavelength shortage, of ensuring political neutrality and of simultaneously satisfying the cravings of commercial and manufacturing interests, the Japanese have created a system which simply parodies the Anglo-Saxon; public and private systems compete together each in the belief that it will ultimately be driven out of existence if some scores of millions of faces are not turned simultaneously towards its screens for several hours a day. The tyranny of television is a tyranny of supply based upon false assumptions of demand.

From that brief recapitulation of my argument it is clear that there is no simple way to turn 'bad' television into 'good'. For a long time we in Britain thought that the success of our broadcasting lay in the 'quality' of the programmes. That was in part true, but in reality the success of the BBC (and ITV, at certain periods) has been that it conscientiously reflects the success of a whole culture in finding some kind of valid relationship with the mass audience, the society at large. That relationship, in Britain as elsewhere, is now under strain and to that extent our 'system' is no longer adequate, no matter how great the quality of individual programmes. The skills of television production cannot be developed without a healthy broadcasting system, they cannot be imported, they cannot be put into cold storage while certain problems rage. A broadcasting industry is healthy only when it is free to hold discourse with its society and when that society is free to influence it, to criticise it and to be challenged and at times affronted by it. Public television in the United States has failed for the most part because it has never really gained any important relationship with the bulk of the American audience or even with any really important segment of it. Many of its best programmes are now imported from Britain. That might be good for those Americans who want to watch British television (there is always of course great value to be obtained from seeing the culture of another nation) but only American society can throw up broadcasting of high quality which is of real value to itself. Prestige is meaningless in television, if it is the prestige of a minority. The inadequacies of American public television are, however, directly the fault of a commercial system so avaricious of its hegemony over the audience that no differently motivated group of broadcasters can establish themselves with the mass audience.

A television producer needs to live within line-of-sight of those who are mainly intended to be entertained or affected by what he does. The real prostitution of American broadcasting lies in the fact that its products are made to be shipped old and stale around the globe to be used to rake up large audiences for foreign television companies and their advertisers. The only really good television is that which is made by a man to earn the shock of recognition of a mass audience whose personality he has felt from birth. He has to enjoy an audience image which actually inspires him and does not leave him cynically manufacturing meretricious products for an unknown, uncaring audience. Broadcasting, at its most active, is a national medium. The peril of commercial television is not that it transmits for money but that it bases itself upon false beliefs about its audience. The peril of public broadcasting is not that it expresses an 'official' view of events and issues but that it is sometimes tempted to see its audience in a bureaucratic manipulative way, as is classically the case in France. Each nation has to finance broadcasting as best it can, each must find the most talented professionals that it can inspire, each must leave its broadcasting to build a rich and uncorrupt relationship with the audience.

There are presently available many exciting technical

possibilities which could transform the relationship between broadcasting in general and the mass audience. The new coaxial cable and the even more revolutionary waveguide-systems could send hundreds of simultaneous messages into homes and offices and could alter the whole way in which we organise our work and leisure. But it would be foolish to found all hopes of future transformation of our present enigmatic broadcasting problems upon new machinery which we have not fully developed, may not be able to afford, and which may well find its way into the existing systems of control when it does arrive.

It would be equally foolish to speak of broadcasting change only in the context of a structurally transformed society. Such a social transformation which would allow a truly democratic system of ownership and control of the means of communication might be wholly desirable, but we might all be dead long before it comes; and when it comes we might not like the new society any more than its predecessor. Nonetheless we do not want now to sit idly confronting a broadcasting culture which has ceased to satisfy us in many respects and which enriches our lives less than it could.

It is clear therefore that I do not take the view that the solution of the problems of 'one big audience' is to find technical and administrative means for splitting the audience up into tiny groups; that may come, through pay television, wired broadcasting, or by the splitting of broadcasting power among a series of confessional groups as in the Dutch pattern. Pluralism is a worthy cause in broadcasting as it is in other areas of society, but only a pluralism which has been interpreted into valid and intelligible roles within the medium itself. The prerequisite of any effort to render more democratic the enormous unitary aggregations of editorial power in broadcasting is the ending of the fusion of content control with administration of the means of dissemination, that defining characteristic of all traditional broadcasting. Those who control the wavelengths, and the cables, should not necessarily be the programme controllers. There have been many proposals, for instance, for splitting up the existing broadcasting institutions; the BBC, it is sometimes argued, should be divided into three or more parts. That would not, however, deal with the problem of the fusion of functions. What is needed is a means by which the controller of the wavelength regards his function as a technical one merely, willingly distributing some or all of his decision-making power over what is put into the programmes. The cause of pluralism in broadcasting can only be usefully pursued by whole broadcasting industries founded on an ideal of pluralism. Making certain hours of programme time available, or setting up broadcasting councils to oversee broadcasting affairs can be parts of a valuable pluralistic pattern but do not constitute such a pattern in themselves. The question of access has many answers, all of them partly helpful. The time has come, it is clear, for a considerable increase in the extent to which broadcasting organisations give away editorial control over certain parts of their transmitting time, in order that anyone who wishes to can have access for a specific propaganda message to the audience created by that organisation. The time has also come for public accountability in broadcasting to be extended beyond, in the case of Britain, a network of manipulated and disregarded advisory committees, into an area in which groups and individuals with an interest in the overall policies of broadcasting may be able, in a practical way, to participate in broadcasting management.

There is, however, a third and more important kind of pluralism, but the path toward it is the hardest and stoniest to tread. Broadcasting will inevitably remain in the hands of large and powerful bodies who will continue to act as giant impresarios and considerable employers in the future as in the past. Broadcasting, in all its main streams, will stay in the hands of the tiny unelected élite of professionals whose knowledge and understanding of their mass clientele will be the main mesh through which most of the messages have to pass. There is no way of avoiding this. The real question of 'access' therefore resolves itself into one of access to the interest and good judgement of the professionals who mediate the entire process. It is the broadcasters' minds which have to be opened up, their working practices, their own personal outlooks on life.

The chains of responsibility within broadcasting are the conveyor belts on which the programmes and messages for mass dissemination are prepared. The open society is one which

284

is able freely to feed its communication spare parts into that assembly system. Broadcasters and producers need to become a breed who cease to look inwards to their institutions and its codes, but to take their own honest sounding of their own social environments as a path towards repersonalising the mass audience whose features they have never truly examined. New rules and regulations, new rights and privileges will only go a short distance along the route to a free broadcasting system; the general consciousness and self-awareness of those who occupy positions of responsibility within broadcasting is the real area of contact between society and mass communicator.

The very fact that the questions I have been examining have become urgent political issues is a heartening sign. One of the characteristics of the mass society of which radio and television have become the principal structuring machinery is the sense of powerlessness, the feeling on the part of the individual that there no longer exists any part of the overpowering mechanism of society in which he can intervene. Broadcasting, however, is a source of power; it is visible and it can be made, in certain ways, available to all. It may prove to be a last resource of power which the individual can use before the sense of total helplessness engulfs mass society. It can be a means by which the articulate can reconnect themselves to the stream of active consciousness and a means by which the inarticulate, if truly served by the community of broadcasters, can see their experience actually being made to carry weight.

With the proper use of new mechanics of communication, as these arrive, we could bring ourselves towards the beginning of the end of mass society. That would mean many profound and valuable changes in the relationships between human beings. We would no longer judge our fellow creatures according to their position within a stultifying hierarchy of intellectuality. We would be no longer trapped between the cliffs of admass and élitism. The fogs of mutual stereotype between communicator and audience would lift. We would begin again to perceive one another as individual people.

There are ways of being serious, without being thought to be obscure. There are ways of expressing beliefs which do not leave in their wake the feeling of being propagandised. There are ways of entertaining which are neither mechanical nor synthetic. All those possibilities would open up, as the struggle for one big audience for four prime hours a day receded.

The communicator too could lay his skills and his machinery at the disposal of an audience, newly and more richly perceived. Empty professionalisms would be rededicated to the societies which had nurtured them. The new technologies of cable and cassette, if they are put into the correct hands, could therefore do much more than reorganise the machinery of mass entertainment and its content. They could change the contours of society.

Notes

Preface

[1] The whole of the speech is reprinted in *The Alfred I. DuPont-Columbia University Survey of Broadcast Journalism 1969–70*, ed. Marvin Barrett, Appendix A, pp. 131–9; 'Year of Challenge, Year of Crisis'; also as an appendix in Joseph Keeley, *The Left-leaning Antenna: Political Bias in Television* (Arlington House, New Rochelle, N.Y. 1971).

[2] At a meeting of the International Radio and Television Society on 25 November, quoted by Barrett, p. 37.

[3] *Broadcasting Magazine*, Dec. 1969, vol. 77, no. 22.

[4] The most trenchant available examination of the implications of the Agnew interventions is to be found in Fred Powledge's paper, 'The Nixon Administration and the Press: the Engineering of Restraint' (American Civil Liberties Union, New York, Sept. 1971). See also Theodore H. White, an interview entitled 'America's Two Cultures' in *Columbia Journalism Review*, Vol. VIII No. 4, Winter 1969–70.

[5] Richard S. Lambert, *Ariel and all his Quality – An Impression of the BBC from within* (Gollancz 1940), p. 317.

[6] The best overall comparative description of world systems of broadcasting is undoubtedly Walter B. Emery's *National and International Systems of Broadcasting: Their History, Operation and Control* (Michigan State University Press, East Lansing 1969). Despite its thoroughness it is already slightly out of date.

Chapter 1

[1] See Asa Briggs, *The History of Broadcasting in the United Kingdom*, vol. 1, *The Birth of Broadcasting* (Oxford University Press 1961), pp. 25–6.

[2] See Degna Marconi, *My Father Marconi* (McGraw Hill, New York 1962), p. 25.

[3] Gabriel Tarde, *Les Lois de l'Imitation*, (Étude psychologique, Paris 1895). Also in 1896, Gustave le Bon published his *La Psychologie des Foules* which emphasised the political problems caused by the new political prominence of the electorate.

[4] *Ibid.*, p. 79. See the discussion of Tarde and Le Bon's theories in Graham Wallas, *The Great Society*, Ch. VIII (Macmillan, London 1941).

[5] See John Bowle, *Politics and Opinion in the 19th Century: An Historical Introduction* (Jonathan Cape 1954, paperback 1963 and 1966); and also Asa Briggs, *The Age of Improvement* (Longmans 1959), Ch. 9, 'Victorianism'.

[6] Wallas, *Great Society*, p. 123.

[7] 1906 ed. p. 92. The earlier edition of Bagehot's work in 1873 had influenced William James in his *Principles of Psychology* (1890).

[8] Wilkie Collins, *The Unknown Public* (1858).

[9] See R. K. Webb, *The British Working Class Reader 1790–1848* (George Allen & Unwin 1955), p. 160.

[10] *Ibid.*, p. 161.

[11] Matthew Arnold, *Culture and Anarchy 1859*, ed. J. Dover Wilson (Cambridge University Press 1932; paperback 1969), p. 69.

The Shadow in the Cave

[12] *Ibid.*

[13] See Raymond Williams, *Culture and Society* (Chatto & Windus 1958), Ch. VI, pp. 110–29 for a detailed discussion.

[14] Arnold, *Culture and Anarchy*, p. 69.

[15] Williams, *Culture and Society*, p. 300.

[16] Wallas, *Great Society*, pp. 132–5.

[17] Arnold, *Culture and Anarchy*, pp. 83–5.

[18] Graham Wallas, *Human Nature in Politics* (Constable & Co. 1908), edition of 1948, p. 54–5. Morris Ginsberg in *Psychology of Society* (Methuen 1921) analyses the role of instinct in mass society and codifies the existing literature on the subject.

[19] Guinevere L. Griest, *Mudie's Circulating Library and the Victorian Novel* (David & Charles 1970), from which most of this account is drawn.

[20] In the *Athenaeum*, 6 Oct. 1860; quoted by Griest, *Mudie's Circulating Library*, p. 145.

[21] See Briggs, *History of Broadcasting*, vol. 1.

[22] Reproduced in Fritz Barnouw's History of *Broadcasting in the United States* (Oxford University Press, New York 1966), vol. 1, p. 6.

[23] See J. A. C. Brown, *Techniques of Mass Persuasion: From Propaganda to Brainwashing* (Pelican Original 1963); Walter Lippmann, *Public Opinion* (Macmillan, New York 1922) and *The Phantom Public* (Macmillan, New York 1925).

[24] J. A. C. Brown, *Psychological Warfare*, Ch. 4, pp. 82–104.

[25] This idea is elaborated in Ernst Kris and Nathan Leites 'Trends in Twentieth Century Propaganda', article in *Psychoanalysis and the Social Sciences*, vol. 1, pp. 393–409 (International Universities Press 1947). The article is reprinted in a volume of essays edited by Bernard Berelson and Morris Janowitz, *Reader in Public Opinion and Communication* (2nd edition, Free Press, New York 1966), pp. 267–77.

[26] Lippmann, *Public Opinion*, p. 249 (edition of 1929).

[27] *Ibid.*, p. 415.

[28] Reported in *New Republic* 31 December 1919, referred to by Lippmann in *Public Opinion*, p. 344.

[29] *Ibid.*, p. 248.

[30] I am greatly indebted to 'The First Casualty', a Thames Television documentary on the propaganda of World War I, transmitted on 16 November 1971, written and narrated by John Terraine, Research: Kate Haste, Director: Peter Morley, and Producer: Jeremy Isaacs.

[31] 'The First Casualty'.

[32] See A. R. Burrows, *The Story of Broadcasting* (Cassell 1924). Burrows was one of Reith's inner group who began the radio service. Some of the points I am stressing can be found between the lines of Burrows' reminiscences of the early months of broadcasting work. 'At present, for instance, we are wrestling with the subtle question of whether our programmes should be of the scrapbook character or possess continuity. On the one hand we have the experience of the British gramophone companies, which in a quarter of a century of contact with the public have found it inadvisable to produce in large numbers records which will play for more than five or ten minutes. Yet on the literary side of things we have an ever-increasing demand for the novel and the serious book, requiring for their full enjoyment long sessions of close reading. ... We broadcasters are not in the fortunate position of newspapers or places of entertainment, which have

Notes

their circulations and box-office returns as evidence of their success or failure.' p. 113.

33 *Report of the Broadcasting Committee August 1923*, Cmd. 1951, Chairman: Maj. Gen. Sir Frederick Sykes, KCB CMG MP, p. 5.

34 *Report of the Broadcasting Committee 1925*, Cmd. 2599 (1926), Chairman: Rt Hon. the Earl of Crawford and Balcarres KT, p. 12.

35 See Asa Briggs, *History of Broadcasting*, vol. 2, *The Golden Age of Wireless*, Introduction: 'Personalities and Performances' (Oxford University Press 1965).

36 J. C. W. Reith, *Into the Wind* (Hodder & Stoughton 1949), p. 101.

37 Ortega y Gasset, *The Revolt of the Masses* (first edition in Spanish 1930, in English 1932). Unwin paperback 1969, p. 10.

38 See R. J. White's introduction to his edition of *Liberty, Equality, Fraternity* by James Fitzjames Stephen (Cambridge University Press 1967).

39 *Ibid.*, p. 13.

40 John Stuart Mill, *On Liberty* (1859), p. 10.

41 *Ibid.*, p. 22.

42 Stephen, *Liberty* (Cambridge edition), p. 57.

43 Mill, *On Liberty*, p. 33.

44 Stephen, *Liberty*, p. 107.

45 James Carey, 'The Communication Revolution and the Professional Communicator' in *The Sociological Review*, Monograph No. 13 (University of Keele 1969), pp. 23–38. See also Fred S. Siebert, Theodore Peterson and Wilbur Schramm, *Four Theories of the Press* (University of Illinois Press 1971).

46 Wilbur Schramm, *Responsibility in Mass Communication* (Harper & Row 1957). A relevant extract is reprinted in Berelson and Janowitz, *Reader*, pp. 206–19 entitled 'Two Concepts of Mass Communication'.

47 *Ibid.*, pp. 212–13.

48 *Ibid.*, pp. 208–11. See also E. G. Wedell, *Broadcasting and Public Policy* (Michael Joseph 1968), pp. 22–6, for a factual account of the evolution of the inhibitory newspaper taxes.

49 In 1779. Quoted by William Ernest Hocking, *Freedom of the Press: A Framework of Principle – a Report from the Commission on the Freedom of the Press* (University of Chicago Press, Illinois 1947).

50 *The Writings of Thomas Jefferson*, edited by A. A. Lipscomb (The Thomas Jefferson Memorial Association ,Washington DC 1904), vol. 2, p. 33. Like Locke and Adam Smith in England, Jefferson saw popular freedom of discussion as a mechanism for limiting the expansion of the role of government as one of 'the most effectual manacles we can rivet on the hands of our successors'.

51 There are many recent contributions to the discussion of 'areas of discourse' within the mass audience. Richard D. Altick, *The English Common Reader: A Social History of the Mass Reading Public 1800–1900* (University of Chicago 1957; Phoenix edition 1963); Malcolm Bradbury, *The Social Context of Modern English Literature* (Basil Blackwell, Oxford 1971); Raymond Williams, *Culture and Society* and *The Long Revolution* (Chatto & Windus 1961); Harold L. Wilensky, 'Mass Society and Mass Culture' in *American Sociological Review*, vol. xxix, April 1964, (reprinted in Berelson and Janowitz, *Reader*, pp. 293–327); also the essay entitled 'An Historical Preface to the Popular Culture Debate' by Leo Lowenthal in

The Shadow in the Cave

Culture for the Millions, ed. Norman Jacobs (D. Van Nostrand Co. Inc., Princeton, N.J. 1961).

[52] An account of this episode is given by Zechariah Chafee Jr in *Freedom of Speech* (Harcourt Brace and Howe, New York 1920), pp. 3–5.

[53] *Ibid.*, p. 5.

[54] See Wilbur Schramm, *Two Concepts of Mass Communication*.

[55] Edition of 1834, p. 122.

[56] *Ibid.*, p. 135.

[57] See James Carey, 'Communication Revolution', p. 32.

[58] Sir Edward Cook, *Delane of 'The Times'* (Constable, London 1915), p. 289.

[59] See Wilson Harris, *The Daily Press* (Cambridge University Press 1943) p. 106, in Current Problems series edited by Ernest Barker, for a typical expression of this view, and for the story of the problem-ridden career of Sir Edward Cook, which I refer to below.

[60] Van Wyck Brooks, *The Confident Years 1885–1915* (J. M. Dent & Sons for the Readers Union, 1953); Frank Luther Mott, *American Journalism* (various editions); Robert E. Pork, 'The Natural History of the Newspaper' written in 1925 and reprinted in Schramm's *Mass Communication*, pp. 8–23.

[61] Upton Sinclair, *The Brass Check: A Study of American Journalism* (published by the author, Pasadena, Cal. 1920).

[62] H. L. Mencken, *Prejudices: a selection made by James T. Farrell* (Vintage Books, New York 1955), p. 215.

[63] *Ibid.*, p. 216.

[64] *Ibid.*, p. 229; see also Douglas Stenerson, *H. L. Mencken: Iconoclast from Baltimore* (University of Chicago Press, Ill. 1971); and Louis G. Geiger, 'The Muckrakers – Then and Now' in *Journal of Broadcasting*, vol. 43, no. 3, Autumn 1966, pp. 469–76.

[65] James Carey, 'Communication Revolution', *passim*.

[66] *Ibid.*, p. 33.

[67] For a profound study of the concept of 'modernity' in England see the opening chapters of Malcolm Bradbury, *Modern English Literature*.

[68] Roger L. Brown's essay 'Approach to the Historical Development of Mass Media Studies' which leads Jeremy Tunstall's series of essays, *Media Sociology* (Constable, London 1970), provides a valuable brief history of mass communication research. Two very interesting essays which develop the discussion on the 'after effects' of the propaganda of World War I are by Ralph D. Casey, 'The Press, Propaganda and Pressure Groups' from the *Annals of the American Academy of Political Science*, 1942, reprinted in Wilbur Schramm's *Mass Communications* (University of Illinois Press 1960); and Shils and Janowitz, 'Cohesion and Disintegration in the Wehrmacht' *Public Opinion Quarterly*, vol. xii, 1948, pp. 300–15 (reprinted in Berelson and Janowitz, *Reader*. There are some relevant chapters also in Melvin L. de Fleur, *Theories of Mass Communication* (David McKay Co. Inc., New York 1966).

[69] Harcourt Brace and Howe, New York 1920.

[70] *Ibid.*, p. 38.

[71] *Free Speech in the United States* (Harvard University Press, Cambridge, Mass. 1941).

[72] *Government and Mass Communications* (University of Chicago Press 1947). (A section is reprinted in Berelson and Janowitz, *Reader*, pp. 220–32.)

290

Notes

See also Alan Barth, *The Loyalty of Free Men* (Gollancz 1951), an examination of the 'cult of loyalty oaths' in post-war America, introduced by Chafee.

73 See Harold L. Wilensky 'Mass Society and Mass Culture' and T. W. Adorno 'Television and the Patterns of Mass Culture' in the *Quarterly of Film, Radio and Television*, vol. 8, 1954 (reprinted in Schramm, *Mass Communications*, pp. 594–612).

74 See A. R. Burrows, *Story of Broadcasting* and Asa Briggs, *History of Broadcasting*, vol. 1 *passim*.

75 See the section of Reith's *Into the Wind* on 'The Brute Force of Monopoly' pp. 99–101. 'So the responsibility at the outset conceived, and despite all discouragements pursued, was to carry into the greatest number of homes everything that was best in every department of human knowledge, endeavour and achievement; and to avoid whatever was or might be hurtful. In the earliest years accused of setting out to give the public not what it wanted but what the BBC thought it should have, the answer was that few knew what they wanted, fewer what they needed.'

76 Reith, *Into the Wind*, pp. 93–4. For a description of the struggle between American radio and the American press which exactly parallels the simultaneous controversy in Britain, see *Journal of Broadcasting*, vol. XIV, no. 3, Summer 1970, pp. 275–86, George Lott, 'The Press–Radio War of the 1930s'. The newspapers attempted to force an agreement on the radio networks by which their founts alone would supply news. The independent local stations ignored the arrangement, which soon broke down.

77 *Sykes Report*, p. 31.

78 *Crawford Report*, p. 12.

79 In terms of international law, freedom of expression as far as broadcasting is concerned has always been felt to be hard to codify. The European Convention for the Protection of Human Rights and Freedoms (Rome 1950) in Article 10, attempts to make a formal acknowledgement of the existence of a freedom of expression in broadcasting. It accompanies this recognition, however, with a reservation which permits governments to subject radio and television enterprises to a licensing system.

80 *Sykes Report*, p. 31.

81 *Crawford Report*, p. 5.

82 See Ch. 5 below.

83 *A Free and Responsible Press*; A General Report on Mass Communication: Newspapers, Radio, Motion Pictures, Magazines and Books (University of Chicago Press 1947), known as the Hutchins Commission. There is an excellent review of the present status of this report and a discussion of whether a similar large-scale commission on the mass media is now needed in *Columbia Journalism Review*, vol. vi, no. 2, Spring 1967, pp. 5–20, entitled 'The Hutchins Report – a Twenty-Year View'.

84 *A Free and Responsible Press*, p. 131.

Chapter 2

1 For a development of this idea see Edward Sapir, 'Communication', quoted in B. Berelson and M. Janowitz, *Reader in Public Opinion and Communication* (2nd edition, Free Press, New York 1966), originally published in the *Encyclopaedia of the Social Sciences*, ed. Edwin R. Seligman, vol. IV (Macmillan & Co. New York 1931), pp. 78–80.

[2] An account of these early experiments is given in an article by David L. Woods, 'Semantics versus the First Broadcasting Station', in *Journal of Broadcasting*, vol. xi, no. 3, Summer 1967.

[3] Both the brothers Puskás died in the early 1890s and the work in Budapest was continued by an engineer called Etienne Popper. A description of the service is given in *The Scientific American* 26 October 1895, p. 267.

[4] Barnouw quotes Sarnoff's memo in *A Tower in Babel*, vol. I of *History of Broadcasting in the United States* (Oxford University Press, 1970), p. 78.

[5] In the essay in the *Political Quarterly*, cited above.

[6] See Ch. 10 of Herbert I. Schiller, *Mass Communications and American Empire* (Augustus M. Kelley, New York 1969).

[7] See Terry Ramsay's essay 'The Rise and Place of the Motion Picture' in W. Schramm's collection *Mass Communication* (University of Illinois Press 1960), pp. 24–38; originally published in *The Annals of the American Academy of Political and Social Science*, Feb. 1947. Also Samuel McKechnie, *Popular Entertainment through the Ages* (Sampson, Low, Martson & Co., London 1932), pp. 75–94.

[8] See Terry Ramsay's essay, and another essay in Berelson and Janowitz *Reader*, by W. W. Charters, 'Motion Pictures and Youth', written originally in 1933.

[9] The Production Code of the Motion Picture Association of America is printed on pp. 626–35 of Schramm's collection of essays, *Mass Communication*.

[10] Roger Manvell describes the early history of cinema censorship in an essay 'Cinema and Television' to be found in Christopher Macy (ed.) *The Arts in a Permissive Society* (Pemberton Books 1971).

[11] Schiller, *Mass Communication and American Empire*, p. 154.

[12] Les Brown has a great deal to say about this, and of course Erik Barnouw in vol. 1 of his *History of Broadcasting* gives an account of the development of commercialism in American broadcasting. See also Gleason L. Archer, *History of Radio to 1926* (American Historical Society 1938).

[13] Schiller, *Mass Communications and American Empire*, p. 22.

[14] John Kenneth Galbraith, *The New Industrial State* (André Deutsch 1972), p. 218.

[15] *Ibid.*

[16] *Ibid.*, p. 384.

[17] P. P. Eckersley, *The Power Behind the Microphone* (Scientific Book Club, London 1942) p. 48.

[18] Asa Briggs, *The Birth of Broadcasting* (vol. 1 of the *History of Broadcasting in the United Kingdom*, Oxford University Press 1961), p. 97.

[19] See Ch. 10, on the crisis of broadcasting in Holland.

[20] Burton Paulu, *Radio and TV Broadcasting on the European Continent* (University of Minnesota Press, Minneapolis 1967).

[21] Gerald Beadle, *Television – a Critical Review* (George Allen & Unwin 1963), p. 64.

[22] Asa Briggs, *The Golden Age of Wireless* (vol. 2 of *History of Broadcasting*, 1965), pp. 476–504 and 640–659.

[23] Sir Hugh Greene, *The Third Floor Front: a View of Broadcasting in the Sixties* (The Bodley Head 1969), pp. 58–63.

[24] BBC *Handbook* 1972, p. 205.

[25] C. F. Pratten, 'The Economics of Television', PEP Broadsheet 520, Sep. 1970, p. 55.

[26] BBC *Handbook* 1972, pp. 213–14; and Pratten, *Economics* p. 22.

[27] *Ibid.*

[28] Les Brown, *Television – the Business Behind the Box* (Harcourt-Brace-Jovanovich Inc. New York 1971), p. 273.

[29] BBC *Handbook* 1972, p. 44.

[30] *Ibid.*, p. 54.

[31] *Ibid.*, p. 68.

[32] The Legal Adviser to ZDF, Dr Ernst W. Fuhr, provides a very useful summary of the complex origins of the channel in his commentary on the ZDF statutes. 'ZDF Staatsvertrag' (von Hase and Koehler Verlag, Mainz 1972), pp. 9–29.

[33] The only published account of the battle of the Intendanten can be found in *Funk-Korrespondenz* vol. 18, no. 47, 19 Nov. 1970; vol. 19, no. 15–16, 8 Mar. 1971; vol. 19, no. 19, 6 May 1971 (Katholisches Rundfunk-Institut, Cologne).

[34] See Herbert J. Gans, 'The Creator-Audience Relationship in the Mass Media: an Analysis of Movie-Making' in Bernard Rosenberg and David Manning White (eds.) *Mass Culture: The Popular Arts in America* (The Free Press of Glencoe 1963), pp. 313–25. It provides a most interesting parallel between television provoked by a consideration of the cinema. 'It can be shown that the role of the audience extends beyond the creation and the contents of the mass media product, but affects the structure and the culture of the mass media industries themselves. ... Every mass media creator, whatever his skill, is to some degree dependent on the validity of his audience image for his status and standing in the industry.'

[35] For the story of Father Coughlin see Charles J. Tull, *Father Coughlin and the New Deal* (Syracuse University Press 1965). But Erik Barnouw also provides a very good account of the radio antics of both Coughlin and Huey Long in vol. 2 of his *History of Broadcasting, The Golden Web*, pp. 44–51.

[36] Barnouw, *ibid.*, pp. 101–2.

[37] Accounts of this episode are given by John Coatman (formerly chief News Editor, North of England Regional Controller of the BBC) 'The BBC, Government and Politics' in *Public Opinion Quarterly*, vol. xv, no. 2 1951, pp. 287–98; and also by W. A. Robson, 'The BBC as an Institution' in *Political Quarterly* Oct.–Dec. 1935, vol. vi, no. 4, pp. 468–88.

[38] I am virtually paraphrasing here an article by J. G. Blumler and Denis McQuail 'British Broadcasting, its Purposes, Structure and Control' in *Gazette* (Leiden), vol. xi, no. 2/3, 1965, pp. 166–91.

[39] The best examples are R. S. Lambert, *Ariel and all his Quality – An Impression of the BBC from within* (Gollancz 1940); C. A. Lewis, *Broadcasting from Within* (George Newnes 1923); A. R. Burrows, *The Story of Broadcasting* (Cassell 1924); Maurice Lane-Norcott, *Up the Aerial* (Grayson and Grayson 1933); D. Cleghorn Thomson, *Radio is Changing Us* (Watts & Co. 1937); and of course Eckersley, *Power behind the Microphone*.

[40] Eckersley, p. 59.

[41] R. H. Coase in *British Broadcasting: A Study in Monopoly* (Longmans 1950) p. 195, argues that the combination of forces which ensured the retention of the monopoly until well after the war was virtually an accident. 'Had the Labour Party been in power at the time of the formation of the BBC; had the independent broadcasting systems not been associated

in the minds of the Press with commercial broadcasting and finance by means of advertisements; had another department, say the Board of Trade, been responsible for broadcasting policy; had the views of the first chief executive of the British broadcasting authority been like those of the second; with this combination of circumstances, there would be no reason to suppose that such a formidable body of support for a monopoly of broadcasting would ever have arisen.'

[42] Reith, *Into the Wind*, p. 103.

[43] *Ibid.*, p. 99.

[44] Charles Hill, *Both Sides of the Hill: the Memoirs of Lord Hill of Luton* (Heinemann 1964), p. 118.

[45] C. A. Lewis, *Broadcasting from Within*, p. 37.

Chapter 3

[1] Gilbert Seldes, *The Great Audience* (Viking Press, New York 1951), p. 207.

[2] From A. William Bluem's introduction to William Small's *To Kill a Messenger: Television News and the Real World* (Communication Arts Books, Hastings House, N.Y. 1970), p. xiii.

[3] A typical story of one of these is told in Fred Friendly's *Due to Circumstances Beyond our Control* (MacGibbon and Kee 1967).

[4] It is hardly surprising that news, when built around a single individual, created a number of powerful personalities, because of the enormous coverage which a daily or twice-daily bulletin provides.

[5] See Maury Green *Television News: Anatomy and Process* (Wadsworth Publishing Company Inc. Belmont Calif. 1969). Chapter 1 looks at some of the economic and structural background to the inauguration of television news.

[6] In the Communications Act of 1934, Public Law 416, 73rd Congress, 19 June 1934.

[7] Stuart Hood, former head of the BBC's News Department, explains in *A Survey of Television* (Heinemann, London 1967) p. 105 that television in the early years was in the hands of men from the theatre and show business who thought radio was the appropriate medium for news. 'In Britain their attitude was reinforced by the extreme conservatism of the BBC's News Division whose upper echelons manifested an almost pathological fear of the new medium. It was, they felt, not serious.'

[8] Green, *Television News*, p. 9.

[9] *Television and the Wired City* by Herman W. Land Associates Inc. (Washington DC National Association of Broadcasters 1968).

[10] Their research is summarised in, Roper Research Associates: *A Ten-year View of Public Attitudes towards Television and Other Mass Media 1959–1968*, 26 March 1969 (TV Information Office, New York), and updated in *An Extended View of Public Attitudes toward Television and Other Mass Media 1959–1971* (Roper Organisation Inc. TV Information Office, N.Y. June 1971).

[11] *Richard Dimbleby – Broadcaster* by his colleagues (BBC 1966), pp. 18–25.

[12] *Ibid.*, p. 19.

[13] Alexander Kendrick, *Prime Time : The Life of Edward R. Murrow* (Avon Books, N.Y. 1969), p. 278.

[14] Asa Briggs, *The History of Broadcasting in the United Kingdom*, vol. 1, *The Birth of Broadcasting* (Oxford University Press 1961), pp. 131–3.

[15] See J. C. W. Reith, *Broadcast Over Britain*, p. 138. 'I do not think there is much demand for an earlier bulletin. A comparatively small proportion of the people are in a position to listen for news before 7 p.m.'

[16] The Sykes Committee treated the press interests as something of national concern which was not to be interfered with.

[17] Oral evidence of Riddell before the Sykes Committee, 29 May 1923. Quoted by Briggs, *History of Broadcasting*, vol. 1, p. 174.

[18] *Ibid.*, p. 173.

[19] The crisis in Ireland has provided the most recent illustration of this general and collective inhibition on the part of broadcasting. See my article in *Index*, No. 2 'Broadcasting and Ireland', Summer 1972. A well-known television reporter wrote to me on reading the article, urging the need 'to underline the crippling effects of second-hand newsgathering' which resulted from the endemic desire of the broadcasting authorities not to report any fact which hadn't already been known and digested by the public from other media.

[20] In a leader in *The Times*, 6 February 1852 (a second leader followed on the same subject the following day), quoted *in extenso* in Sir Edward Cook, *Delane of the 'Times'* (Constable, London 1915), pp. 277–8.

[21] *Ibid.*

[22] Some good examples are given in Ch. 2 of Robert Macneil's *The People Machine* (Harper & Row, New York 1967) entitled 'The Frailties of Television News'.

[23] The first use of the concept (and the term) 'gatekeeper', applied to the phenomenon of news passing along various paths through a society but having to get through a series of 'gates' in the process, is in the work of Kurt Lewin (see his 'Channels of Group Life' in *Human Relations*, vol. 1, no. 2). Walter Gieber's 'News is What Newspapermen Make It' can be found on pp. 173–82 of Lewis A. Dexter and David Manning White (eds.) *People, Society and Mass Communications* (Free Press, New York 1964). David Manning White's own essay in the same collection (pp. 160–72) 'The "Gatekeeper": A Case Study in the Selection of News' presents a fascinating picture of how incoming information is processed through the mind of a news-editor-gatekeeper.

[24] Figures from Bagdikian, *The Information Machines: Their Impact on Men and the Media* (Harper & Row 1971), pp. 170–1.

[25] Harold Herd, *The March of Journalism* (George Allen & Unwin 1952), p. 17.

[26] See Stanislaw Orsini-Rosenberg 'Les Mercures français et polonais du XVIIème siècle' in *Kwartalnik Prasonawczy* (Warsaw), vol. II, no. 2 (6), pp. 11–21.

[27] *Ibid.* The French press, on the other hand, was far more lavishly produced and completely given over to the propaganda of Louis XIV.

[28] Bagdikian, *Information Machines*, p. 9.

[29] Useful facts and figures from A. M. Lee, *The Daily Newspaper in America* (Macmillan, 1937). Also from Bernard A. Weisberger, *The American Newspaperman* (University of Chicago Press 1961).

[30] Bagdikian, *Information Machines*, pp. 92–6.

[31] Daniel Boorstin, *The Image: What Happened to the American Dream* (Weidenfeld & Nicolson, London 1961), pp. 12–13.

[32] See James W. Carey, 'The Communications Revolution and the Professional Communicator' in *The Sociological Review* Monograph No. 13 (Keele University, January 1969), pp. 23–8.

The Shadow in the Cave

[33] Boorstin, *The Image*, p. 14.
[34] Editorial in *The Nation*, 28 January, 1869.
[35] 'Introduction' to Boorstin, *The Image*.
[36] Figures from the *Editor and Publisher Yearbook*, analysed by Bagdikian, *Information Machines*, p. 129.
[37] See an excellent broadcast talk by Stuart Hall, reprinted in *The Listener*, 16 March 1972, vol. 87, no. 2242, pp. 328–9.
[38] See *Rundfunk und Fernsehen*, Heft 4 1971, pp. 406–28; Thomas N. Stemmle, *Der Fernsehschaffende im Spannungsfeld von Institution und Massenkommunikation*, which also provides an excellent short bibliography of studies of reporting and its ideological perspectives in various media.
[39] Edith Efron, *The News Twisters* (Nash Publishing Co. 1971).
[40] See, for instance, the study commissioned by CBS News from Dr Charles Winick of the City University of New York, summarised in *Broadcasting Magazine*, 18 October 1971.
[41] *The Public Interest*, No. 26, Winter 1972, pp. 57–74.
[42] *Ibid.*, p. 73.
[43] Fred Friendly's *Due to Circumstances* gives an account of the development of journalism in American television; and Alexander Kendrick's biography of Ed Murrow, *Prime Time*, also shows how the American broadcast journalist draws on a tradition older than his own medium.
[44] See Donald Edwards 'BBC News and Current Affairs' (BBC Lunchtime Lectures No. 2, December 1962).
[45] Olof Rydbeck of Swedish Radio discusses the conflict between impartiality and factuality in an essay in *EBU Review* 1218, May 1970, pp. 10–13. Broadcasting in Sweden has a legal obligation to be impartial. Mr Rydbeck, the Director-General of SR, indicates some of the difficulties entailed in the pursuit of pure impartiality: 'The public powers did not intend to make the SR operate in a kind of absolute ideological vacuum. The principle of impartiality should be applied in the context of superimposed common democratic ideology and the criteria employed should bear the stamp of the fundamental democratic norms. . . . It does happen, however, that in some cases this principle of strictly mathematical equality comes into conflict with other requirements or other important interests.'
[46] The origin of the division was in the broadcast 'Talk' of the 1930s. Under the direction of Miss Hilda Matheson a department, quite separate from news, education and religion, sprang up around the discipline of this new genre. Asa Briggs, in vol. 2 of his history (*The Golden Age of Wireless*, p. 125): 'In philosophizing about the "technique" or "art" of the talk, therefore, Miss Matheson did not start with the "essay" or the "article" in her mind. She started with the broadcasting medium itself.' The Talks Department, which took various forms according to the state of various internal power divisions within the BBC, eventually spread to television where it caused a whole new series of documentary disciplines to flourish in the 1950s. The term 'current affairs' although narrower in scope emerged later.
[47] One of the key figures in the founding of Israeli television was Professor Elihu Katz who attempted, in the brief period in which his influence remained in the Israeli television service, to avoid the wasteful consumption of precious resources in the news division. 'From the beginning, then, we moved away from the traditional news programme format toward the development of a news magazine based on the assumption that it was

better to present a few items visually and in depth than to try to keep up with radio news. . . . We began with a 45-minute show against the advice of the American experts and some of our own news people, and emphasised short documentary items of five minutes or more using archive materials, interpretative artists, commentary by guest panelists and so forth, as well as long items on local activities. Even at the rate of three times a week, this show proved terribly difficult to sustain. . . .' (*Transaction*, vol. 8, no. 8 pp. 42–9, June 1971, 'Television Comes to the Middle East').

48 Efron, *News Twisters*.

49 See chapter 5 of *Broadcaster/Researcher Co-operation in Mass Communication Research*, ed. James D. Halloran and Michael Gurevitch (Centre for Mass Communication Research, Leicester University 1971) in which Herbert Gans contributes a paper 'The Sociologist and the Television Journalist: Observations on Studying Television News'. This quotation is on p. 96.

50 The most systematic attempt to survey anti-union bias in television news and current affairs coverage was made by the ACTT Television Commission in January 1971. Their publication *One Week* commented on every mention of trade union affairs between 8 and 14 January and concluded 'That industrial affairs are covered in a superficial and haphazard fashion; that the BBC in particular scandalously failed to maintain impartiality in dealing with three issues during the week monitored; that ITV shows conscientious effort to achieve impartiality; that Unions may be partly at fault in failing to supply news and check its coverage.'

51 See 'Strikes and the Media' by Stuart Hood in *The Listener* 25 Feb. 1971, vol. 85, no. 2187.

Chapter 4

1 *Areopagitica* (1644).

2 David Hume, *On the Liberty of the Press* (1751).

3 1810. Sheridan made an extraordinary frenzied exclamation on press freedom. It is worth quoting in full. 'Give me but the liberty of the Press and I will give to the Minister a venal House of Peers: I will give him a corrupt and servile House of Commons: I will give him the full sway of the patronage of office: I will give him the whole of Ministerial influence: I will give all the power that place can confer upon him to purchase up submission and overawe resistance – and I will go forth to meet him undismayed. I will attack the mighty fabric he has reared with that mightier engine: I will shake down from its height corruption and bury it amidst the ruins of the abuses it was meant to shelter.'

4 See his delightful essay to Queen Victoria (*Letters of Victoria*, vol. 3, p. 590) in which he describes the market mechanism which determines the nature and contents of *The Times*.

5 Graham Wallas, *Human Nature in Politics* (Constable & Co. 1908), edition of 1948.

6 Memorandum to Lord Malmesbury, July 1867.

7 Szulczewski, shortly after the start of the Gomulka era, wrote an interesting essay on 'The Problem of Journalistic Ethics' (*Kwartalnik Prasonawczy*, vol. 2, No. 2 (6), pp. 30–45) in which he describes the development of a craft-ethic for journalism, which was recovering from the Stalinist era in which public confidence in the press had been severely undermined. 'What are the ethical ideals of the journalist? In our opinion they are:

truth and the sense of responsibility towards those of whom he writes and towards those for whom he writes.'

8 For a longer account of Trybuna Obywatelska see my article in *The Listener*, 28 October 1971.

9 *Political Quarterly*, Oct.–Dec. 1935, vol. vi, no. 4, pp. 463–7, G. B. Shaw, 'The Telltale Microphone'. George Baker, the chief of the Republican National Publicity Bureau in the 1924 election, anticipated Bernard Shaw: 'The man who talks politics over the radio has got to talk sense in order to get a hearing. If he doesn't his audience walks out on him. . . . The radio will entirely change political methods, I believe; it will knock the nonsense out of politics.' Quoted by Edward W. Chester in *Radio, Television and American Politics* (Sheed & Ward, New York 1969), p. 283.

10 J. Trenaman and Denis McQuail, *Television and the Political Image* (Methuen, London 1961).

11 *Ibid.*, p. 192.

12 See Ch. 10 on 'Television and Radio' in David E. Butler and Anthony King, *The British General Election of 1964* (Macmillan, London 1965), p. 156.

13 Jay G. Blumler and Denis McQuail, *Television in Politics: Its Uses and Influence* (Faber 1968).

14 Joseph T. Klapper, *The Effects of Mass Communication* (The Free Press, New York 1960).

15 Kurt Lang and Gladys Engel Lang, *Politics and Television* (Quadrangle Books, Chicago 1968).

16 The FCC hearings on the complaint brought by Congressman Smith against NBC contain the best brief summary of the issues and the positions taken by various parties. See FCC 68–931, pp. 713–41, 11 Sept. 1968, 14 FCC 2d. William Small, *To Kill a Messenger: Television News and the Real World* (Communication) Arts Books, Hastings House, New York 1970) pp. 192–217, gives in Ch. 11 an excellent summary of the running battle at the convention between newsmen, police and politicians.

17 Reuven Frank provides a spirited riposte to the barrage of criticism in an essay entitled 'The Ugly Mirror' in *Television Quarterly*, vol. vii, no. 1, Winter 1969, pp. 82–95. 'And here today in the United States, facing a frightening jigsaw of crises for which we are unprepared, many people seem to think that American television journalism should be governed by ennobling purposes. We are castigated for not promoting unity, for not opening channels of inter-racial communication, for not building an edifice of support for our fighting men, for not ignoring dissent, for not showing good news.'

18 Howard Monderer, 'Response to an FCC Inquiry', *Television Quarterly*, vol. vii, no. 1, Winter 1969, pp. 97–106.

19 Quoted by George A. Miller in *The Psychology of Communication* (Pelican 1965), p. 7.

20 John Coatman, 'The BBC, Government and Politics' in *Public Opinion Quarterly*, vol. xv, no. 2, 1951, pp. 287–98.

21 See *Hansard*, vol. 285, col. 1577 for the questions to the PMG which arose from the Bartlett broadcast.

22 For a detailed account of the origins of the Fourteen-Day Rule see Burton Paulu, *British Broadcasting: Radio and Television in the United Kingdom* (University of Minnesota Press, Minneapolis 1967), pp. 168–70; and *British Broadcasting in Transition* (University of Minnesota Press, Minneapolis 1961), pp. 94–7.

²³ The full statement is in *The Times*, 28 July 1955, p. 8.
²⁴ Report of the Broadcasting Committee (1949) Cmd. 8116, 1951, p. 68, para. 264; see also the BBC Memorandum in Appendix H to the Beveridge Committee Report, pp. 109–10.
²⁵ *Hansard*, 23 Feb. 1955, vol. 537, col. 1277.
²⁶ Report from the Select Committee on Broadcasting (Anticipation of Debates) 1955.
²⁷ Lord Simon, *The BBC from Within*, p. 134.
²⁸ Fred Powledge, *The Nixon Administration and the Press: The Engineering of Restraint* (American Civil Liberties Union, New York, September 1971).
²⁹ The Broadcasting Authority Law. Israel Broadcasting Authority 1970, para. 7 (a), p. 3.
³⁰ *Studies in Political Development* 1 ed. Lucien Pye, *Communications and Political Development*, p. 78.

Chapter 5
¹ See Asa Briggs, *The History of Broadcasting in the United Kingdom*, vol. 1, *The Birth of Broadcasting* (Oxford University Press, 1961), pp. 360–84. The best detailed accounts, however, are Julian Symons, *The General Strike* (Cresset Press, 1957), pp. 177–82; and Andrew Boyle *Only the Wind Will Listen: Reith of the BBC* (Hutchinson, London 1972), pp. 189–205.
² See Harman Grisewood, *One Thing at a Time* (Hutchinson, London 1968) pp. 190–204.
³ The Whitley document is reproduced in Lord Simon of Wythenshawe's *The BBC from Within* (Gollancz, London 1953), pp. 46–7.
⁴ *Ibid.*, p. 32.
⁵ See Greene's chapter 'Onward to Pilkington' in *The Third Floor Front: A View of Broadcasting in the Sixties* (Bodley Head 1969), pp. 58–63.
⁶ See Greene in *Third Floor Front*, p. 103. 'Relevance is the key – relevance to the audience and to the tide of opinion in society. Outrage is impermissible. Shock is not always so. Provocation may be healthy and indeed socially imperative.'
⁷ See Greene's Granada Lecture delivered at the Guildhall, 16 October 1972, and reprinted in the *New Statesman*, vol. 84, no. 2170, 20 October 1972.
⁸ Normanbrook defended his constitutional authority to ban an appearance of Ian Smith, Prime Minister of Rhodesia on the programme '24 Hours' in a BBC lunch-time lecture, 'The Functions of the BBC's Governors' (BBC December 1965).
⁹ Reprinted in *The Listener*, 15 July 1971, vol. 86, no. 2207, pp. 67–9.
¹⁰ *New Statesman*, 16 July 1971.
¹¹ Julian Critchley, *Counsel for Broadcasting*, Conservative Political Centre No. 475, January 1971.
¹² They dealt with three cases in the first year. In the first they criticised a reporter for harassing a factory-owner who had refused to give an interview concerning a strike in the North of England.
¹³ 'BBC Programmes and the Public' in *The BBC Record*, no. 76, October 1971, p. 4.
¹⁴ A. Namurois, 'Freedom of Speech on Radio and Television: A Myth?', Part 1 in *EBU Review* 988, July 1966, pp. 44–54; Part 2 in *EBU Review* 998, Sept. 1966, pp. 34–41.

[15] *A Free and Responsible Press* (University of Chicago Press 1947), pp. 100–107.

[16] Royal Commission on the Press 1947–9, presented June 1949, Cmd. 7700 (under the chairmanship of Sir William Ross) para. 619, p. 165.

[17] Second Report from the Select Committee on Nationalised Industries, session 1971–2 on the IBA (formerly ITA) para. 917. Evidence of Lord Aylestone.

[18] *Ibid.*, Appendix 10, pp. 332–3.

[19] Walter B. Emery, *National and International Systems of Broadcasting: Their History, Operation and Control* (Michigan State University Press, East Lansing 1969), p. 208.

[20] *EBU Review* 608, March 1960, pp. 23–4. See also Claude Durieux, 'Suède: un exemple de monopole bien compris' in *Le Monde*, 24 May 1972, p. 31.

[21] Henrik Hahr, director and chief assistant to the Director General of Swedish Radio, describes the Code in some detail in *EBU Review* 768, November 1962, p. 43; and also in *EBU Review* 778, January 1963, pp. 25–7, where he writes about how the Code deals with news.

[22] See Staffan Vängby, *Opartiskhet och saklighet* (Sveriges Radio forläg, Stockholm 1971), p. 7.

[23] Vängby, *Opartiskhet och saklighet*, pp.191–215.

[24] *Ibid.*, p. 112.

[25] *Ibid.*, pp. 181–2.

[26] *Ibid.*, pp. 201–3.

[27] *Ibid.*, p. 20.

[28] Professor Jörgen Westerstähl, 'Objectivity is measurable', in *EBU Review* 1218, May 1970, pp. 13–17.

Chapter 6

[1] Quoted by Professor Henri Mercillon in a paper entitled 'Quelques réflexions sur le monopole de l'ORTF' in *Droit Social*, No. 12, Dec. 1970, pp. 75–81. Special edition on ORTF and its problems.

[2] Most of my information on broadcasting in France prior to the outbreak of war comes from Walter B. Emery, *National and International Systems of Broadcasting; Their History, Operation and Control* (Michigan State University Press, East Lansing 1969), pp. 237–44.

[3] Broadcasting France. *EBU Bulletin*, Sept.–Oct. 1956, p. 639.

[4] See Raymond Aron, 'Signification Politique de la Radio-Télévision dans le Monde Présent' in *Cahiers d'Études de Radio-Télévision*, No. 15, p. 240.

[5] I am very considerably indebted to the research work of Dr Ann Saldich (and to her whole train of thought) whose unpublished Sorbonne doctorate thesis 'Politics and Television in France during the de Gaulle Years' has been made available to me.

[6] Philip Williams and Martin Harrison, *Politics and Society in de Gaulle's Republic* (Longmans 1971), p. 243.

[7] Michel Piccoli quoted by Jaques Thibau in '*Une Télévision pour tous les Français*' (Editions du Seuil 1970). M. Thibau worked in the office of the Minister of Information in the time of Peyrefitte and was Assistant Director of the ORTF 1965–8 (January).

[8] Quoted by Thibau, p. 85.

[9] *Ibid.*, p. 85.

[10] In a conversation with Dr. Saldich. But Peggy Taylor and Bernard Redmont in 'French Television: A Changing Image' (*Television Quarterly* vol. viii, no. 4, Autumn 1969, pp. 39–49) deny this, saying that instructions would pass daily at 11 a.m. from SLII to the ORTF directors. By this direct means, for instance, film of de Gaulle's misfired visit to Quebec was kept from French television screens.

[11] This meant that the civil servants at the Finance Ministry supervised three categories within the budget: investment, salaries and the size of staff (Taylor and Redmont). Thibau says (p. 124) that in 1962 the ORTF had to submit about two-thirds of its individual payments to higher authority, but this decreased gradually in the ensuing three years.

[12] In 'Modern Television', an article by Sylvain Moumette in *Les Temps Modernes*, no. 270, December 1968, p. 1146.

[13] See Richard Hauser, 'Small Screens and Serving Girls – TV in France', *Television Quarterly*, vol. 5, no. 2, Spring 1966, pp. 43–50.

[14] See *New York Herald Tribune* (Int. Ed.) 21 May 1965, where French government is shown to own 100 per cent of Europe No. 1, 83 per cent of Radio Monte Carlo (35 per cent of Tele Monte Carlo), and 97 per cent of Andorra Radio. All are profitable stations. See also the interesting history of Radio Luxembourg given by Walter B. Emery in 'Radio Luxembourg – The Station of the Stars' in *Journal of Broadcasting*, vol. x, no. 4, Autumn 1966, pp. 311–26.

[15] See *Television Quarterly*, Autumn 1969, pp. 47–8.

[16] Quoted from David Schoenbrun's *The Three Lives of Charles de Gaulle* (Atheneum Press, New York 1966), p. 105.

[17] *Television Quarterly*, Autumn 1969, p. 40.

[18] For a detailed description of the Commission's terms of reference see *La Documentation Française*, no. 3283, 'Textes et Documentes relatifs à l'élection Présidentielle du 5 et 19 Décembre 1965', 19 April 1966. Notes et Etudes Documentaires, p. 32.

[19] Assemblée Nationale. Senate Rapport No. 118.

[20] It should be pointed out that the issue of television news reporting came to a head as a source of popular discussion throughout the world in 1968, partly because of the events in France and Czechoslovakia, partly because of the situation in Vietnam. It was the year in which many people realised that news events were somehow beginning to overlap with their coverage. People demonstrated because demonstrations were televised, or so went the argument.

[21] The debate on the third of these motions on 19 May was televised – the first time that cameras were allowed into the National Assembly.

[22] The most eloquent single account of the details of the coverage of the events by different ORTF programmes is given by Jacques Thibau, *Une Télévision*, pp. 155–9. 'Entre-temps, il y avait eu, le 11 mai à *Télé-Soir*, une rubrique spéciale destinée à faire le point sur des événements qu'il n'était plus possible d'ignorer. Elle fut à la mesure du système de cette information: dépourvue d'honnêteté, ne donnant aucun élément de sélection, d'approfondissement – se contentant de présenter quelques carcasses de voitures brûlées.'

[23] See Thibau, *Une Télévision*, p. 161. 'Quand j'étais debout, ils étaient couchés, j'ai été obligé de mettre un genou en terre, ils se sont précipités pour me poignarder.'

[24] See Roger Louis's highly coloured account of this episode in '*L'ORTF – un combat*' (Editions du Seuil 1968), pp. 19–23. M. Louis was one of the reporters on 'Cinq Colonnes à la Une.'

[25] *Ibid.*, p. 24.

[26] François de Closets, 'La Télévision, Instrument de la Participation', *Le Monde*, 3 July 1969.

[27] Edouard Sablier, 'De L'Objectivité', *Le Monde*, 3 July 1968.

[28] Ann Saldich obtained definitive statements from none of them on this issue.

[29] Sud-Ouest conducted the poll which was reported in *Le Monde* on 5 July 1968.

[30] *Le Fait Public*, 14 January 1970, p. 28. 'L'ORTF. Ce que coûte une répression'.

[31] After a long and bitter argument with all the other networks in Europe the French decided to use their own colour system, SECAM, which was compatible with none of the other systems in use; the Russians opted for SECAM also and until the present day the French government has been using a variety of methods to persuade other countries to use their system instead of either the American or German methods.

[32] Thibau, *Une Télévision*, p. 164.

[33] *Ibid.*, pp. 174–5.

[34] *L'Express*, 6–12 July 1970, pp. 84–94.

[35] *Le Monde*, 31 December 1971.

[36] Pierre Emmanuel, *Pour une Politique de la Culture* (Editions du Seuil 1971).

[37] This system, decided in October 1970 and enacted on 1 January 1971, is amply described in a series of articles in *Le Monde* by Claude Durieux entitled 'La Télévision en Mutation', 1 December 1971 and 1 January 1972.

[38] *Le Monde*, 21 December 1971.

[39] Pierre Viansson-Ponté in *Le Monde*, 15 December 1971.

[40] *Figaro*, 14 December 1971.

[41] *L'Humanité*, 22 December 1971, 'La Télévision en proie à la Censure'.

[42] *Journal Officiel – Sénat*, 29 November 1971, p. 2454.

[43] *Ibid.*

[44] *Le Monde*, 24 May 1972.

[45] *Paris-Match*, 12 August 1972, p. 21.

[46] Internal document of ORTF dated 25 July 1972.

[47] *Variety*, 26 July 1972, p. 42.

Chapter 7

[1] Timothy Green, *The Universal Eye – World Television in the Seventies* (The Bodley Head 1972), p. 13.

[2] Herbert Schiller, *Mass Communications and American Empire* (Augustus M. Kelly, New York 1969), p. 82.

[3] *Ibid.*

[4] *Ibid.*, p. 83. See also Harry J. Skornia, *Television and Society: An Inquest and Agenda for Improvement* (McGraw-Hill 1965) p. 189 for the history of this phenomenon.

[5] H. Comor, 'American TV: What Have You Done to Us?' *Television Quarterly*, vol. vi, no. 1, Winter 1967, pp. 50–1.

[6] I have borrowed this method for dividing up the various strands from a most interesting interview by Jack Gould, formerly television critic of the *New York Times*, on 'The American Character' (Center for the Study of Democratic Institutions, California, October 1961).

[7] *Variety*, 15 September 1971, p. 29.

[8] *Ibid.*, p. 30.

[9] Les Brown, *Television: The Business Behind the Box* (Harcourt-Brace-Jovanovich Inc., New York 1971), p. 95.

[10] Bagdikian, *The Information Machines: Their Impact on Men and the Media* (Harper & Row 1971), p. 172.

[11] *Variety*, 15 Sept. 1971, p. 29.

[12] Les Brown, *Television*, pp. 34–5; see also Skornia *Television and Society* pp. 120–42.

[13] *Ibid.*, p. 59.

[14] See Nicholas Johnson, *Test Pattern for Living* (Bantam Books, 1972), p. 140, quoting from Edward H. Meyer.

[15] Fred Friendly, *Due to Circumstances beyond our Control* (MacGibbon & Kee 1967), pp. 287–8.

[16] Conversation with staff of WHDH, Boston.

[17] Skornia, *Television and Society*, p. 114.

[18] Bagdikian, *Information Machines*, p. 173.

[19] Ben H. Bagdikian, 'News as a By-product; What Happens when Journalism is Hitched to a Great Diversified Corporation?' in *Columbia Journalism Review*, vol. vi, no. 1, Spring 1967, pp. 5–10.

[20] Bagdikian, *Information Machines*, p. 176.

[21] The going rate in autumn 1972 was 60–68,000 dollars per minute of prime time.

[22] *Variety*, 20 Sept. 1972, p. 25.

[23] Information from *Variety*, 4 October 1972, p. 33.

[24] *Variety*, 4 October 1972.

[25] *Love Story* raised the entire rating of the network over a week by as much as 2 points.

[26] The Radio Act of 1912 made the Secretary of Commerce and Labor responsible for licensing radio but provided no criteria for his accepting or rejecting applications. When the Court ruled that the Secretary (in the time of Herbert Hoover) had no power to deny applications, the chaos of overlapping signals increased to an intolerable extent. The Radio Act of 1927 was the result, the first attempt to impose order by giving the government power to authorise wavelengths (and deny them) and to impose transmitting strengths, through a new agency, the Federal Radio Commission.

[27] Section 301 of the Communications Act of 1934 (S. Doc. 144 73d Congress 2d Session, 26 February 1934) states: 'It is the purpose of this Act, among other things, to maintain the control of the United States over all the channels of interstate and foreign radio transmission; and to provide for the use of such channels, but not the ownership thereof, by persons for limited periods of time, under licences granted by Federal authority, and no such licence shall be construed to create any right, beyond the terms, conditions and periods of the licence.'

[28] See Nicholas Johnson and Tracy Westen, 'A Twentieth Century Soapbox: The Right to Purchase Radio and Television Time', in *Virginia Law Review*, vol. 57, no. 4 1971, pp. 574–634.

The Shadow in the Cave

²⁹ See Skornia, *Television and Society*, pp. 78–9.
³⁰ Fred Friendly, *Due to Circumstances*, p. 297, reports this widespread belief. *Broadcasting Magazine* (May 1965) reported however that only 9 senators and 14 members of the House of Representative had interests in radio and television stations.
³¹ The origins of the FCC's now much publicised indolence in regard to scrutinising the performance of stations lie in the 1940s when starting a television station was an expensive and risky business. The FCC felt a responsibility to help the first generation of pioneers in television; thereafter the habit of relicensing stations wholesale seemed to stick. Every applicant for a licence renewal had to fill in a searching questionnaire, explaining what proportion of his programming would consist of news, public affairs, etc.; the information is scarcely perused by the seven commissioners in making their decision, and frequently not even checked. Even Newton Minow, who as Chairman of the FCC rapidly became the scourge of the networks in the Kennedy days, on retirement to his law practice found himself handling the extremely lucrative legal affairs of CBS.
³² Skornia, *Television and Society*, p. 78.
³³ See Satellite Communications: Report prepared by Military Operations Subcommittee, Committee on Government Operations, 88th Congress, 2nd Session, Washington 1964, p. 82.
³⁴ Newton N. Minow, *Equal Time: The Private Broadcaster and the Public Interest* (Athenaeum, New York 1964), p. 97.
³⁵ *Ibid.*, p. 287.
³⁶ The removal of the licence of WHDH is described in '"Spare the Golden Goose" – The Aftermath of WHDH in Licence Renewal Policy' by Hyman H. Goldin, *Harvard Law Review*, vol. 83, pp. 1014–35, 1970, and in *Broadcasting Magazine*, 23 August 1971, pp. 26–31. The Boston *Sunday Globe* of 23 January 1972, tells the story of the seventeen years of intrigue and struggle which lay behind the removal of the previous station owners.
³⁷ See *Columbia Journalism Review*, vol. vi, no. 1, Spring 1967, pp. 42–6, 'The FCC's Wholesale Licensing' for a description of how Kenneth Cox and Nicholas Johnson, two of the commissioners, fought against the renewal of a group of stations in Florida.
³⁸ Minow, *Equal Time*, p. 294.
³⁹ 'In the Matter of the Mayflower Broadcasting Corporation and the Yankee Network Inc.' (WAAB) 8 FCC 333, 338, 16 January 1941.
⁴⁰ The 'Fairness Doctrine' is spelt out in the FCC document 13 FCC 1246, 'In the Matter of Editorializing by Broadcasting Licensees', 1 June 1949.
⁴¹ *Ibid.*, para. 21.
⁴² There are two important extended statements by the FCC which clear up many of the details of the application of the Fairness Doctrine. In 29 Fed. Reg. 10416 'Applicability of the Fairness Doctrine in the Handling of Controversial Issues of Public Importance' adopted 1 July 1964, the FCC codified a series of its past rulings. In 31 Fed. Reg. 6660 'Use of Broadcast Facilities for Public Office' adopted 27 April 1966, the FCC codifies its rulings on the 'equal time' question, under which section 315 of the 1934 Communications Act was deemed to oblige every station to keep exactly equal broadcasting time to *every* candidate for election.
⁴³ In a speech to the International Radio and Television Society Newsmaker Luncheon, 6 October 1971, at the Waldorf Astoria Hotel, New York.

304

⁴⁴ In FCC 67–641, 2 June 1971, a new era began for the Fairness Doctrine, when the FCC decreed that cigarette advertising having become a public issue attracted the application of the doctrine. The FCC explained to WCBS station in New York that the doctrine now 'requires a station which carries cigarette commercials to provide a significant amount of time for the other viewpoint'.

⁴⁵ See Les Brown, *Television*, pp. 353–60.

⁴⁶ Kenneth Cox was drawing to the end of his seven-year tenure as a commissioner.

⁴⁷ Les Brown, *Television*, p. 236.

⁴⁸ *Variety*, 13 Sept. 1972.

⁴⁹ The blacklist mania is described by Erik Barnouw in his *History of Broadcasting in the United States*, vol. 3, *The Image Empire* (Oxford University Press, New York 1970), pp. 8–21.

⁵⁰ A good account of the 'quiz scandals' is given by Skornia, *Television and Society*, pp. 48–50, and by Barnouw, *History of Broadcasting*, vol. 3, *The Image Empire*, pp. 122–5.

⁵¹ *Ibid.*, p. 36.

⁵² See Friendly's own account in *Due to Circumstances*; and Alexander Kendrick's *Prime Time – the Life of Edward R. Murrow* (Avon Books 1969), pp. 380–475.

⁵³ Friendly, *Due to Circumstances*, Ch. 9, 'Air Time for Vietnam', pp. 212–65.

⁵⁴ Marvin Barrett, *A State of Siege. The Alfred I. Dupont-Columbia University Survey of Broadcast Journalism 1970–1* (Grosset & Dunlap Inc., New York 1971), p. 13.

⁵⁵ *Ibid.*, p. 83.

⁵⁶ *Ibid.*, p. 85.

⁵⁷ Fred Powledge, *The Nixon Administration and the Press: The Engineering of Restraint* (American Civil Liberties Union, New York, September 1971).

⁵⁸ The investigators wanted *unused* material, copy, photographs etc. and thus inaugurated an important piece of heartsearching over whether the waste products of broadcast journalism should be destroyed or locked away to prevent access to authority.

⁵⁹ They also wanted notes of telephone calls, correspondence and unused film.

⁶⁰ Wallace was interviewed by someone who knew him personally and Wallace thought that this informal contact would, if successful, be used as a thin end of a wedge to persuade all prominent journalists to comply with such requests.

⁶¹ He was finally released after extensive appeals. The US Court of Appeal said that if a grand jury could force a reporter to produce information obtained by him in secrecy, it would in effect 'have the power to convert him after the fact into an investigative agent of the government'.

⁶² Powledge, *The Nixon Administration*, p. 5.

⁶³ *Variety*, 2 August 1972, an article by Les Brown, p. 1.

Chapter 8

¹ See *Broadcasting Magazine*, 1 February 1971, vol. 80, no. 5, pp. 22–3, 'A Huge Growth in the TV Audience' – account of a report published by the National Association of Broadcasters and the Television Bureau of Advertising. Television viewing in America, for an unaccountable reason,

rose between late 1969 and late 1970. In the previous years it had been showing a slight decline.

[2] See Erik Barnouw, *A Tower in Babel*, vol. 1 of *History of Broadcasting in the United States*, to 1933 (Oxford University Press, New York 1966), pp. 172–4, 218–19, 259–261.

[3] When the 'freeze' on new station licensing began there were 107 television stations in operation. 700 applicants were waiting for channels.

[4] See Erik Barnouw, *The Golden Web*, vol. 2 of *History of Broadcasting*, to 1953, pp. 293–4.

[5] *Broadcasting Magazine*, 8 November 1971, p. 33.

[6] See Hyman H. Goldin's supplementary paper to 'Public Television: a Programme for Action' – the report and recommendations of the Carnegie Commission on Educational Television (Bantam 1967), pp. 229–234.

[7] See *Television Quarterly*, vol. ix, no. 1, Winter 1970, pp. 24–8, quoted in an article by James Day, President of National Educational Television, 'Cultured Beggars and Social Responsibilities'.

[8] Public Law 87–447, 87th Congress, 1 May 1962.

[9] Apart from the Carnegie Commission report, quoted above, there is a good short account of the history of public television in *Broadcasting*, 8 November 1971, pp. 30–6.

[10] CPB, on the other hand, had a council which met regularly in Washington, consisting of the managers of the local stations.

[11] See Friendly, *Due to Circumstances Beyond our Control* (MacGibbon & Kee 1967), pp. 300–25.

[12] *Ibid.*, p. 309.

[13] *Ibid.*, p. 315.

[14] *Ibid.*, p. 315.

[15] Johnson's message, however, included a promise to study the possibilities of the Friendly/Bundy/Carnegie proposal to establish an educational radio and television network using communication satellites.

[16] Public Law 90–129, 90th Congress, 7 November 1967.

[17] Title II, Part IV Subpart B, para. 9–1.

[18] There was a steady barrage of carping from Congressmen. A random example taken from the Congressional Record of Wednesday 23 February 1972 (E 1519) provides a transcript of some remarks by Richard H. Ichord, representative from Missouri: 'And when one is discussing the Public Broadcasting System in general, I must say that I was aghast to discover that it was paying the very handsome salary of 85,000 dollars – twice what Congressmen and Senators earn – to one Sander Vanocur to impose his special slants and prejudices on the PBS news operation. If the PBS continues to utilize congressionally appropriated funds to directly or indirectly smear the operations of Congress, I assure you that I can hardly be persuaded to continue to vote approval of these funds.'

[19] In an interview on National Public Radio in February 1972. Whitehead's attack on PBS for developing, unconstitutionally, into a network, instead of a loosely organised educational broadcasting industry, was developed throughout 1971, as the funding bill for CPB passed through Congress. At the Miami convention of the National Association of Educational Broadcasters (reported in *Broadcasting*, 25 October 1971, p. 140) Whitehead attacked CPB for being in contravention of the intention of the 1967 Act: 'I honestly don't know what group I'm addressing today. . . . What

is your status ? To us there is evidence that you are becoming affiliates of a centralised, national network.'

20 See 'That Was the PTV That Was' in *Variety*, 23 August 1972.
21 See editions of *Variety* (front page stories) throughout September and October 1972.
22 *Variety*, 23 August 1972, p. 35.
23 Carnegie Report, pp. 98–9.
24 The speaker was Ronald H. Coase at a conference sponsored by the Johnson Foundation of Racine, Wisconsin, in January 1968. Reprinted in *Television Quarterly*, vol. vii, no. 1, Winter 1968 (special issue), p. 82.
25 See *More* magazine, vol. 1, no. 3, December 1971, Malcolm Carter, 'Policing Public Television'. Also a speech by Commissioner Johnson at the Harvard Law School Forum of 11 February 1972, entitled 'Death before Life – a case study of public broadcasting'. In both of these the disputed programmes were described and the charges of interference and manipulation laid out.
26 Because the FCC's power is concerned with stations and not with networks, the operation of enforcing NBC to divest was undertaken in a curious roundabout way. The FCC's order said that no licence shall in future be issued 'to a standard broadcast station affiliated with a network organisation which maintains more than one network'.
27 The fines, when levied, are normally $100.
28 It is now run by an integrated citizens' group.
29 See Kenneth A. Cox and Nicholas Johnson, 'Broadcasting in America and the FCC's License Renewal Procedure – an Oklahoma Case Study' in *Columbia Journalism Review*, vol. vii, no. 3, Winter 1968.
30 *Ibid.*, pp 1–2. 'Americans have a sense of the inevitability of TV being the way it is – but the system was built by the Government and the FCC, and the assumptions on which everything is based are theirs.'
31 They had previously started challenging a number of other licence renewals in small groups.
32 *Ibid.*
33 See *Broadcasting*, 17 May 1971.
34 Much of my information on the licence-challenging movement comes from an unpublished dissertation by Mr Peter A. Lance at the University of Columbia, to whom I am indebted. Some of his information has been published in *More*, June 1972, vol. 2, no. 6, 'The People *v.* The Wasteland'. Another valuable source of material on the radical movement in American broadcasting is *Television Today*, a handbook published for the Institute for Policy Studies by the Communication Service Corporation, Washington, DC 1969.
35 *Broadcasting*, 17 May 1971; and 1 November 1971, pp. 26–7, 'D-Day Approaches for California Stations'.
36 Quoted from Lance.
37 The Progress Reports of the Citizens Communication Center in Washington are the best source of information on this rapidly developing field.
38 It began its activities in August 1969.
39 See the profile of Nicholas Johnson in *Penthouse* Magazine) Feb. 1972), p. 36.
40 The titles of his two books amply illustrate Johnson's style: *How to Talk Back to Your Television Set* (Little, Brown & Co., Boston 1967); *Test Pattern for Living – A Twentieth-Century Guide to Coping with Life, Liberty and the Pursuit of Happiness – Without Dropping Out* (Bantam 1972).

⁴¹ Like Canada and Hong Kong, two other countries in which cable broadcasting has become a principal means for disseminating television and/or radio, the Soviet Union adopted it for political reasons; it enables a country to control more closely the input of messages into their society, provided that receiving sets are manufactured only with the capacity to receive cable communications. Similarly in China, since 1959, there has been a phenomenal growth of wired broadcasting. (See Walter S. Emery, *National and International Systems of Broadcasting* (Michigan State University Press 1969), pp. 62–3, 496–71, 385–6. For a European view of cable development see Helmut Lenhardt, *Die Zukunft von Rundfunk und Fernsehen in der Auseinandersetzung mit den neuen elektronischen Medien*, (Verlag Fritz Molden, Vienna 1972); and Brenda Maddox, *Beyond Babel* (André Deutsch 1972).

⁴² See *On the Cable – the Television of Abundance*, Report of the Sloan Commission on Cable Communications (McGraw-Hill, New York 1971), pp. 22–3.

⁴³ *Ibid.*, p. 24.

⁴⁴ Leonard Ross, 'The TV Racket', *New York Review of Books* vol. xviii, no. 4, 9 March 1972, p. 28.

⁴⁵ Monroe Price and John Wicklein, *Cable Television – A Guide for Citizen Action*, with foreword by Everett C. Parker (Pilgrim Press Book, Philadelphia 1972); Charles Tate (ed.), *Cable Television in the Cities: Community Control, Public Access, Minority Ownership* (Urban Institute, New York 1972).

⁴⁶ See 'Plan for Minority Participation in a Cypress Cable System in Dayton, Ohio' (Cypress Communications' Corporation, Los Angeles, Calif., February 1972).

⁴⁷ Report of the Sloan Commission.

⁴⁸ *Ibid.*, pp. 92–5 and 130.

⁴⁹ *Ibid.*, pp. 132–4.

⁵⁰ *Ibid.*, pp. 135–49.

⁵¹ *Ibid.*, p. 141.

⁵² *Ibid.*, p. 39.

⁵³ Goldmark was President of cbs Laboratories. The Report of the National Academy of Engineering's Committee on Telecommunications is published as 'Communications Technology for Urban Improvement' (Commerce Department, Springfield, Virginia 1970).

Chapter 9

¹ See Keizo Okabe, 'Broadcast Research Today' in *International Studies of Broadcasting, with special reference to the Japanese studies*. Ed. H. Eguchi and H. Ichinohe (nhk Radio and tv Culture Research Institute, Tokyo 1964).

² Much of my material on the early journalistic history of Japan comes from Shuichi Kato, 'The Mass Media in Japan', which is Ch. 6 of *Political Modernisation in Japan and Turkey*, ed. Robert E. Ward and Dankwart A. Rustow (Studies in Political Development, No. 3, Princeton University Press 1964; paperback 1968).

³ Quoted by Walter B. Emery in *National and International Systems of Broadcasting* (Michigan State University Press, East Lansing 1969), p. 480.

4 Some of the important stages in this period of government–press relations are listed by Emery, *Systems of Broadcasting*, p. 482–3.

5 An excellent account of early broadcasting in Japan is given in Iwao Nakajima, 'The Broadcasting Industry in Japan: Its Historical, Legal and Economic Aspects' in Eguchi and Ichinohe, *International Studies*.

6 The reasons for Japan starting with a non-profit corporation are to some extent accidental. Takeshi Inukai, the Minister of Communications in 1924, had grown exasperated at the attempt to bring the various competing businessmen in Tokyo, Nagoya and Osaka into any kind of harmony. He therefore set up the corporation instead of a joint-stock company in order that those clamouring for the franchise – mainly newspaper owners and equipment manufacturers – would realise that there was no money to be made out of the prize.

7 Emery, *Systems of Broadcasting*, p. 482.

8 The best account of the conflict between the Japanese and GHQ over the foundation of the NHK after the war is given by Yoshima Uchikawa, *Process of Establishment of the New System of Broadcasting in Post-War Japan Studies of Broadcasting* (NHK Radio and TV Culture Research Institute, Tokyo 1964), pp. 50–80.

9 See Shuichi Kato, 'The Mass Media'.

10 A good description of newspaper distribution in Japan is given by Mitsugi Kondo, 'Newspaper Competition in Japan' *Gazette* (Leiden – *International Journal of the Science of the Press*, vol. 11, no. 2, 1956), pp. 97–112.

11 For general summary of the media spread in Japan see *Gazette* (Leiden) vol. 6, no. 1, 1960, which devotes the entire issue to a series of essays on press, broadcasting and the law in Japan.

12 See Iwao Nakajima, *Revenue Resources of the Broadcasting Industry in Japan, Studies of Broadcasting No. 7* (NHK Radio and TV Culture Research Institute, Tokyo 1969).

13 See *NHK Handbook 1971* for a detailed account of the law, and also for the most recent statement of NHK's internal rules and code of broadcasting. 'NHK was founded on the basic policy of serving the nation as its public service broadcasting medium without intervention from any other sources, zealously safeguarding its stand of being a non-partisan and independent organisation, maintaining its code of upholding the freedom of speech and expression, and to exert its utmost towards the presentation of affluent and well-knit broadcasts, thus promoting the welfare of the public and exerting the best possible efforts towards the elevation of the nation's cultural standards.'

14 See Nakajima, *Revenue Resources*.

15 Hideya Kumata, *Broadcasting and Social Change, Studies of Broadcasting* (NHK Radio and TV Culture Research Institute, Tokyo 1964), pp. 41–9.

16 Viewing statistics given by Iwao Nakajima in Eguchi and Ichinohe, *International Studies*, p. 57, and Walter B. Emery, *Systems of Broadcasting*, p. 489).

17 Statistics for industrial growth and broadcasting given by Nakajima in Eguchi and Ichinohe, *International Studies*, pp. 62–5.

Chapter 10

1 See Harman Grisewood in *One Thing at a Time* (Hutchinson 1968) pp. 175-9, for some perceptive reminiscences of the BBC's longstanding dilemma about its precise place in the political spectrum.

² Agnew's pronouncements, referred to in the Preface, are characteristic expressions of this fear among modern democratic politicians. For a German version of this reaction to television see *Fernseh-Kritik II Die Gesellschaftskritische Funktion des Fernsehens, Herausgegeben von Diether Stolte* (von Hase und Koehler Verlag, Mainz 1970).

³ I have taken one example of Mr Wedgwood Benn's many presentations of his argument, his paper delivered at the Fourth Symposium on Broadcasting Policy at Manchester University, 'External Influences on Broadcasting'. It was published in *The Guardian* on 9 February 1972. A presentation of the case for a 'publishing' function in television which personally I admire more than Mr Benn's is Robin Day's 'Television in a Democracy' (in the *Society of Film and Television Art's Journal* for Spring 1965, and reprinted in A. William Bluem and Roger Manvell (eds.) *Progress in Television*, Focal Press Ltd 1967). 'Hitherto the timorous answer to the challenge of television's power has been to contain it, by keeping it in a very few "impartial" hands. During the next quarter of a century let us distribute the power of television, so that in 1984 television will not be an Orwellian instrument of mass hypnosis, but will have long been built into a broad and open platform of democratic opinion.'

⁴ 'One Week' – a survey of television coverage of Union and Industrial Affairs in the week 8–14 January 1971. ACTT Television Commission, London.

⁵ This point is eloquently argued by Stuart Hood in *The Listener*, vol. 85, no. 2187, 25 February 1971, pp. 1–2.

⁶ Benn, 'External Influences', p. 5.

⁷ Cable, of course, introduces a new element into the discussion. I deal with this in Ch. 8.

⁸ See Ch. 8.

⁹ French governments have tended (especially Gaullist ones) to defend their hegemony over television by arguing that it helped negate the hostility of the press and therefore rendered an unequal situation more fair.

¹⁰ Two powerful articulations of this view: P. P. Eckersley, *The Power Behind the Microphone* (The Scientific Book Club 1942); and Henry Fairlie's essay on 'The BBC' in *The Establishment*, edited by Hugh Thomas (Anthony Blond 1959).

¹¹ Most of my information on the early history of Dutch Broadcasting (pre-1965) comes from 'Legislation and the broadcasting institutions in the Netherlands' by Dr J. van Santbrink, Legal Adviser to Nederlandsche Unie, in *EBU Review* No. 988, July 1966; and from Walter B. Emery's *National and International Systems of Broadcasting* (Michigan State University Press, East Lansing 1969) Ch. viii, as well as from private conversations with Dutch broadcasters.

¹² See N. Ti Swierstra, 'The Birth of Broadcasting' in *EBU Review*, no. 1148, March 1969.

¹³ See Barnouw, *Tower in Babel*, vol. 1 of *History of Broadcasting in the United States* (Oxford University Press, New York 1970), pp. 64–74, 'Decision in Pittsburgh'.

¹⁴ See 'The Origin, Development and Present Organization of Sound and Television Broadcasting in the Netherlands' in *EBU Review*, no. 488, April 1958.

¹⁵ *Ibid.*

¹⁶ See *EBU Review's* special religious broadcasting number, No. 978, May 1966, which contains a short description of the memberships of the religious broadcasting organisation in the Netherlands by Bernard F. Takkenberg (from the religious broadcasting section of KRO).

¹⁷ The best descriptions of the provisions of the 1965 transitional arrangements and the eventual reorganisation see two further articles by Dr Santbrink in *EBU Review*, nos. 1028 (March 1967) and 1168 (July 1969). They both bear the same title as the first article.

¹⁸ See Netherlands Broadcasting Act of 1967, Section 61.

¹⁹ Netherlands Broadcasting Act of 1967, Section 33 para 4.

²⁰ *Ibid.*, Section 41.

²¹ *Ibid.*, Sections 49 and 50; Broadcasting Decree of April 1st 1969, Articles 20, 21 and 22. For further details of how the advertising system operates see 'Advertising on Radio and Television in Holland' published by NOS Press Department.

²² Act, Sections 27–31.

²³ See Timothy Green, *The Universal Eye – World Television in the Seventies* (The Bodley Head 1972) pp. 172–3.

²⁴ Act, Section 19.

²⁵ Act, Section 14.

²⁶ See 'Dutch Television' by Joan Bakewell, *Listener*, 12 March 1970.

²⁷ See Green, *Universal Eye*, p. 174.

A Broadcasting Bibliography

A. *British Government Publications*

Broadcasting Committee: Report (Cmnd. 1951), 1923 (The Sykes Report)

Report of the Broadcasting Committee, 1925 (Cmnd. 2599), 1926 (The Crawford Report)

Report of the Television Committee (Cmnd. 4793), 1935 (The Selsdon Report)

Report of the Broadcasting Committee, 1935 (Cmnd. 5091), 1936 (The Ullswater Report)

Memorandum on the Report of the Broadcasting Committee, 1935 (Cmnd. 5207), 1936

Report of the Television Committee, 1943, Privy Council Office (The Hankey Report), 19 December 1944

Broadcasting Policy (Cmnd. 6852), 1946

Royal Commission on the Press 1947–9 Report (Cmnd. 7700), 1949

Report of the Broadcasting Committee, 1949 (Cmnd. 8116), 1951 (The Beveridge Report), Appendix H: Memoranda Submitted to the Committee (Cmnd. 8117), 1951

Broadcasting: Memorandum on the Report of the Broadcasting Committee 1949 (Cmnd. 8291), 1951

Broadcasting: Memorandum on the Report of the Broadcasting Committee, 1949 (Cmnd. 8550), 1952

Broadcasting: Memorandum on Television Policy (Cmnd. 9005), 1953

The Television Act 1954 2 & 3 Eliz. 2 Ch. 55

Broadcasting (Licence granted on 6 April 1955, to the ITA) (Cmnd. 9451), 1955

Report of the Committee on Broadcasting, 1960 (Cmnd. 1753), 1962 (The Pilkington Report), Appendix E: Memoranda submitted to the Committee (two volumes) (Cmnd. 1819–1), 1962

Broadcasting Memorandum on the Report of the Committee on Broadcasting, 1960 (Cmnd. 1770), 1962

Broadcasting: Further Memorandum on the Report of the Committee on Broadcasting, 1960 (Cmnd. 1893), 1962

The Future of Sound Radio and Television: a short version of the Report of the Pilkington Committee (HMSO 1962)

Royal Commission on the Press 1961–2 (Cmnd. 1811), 1962

Television Act 1964 12 & 13 Eliz. 2 Ch. 21

The University of the Air (Cmnd. 2992), 1966

Broadcasting (Cmnd. 3169), 1966

An Alternative Service of Radio Broadcasting (Cmnd. 4636), 1971

Sound Broadcasting Act 1972 19 and 20 Eliz. 2 Ch. 31

Second Report from the Select Committee on Nationalised Industries

Session 1971–2 Independent Broadcasting Authority (formerly Independent Television Authority) (sub-committee B) House of Commons Paper 465, 1972

Report of the Technical Advisory Committee of the Minister of Posts and Telecommunications 1972 (The Cockburn Report)

Observations (on the Second Report of the Select Committee of the Nationalised Industries) by the Minister of Posts and Telecommunications and the Independent Broadcasting Authority (Cmnd 5244) March 1973.

In addition there are the various successive Licences and Charters of the BBC and the ITA, the annual volume published by the BBC (variously called the Yearbook or the Handbook), the Annual Reports of the BBC and the Annual Reports of the ITA.

B. *American Government and Federal Communications Commission Publications.* (All these documents are available in Frank J. Kahn (ed.) *Documents of American Broadcasting* (Appleton-Century-Crofts, New York 1968)

The Wireless Ship Act
    Public Law 262, 61st Congress, 24 June 1910
The Radio Act of 1912
    Public Law 264, 62nd Congress, 13 August 1912
The Radio Act
    Public Law 632, 69th Congress, 23 February 1927
The Communications Act
    Public Law 416, 73rd Congress, 19 June 1934
The Blue Book
    Public Service Responsibility of Broadcast Licensees 7 March 1946
The Fairness Doctrine
    In the Matter of Editorialising by Broadcast Licensees 13 FCC 1246, 1 June 1949
Third Notice of Proposed Rule Making
    16 Fed. Reg. 3072, 3079
    Adopted 21 March 1951, printed 7 April 1951
'The Freeze'
    17 Fed. Reg. 3905, 3908
    Adopted 14 April 1952, printed 2 May 1952
'The Educational Reservation'
Report and Statement of Policy re: Commission *in blanco* Programming Enquiry. FCC 60–970, 29 July 1960
The ETV Facilities Act of 1962
    Public Law 87–447, 87th Congress, 1 May 1962
The Communications Satellite Act
    Public Law 624, 87th Congress 2nd session, 31 August 1962
Broadcast Licensees Advised Concerning Stations' Responsibilities Under the Fairness Doctrine as to Controversial Issue Programming FCC 63–734, 25 July 1963

The Pacifica Case
  36 FCC 147, 22 January 1964
'The Section 315 Primer'
  Use of Broadcast Facilities by Candidates for Public Office. 31 Fed.
  Reg. 6660. Adopted 27 April 1966. Printed 4 May 1966
The Public Broadcasting Act
  Public Law 90–129, 90th Congress, 7 November 1967

C. *Principal Journals* (all are American publications unless indicated
  otherwise)
American Journal of Sociology
American Sociological Review
Audio-Visual Communications Review
Broadcasting
Chicago Journalism Review
Columbia Journalism Review
Contrast (London – defunct in 1964)
European Broadcasting Union Review (Brussels)
Gazette (Leiden)
Journalisme (Strasbourg)
Journalism Quarterly
Journal of Broadcasting
Journal of Communication
Journal of Conflict Resolution
Journal of Social Forces
Journal of Social Issues
Journal of the Society of Film and Television Arts (London)
Journalism Today (London)
Kwartalnik Prasonawczy (Warsaw)
Listener (London)
More (New York)
New Society (London)
Novinarsky Sbornik (Prague, now defunct)
Polish Sociological Bulletin (Warsaw)
Political Quarterly (London)
Public Opinion Quarterly
Publizistik (Frankfurt)
Quarterly of Film, Radio and Television
Reports of the International Press Institute (Zurich)
Rundfunk und Fernsehen (Hamburg)
Social Problems
Television Quarterly
TV Guide
Variety

D. *Research Collections*
Since the end of the Second World War something approaching

fifteen thousand research projects have been undertaken and published in the field of mass communication. Much of the best work has appeared in the periodicals listed in Section C of this bibliography. However, the most accessible source for most of the best work is in one or other of the following collections. Each collection of papers has been designed according to the personal ideology or private bias of the editor, and is all the better for that. Each covers a broader area than that of this book and has exercised some influence or other on the present writer's train of thought.

Bernard Berelson and Morris Janowitz, *Reader in Public Opinion and Communication* (The Free Press, New York 1966), (earlier editions in 1950 and 1953).

A. William Bluem and Roger Manvell, *Progress of Television: An Anglo-American Survey* (Focal Press 1967).

John E. Coons, *Freedom and Responsibility in Broadcasting* (Northwestern University Press 1961).

Lewis A. Dexter and David Manning White, *People, Society and Mass Communications* (The Free Press, New York 1964).

James Halloran, *The Effects of Television* (Panther Books 1970).

Paul Halmos, *The Sociology of Mass-Media Communicators*. The Sociological Review Monograph No. 13 (University of Keele, January 1969).

Denis McQuail, *Sociology of Mass Communications: Selected Readings* (Penguin 1972).

Lucien W. Pye, *Communications and Political Development* (Princeton University Press, New Jersey 1963).

Bernard Rosenberg and David Manning White, *Mass Culture: The Popular Arts in America* (The Free Press of Glencoe 1956).

Wilbur Schramm, *Mass Communications: a Book of Readings* (University of Illinois Press 1960).

Wilbur Schramm, *The Science of Human Communication: New Directions and New Findings in Communication Research* (Basic Books Inc. New York 1963).

Jeremy Tunstall, *Media Sociology: A Reader* (Constable, London 1970).

E. *Biography, Memoir and Reminiscence*

There is, of course, a great wealth of biographical and autobiographical material available concerned with the careers of people intimately involved in half a century of broadcasting. Most modern political biographies contain useful material with a bearing on broadcasting policy. The following list, therefore, is to some extent arbitrary; I have selected works which have been particularly relevant to the content of this book or which appear to me to be amusing or stimulating.

Richard Baker, *Here is the News* (Leslie Frewin 1966).

Thomas Barman, *Diplomatic Correspondent* (Hamish Hamilton 1968).

Gerald Beadle, *Television: a Critical Review* (Allen & Unwin 1963).

Reginald Bevins, *The Greasy Pole* (Hodder & Stoughton 1965).
Andrew Boyle, *Only the Wind will Listen, Reith of the BBC* (Hutchinson 1972).
Russell Braddon, *Roy Thomson of Fleet* (Collins 1965).
A. R. Burrows, *The Story of Broadcasting* (Cassell 1924).
Stuart Chesmore, *Behind the Microphone* (Nelson 1935).
P. P. Eckersley, *The Power Behind the Microphone* (The Scientific Book Club 1942).
Roger Eckersley, *The BBC and All That* (Low, Marston 1946).
Lionel Fielden, *The Natural Bent* (André Deutsch 1960).
Fred W. Friendly, *Due to Circumstances Beyond our Control* (MacGibbon & Kee 1967).
Val Gielgud, *Years of the Locust* (Nicholson & Watson 1947).
Maurice Gorham, *Sound and Fury* (P. Marshall 1948).
Harman Grisewood, *One Thing at a Time* (Hutchinson 1968).
Leonard Henry, *My Laugh Story* (S. Paul 1937).
Stuart Hibberd, *This – is London* (MacDonald & Evans 1950).
Lord Hill of Luton, *Both Sides of the Hill* (Heinemann 1964).
Alexander Kendrick, *Prime Time: The Life of Edward R. Murrow* (Little, Brown & Co., Boston, Mass. 1969).
C. A. Lewis, *Broadcasting From Within* (George Newnes 1924).
Eugene Lyons, *David Sarnoff: a biography* (Harper & Row 1966).
Degna Marconi, *My Father Marconi* (McGraw-Hill, New York 1962).
Eric Maschwitz, *No Chip on My Shoulder* (Jenkins 1937).
Leonard Miall, *Richard Dimbleby, Broadcaster* (BBC 1966).
Sydney Moseley, *Broadcasting in My Time* (Rich & Cowan 1935).
——, *John Baird: The Romance and Tragedy of the Pioneer of Television* (Odhams 1952).
Jack Payne, *Signature Tune* (S. Paul 1947).
J. C. W. Reith, *Broadcast Over Britain* (Hodder & Stoughton 1924).
——, *Into the Wind* (Hodder & Stoughton 1949).
Gordon Ross, *TV Jubilee 25 Years* (W. H. Allen 1961).
Lord Simon of Wythenshawe, *The BBC from Within* (Gollancz 1953).
S. W. Smithers, *Broadcasting from Within* (Pitman 1938).
D. Cleghorn Thomson, *Radio is Changing Us* (Watts & Co. 1937).
Mary Whitehouse, *Who Does She Think She Is* (New English Library 1971).
Lord Woolton, *Memoirs* (Cassell 1959).

F. *History of broadcasting, and other media, relevant to the present study*

Richard D. Altick, *The English Common Reader: A Social History of the Mass Reading Public 1800–1900* (University of Chicago Press 1957, Phoenix Press 1967).
Erik Barnouw, *A Tower in Babel.* Vol. 1 of *A History of Broadcasting in the United States* to 1933 (Oxford University Press, New York 1966).
——, *The Golden Web.* Vol. 2 of *A History of Broadcasting in the United States, 1933–1953* (Oxford University Press 1968).

——, *The Image Empire*. Vol. 3 of *A History of Broadcasting in the United States*, from 1953 (Oxford University Press 1970).

Marvin Barrett (ed.), *The Alfred I. Dupont-Columbia University Survey of Broadcast Journalism 1968–9* (Grosset & Dunlap Inc., New York 1969).

——, (ed.), *Year of Challenge, Year of Crisis. The Alfred I. Dupont-Columbia University Survey of Broadcast Journalism 1969–70* (Grosset & Dunlap Inc., New York 1970).

——, (ed.), *A State of Siege. The Alfred I. Dupont-Columbia University Survey of Broadcast Journalism 1970–1* (Grosset & Dunlap Inc., New York 1971).

Daniel J. Boorstin, *The Image: What Happened to the American Dream* (Weidenfeld & Nicolson 1962).

Malcolm Bradbury, *The Social Context of Modern English Literature* (Basil Blackwell, Oxford 1971).

Asa Briggs, *The Birth of Broadcasting*. Vol. 1 of *The History of Broadcasting in the United Kingdom* (Oxford University Press 1961).

——, *The Golden Age of Wireless*. Vol. 2 of *The History of Broadcasting in the United Kingdom* (Oxford University Press 1965).

——, *The War of Words*. Vol. 3 of *The History of Broadcasting in the United Kingdom* (Oxford University Press 1970).

Van Wyck Brooks, *The Confident Years 1885–1915* (the last of a series of five volumes under the general title *Makers and Finders: A History of the Writer in America 1800–1915*) (J. M. Dent & Sons Ltd 1953).

Walter B. Emery, *National and International Systems of Broadcasting: Their History, Operation and Control* (Michigan State University Press 1969).

J. J. Fahie, *A History of Electric Telegraphy to the Year 1837* (E. and F. N. Spon 1884).

Maurice Gorham, *Broadcasting and Television since 1900* (Dakers 1952).

Guinevere L. Griest, *Mudie's Circulating Library and the Victorian Novel* (Indiana University Press 1970; David & Charles 1970).

Harold Herd, *The March of Journalism: The Story of the British Press from 1622 to the Present Day* (George Allen & Unwin 1952).

Harold Hobson, Philip Knightley and Leonard Russell, *The Pearl of Days: An Intimate Memoir of 'The Sunday Times' 1822–1972* (Hamish Hamilton 1972).

Henry Jephson, *The Platform* (London 1897).

Samuel McKechnie, *Popular Entertainments through the Ages* (Sampson Low, Marston & Co. Ltd 1931).

Marshall McLuhan, *The Gutenberg Galaxy: The Making of Typographic Man* (University of Toronto Press 1962; Routledge & Kegan Paul 1962).

Frank Luther Mott, *A History of American Magazines* (4 vols.) (Macmillan Co., New York 1938).

Bibliography

Frank Luther Mott, *American Journalism* (Macmillan, New York. Revised ed. 1950).

——, *The News in America* (Macmillan, New York 1952).

R. K. Webb, *The British Working-Class Reader 1790–1848* (George Allen & Unwin 1955).

Dixon Wecter, *The Age of the Great Depression 1929–1941* (Macmillan Co. 1948; Quadrangle Books 1971) (Vol. XIII in the History of American Life series).

Raymond Williams, *Culture and Society 1780–1950* (Chatto & Windus 1958).

——, *The Long Revolution* (Chatto & Windus 1961).

G. *A short bibliography on broadcasting in France*
Other short articles are referred to in the Notes to Chapter 6.

L'Année 1968 (Presses Universitaires de France, 1969).

Raymond Aron, *Signification politique de la Radio-Télévision dans le Monde Présent*. Cahiers d'études de Radio-Télévision No. 15 (Flammarion, Paris 1957).

André Bailly, René de Roche, *Dictionnaire de la Télévision* (Librairie Larousse, Paris 1967).

Jean Cazeneuve, *Les Pouvoirs de la Télévision* (Gallimard, Paris 1970).

Communications No. 5, Les Intellectuels et la Culture de Masse (Seuil, Paris, May 1965, pp. 1–45).

Communications No. 12, an issue devoted entirely to the Events of May 1968 (Seuil, Paris, May 1968).

Charles Debbasch, *Le Droit de la Radio et de la Télévision* (in the series 'Que sais-je?') (Presses Universitaires de France, Paris 1969).

André Diligent, *La Télévision: Progrès ou Décadence?* (Hachette, Paris 1965).

Droit Social No. 12, L'ORTF et ses problèmes (December 1970).

Roger Errera, *Les libertés à l'Abandon* (Seuil, Paris 1968).

Claude Frédéric, *Libérer l'ORTF* (Edition Combats, Seuil, Paris 1968).

Jules Gritti & M. Souchon, *La Sociologie Face aux Média* (Collection Medium. Mame, Paris 1968).

Roger Louis, *L'ORTF: Un Combat* (Seuil, Paris 1968).

Jean-Pierre Manuel and Alomee Planel, *La Crise de l'ORTF* (Jean-Jacques Pauvert, Paris 1968).

Jean-Guy Moreau, *La Règne de la Télévision* (Seuil, Paris 1968).

Rapport de la Commission d'Etude du Statut de L'ORTF (the 'Paye Report') 30 June 1970. (Journaux Officiels, Paris 1970).

Sylvain Roumette, 'Shadow Television' in *Les Temps Modernes* (two articles) December 1969 and January 1970.

David Schoenbrun, *The Three Lives of Charles de Gaulle* (Athenaeum Press, New York 1966).

Jacques Thibau, *Une Télévision pour tous les Français* (Collections Esprit 'La Cité Prochaine', Seuil, Paris 1970).

Union des Journalistes de la Télévision: 'Notes d'Information concernant la crise de l'ORTF et la grève des Journalistes de la Télévision' (the strikers' 'White Paper') July 1968.

Alexander Werth, *De Gaulle: A Political Biography* (Simon & Shuster, New York 1965).

Philip M. Williams, *The French Parliament 1958–1967.* Studies in Political Science (George Allen & Unwin 1968).

Philip M. Williams and Martin Harrison, *Politics and Society in de Gaulle's Republic* (Longman 1971).

French Official Papers
The following represent some of the most interesting debates and state papers of recent years.

Journal Officiel

No. 150. Loi no. 64–621 du 27 Juin 1964 portant statut de l'Office de Radiodiffusion-télévision Française (p. 5636) 28 Juin 1964.

No. 170. Décret no. 64–736 du 22 Juillet 1964 pris pour l'application de la loi no. 64–621 du 27 Juin 1964 portant statut de l'Office de Radiodiffusion-télévision Française (p. 6552) 23 Juillet 1964.

No. 269. Décret no. 69–1024 du 12 Novembre 1969 modifiant le décret no. 64–739 du 22 Juillet 1964 portant statut des journalistes de l'Office de Radiodiffusion-télévision Française (p. 11213) 17–18 Novembre 1969.

No. 66 S – contains the Senate budget debate (pp. 2436–2489) of November 1971, at which André Diligent presented his report on the ORTF.

No. 27 A.N. questions orales avec débat (p. 1482–1501) on the corruption scandal in the ORTF in National Assembly, 11 May 1972.

No. 29 S – the Senate Debate of 20 June 1972 on the report of the special commission into the affairs of the ORTF (pp. 1022–1030) 21 June 1972.

No. 325. Senate debate of 26 June 1972 on the new statute for the ORTF (pp. 1201–1217) 27 June 1972.

No. 35 S. which contains the continuation of the Senate debate on the statute of the ORTF (pp. 1382–1412) 30 June 1972.

No. 54 A.N. which contains the record of the National Assembly's debate on the statute (pp. 3002–3008) 30 June 1972.

No. 55 A.N. – continuation of National Assembly debate of 30 June 1972 on the new statute for the ORTF (pp. 3082–3084) 1 July 1972.

H. *Broadcasting Policy and Broadcasting Structures*

ACTT Television Commission – Report to Annual Conference (ACTT March 1972).

W. Altman, D. Thomas and D. Sawyers, *TV: From Monopoly to Competition and Back?*, Hobart Paper 15. (Institute of Economic Affairs 1962).

F. S. Badley (ed.), *Second Symposium on Broadcasting: Determinants of Broadcasting Policy* (University of Manchester, Department of Extra-Mural Studies, November 1970).

Ben Bagdikian, 'Right of access: a modest proposal', *Columbia Journalism Review*, vol. 8, no. 1, Spring 1969, pp. 10–13.

Joan Bakewell and Nicholas Garnham, *The New Priesthood: British Television Today* (Allen Lane, The Penguin Press 1970).

Jerome A. Barron, 'Access to the press: a new first amendment right' *Harvard Law Review*, June 1967.

——, 'An enlarging first amendment right of access to the media?' *George Washington Law Review*, March 1969.

Reinhard Bendix, Article on Bureaucracy in *International Encyclopedia of the Social Sciences*, vol. 2, pp. 206–17. (Macmillan and Free Press, New York 1968).

Hal Bethell, *Education and BBC Local Radio* (BBC, November 1972).

Peter Black, *The Mirror in the Corner – People's Television* (Hutchinson 1972).

Joseph L. Brehner, 'A Statement on the Fairness Doctrine,' *Journal of Broadcasting*, vol. 9, no. 2, pp. 103–12, Spring 1965.

Les Brown, *The Business Behind the Box*, (Harcourt-Brace-Jovanovich, New York 1971).

Dean Burch, 'Another type of air pollution', *Television Quarterly*, vol. 9, no. 1, Winter 1970, pp. 5–10.

Sir Sydney Caine, *Paying for Television* (Institute of Economic Affairs 1968).

Carnegie Commission, *Public Television: A Program for Action* (Bantam Books 1967).

Peter Clarke and Lee Ruggels, 'Preferences among news media for coverage of public affairs', *Journalism Quarterly*, vol. 47, no. 3, Autumn 1970, pp. 464–71.

Deena Clark, 'Public television speaks out – An Interview with John Macy'. *Television Quarterly*, vol. 9, no. 2, Spring 1970, pp. 26–33.

Beresford Clark, 'The BBC's external services', *International Affairs*, vol. 35, no. 2, April 1959.

R. H. Coase, *British Broadcasting: A Study in Monopoly* (Longmans 1950).

John Coatman, 'The BBC, government and politics', *Public Opinion Quarterly*, vol. xv, no. 2, pp. 287–98.

George A. Codding Jr, *Broadcasting without Barriers* (UNESCO 1960).

Robert L. Coe, 'The National Citizens Committee for Broadcasting: What is It?' *Television Quarterly*, vol. 8, no. 3, Summer 1969, pp. 48–55.

Marcus Cohn, 'Rebels, the FCC and the structure of broadcasting', *Television Quarterly*, vol. 9, no. 4, Autumn 1970, pp. 6–12.

John E. Coons (ed.), *Freedom and Responsibility in Broadcasting* (Northwestern University Press 1961).

The Shadow in the Cave

Kenneth A. Cox, 'Does the FCC really do anything?' *Journal of Broadcasting*, vol. xi, no. 2, Spring 1967, pp. 97–114.

Kenneth A. Cox and Nicholas Johnson, 'Broadcasting in America and the FCC's license-renewal process – an Oklahoma case study', *Columbia Journalism Review*, vol. vii, no. 2, Summer 1968.

Julian Critchley, *Counsel for Broadcasting* (Conservative Political Centre 1971).

Mary Crozier, *Broadcasting: Sound and Television* (Oxford University Press 1958).

Charles Curran, 'The BBC's advisory bodies', *EBU Review* 958, January 1966, pp. 10–15.

——, *Breaking Up the BBC?* (BBC 1972).

——, *The BBC and its Educational Commitment* (BBC 1972).

James Day, 'Cultural beggars and social responsibilities', *Television Quarterly*, vol. 9, no. 1, Winter 1970, pp. 24–8.

M. E. Dimmock, *British Public Utilities and National Development* (Allen & Unwin 1933).

Jack Dowling and Lelia Doolan (and Bob Quinn), *Sit Down and be Counted: The Cultural Evolution of a Television Station* (Wellington, Dublin 1969).

Peter Draper (ed.), 'Towards an open society; ends and means in British politics'. Proceedings of a seminar organised by the British Humanist Association (Pemberton Books 1971).

Walter B. Emery, *Broadcasting and Government: Responsibilities and Regulations* (Michigan State University Press 1971).

FCC, 'The Pacifica decision – broadcasting and free expression', *Journal of Broadcasting* vol. ix, no. 2, Spring 1965, pp. 177–82.

Sir Dingle Foot, 'The relationship and interplay between the law, the government, press and parliament', *Journalism Today*, vol. 1, no. 1, Autumn 1970.

Frederick W. Ford, 'The Fairness Doctrine' *Journal of Broadcasting*, vol. viii, no. 1, Winter 1963–64, pp. 3–16.

Bernard Frank (ed.), *Fernseh-Kritik: fernsehen von morgen – ende eines monopolbewusstseins*, (von Hase and Koehler Verlag, Mainz 1972).

Richard Fraser, *The Coming of Independent Television* (ITA 1955).

Fred W. Friendly, 'TV at the turning point', *Columbia Journalism Review*, vol. ix, no. 4, Winter 1970/71, pp. 13–20.

Ernst W. Fuhr, *ZDF – Staatsvertrag*, (von Hase and Koehler Verlag, Mainz 1972). Staatsvertrag über die Errichtung der gemeinnützigen Anstalt des öffentlichen Rechts 'Zweites Deutsches Fernsehen'.

John Kenneth Galbraith, *The New Industrial State* (André Deutsch 1972).

Hyman H. Goldin, 'The 50–50 Rule: or how to parlay a Game show into program diversity'. *Television Quarterly*, vol. 9, no. 1, Winter 1970, pp. 50–8.

Bibliography

L. Gordon, *The Public Corporation in Great Britain* (Oxford University Press 1938).

Timothy Green, *The Universal Eye: World Television in the Seventies* (The Bodley Head 1972).

Hugh Greene, *The BBC as a Public Service* (BBC 1960).

——, 'Local broadcasting and the local authority,' *Public Administration*, Winter 1961.

——, *The Broadcaster's Responsibility* (BBC 1962).

——, *Future Prospects in Broadcasting* (BBC 1963).

——, *The Third Floor Front: A View of Broadcasting in the Sixties* (The Bodley Head 1969).

Brian Groombridge, *Television and the People: A Programme for Democratic Participation* (Penguin Education Special 1972).

Sir William Haley, *The Central Problem of Broadcasting* (BBC 1948).

——, *The Responsibilities of Broadcasting* (BBC 1948) (The Lewis Fry Memorial Lectures of May 1948).

James D. Halloran, *Control or Consent: A study of the challenge of mass communication* (Sheed & Ward 1963).

A. H. Hanson (ed.), *Nationalisation: a book of readings* (Allen & Unwin 1963).

Alvin Harlow, *Old Wine and New Waves* (D. Appleton-Century 1936).

Kenneth Harwood, 'Communes as broadcasters', *Television Quarterly*, vol. 9, no. 4, Autumn 1970, pp. 80–5.

E. William Henry and Hubbell Robinson, 'The 50–50 rule: angels, saints and sinners'. *Television Quarterly*, vol. 4, no. 4, Autumn 1965.

E. William Henry, Charles E. Goodell, Julian Goodman, Leon Brooks and John de J. Pemberton Jr, 'Section 315 – the prospects'. *Television Quarterly*, vol. 5, no. 1, Winter 1965, pp. 33–46.

Charles Hill, 'The future of television'. *Journalism Today*, vol. 1, no. 3, Autumn 1968.

Stuart Hood, *A Survey of Television* (Heinemann 1967).

——, *The Mass Media* (Macmillan 1972).

Roland Huntford, *The New Totalitarians* (Allen Lane, The Penguin Press 1971). (See Chapter 7 on 'The Mass Media and the Creation of Conformism'.)

Alex Inkeles, 'Recent developments in Soviet mass communications', *Gazette*, vol. 4, no. 4, 1958, pp. 285–97.

Institutes for Policy Studies, *Television Today* (Communication Service Corporation, Washington D.C. 1969).

International Press Institute, 'IPI survey on the press in authoritarian countries' (IPI Zurich 1959).

Sir Ian Jacob, *The BBC: a national and international force* (BBC 1957).

Louis L. Jaffe, 'The editorial responsibility of the broadcaster: reflections on fairness and access'. *Harvard Law Review*, vol. 85, no. 4, Autumn 1972.

Clive Jenkins, *Power behind the Screen* (MacGibbon & Kee 1961).

Johnson Foundation of Racine, Wisconsin, Proceedings of, January 1968: 'Public television – search for identity'. *Television Quarterly*, vol. 7, no. 1, Winter 1968.

Nicholas Johnson, *How to Talk Back to Your Television Set* (Atlantic, Little, Brown, Boston (Mass.) 1967).

——, 'What the FCC Must Do' *Columbia Journalism Review*, vol. viii, no. 4, Winter 1969, pp. 28–33.

——, 'Just how good *is* British TV? Comparisons and lessons for America'. *Television Quarterly*, vol. 9, no. 4, Autumn 1970, pp. 13–32.

——, *Test Pattern for Living* (Bantam Books 1972).

—— and Tracy Westen, 'A twentieth-century soapbox: the right to purchase radio and television time'. *Virginia Law Review*, vol. 57, no. 4, 1971.

La Concentration des entreprises de press et la liberté de l'information. Special issue of *Journalisme*, no. 34, 1971.

Dan Lacy, 'Freedom and Communications' (The Windsor Lectures for 1959) (University of Illinois Press, Urbana 1965), 2nd edn.

Norman Lobsenz, 'Everett Parker's Broadcasting Crusade'. *Columbia Journalism Review*, vol. viii, no. 3, Autumn 1969, pp. 30–6.

Local Radio in the Public Interest – the BBC's plan (BBC 1966).

Lee Loevinger, 'The future of television'. *Television Quarterly*, vol. 4, no. 4, Autumn 1965, pp. 41–52.

Elmer W. Lower, 'Television, Soviet style – 1967'. *Television Quarterly*, vol. 6, no. 3, Summer 1967.

David McKie, *TV File* (Panther record 1967).

Salvador de Madariaga, *Essays with a Purpose* (Hollis & Carter 1954).

Alexander Matejko, 'Newspaper staff as a social system', *Polish Sociological Bulletin*, vol. 15, no. 1, 1967, pp. 58–68.

Hilda Matheson, *Broadcasting* (Thornton Butterworth 1933).

Martin Mayer, *About Television* (Random House, New York 1973).

Henrique Melon-Martinez, *La Télévision dans la famille et la société modernes* (Marabout universitaire 1970).

Newton Minow, *Equal Time: the private broadcaster and the public interest* (Athenaeum, New York 1964).

——, Review of Erik Barnouw's 'The Image Empire' in *Political Science Quarterly*, vol. lxxxvii, no. 1, March 1972, pp. 109–10.

Howard Monderer, 'Response to an FCC inquiry'. *Television Quarterly*, vol. 7, no. 1, Winter 1969, pp. 97–106.

Lord Normanbrook, *The Functions of the BBC Governors* (BBC 1965).

T. H. O'Brien, *British Experiments in Public Ownership and Control* (Allen & Unwin 1937).

Burton Paulu, *British Broadcasting: Radio and Television in the United Kingdom* (Oxford University Press 1957).

——, *Radio and Television Broadcasting on the European Continent* (University of Minnesota Press 1967).

Bibliography

Burton Paulu, *British Broadcasting in Transition* (Macmillan 1961).

John de J. Pemberton Jr, 'The Right of Access to Mass Media', from Norman Dorsen (ed.) *The Rights of Americans – What They Are, What They Should Be* (Pantheon Books, New York 1970)

Avner Perry, 'The Enigma Called Israeli Television', *Television Quarterly*, vol. 7, no. 3, Summer 1968, pp. 85–93.

Thomas Petry, 'West German TV – The Way Ahead', *Television Quarterly*, vol. 2, no. 3, Summer 1963, pp. 58–67.

Political Quarterly (special issue on BBC), Oct–Dec. 1935.

Raymond Postgate, *What to do with the BBC* (Hogarth Press 1935).

R. Powell, 'Possibilities for local radio' (Centre for Contemporary Studies, University of Birmingham 1965).

Fred Powledge, *The Nixon Administration and the Press* (American Civil Liberties Union, September 1971).

A. W. Pragnell, 'British Independent Television after fifteen years'. *EBU Review*, 1208, March 1970, pp. 16–21.

C. F. Pratten, 'The Economics of Television' (PEP Broadsheet 520, September 1970).

Hubbell Robinson, 'What makes Nick tick' (Review of Nicholas Johnson's 'How to Talk Back to Your Television Set'), *Television Quarterly*, vol. 9, no. 2, Spring 1970, pp. 51–6.

W. A. Robson, 'The BBC as an institution', *Political Quarterly*, vol. vi, no. 4, Oct.–Dec. 1935, pp. 468–88.

—— (ed.), *Public Enterprise* (Allen & Unwin 1937).

——, *British Government since 1918* (Allen & Unwin 1950).

Roper Organisation Inc., 'An extended view of public attitudes toward television and other mass media, 1959–1971' (Television Information Office, New York 1971).

Richard Rose, *Politics in England* (Faber & Faber 1965).

——, *Studies in British Politics* (Macmillan 1966).

Olof Rydbeck, 'Coordinating the two Swedish Services'. *EBU Review*, 918, May 1965, pp. 40–2.

Herbert I. Schiller, *Mass Communications and American Empire* (Augustus M. Kelley, New York 1969).

Jean Schwoebel, 'The coming newsroom revolution – the miracle *Le Monde* wrought', *Columbia Journalism Review* vol. ix, no. 2, Summer 1970, pp. 8–11.

John Scupham, *Broadcasting and the Community* (Watts 1967).

Harry J. Skornia, *Television and Society: an inquest and agenda for improvement* (McGraw-Hill, New York 1965).

John Snagge and Michael Barsley, *Those Vintage Years of Radio* (Pitman 1972).

P. O. Steiner, 'Monopoly and competition in television: some policy issues', Manchester School, vol. 29, no. 2.

N. Ti Swiertra, 'The Birth of Broadcasting', *EBU Review*, 1148, March 1969.

325

Bernard F. Takkenberg, 'The structure of religious broadcasting in Netherlands radio and television', *EBU Review*, 978, May 1966 (special issue on religious broadcasting), pp. 29–31.

Peggy Taylor and Bernard Redmont, 'French television – a changing image', *Television Quarterly*, vol. 8, no. 4, Autumn 1969, pp. 39–49.

Trygve R. Tholfson, 'The intellectual origins of mid-Victorian stability', *Political Science Quarterly*, vol. lxxxvi, no. 1, March 1971, pp. 57–91.

Howard Thomas, *The Truth about Television* (Weidenfeld & Nicolson 1962).

Ivor Thomas, 'Systems of Broadcasting'. *Political Quarterly*, Oct.–Dec. 1935, vol. vi, no. 4, pp. 489–505.

The Uncertain Mirror: Report of the Special Senate Committee on Mass Media, 3 vols. Vol. 1, *Broadcasting Section*, pp. 193–226 (Queen's Printer for Canada, December 1970).

Egon Wagner, 'Report from the Federal Republic of Germany', *EBU Review*, 1218, May 1970, pp. 58–62.

E. G. Wedell, *Broadcasting and Public Policy* (Michael Joseph 1968).
—— (ed.), *Structures of Broadcasting: A Symposium* (Manchester University Press 1970).

Geoffrey Wigoder, 'Radio is Israel', *Gazette*, vol. vii, no. 1, 1961, pp. 129–36.

Colin Welch, 'Between commerce and the state – a dissent'. *Encounter*, vol. 18, no. 5, May 1962, pp. 49–54.

Av Westin, 'An Open Memorandum to Mr John W. Macy Jr, President of the Corporation for Public Broadcasting', *Television Quarterly*, vol. 8, no. 2, Spring 1969, pp. 31–46.

Raymond Williams, *Communications* (revised) (Chatto & Windus, 1969).

H. H. Wilson, *Pressure Group – The Campaign for Commercial Television* (Secker & Warburg 1961).

Hermann H. Wolff, 'West German television and television in the Soviet zone', *Gazette*, vol. 2, no. 4, 1956, pp. 235–42.

Donald N. Wood, 'The first fifteen years of the "Fourth Network"', *Journal of Broadcasting*, vol. xiii, no. 2, Spring 1968, pp. 131–44.

David L. Woods, 'Semantics versus the "First Broadcasting Station"'. *Journal of Broadcasting*, vol. xi, no. 3, Summer 1967.

World Radio and Television (UNESCO, Paris; and Publications Center, New York 1965).

V. N. Yaroshenko, 'Soviet radio – is anyone listening?' Vestnik Moskovskovo Universiteta, Seriya xi, *Zhurnalistika*, no. 1, 1966.

Whitney M. Young, Jr, 'The social responsibility of broadcasters', *Television Quarterly*, vol. 8, no. 2, Spring 1969, pp. 7–17.

Harry Zinder, 'Television in Israel'. *Gazette*, vol. vii, no. 1, 1961, pp. 137–40.

The IBA (ITA) has published regular policy bulletins, entitled *ITA NOTES* (Nos. 1–25, 1963–1973). The BBC's equivalent is The *BBC*

Bibliography

RECORD (Nos. 1–85, 1961–1973). The *Annual Reports and Accounts* of both organisations contain much valuable material.

I. *Material on the impact and effects on society of broadcasting and other media of mass communication*

Elkan and Dorothea Allen, *Good Listening: a survey of broadcasting* (Hutchinson 1948).

Rudolf Arnheim, *Radio* (Faber & Faber 1936).

——, *Film as Art* (Faber & Faber 1969).

Matthew Arnold, *Culture and Anarchy* (1869).

L. Arons and M. A. May, *Television and Human Behaviour* (Appleton-Century-Crofts 1963).

Alan Barth, *The Loyalty of Free Men* (with foreword by Zachariah Chafee Jr) (Gollancz 1951).

Z. Baumann, 'Two notes on mass culture', *Polish Sociological Bulletin*, vol. 14, no. 2, 1966, pp. 58–74.

Daniel Bell, *The End of Ideology* (The Free Press, New York 1960).

William A. Belson, *The Impact of Television: Methods and Findings in Programme Research* (Crosby Lockwood 1967).

Edward Bliss Jr (ed.), *In Search of Light: Broadcasts of Edward R. Murrow 1938–61* (Alfred A. Knopf, New York 1967).

A. William Bluem, 'Media mononucleosis'. *Television Quarterly*, vol. 6, no. 4, Autumn 1967, pp. 45–51.

J. G. Blumler and Denis McQuail, 'British broadcasting: its purposes, structures, and control', *Gazette*, vol. xi, no. 2/3, 1965, pp. 166–91.

Leo Bogart, *The Age of Television: A Study of Viewing Habits and the Impact of Television on American life* (Crosby Lockwood & Son 1956, 1958).

Lloyd R. Bostian, 'The two-step flow theory: cross-cultural implications', *Journalism Quarterly*, vol. 47, no. 1, Spring 1970, pp. 109–17.

John Bowle, *Politics and Opinion in the Nineteenth Century: An Historical Introduction* (Jonathan Cape 1954, 1966).

Bertolt Brecht, 'Theory of radio', *Gesammelte Werke*, Band VIII (1932), pp. 129–34.

Asa Briggs, *The Communications Revolution* (Leeds University Press 1966).

J. A. C. Brown, *Techniques of Persuasion: From Propaganda to Brainwashing* (Pelican 1963).

Edmund Carpenter and Marshall McLuhan (eds.), *Explorations in Communication – An Anthology* (Beacon Press, Boston 1960).

Richard F. Carter and Bradley S. Greenberg, 'Newspapers or television: which do you believe?' *Journalism Quarterly*, vol. xlii, no. 1, Winter 1965, pp. 29–34.

Douglas Cater, *The Fourth Branch of Government* (Houghton Mifflin, Boston 1959).

327

Zachariah Chafee Jr, *Free Speech in the United States* (Harvard University Press, Cambridge Mass. 1941), replaces the classic work of 1920.

David Chaney, *Processes of Mass Communication* (Macmillan 1972).

Cedric Clark, 'Television and social controls: some observations on the portrayal of ethnic minorities'. *Television Quarterly*, vol. 8, no. 2, Spring 1969, pp. 18–22.

Royal D. Cole, 'Negro image in the mass media – a case study in social change', *Journalism Quarterly*, vol. xlv, no. 1, Spring 1968, pp. 55–60.

Kenneth Cox, 'Can broadcasting help achieve Social reform?'. *Journal of Broadcasting*, vol. xiii, no. 2, Spring 1968, pp. 117–30.

John Crittenden, 'Democratic functions of the open mike radio forum'. *Public Opinion Quarterly*, vol. xxxv, no. 2, Summer 1971, pp. 200–6.

C. A. R. Crosland, 'The Mass Media', *Encounter*, vol. 19, no. 5, November 1962, pp. 3–14.

Richard Crossman, 'Thoughts of a captive viewer', *Encounter*, vol. 19, no. 2, August 1962, pp. 46–52.

Melvin L. De Fleur, *Theories of Mass Communication* (David McKay, New York 1966).

Wilson P. Dizard, *Television – World View* (Syracuse University Press 1966).

H. Eguchi and H. Ichinohe (eds.), *International Studies of Broadcasting: With Special Reference to the Japanese studies* (NHK Radio & TV Culture Research Institute, NHK, Tokyo 1971).

Philip Elliott, *The Making of a Television Series: A Case Study in the Sociology of Culture* (Constable 1972).

Jacques Ellul, *Propaganda – the Formation of Men's Attitudes* (Alfred A. Knopf, New York 1965).

Walter B. Emery, 'Radio Luxembourg: "the station of the stars"', *Journal of Broadcasting*, vol. x, no. 4, Autumn 1966, pp. 311–26.

Brian P. Emmett, 'Gratifications research in broadcasting', *Public Opinion Quarterly*, Winter 1968/9, pp. 654–65.

Hans Magnus Enzensberger, 'Constituents of a theory of the media', *New Left Review*, no. 64, Nov./Dec. 1970.

Richard R. Fagen, *Politics and Communication – an analytic study* (Little, Brown, Boston Mass. 1966).

Franz Fassbind, 'Radio and television in Switzerland', *Gazette*, vol. xiii, no. 2, 1967, pp. 145–58.

FCC: Policy Matters and Television Programming: Hearings before the sub-committee on communications of the Committee on Commerce of the US Senate, 91st Congress 1st session. *Crime and Violence on TV*, March 1969.

Jack Gould, *An Interview on the American Character* (Center for the Study of Democratic Institutions, Santa Barbara, Calif. 1961).

Maury Green, 'The Mythology of Television', *Television Quarterly*, vol. 9, no. 2, Spring 1970, pp. 5–13.

Kenneth Gumpertz, Stuart Cooney and Richard Tuber, 'A Bibliography of articles on broadcasting in law periodicals 1920–68'. *Journal of Broadcasting*, vol. xiv, no. 1 (pt. 2), with the *Federal Communications Bar Journal* vol. xxxiii, no. 3 (pt. 2), (joint issue), Winter 1969.

Robert J. Gwyn, 'Political dissent and the free market of ideas: an eight-nation study', *Gazette*, vol. xiii, no. 2/3, 1966, pp. 187–200.

——, 'Some reflections on television and symbolic speech'. *Television Quarterly*, vol. 8, no. 2, Spring 1969, pp. 57–65.

Stuart Hall and Paddy Whannel, *The Popular Arts* (Hutchinson 1964).

J. D. Halloran, 'The Effects of Mass Communication: with special reference to television' (Television Research Committee Working Paper No. 1) (Leicester University Press 1964).

——, 'Attitude Formation and Change', (Television Research Committee, Working Paper No. 2) (Leicester University Press 1970).

—— (ed.), *The Effects of Television* (Panther 1970).

——, R. L. Brown and D. C. Chaney, 'Television and Delinquency', (Television Research Committee, Working Paper No. 3) (Leicester University Press 1970).

—— and Michael Gurevitch (eds.), 'Broadcaster/Researcher co-operation in Mass Communication Research' – a report on an international seminar held at the University of Leicester, December 1970 (University of Leicester Press 1971).

H. T. Himmelweit, A. N. Oppenheim and P. Vince, *Television and the Child* (Oxford University Press 1958).

Richard Hoggart, *The Uses of Literacy* (Chatto & Windus, 1957).

——, 'The Nature and Context of Mass Communication' – Harvey Memorial Lecture 1960.

Richard W. Jencks, 'Is Taste Obsolete?' *EBU Review* 1218, May 1970, pp. 21–4.

Akinori Katagiri and Koichi Motono (eds.), *Studies of Broadcasting* (NHK 1963).

——, *Studies of Broadcasting* (NHK 1964).

Elihu Katz and Paul F. Lazarsfeld, *Personal Influence: the part played by people in the flow of mass communications* (The Free Press, New York 1955, 1964).

Elihu Katz, 'Television comes to the Middle East', *Transaction* (New York), vol. 8, no. 8, June 1971.

——, 'Cultural Problems of Television in New Nations' – lecture at Service de la Recherche de l'ORTF and the International Film and Television Council at UNESCO, Paris, April 1971.

Joseph T. Klapper, *The Effects of Mass Communication* (Free Press, New York 1960).

Antonina Kloskowska, 'Mass Culture in Poland', *Polish Sociological Bulletin* vol. 10, no. 2, 1964, pp. 106–15.

Terry Ann Knopf, 'Media Myths on Violence', *Columbia Journalism Review*, vol. ix, no. 1, Spring 1970, pp. 17–23.

E. John Kottman, 'Towards an understanding of truth in advertising', *Journalism Quarterly*, vol. 47, no. 1, Spring 1970, pp. 81–6.

Maurice Lane-Norcott, *Up the Aerial* (Grayson & Grayson 1933).

Otto N. Larsen (ed.), *Violence and the Mass Media* (Harper & Row, New York 1968).

Gustave Le Bon, *Psychologie des Foules* (Presses Universitaires de France 1947) – published originally in 1896.

James B. Lemert, 'Two studies on status conferral', *Journalism Quarterly*, vol. 43, no. 1, Spring 1966, pp. 25–33.

Walter Lippmann, *Public Opinion* (Macmillan Co. New York 1922 – revised 1929).

——, 'On Understanding Society' (interview on 80th birthday), *Columbia Journalism Review*, vol. viii, no. 3, Autumn 1969, pp. 5–7.

Lee Loevinger, 'Broadcasting and religious liberty', *Journal of Broadcasting*, vol. ix, no. 1, Winter 1964–5, pp. 3–24.

——, 'The Ambiguous Mirror: the reflective-projective theory of broadcasting and mass communications', *Journal of Broadcasting*, vol. xii, no. 2, Spring 1968, pp. 97–116.

Marshall McLuhan, *Understanding Media* (Routledge & Kegan Paul 1964).

Harold Mendelsohn, *Mass Entertainment* (College & University Press, New Haven, Conn. 1966).

George A. Miller, *The Psychology of Mass Communication* (Pelican 1967).

Jonathan Miller, *McLuhan* (Fontana Modern Masters 1971).

Leslie G. Moeller, 'Journalism education, the media and "The New Industrial State"', *Journalism Quarterly*, vol. 45, no. 3, Spring 1968, pp. 496–508.

Malcolm Muggeridge, *The Thirties* (Hamish Hamilton 1940).

Kaarle Nordenstreng, 'Comments on gratifications research in broadcasting'. *Public Opinion Quarterly*, vol. xxxiv, no. 1, Spring 1970, pp. 130–3.

M. Timothy O'Keefe, 'The anti-smoking commercials: a study of television's impact on behaviour'. *Public Opinion Quarterly*, vol. xxv, no. 2, Summer 1971, pp. 242–8.

Ortega y Gasset, *The Revolt of the Masses* (original in Spanish 1930; Unwin Books 1969).

Burton Paulu, 'Recent developments in educational radio and television in the United States', *EBU Review*, 1088, March 1968, pp. 28–31.

Problems of Television Research: a progress report. (Television Research Committee) (Leicester University Press 1966).

Leonhard Reinisch (ed.), *Fernsehen Heute und Morgen* (c. Bertelsman Verlag 1962).

John P. Robinson, 'Television and leisure time; yesterday, today and (maybe) tomorrow', *Public Opinion Quarterly*, vol. xxxiii, no. 2, 1969, pp. 210–22.

Yale Roe, *The Television Dilemma* (Hastings House, New York 1962).

Olof Rydbeck, 'Impartiality – Utopia or reality?'. *EBU Review*, May 1970, pp. 10–13.

Leslie W. Sargent, 'Communicator images and news reception', *Journalism Quarterly*, vol. 42, no. 1, Winter 1965, pp. 35–42.

Wilbur Schramm, *Mass Media and National Development* (Stanford University Press, Calif. 1961).

——, Jack Lyle and Edwin B. Parker, *Television in the Lives of our Children*, (Stanford University Press, Calif. 1961).

—— and Donald F. Roberts, *The Process and Effects of Mass Communications* (revised edn.), (University of Illinois Press, Urbana 1971).

John Scupham, *The Revolution in Communications* (Holt Rinehart and Winston 1970).

David O. Sears and Jonathan L. Freedman, *Selective Exposure to Information: A Critical Review* (pp. 194–213).

Gilbert Seldes, *The Great Audience* (Viking Press 1956).

——, *The Public Arts* (Simon & Shuster, New York 1958).

——, 'Television in peril of change', *Television Quarterly*, vol. 4, no. 2, Spring 1965, pp. 9–16.

Andrzej Sicinski, 'A two-step flow of communication: verification of a hypothesis in Poland', *Polish Sociological Bulletin*, vol. 7, no. 1, 1963, pp. 33–40.

Charles Siepmann, *Radio, Television and Society* (Oxford University Press, New York 1950).

Robert Silvey, *Reflections on the Impact of Broadcasting* (BBC 1963).

Don D. Smith, 'Moscow Radio's North American broadcasts: an exploratory study', *Journalism Quarterly*, vol. 42, no. 4, Autumn 1965, pp. 643–5.

——, 'Some effects of Radio Moscow's North American broadcasts', *Public Opinion Quarterly*, vol. xxxiv, no. 4, 1970, pp. 539–51.

Robert R. Smith, 'Broadcasting and religious freedom', *Journal of Broadcasting*, vol. xiii, no. 1, Winter 1968–9, pp. 1–12.

Charles S. Steinberg, *The Mass Communicators, Public Relations, Public Opinion and Mass Media* (Harper & Bros. New York 1958).

——, *The Communicative Arts: An Introduction to Mass Media* (Communication Arts Books, Hastings House, New York 1970).

William Stephenson, *The Play Theory of Mass Communication* (University of Chicago Press, New York 1967).

Ethel Strainchamps, '*Medinese:* The International Dialect', *Television Quarterly*, vol 4, no. 1, Winter 1965, pp. 29–32.

The Shadow in the Cave

Denys Thompson (ed.), *Discrimination and Popular Culture* (Pelican 1964).

J. M. Trenaman, *Communication and Comprehension* (Longmans 1967).

Graham Wallas, *The Great Society – a Psychological Analysis* (Macmillan 1914).

Theodore H. White, interview on 'America's Two Cultures', *Columbia Journalism Review*, vol. viii, no. 4, Winter 1969–70, pp. 8–13.

Mary Whitehouse, *Cleaning up TV – from Protest to Participation* (Blandford Press 1967).

Oliver J. Whitley, 'Observation, evidence and opinions', *EBU Review* 1218, May 1970, pp. 18–20.

Noel Avon Wilson, 'The thrust of the mob and the media', *Journal of Broadcasting*, vol. xiv, no. 4, Autumn 1970, pp. 441–8.

Charles Wintour, *Pressures on the Press – an Editor looks at Fleet Street* (André Deutsch 1972).

Charles R. Wright, *Mass Communications – a sociological perspective* (Random House, New York 1959).

Max Wylie, *Clear Channels: Television and the American People* (Funk and Wagnalls 1955).

Filson Young, *Shall I Listen? Studies in the Adventure and Technique of Broadcasting* (Constable 1933).

J. *Material on the dual problems of broadcast journalism and the political effects of broadcasting.*

Herbert A. Alexander, 'Political broadcasting', *Television Quarterly*, vol. 5, no. 2, Spring 1966, pp. 65–75.

——, 'Political broadcasting in 1968'. *Television Quarterly*, vol. 9, no. 2, Spring 1970, pp. 41–50.

——, Stimson Bullitt, and Hyman H. Goldin, 'The high cost of TV campaigns', *Television Quarterly*, vol. 5, no. 1, 1966, pp. 47–65.

James Aronson, *The Press and the Cold War* (Bobbs-Merrill, New York 1970).

Ben Bagdikian, 'News as a by-product: what happens when journalism is hitched to great diversified corporations?' *Columbia Journalism Review*, vol. 6, no. 1, Spring 1967, pp. 5–10.

——, *The Information Machines: their impact on Men and the Media* (Harper & Row, New York 1971).

Lord Beaverbrook, *Politicians and the Press* (Hutchinson 1924).

B. Berelson, P. F. Lazarsfeld and W. N. McPhee, *Voting: A Study of Opinion formation in a Presidential Campaign* (University of Chicago Press 1954).

William Blankenburg, 'News accuracy: some findings on the meaning of errors'. *Journal of Communication*, vol. 20, no. 4, December 1970, pp. 375–86.

A. William Bluem and Roger Manvell (eds.), *Progress in Television: an Anglo-American Survey* (Focal Press 1967).

332

Bibliography

J. G. Blumler and Denis McQuail, *Television and Politics: Its Uses and Influence* (Faber & Faber 1968).

David Brinkley, 'TV News and the star system', *Television Quarterly*, vol. 5, no. 2, Spring 1966, pp. 13–18.

James Buckalew, 'News elements and selection by television news editors', *Journal of Broadcasting*, vol. xiv, no. 1, Winter 1969, pp. 47–54.

Angus Campbell, Philip E. Converse, Warren E. Miller and Donald E. Stokes, *The American Voter – an abridgement* (John Wiley & Sons Inc., New York 1964).

Carl J. Cannon (ed.), *Journalism – a bibliography* (The New York Public Library 1924; reprint by Gale Research Co., Detroit 1967).

Leon Chade, 'Freedom of expression and finance', *L'Enseignement du journalisme*, no. 10, Summer 1961, pp. 1–35.

Mitchell V. Charnley, 'The American approach to news broadcasting'. *EBU Review*, 918 (special issue on news broadcasting) May 1965.

Edward W. Chester, *Radio, Television and American Politics* (Sheed & Ward, New York 1969).

Bernard C. Cohen, *The Press and Foreign Policy* (Princeton University Press, New Jersey 1965).

Commission on Freedom of the Press: *A Free and Responsible Press* (University of Chicago Press 1947).

P. Converse and D. Campbell (eds.), *Information Flow and the Stability of Partisan Change in Electors and the Political Order* (Wiley 1966).

Sir Edward Cook, *Delane of 'The Times'* (Constable 1915).

Robin Day, *TV: A Personal Report* (Hutchinson 1961).

Edwin Diamond, 'News-room Revolution – reporter power takes root', *Columbia Journalism Review*, vol. ix, no. 2, Summer 1970, pp. 12–18.

Gordon J. DiRenzo, 'Professional politicians and personality structure', *American Journal of Sociology*, vol. 73, no. 2, 1967–8, pp. 217–25.

——, 'Dollar politics: the issue of campaign spending', *Congressional Quarterly* (Washington DC 1971).

Andrzej Duma, 'Research on TV viewers in Poland: a programme research study of Polskie Radio i Telewizja', *Gazette*, vol. xi, no. 4, 1965, pp. 261–71.

Donald Edwards, *BBC News and Current Affairs* (BBC 1962).

Edith Efron, *The News Twisters* (Nash Publishing, New York 1971).

A. S. C. Ehrenberg, G. F. Goodhardt and I. R. Haldane, 'The News in May', *Public Opinion Quarterly*, vol. xxxiii, no. 4, 1969, pp. 546–55.

Edward Jay Epstein, *News from Nowhere – Television and the News* (Random House 1973).

Henry Fairlie, 'The BBC', in Hugh Thomas (ed.): *The Establishment* (Anthony Blond 1959).

FCC, 'Survey of Political Broadcasting: primary and general election campaigns of 1968' (FCC, Washington DC, August 1969).

Reuven Frank, 'The Making of the Tunnel', *Television Quarterly*, vol. 2, no. 4, Autumn 1963, pp. 9–23.

——, 'The Ugly Mirror', *Television Quarterly*, vol. 7, no. 1, Winter 1969, pp. 82–95.

——, 'An Anatomy of television news', *Television Quarterly*, vol. 9, no. 1, Winter 1970, pp. 11–23.

Peter Frazer, 'The British government's use of parliamentary publicity in the past', *Gazette*, vol. ix, no. 2/3, 1965, pp. 192–202.

G. Ray Funkhouser, 'A probabilistic model for predicting news diffusion', *Journalism Quarterly*, vol. 47, no. 1. Spring 1970, pp. 41–5.

Douglas W. Gallez, 'Pictorial Journalism at War', *Journalism Quarterly*, vol. 47, no. 3, Autumn 1970, pp. 493–9.

Kent Geiger and Robert Sokos, 'Social News in Television Watching', *American Journal of Sociology*, vol. 65, no. 2, September 1959, pp. 174–81.

Louis G. Geiger, 'Muckrakers – then and now', *Journalism Quarterly*, vol. 43, no. 3, Autumn 1966, pp. 469–76.

Maury Green, *Television News: Anatomy and Process* (Wadsworth Publishing Co. Belmont, Calif. 1969).

Sir William Haley, 'Where TV news fails', *Columbia Journalism Review*, vol. ix, no. 1, Spring 1970.

J. D. Halloran, P. Elliott and G. Murdock, *Communications and Demonstrations: A Case Study* (Penguin 1970).

Wilson Harris, *The Daily Press* (Cambridge University Press 1943).

Martin Harrison, 'Television and radio' in D. E. Butler and A. King (eds.), *The British General Election of 1966* (Macmillan 1966).

William Hawes, 'Television censorship: myth or menace?', *Television Quarterly*, vol. 4, no. 3, Summer 1965, pp. 63–73.

Edward Heath, 'Reporting politics: the need for a new idiom'. *Journalism Today*, vol. 1, no. 4, Spring 1969.

M. U. Himmelstrand, 'The Nigeria-Biafra conflict'. *Journalisme*, no. 36, 1969, pp. 11–27, (Strasbourg). (Special issue on 'La distortion du message à travers le circuit de l'information'.)

Gale Durham Hollander, 'Recent developments in Soviet radio and television news reporting', *Public Opinion Quarterly*, vol. xxxi, no. 3, 1967, pp. 359–65.

The Hutchins Report: a twenty-year view. *Columbia Journalism Review*, vol. vi, no. 2, Spring 1967, pp. 5–20.

IBI (International Broadcast Institute) Report: How influential is TV News? *Columbia Journalism Review*, vol. ix, no. 2, Summer 1970, pp. 19–29.

Richard W. Jencks, 'TV news – a dark perception – the price'. *Television Quarterly*, vol. 7, no. 4, Autumn 1968, pp. 15–20.

Kennedy Jones, *Fleet Street and Downing Street* (Hutchinson, 1919).

Joseph Keeley, *The Left-Leaning Antenna: Political Bias in Television* (Arlington House, New Rochelle, New York 1971).

S. Kelly Jr, *Political Campaigning: Problems in Creating an Informed Electorate* (The Brookings Institution, Washington DC 1960).

V. O. Key, *The Responsible Electorate: Rationality in Presidential Voting 1936–1960* (Harvard University Press 1966).

Lord Kilbrandon, 'Conflict of opinions in professional ethics between morals, truth and freedom', *Journalisme* (Strasbourg) no. 37, 1972, pp. 9–20 (Special issue on Morale et liberté de la Presse dans l'Ethique Professionelle).

Cecil King, 'The newspaper in Europe', *Journalism Today*, vol. 1, no. 1, Autumn 1967.

Mitsui Kondo, 'Newspaper competition in Japan', *Gazette*, vol. 2, no. 2, pp. 97–112.

Sidney Kraus (ed.), *The Great Debates* (Indiana University Press 1962).

Andrzej Lam, 'What kind of liberty of the press?' *Kwartalnik Prasoznawczy* 1957, Nos. 1–2.

Kurt Lang and Gladys Lang, *Politics and Television* (Quadrangle Books, Chicago 1968).

P. F. Lazarsfield, B. Berelson and H. Gaudet, *The People's Choice: How the Voter Makes up his Mind in a Presidential Campaign* (Duell, Sloan and Pearce 1944).

Daniel J. Leab, 'Response to the Hutchins Commission', *Gazette*, vol. xvi, no. 2, 1970, pp. 105–13.

Anthony Lewis, 'Press freedom and national security, *Journalism Today*, vol. 1, no. 2, Spring 1968.

Sir Trevor Lloyd-Hughes, 'The government information services and their place in modern democracy', *Journalism Today*, vol. 2, no. 3, Spring 1971.

Lee Loevinger, 'The journalistic responsibility of broadcasting'. *Television Quarterly*, vol. 7, no. 1, Winter 1969, pp. 70–81.

George Lott, 'The press-radio war of the 1930s', *Journal of Broadcasting*, vol. xiv, no. 3, Summer 1970, pp. 275–86.

Elmer W. Lower, 'Fairness, balance and equal time', *Television Quarterly*, vol. 9, no. 4, Autumn 1970, pp. 46–53.

Joe McGinniss, *The Selling of the President 1968* (Trident Press 1969; Penguin 1971).

Bryan Magee, *The Television Interviewer* (Macdonald 1966).

Martin Mayer, 'How television news covers the world (in four thousand words or less)', *Esquire* January 1972, vol. lxxvii, no. 1, whole number 458.

H. L. Mencken, *Prejudices: A Selection* (Vintage Books 1955).

Harold Mendelsohn and Irving Crispi, *Polls, Television and the New Politics* (Chandler Publishing Co. Scranton, Pa. 1970).

Sig Mickelson, *The Electric Mirror: Politics in an Age of Television* (Dodd, Mead, New York 1972).

John Stuart Mill, *Liberty* (Longmans 1859).

Daniel P. Moynihan, 'The presidency and the press', *Commentary*, vol. 51, no. 3, March 1971, pp. 41–53.

Donald P. Mullaly, 'The Fairness Doctrine – benefits and costs'. *Public Opinion Quarterly*, vol. xxxiii, no. 4, 1969, pp. 577–82.

J. Zvi Namenwirth, 'Marks of distinction: an analysis of British mass and prestige newspaper editorials'. *American Journal of Sociology*, vol. 74, no. 4, January 1969, pp. 343–60.

A. Namurois, 'Freedom of speech on radio and television: a myth?' (part 1). *EBU Review*, 988, July 1966, pp. 44–54.

——, 'Freedom of speech on radio and television a myth?' (part 2). *EBU Review*, 998, September 1966, pp. 34–41.

Felix E. Oppenheim, *Dimensions of Freedom – An Analysis* (St Martin's Press, New York 1961).

David L. Peletz, Peggy Reichert and Barbara McIntyre, 'How the Media support Local Government Authority'. *Public Opinion Quarterly*, vol. xxxv, no. 1, Spring 1971, pp. 80–92.

Maurice Pinard, 'Mass society and political movements: a new formulation', *American Journal of Sociology*, vol. 73, no. 6, May 1969, pp. 682–90.

Chapman Pincher, 'Press freedom and national security'. *Journalism Today*, vol. 1, no. 2, Spring 1968.

'The Polish press, radio and television', special issue of *Kwartalnik Prasonawczy* 1959.

James E. Pollard, 'The White House news conference as a channel of communication', *Public Opinion Quarterly*, vol. xv, no. 4, 1951, pp. 663–78.

Ithiel de Sola Pool, review of K. and G. Lang's 'TV and Politics' in *Public Opinion Quarterly*, vol. xxxiii, no. 2, 1969, pp. 287–9.

Enoch Powell, 'Consensus Reporting'. *Journalism Today*, vol. 2, no. 1, Spring 1970, pp. 101–9.

Lucien W. Pye, *Communications and Political Development* (Princeton University Press 1963).

Sir Alfred Robbins, *The Press* (Ernest Benn c. 1931).

Richard Ross, *Influencing Voters: A Study of Campaign Rationality* (Faber & Faber 1967).

Albert J. Rosenthal, *Federal Regulation of Campaign Finance: Some Constitutional Questions* (Citizens' Research Foundation, Princeton New Jersey 1972).

Peter Rossbacher, 'The Soviet journalistic style'. *Gazette*, vol. xii, nos. 2/3, pp. 201–11.

Luca di Schiena, 'Television expeditions Abroad – the story of the Pope's journeys to the Holy Land and Bombay', *EBU Review* 918, May 1965.

Wilbur Schramm, 'The nature of news – the ludenic theory of news-reading', *Journalism Quarterly*, vol. xxvi, 1949, pp. 259–69.

Bernard Shaw, 'The telltale microphone', *Political Quarterly*, vol. vi, no. 4, Oct–Dec. 1935, pp. 463–7.

Fred S. Siebert, Theodore Peterson and Wilbur Schramm, *Four Theories of the Press* (University of Illinois Press, 1956, 1971).

Upton Sinclair, *The Brass Check – A Study of American Journalism* (published by the author, Pasadena, Calif. 1920).

Harry J. Skornia, *Television and the News – a Critical Appraisal* (Pacific Books, Palo Alto, Calif. 1968).

William Small, *To Kill a Messenger: Television News and the Real World* (Communications Arts Books, Hastings House, New York 1970).

Anthony Smith, 'TV coverage of Northern Ireland, *Index*, vol. 1, no. 2, Summer 1972, pp. 15–32.

Howard K. Smith, 'The changing challenge to journalism' (from the Seidman Lectures of 1969), published as *The News Media – A service and a force* (edited by Festus Justin Viser, Memphis State University Press 1970), pp. 1–19.

Howard K. Smith and Stanley Kelley Jr, 'The great debates', *Television Quarterly*, vol. 5, no. 1, Winter 1966, pp. 27–31.

Robert R. Smith, 'The origins of radio network news commentary', *Journal of Broadcasting*, vol. ix, no. 9, Spring 1965, pp. 113–22.

James Fitzjames Stephen, *Liberty, Equality, Fraternity* (Cambridge University Press 1967) (originally published by Smith Elder 1874).

Norman Swallow, *Factual Television* (Focal Press 1966).

Michal Szulczewski, 'Problems of journalistic ethics', *Kwartalnik Prasonawczy*, vol. 2, no. 2 (6), 1958, pp. 30–45.

H. A. Taylor, 'The British concept of freedom of the Press', *Gazette*, vol. xi, no. 2/3, 1965, pp. 123–38.

E. van Thijn, 'Television newsreel and television news services' *Gazette*, vol. viii, no. 3/4, 1961, pp. 313–28.

Ned Thomas (ed.), 'The future of broadcasting' in *Planet, A Journal*, no. 2, Oct./Nov. 1970.

——, 'The air over Europe', in *Planet*, no. 3, Dec. 1970/Jan. 1971.

Joseph Trenaman and Denis McQuail, *Television and the Political Image*, (Methuen 1961).

Sander Vanocur, 'How the media massacred me – my fifteen years of conditioning by network news', *Esquire*, Jan. 1972, vol. lxxvii, no. 1, whole no. 458.

Serena Wade and Wilbur Schramm, 'The mass media as sources of public affairs, science and health knowledge', *Public Opinion Quarterly*, vol. xxxiii, no. 2, 1969, pp. 197–209.

Robert E. Ward and Dankwart A. Rustow (eds.), *Political Modernization in Japan and Turkey* (Princeton University Press, New Jersey 1964).

Paul H. Weaver, 'Is television news Biased?' *The Public Interest*, no. 26, Winter 1972, pp. 57–74.

Jörgen Westerstähl, 'Objectivity is measurable', *EBU Review* 1218, May 1970, pp. 13–17.

John Whale, *The Half-Shut Eye: Television and Politics in Britain and America* (Macmillan, St Martin's Press 1969).

——, *Journalism and Government* (Macmillan 1972).

Thomas Whiteside, 'Corridor of mirrors: the television editorial process', *Columbia Journalism Review*, vol. vii, no. 4, Winter 1968/9, pp. 35–54.

Tom Wicker, Kenneth P. O'Donnell and Rowland Evans, 'TV in the political campaign', *Television Quarterly*, vol. 5, no. 1, Winter 1966, pp. 13–26.

Francis Williams, *The Right to Know: the rise of the world press* (Longmans 1969).

Lord Windlesham, *Communication and Political Power* (Jonathan Cape 1966).

Eugene J. Young, *Looking Behind the Censorships* (Lovat Dickson 1938).

William A. Wood, *Electronic Journalism* (Columbia University Press 1967).

K. *Material dealing with future developments in broadcasting.*

Abderrazak Berrada, *Frequencies for Broadcasting Satellites* (International Broadcast Institute, London 1971).

Robert J. Blakeley, *The People's Instrument: a philosophy of programming for public television.* A Charles F. Kettering Foundation Report (Public Affairs Press, Washington DC 1971).

Frank Browning, 'Cable TV: turn on, tune in, rip off', *Ramparts Magazine*, April 1971, pp. 32–45.

Professor Dr Karl Holzamer, *Fernsehen in den 70er Jahren*, Schriftenreihe des ZDF (Mainz 1971).

Helmut Lenhardt, *Die Zukunft von Rundfunk und Fernsehen in der Auseinandersetzung mit der neuen elektronischen Medien* (Fritz Molden Verlag, Munich 1972).

Brenda Maddox, *Beyond Babel* (André Deutsch 1972).

Roger P. Morgan, 'The New Communications Technology and its Social Implications'. Report of a symposium of the IBI at Ditchley Park, Oxfordshire, November 1970 (IBI, London 1971).

Monroe Price and John Wicklein, *Cable Television – A Guide for Citizen Action* (Pilgrim Press, Philadelphia 1972).

Michael Schamberg, *Guerrilla Television* (Holt, Rinehart & Winston, and the Raindance Corporation, New York 1962).

Sloan Commission on Cable Communications. *On the Cable – The Television of Abundance* (McGraw-Hill, New York 1971).

Charles Tate (ed.), *Cable Television in the Cities – community control, public access and minority ownership* (Urban Institute, New York 1972).

Index

Index

ABC network, USA 99, 195, 228
 constituent companies 196
 old films bought by (1972–3) 199–200
 Worldvision subsidiary 187
Adenauer, Konrad 64
Agnew, Spiro T. xiii, 101, 206, 227, 265
 on broadcaster xiii, 205
 reactions to views of xiv
Agrémy, Jean-Pierre 185
Algemeene Vereeniging Radio Omroep (AVRO), Holland 270, 276
Alice in Wonderland, Lewis Carroll's 264
Allen, Ted 209
American broadcasting,
 airwaves chaos 200
 educational radio stations 218, 219
 involvement of members of Congress in 202
 licensing of stations 202–3, 228–9
 question of common carrier status 201–2, 235–6, 244
American Civil Liberties Union 134, 212
 The Engineering of Restraint report 211
American Commission of the Freedom of the Press (1947) 45
American Council for Better Broadcasts 234
American Marconi Company 48, 49
American TV,
 advertising costs 192–4, 196, 197
 advertising profits 191
 advertising time (%) 193
 anti-commercials 234
 audience figures 191
 cable 189, 217, 237–45, 283
 cassette 189
 cigarette advertising ban 210–11
 constituent elements 189
 educational and public financing 219, 221, 224–5

educational   programme-making 221
educational stations 219–22
freedom of expression and commercial tyranny 189–90, 209–10
licence-challenging 231–3
local stations and broadcasting responsibility 190–1, 194
McCarthyism 209, 210
network conservatism 198–9
network liberalisation (1972) 213–214
network ownership 195–6
network power 193
network revenue drop (1971) 211
network stations 191, 193
networking, means of transmission 220
network reduction in news 210
newspaper stake in 194–5
Nixon government conflict with 211–12
old films 199–200
One Big Audience strategy 236, 244, 283
persistence of programmes 190, 197–8
pressure groups for improvement 233–5
prime source of news 85
profitability 194, 195
programme   investment 59–60, 196–7
programme-making 208
programmes: Bewitched 190; Bonanza 187, 189, 190, 276; Dean Martin Show 190; Gunsmoke 190; Lassie 207; Lucille Ball shows 190, 207; Marty 209; Mash 213; Mission Impossible 190; My Three Sons 190; Peyton Place 276; See It Now 210; That Certain Summer 213; Wild Kingdom 207; World of Disney 190

public broadcasting 189, 216, 223–228, 282
quiz scandals 209
reform, attempts at 216–17
rerun (repeat) profitability 197
sponsors 192–3, 198, 209
viewers' hours of watching 215
viewing research organisations, 191–2
violence on 213, 231
volume of news 84–5
worldwide influence 187, 188, 282
See also ABC, CBS and NBC networks
Amsterdam Stock Exchange, transmitter 269
Annenberg, Walter (group) 232
ARB research organisation 191
Arnold, Matthew 21, 26, 31, 70, 159
as a mass educator 24–5
Arnold Palmer Enterprises 195
Aron, Raymond 157
Asahi 248, 251
Associated Press 94
Audience, mass,
broadcasters' view of 66–7, 129
broadcasting as statutory leisure for 55
early advertising and salesmanship for 25
early newspapers and 29
educationalisn and 23, 24–5
elevating the 28, 32
ignorance of nineteenth-century electorate 112
news reports and 85–6, 108–9
nineteenth-century approaches to 23–8, 111
political emergence 112
political propaganda and 29, 112
propagandist victim of First World War 28–9
puzzling nature of 22
relation to politicians 113–14
suggestion and 26
Aware Inc. 209
Aylestone, Lord 149

Bagehot, Walter 23, 26
Barnes, Thomas 93
Barrère, Igor 172
Bartlett, Vernon 69, 130

Battle for Algiers 177
Baudrier, Jacqueline 177, 186
Baverstock, Donald 78
Beadle, Sir Gerald 57
Beaverbrook, Lord 112
Belgium, RTB of 148
Bellemare, Pierre 178
Benamon, Roger 172
Benn, Anthony Wedgwood, on access to broadcasting 265–7
Bentham, Jeremy 26
Beveridge Committee and Report 59, 132
Bill of Rights, American 37
Birkin, Jane 152, 186
Bismarck, Herr von 65
Black Efforts for Soul in Television 233–4
Black Panthers 212
Blumler, Jay 121–2
Boorstin, Daniel 95
Boothby, Robert 69, 132
Boston Broadcasters Inc. 203
Bottomley, Horatio 30
Brecht, Bertholt 264, 273
Britain,
propaganda media in First World War 30
radio and TV coverage (1974) 91
British Board of Film Censors 52
British Broadcasting Company 71, 150
British Broadcasting Corporation (BBC) 261, 266, 281
chairman's rise to power 145
Complaints Commission 146–8, 152
continuing public scrutinies of 58–59
cultural influence 71
early influence defined xv
early presentation of TV news 81
early restrictions on radio news 87–9
executive supremacy of DG ended 144–5
formation 56, 249
Fourteen Day rule and 131–2
General Advisory Council 147
hours of TV transmission categorised (1970–1) 60
income and expenditure (1971) 59

independence of state 141–3
inter-war support for 69
jeopardised by General Strike 58
position vis-à-vis Parliament 70,
  129–34
programmes: British Empire 61–
  62; Forsyte Saga 220; In the
  News 132; Panorama 247;
  Six Wives of Henry VIII 207;
  Softly, Softly 276; Tonight
  78, 79, 82; War and Peace 198;
  Yesterday's Men 145–6; Z Cars
  276
violence code 120
wartime rise 130
Whitley document and 143–4
Broadcasting,
access in 264–8, 273, 274–5, 284
approach to mass audience 32–3,
  126–9
battle with the press 43
buffer institutions proposed between govt and 148–50
central control in Britain 52–3, 56
central control in Europe 57
characteristics and problems xvii,
  xviii
commercial control in USA 53–4,
  56–7
controversy in 44, 52
early degradation by advertising 33
education v entertainment dilemma
  46, 52
fear of govt control 31, 140
freedom of expression and 45–6
independence in Britain 141–3
news bias 99–102
news by 74–91, 96–7
news judgement, criteria of 103–7
news sense, changing 97–8
political power of 67–9, 118
problem of power of xv–xvi
publishing function possible 265,
  267
relations with Parliament 129–34
role compared with press 89–90,
  101
shaped by society 22
siege mentality in xiv
wire broadcasting 237
See also BBC, ORTF and under
  countries

Broadcasting Committee (Crawford
  Committee, 1925) 58
on standards 32
Report 71
Broadcasting Council (British) pro-
  posed 149–50
Brown, F. J. 56
Bundy, McGeorge 222
Bunku Broadcasting, Japan 258
Burch, Dean 206, 211, 233
Burke, Edmund 115

Cals, Dutch PM 269, 272
Canada, broadcasting in 280
Capitol Cities Broadcasting 232
Carlyle, Thomas 26
Carnegie Commission on Public Tele-
  vision (US) 223, 226
Report 225–6
Catholic Broadcasting Foundation
  (KRO), Holland 270, 276
Cazeneuve, Mons. 178
Chaban-Delmas, Pierre 177–8
Chaffee, Zechariah 37, 42–3
Channel Television 150
Chaptal, Mons. 155
Chayevsky, Paddy 209
Chrysler motors 195
Churchill, Winston 101, 131–2,
  141
Cinema,
American movie code 51
censorship in 52–3
development 50–1
Japanese censorship 250
Propagandist use in Britain (First
  World War) 30
Topical War Film Committee
  (British) 30
Citizens' Commonwealth Center,
  Washington, 232, 234
Clarendon, Lord 143
Clavel, Maurice 182
Coatman, John 130
Cobbett, William 24
Collins, Wilkie 23
Columbia Broadcasting System (CBS)
  xiv, 99, 193, 206, 212–13
CBS News 78, 210, 261
companies owned by 195
KNXT's 'The Big News' 82–3
news cutback by 211

Columbia University, Graduate School of Journalism xiv, 193
Communications and Political Development, Lucien Pye's 136
Community Coalition on Broadcasting (US) 231
Compagnie Sans Fil (CSF) 168
Conservative Party, British 69, 131
Conte, Arthur 185–6
Coolidge, Calvin 33
Corporation for Public Broadcasting (CPB), American 223–5, 227
Coughlin, Father 67–8
Cowper, William 73
Cox, Kenneth A. 230, 239
Crabbe, Rev. George 37–8
his poem 'The Newspaper' 38
Crawford, Lord 32
Critchley, Julian 146
Crossman, Richard 146
Culture and Anarchy, Matthew Arnold's 21
Curran, Charles 145
Cypress Communications Corporation 241
Czechoslovakia, Russian Invasion of 80

Daily Graphic, New York 28
Daily Mail 27, 269
Daily Mirror, The 30
Daley, Mayor, of Chicago 124, 137
D'Arcy, Jean 175
Darget, Claude 176
Darwin, Charles 22, 23
effects of Theory of Evolution 22–23
David Copperfield, Charles Dickens' 111
Dayton, Ohio,
CATV in 241
Citizens' Cable Corporation 241
De Bresson, Jacques 175–6, 180, 184–5
De Closets, Mons. 174
De Gaulle, Charles 157–8, 172, 173, 178
creates RTF 158
on influence of radio 168–9
personal style on TV 169–71
Delane, John Thaddeus 39
on role of press 89–90

Delaunay, Mons. 161
Democracy,
eighteenth-century censorship 36
Jeffersonian 36
liberty *v* coercion (Stephen *v* Mill) 33–5
Democratic Party, American,
Chicago Convention (1968) 76, 124–5, 137
Nominating Convention (1948) 73–4
Derby, Lord 89, 90
De Sédouy, Alain 172, 178
Desgraupes, Pierre 78, 165, 172, 177, 180, 185, 186
Des Moines, Iowa xiii, 205
De Tocqueville, Alexis 155
De Turenne, Henri 172
Diligent, Senator André 162, 171, 183
Diligent Report 172
on financial scandal in ORTF 183–4
Dillingham, John 91
Dimbleby, Richard 86–7
Disraeli, Benjamin 111, 114, 117
Domei Tsushin news agency 250
Doubleday Broadcasting Company 231
Duhamel, Jacques 168
Dumayet, Mons. 172
Dutch Television Foundation (NTS) 272

Eckersley, Captain Peter 56, 70
'Eclaire' camera 78
Ede, J. Chuter 149
Eden, Anthony 142
Edison, Thomas Alva 48
Efron, Edith 99, 100, 108
Eisenhower, Dwight D. 137
Encounter 21
Erskine, Thomas 36
Essay on Liberty, J. S. Mill's 33
Europe No. 1 radio station 167–8
Evangelical Union (EO), Holland 275
Evening Bulletin, Philadelphia 95

Fairlie, Henry 21
Fauvet, Jacques 161
Federal Communications Commission (FCC) 53, 57, 79, 190, 195–7, 200, 202, 216–17

'access doctrine' 205, 229
anti-trust actions 228
Blue Book 201
cable TV and 238, 240
educational channels 219–20
'fairness doctrine' 204–5, 217,
  229, 233, 234, 235, 242
First Amendment and 235
Inquiry into Chicago Convention
  coverage (1968) 124–5
investigation into licence-holders
  229, 230–1
laxity in licensing 229–30
licence challenges made to 231–3
licensing duties 202–3, 228–9
Prime Time Access Rule 206–7
waveband policy 218–19, 238–9
Federal Radio Bureau 218
Federal Radio Commission 57, 200
Fender Musical Instrument Company
  195
Figaro 183
Fletcher, Andrew 215
Foot, Michael 132
Ford Foundation 219, 221–2
Ford motor company 195
France, broadcasting in 280, 282
  Administrative Council 163, 164
  censorship 163, 173, 175, 182–3
  effect of border commercial radio
    on 167–8
  French shares in border radio 168
  growth of TV 159, 160
  instability of 156–7
  Paye Commission (1970) 179–80
  radio in 1940s 160
  RTF created 158, 160
  Service de Liaison Interministeriel
    pour l'Information 163, 176
  state monopoly of 158–9
  under Administration of Posts and
    Telegraphs 156, 157, 160–1
  under Vichy govt 157
  See also ORTF
Freedom,
  delegated to the expert 35
  guaranteed in American Constitu-
    tion 37
  of expression, and broadcasting
    45–6
  of expression, and the press 113
  of speech 42–3

Freedom of Speech, Z. Chaffee's 42
Fréville, Henri 172
Friendly, Fred 78, 210, 221–2
Fuji Television 258
Funny Girl 199

Galbraith, John Kenneth 236
  on US radio and TV 54
Gans, Prof. Herbert 108
Gaullaud, Jean-Louis 185
General Motors 195, 199
General Strike (1926) 58, 130, 141
*General View of the Criminal Law of
  England, A* J. F. Stephen's 33
Germany, broadcasting in 62–5
  ARD federal union 62, 63, 64
  central code 63
  decentralisation 62
  politicians' relations with 134
  ZDF commercial channel 64
Gierek, Edward 116
Giscard d'Estaing, Mons. 163
Gladstone, William Ewart 111
Glasgow Record, The 30
Goldmark, Dr Peter C. 242
Gomulka, Wladislaw 116
Gorse, Mons. 155–6
Greene, Sir Hugh 59, 63, 144–5,
  148
Gutenberg, Johann G. 92–3

Hamilton, Alexander 37
Hammerschmidt, Herr 65
Harris, André 165, 172, 178
Harrison, Martin 121, 159
Hartnett, Vincent W. 209
Havas agency 168, 183, 184
Hennock, Frieda B. 219
Henry IV, Shakespeare's 140
Herald Traveller, Boston 203
Herrold, Charles D. 48
Hertz car-rental company 195
Hewitt, Slim 69
Hill, Dr (later Lord) 71, 147
  becomes BBC chairman 145
Hilliard, David 212
Hilversum 270, 274, 278
Hilversumsche Draadloze Omroep
  (HDO) 270
Hitler, Adolf 42
Hobbes, Thomas 26
Hoffman-La Roche drugs 195

Hole, Tahu 81
Holland, TV and broadcasting in 280–1
'access' in 268, 273–5
advertising 274
beginning of radio transmission 265
Broadcasting Council (Radio raad) 270
broadcasting organisations 270–1, 275
dullness of TV 276
early radio 270
faults of system 278
inauguration of new system (1969) 269, 273
licence fee 274
NOS formed 273
pirate stations and 272
post Second World War reorganisation 272
qualifications for broadcasting organisations 274–6
radio and TV foundations 271–2
Hollywood 225, 237
TV programme-making in 208
Holt Rinehart publishing company 195
Hooper research organisation 191
Hoover, Herbert 33, 187, 200
Howarth, David 86
Huizen, Holland 270
Humanist Movement, Holland 275–276
Hume, David 113
Humphrey, Hubert 99
Hutchins Commission (Freedom of the Press), US 148
Hutchins, Robert M. 148
Huxley, Aldous 42, 123
Hyde, Rosel H. 222

IBA (Independent Broadcasting Authority) 149
violence code 120
Idzerta, Hanso 269
his PCGG radio station 269
Information, right of 35
Institute of American Democracy 234
Israeli TV,
news coverage costs 107–8

politicians' relations with broadcasting 134–5
IT & T 196
ITA (Independent Television Authority) 57
now IBA 149
ITV (Independent Television) 150, 281
formed 57
News 81
programmes: 'Coronation Street' 276; 'Free Speech' 132–3; 'News at Ten' 79
'James Bond' films 199
Japan Broadcasting Corporation 249
Japanese broadcasting and TV 281
censorship 250–1
commercial 257
commercial owners 258
growth of radio 249–50
growth of TV 259
post Second World War 252–63
production of sets, and exports 259–60
Radio Regulatory Commission 254–5
restrictions on broadcasting (1931–1946) 249, 250
samurai westerns 262
style of TV 262
TV based on Western model 246–7
viewers' watching hours 259
See also Nippon Hoso Kyokai
Jefferson, Thomas 36
Jiru Minken Windo (Japanese Freedom and Popular Rights Movement) 248
John Bull 30
Johnson, Lyndon B. 223, 224, 237
Johnson, Nicholas 215, 216, 225, 230, 236–7
Johnson, Samuel 36

Kaltenborn, H. V. 76
KDKA station, Pittsburgh 269
Kennedy, John F. 95, 202
Killian, James R. 223
Klapper, Joseph 122, 123
Klein, Herb 211
Kramer, Al 232
KTAL station, Texarkana 233

Kumata, Prof. 258

Labour Party, British 69, 137
  controversy over 'Yesterday's Men'
  145–6
Labro, Philippe 172
Lambert, R. S. xv
Landis, James 202
Lang, Kurt and Gladys 123, 124
Lawrence of Arabia 199
Le Bon, Gustave 26
Lecanuet, Mons. 170, 173
Leeds Mercury, The 30
Le Monde 161, 174, 175, 183
Lewis, C. A. 71
L'Express 180
L'Humanité 183
Liberal Party, British 132
Liberal Protestant Broadcasting Asso-
  ciation, Holland 270, 275
Liberty, Equality, Fraternity, J. F.
  Stephen's 33
Life 211
Life-NBC TV news unit 74
Limburg, Holland 273
Lincoln, Abraham 111
Lippmann, Walter, on propaganda 29
Lois de l'Imitation, Les, Gabriel
  Tarde's 21
Long, Huey 67, 68
  'Share-Our-Wealth' movement
  68
Lorenzi, Stellio 166
Los Angeles 82, 237
  as TV market 83
  news, volume of 85
Louis, Roger 173
Love Story 199
Lux, Guy 178
Luxembourg, Grand Duchy of 168

MacArthur, General 253, 254
McCarthy, Senator Joseph 101, 210
McCartney, Paul 104
McGraw-Hill publishing company
  232
MacNeil, Robert 224
McQuail, Denis 121, 122
Mainichi 251
Mannes, Mary 219
Marconi, Guglielmo 22, 26, 33
  early work on wireless 21

Marijnen, Dutch PM 268, 272
Mass audience, *see* Audience, mass
Mass communication,
  birth of 36
  TV news and 85–6
Mass psychology 25
  imitation in 23, 26
Matignon 177
Mauriac, François 172
Mayflower Broadcasting Company
  204
Mead, George Herbert 128
Mein Kampf, Adolf Hitler's 42
Mencken, H. L. 40
Michigan State University 258
Mill, John Stuart 33, 35, 36, 44, 113,
  268
  on liberty 34, 35
Milton, John 113
Minow, Newton 202, 203
Mitterand, François 170, 171, 174
Mobil Oil 227
Monderer, Howard 125
Monod, Jacques 173
Moral Rearmament 275
Mudie, Charles Edward 27, 28, 31
  Victorian moral code and 28
  victory of the middle-man 27
Mudie's Circulating Library 27–8
Murrow, Ed 77, 87, 210

Nader, Ralph 237
  on Mobil Oil commercials 227
Namurois, A. 148
National Association of Broadcasters,
  US 84
  Land Report 84
  violence code 120
National Educational Television
  (NET), US 221, 222, 223
  programmes: Banks and the Poor
  227; Great American Dream
  Machine 227; Who Invited
  Us 227
National Public Affairs Centre for
  Television (NPACT), US 224.
  227
National Union for Social Justice 68
National Viewers' and Listeners'
  Association 214
NBC network, USA 96, 99, 187,
  206, 213, 228

cameras at Chicago Convention (1968) 124–5
Kansas City TV station 194
owned by RCA 195
NDR broadcasting company, Hamburg 65
Nederlandse Omroep Stichting 273, 278
organisation of 274
Netherlands Christian Radio Society (NCRV) 270, 276
New York Times 212
New York Yankees 195
News, broadcasting of 74–91, 96–7
BBC developments 82
BBC's early restrictions on 87–9
bias in 99–102
changing news sense 97–8
development of radio news reporting 86–7
distortion 74–5, 76
early TV presentation 80–1
French failures in 161
Land Report 84
news judgment, criteria of 103–7
pluralism in 108–9
revolution in camerawork 79–80
US developments 82–4
volume of news, US 84
Newspaper Proprietors' Association, London 43, 87
Newsweek 211
Nielsen research organisation 191, 192
Nieuwe Rotterdamse Courant 269
Nippon Hoso Kyokai (NHK), Japan 247, 249, 256–7
automation in 261
financing 255–6
news on 261
parody of BBC 260
post Second World War development 253–5
research by 261–2
under govt control 250
Nippon TV 258
Nixon, Richard M. 99, 100–2, 134, 197, 205, 212–13, 224–5
Normanbrook, Lord 144–5
Northcliffe, Lord 27, 30, 112
North Rhine-Westphalia, broadcasting organisation 63

Nouvel Observateur 177

Odd Couple 199
Oklahoma, FCC investigation into TV stations in 230–1
Olszowski, Stefan 116–17
ORTF (L'Office de la Radiodiffusion et Télévision Française) and RTF 155, 160
bureaucracy vis-à-vis 165–6
censorship 163, 173, 175
censorship of 'Armes Egales' programme 182–3
coming of colour 177–8
controlled by Minister of Information 162–3
effect of Paye and Riou commissions 180
effects of 1968 strike 176–9
financed from Ministry of Finance 162
financial scandal (1971) 183–4
founding of ORTF 159, 162
gaps in coverage 165
Gaullist control of news 164
growth of viewers and channels 167
news division 164, 165
programme harmonisation 185, 186
programmes: Caméra III 173, 177; Cinq Colonnes à la Une 78, 165, 173, 177; Journal Télévisé 161; La Caméra explore le Temps 166; L'Affaire Ledru 166; Panorama 165, 172, 177; Zoom 165, 173, 177
programmes axed after 1968 strike 176–7
protected position of 164
reorganisation (1972) 185
RTF created 158
strike of 1968 172–6
Orwell, George 123
Osaka 247, 248

Paine, Tom 36
Paley 193
Pall Mall Gazette, The 33
Palmerston, Lord 113
Paris-Match 185
Parker, Dr Everett 231

Parliament,
  'access' to broadcasting 267
  Fourteen Day rule 131–2
  relations with broadcasting 129–134
Parodi, Alexandre 170
Party Political Broadcasts 133
Pasteur, Joseph 185
Patton 199
Paye, Mons. 180
Payrefitte, Mons. 162–3
Physics and Politics, Walter Bagehot's 23
Picture Post 82
Pilkington Committee 59
Plato 36
Poland,
  political use of TV 116–17
  Trybuna Obywatelska 116
Polish Mercury 92
Politicians,
  relations with broadcasters and broadcasting xiii, xiv, 115–17, 129, 133–7, 162–4, 170–1, 172–4, 183–5, 205, 209–10, 211–12, 223, 224–5, 227, 250
  relations with mass audience 113–114
Pompidou, Georges 155, 163, 178, 182, 185, 186
Post Office (GPO), British 69, 70, 88
Powell, Enoch 101
Powledge, Fred 212
Pozzo di Borgo, Roland 184
Presidential press conference, US 95
  first televising of 95
Press Council 149
Press, the,
  coming of telegraph and 94
  Cowper on 73
  eighteenth-century development 37–8
  First World War propaganda in 30, 42
  gains freedom through advertising revenue 38–9
  Japanese 247–9, 251–3, 258
  Japanese censorship 250, 251
  nineteenth- and twentieth-century developments 95–6
  nineteenth-century principles 39, 112

nineteenth-century US muckrakers 39
Nixon govt conflict with 211–12
printing improvements and 92–5
professionalisation of journalists 41
role compared with broadcasting 89–90, 101
seventeenth-century news gathering 91–2
twentieth-century US reportage 40
wire services and 94
Printing, development of 92–3
Propaganda,
  First World War 30–1, 42
  mass audience First World War victim of 28–9
  mass control by elitist 42
Public Advertiser 38
Public broadcasting, US 189, 216, 223–8, 282
  Children's TV Workshop 227
  documentaries 227
  financing of 224–5
  opposition to 225–6, 227
  programme making 223–6
  Public Broadcasting Act (1967) 223
  Public Broadcasting Service (PBS) 223–4
  Sesame Street 226
  successes of 226–7
Public Ledger, Philadelphia 94
Public opinion 30, 113
Puskás brothers 48
Puskás, Theodore 48

Radio,
  development of 49, 50
  development of news reporting 86–7
  early restrictions on BBC news 87–9
  given impetus by First World War 48
  US educational 218, 219
  wavelength problem 56, 200
Radio Monte-Carlo 168
Radio Tele-Luxembourg (RTL) 167, 168
Radiotherie, Bertolt Brecht's 264

Ramadier, Paul 169
Random House publishing company 195
RCA (Radio Corporation of America) 96
  owner of NBC 195
RCA Victor records 195
Reed, John 40
Reith, John 28, 32, 43, 70, 88, 141, 143, 249, 262
Riddell, Lord 87–8
Robson, W. A. 50
Roosevelt, Franklin D. 68, 95
Roosevelt, Theodore 95
Roper, Burns 85
Roper, Elmo 85
Rothermere, Lord 30, 112
Royal Commission on the Press (1947–1949) 149
Royer, Jean 182
Ruskin, John 70

Sablier, Edouard 175
St Mark 215
Sarnoff, David 48–50
Satellites, communications 222
Schiller, Herbert 54
Schramm, Wilbur 36
Screen Actors Guild, US 197
Schröder, Herr 65
Select Committee on Nationalised Industries 149
Serling, Rod 209
Sexual Reform Society, Holland 275–6
Shaw, George Bernard 118
Sheridan, R. B. 113
Shigeo, Mizuno 258
Simmons research organisation 191
Simon, Lord, of Wythenshawe 132, 143
Sinclair, Upton 40
Sindlinger research organisation 191
Sloan Commission, US, Report on CATV 241–2
Smith, Howard K. 73
Smith, W. H. 27
SOFIRAD (La Société Financière de Radiodiffusion) 168
Speech, freedom of 42–3
  eighteenth-century suppression 37–8

Spiers, Brig-Gen. 68
Stalin, Joseph 187
Stanton, Dr Frank xiv
Steffens, Lincoln 95
Stephen, James Fitzjames 33–4
  on society 34–5
Stern Community (Concern), Los Angeles 233–5
Stichting Radio Unie (NRU, Netherlands Broadcasting Foundation) 271–2
Sud-Radio 167, 168
Swann, Prof. Sir Michael 147–8
Sweden, broadcasting in,
  Broadcasting Council 151–2, 153
  Code of Broadcasting Practice 151
  dealing with complaints 150–3
  Swedish Radio company 150–3
SWF broadcasting company, Baden-Baden 65
Swing, Raymond 77
Sykes Committee 88
  on radio-telephony 31
Szulczewski, Michal 116

Tadashi, Adach 258
Tarde, Gabriel 22, 26
  on crowd-psychology 21–2
Task Force on Communications Policy, US 84
Telephone 31
  attempts to broadcast by 48
  Terrors of the . . . (cartoon) 28
Tele-7 Jours 166
Television,
  actuality of 74, 80
  BBC monopoly broken 57
  distorting effects on 74–6, 124
  effect on voters 121–2
  incomes and expenditure of BBC and ITV 59
  influence in home xvi
  investigating influence of 120–4
  news transmission 76–91, 96–7
  political effects of 119–20, 125–6
  violence on 120, 213, 231
  See also BBC, ITV and under countries
Ten Commandments 199
Thibau, Jacques 162, 163, 178, 184
Thirties, The, Malcolm Muggeridge's 47

Time 211
Time-Life Corporation 61, 232
Times, The 30, 39, 89, 93
Todd, Olivier 177
Tokyo 247, 248
  Radio Tokyo 258
TOPICS computer 261
Trade unions 267
  dissatisfaction with industrial report-
    ing on TV1 09–10, 138, 266
  One Week 266
Trenaman, Joseph 121
Trendex research organisation 191
Tribune, New York 40
TROS broadcasting organisation,
  Holland 275
TvQ research organisation 191

United Church of Christ, US 228,
  231–2

Vanocur, Sander 224, 227
Variety 207, 213

WAAB station, Boston 204
Wallace, George 99
Wallace, Mike 212
Wallas, Graham 23, 29, 113
  on crowd behaviour 26

Walpole, Sir Robert 36
Warner Brothers 241
WDR broadcasting company, Cologne
  65
Weathermen, the 211
Weaver, Prof. Paul 99–101
Wells, H. G. 42
Westen, Tracy 233
Westerstähl, Prof. Jörgen 153–4
WHDH station, Boston 203, 228
Whitehead, Dr Clay T. 205, 212–13,
  224–5, 227, 233, 235
Whitehouse, Mary 214, 247
White House, Washington 227
  Office of Telecommunications
    Policy 205, 212, 224–5
Whitley, J. H. 143
Williams, Philip 159
Williams, Raymond 25
Wilson, Harold 145–6
Winchell, Walter 68
Wireless World 269
WLBT station, Jackson, Mississippi
  228, 231
Wood, Robert D. 82–3
Woodfall, Henry-Samson 38

Yokohama Mainichi 247–8
Yomiuri 251